CROSSING SEX AND GENDER IN LATIN AMERICA

CROSSING SEX AND GENDER

IN LATIN AMERICA

Vek Lewis

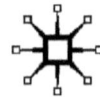

CROSSING SEX AND GENDER IN LATIN AMERICA
Copyright © Vek Lewis, 2010.
Softcover reprint of the hardcover 1st edition 2010 978-0-230-10402-0
All rights reserved.

Cover photograph from the series *La manzana de Adán* by Paz Errázuriz

Chapter 2 was previously published in May 2009 in *Chasqui: Revista de literatura latinoamericana* 38, no. 1:104–24 in a slightly different form.

First published in 2010 by PALGRAVE MACMILLAN® in the United States—a division of St. Martin's Press LLC, 175 Fifth Avenue, New York, NY 10010

Where this book is distributed in the UK, Europe and the rest of the world, this is by Palgrave Macmillan, a division of Macmillan Publishers Limited, registered in England, company number 785998, of Houndmills, Basingstoke, Hampshire RG21 6XS.

Palgrave Macmillan is the global academic imprint of the above companies and has companies and representatives throughout the world.

Palgrave® and Macmillan® are registered trademarks in the United States, the United Kingdom, Europe and other countries.

ISBN 978-1-349-28849-6   ISBN 978-0-230-10996-4 (eBook)
DOI 10.1057/9780230109964

Library of Congress Cataloging-in-Publication Data

Lewis, Vek.
  Crossing sex and gender in Latin America / Vek Lewis.
    p. cm.
  Includes bibliographical references and index.

  1. Latin American literature—20th century—History and criticism. 2. Latin American literature—21st century—History and criticism. 3. Transgender people in literature. 4. Gender identity in literature. 5. Motion pictures—Latin America—History—20th century. 6. Motion pictures—Latin America—History—21st century. 7. Transgender people in motion pictures. 8. Gender identity in motion pictures I. Title.

PQ7081.L4535 2010
860.9'35266—dc22   2009053916

Design by Scribe Inc.

First edition: August 2010

Este libro se lo dedico a mi amigo del alma, N. D. You know who you are.
Your influence is alive in these pages.

Contents

Acknowledgments	ix
Introduction: The Persistence of Vision(s): Sex and Gender Variance in the Past and Present	1
1 Thinking Figurations Otherwise: Reframing Dominant Knowledges of Sex and Gender Variance in Latin America	17
2 Grotesque Spectacles: The Janus Face of the State and Gender-Variant Bodies in Reinaldo Arenas	45
3 Life Is (More than) a Cabaret: Gender Crossing and "Trans" Signification in Contemporary Cinema from Latin America	73
4 Authorizing Subjectivity: Eroticism, Epidemia, and the (In)validation of Bodies in Pedro Juan Gutiérrez's *El Rey de La Habana* and Mario Bellatin's *Salón de belleza*	107
5 Trans Bodies, Popular Culture, and (National) Identity in Crisis: Luis Zapata's *La hermana secreta de Angélica María* and Mayra Santos-Febres's *Sirena Selena vestida de pena*	143
6 Scandalous Embodiments, Shameful Citizenships: *Loca* and *Travesti* Subjectivities in the Work of Pedro Lemebel	181
Epilogue	221
Notes	227
References	249
Index	265

Acknowledgments

I would like to thank Diana Palaversich and Stewart King, who helped me with the initial work conducted for this book. Thanks should also go to those who assisted me in its final phases: Debra Castillo, Paul Allatson, and Jeffrey Browitt. Finally, without the intellectual exchange and friendship of Viviane Namaste, Talia Mae Bettcher, Ben Singer, Natalia Anaya, Rosío Córdova Plaza, Mauro Cabral, Rodrigo Parrini, and Ntennis Davi, I would not have had the context or the faith to see this project to completion.

Sincere thanks also to friends and family in Australia, Mexico, and Puerto Rico for your love and solidarity.

Introduction

The Persistence of Vision(s)

Sex and Gender Variance in the Past and Present

Travestismo, or male-to-female gender crossing, notes critic Anke Birkenmaier (2002), has become a fashionable feature of contemporary Latin American literature. This is by no means restricted, of course, to the literary domain. There has been an explosion in the depiction of "trans" subjects and acts in contemporary cultural production, particularly in television and print media. Three countries have run soap operas that feature *travesti* characters (male born individuals who live in feminine mode) played by real-life *travestis* and transsexuals to great acclaim: *Los Roldán* (*The Roldán Family*) in Argentina, starring Florencia de la V., *Los Sánchez* (*The Sánchez Family*) in Mexico with Libertad, and *Los Reyes* (*The Reyes Family*) with Endry Cardeño in Colombia. In particular, de la V has gained the status of megastar in Argentina. An increasing number of films feature *locas*, or gender-crossing characters. There have also been several high-profile documentaries, some of which are mentioned in the course of this book. Other examples of representation include performance by transvestites in art and on stage in academic and cultural settings, as well as *La manzana de Adán* (*Adam's Apple*), a coffee-table book with photographs from the 1980s of *colas* (*locas*) from Chile, an image from which adorns this book's cover. Puerto Rican *salsero* Willy Colón is still heard singing on the radio about a *travesti* who defies patriarchal control and dies of AIDS in "El gran varón" ("The great man"). Newspapers, magazines, and television networks have devoted considerable column inches and airtime to the subject of *travestis* and their place in society in venues such as *Página 12* in Argentina, *Letra S* in Mexico's daily *La Jornada*, and Chile's *Teletrece*, to name just a respectable few, that is, aside for the more voluminous popular and tabloid press.

This book is concerned with contemporary visions of nonnormative sexualities and genders in Latin America. It looks at cinematic and literary texts produced over a twenty-year period from 1985 to 2005. In these texts, as in the majority of contemporary representations in other popular forms, change in sexual identity and gender refers principally to crossings from male to female. Only a small number of novels have been published in recent years that deal with female-to-male changes.[1] This fact is not in itself new. Birkenmaier notes that even in the golden age of *Novohispano (New Spain)* literature, during the time of Sor Juana Inés de la Cruz, for instance, gender crossing was principally from male to female. If in time past, transvestite figures were used in Latin American literary works in the name of a certain exoticism that recalled disguise and festivity, the mask and the pageant, the inversion of orders, and the play of desires between man and woman or man dressed as woman, then the new subject of the *travesti* in modern and contemporary literature still points to a critique of the social order. Birkenmaier sustains that contemporary representations of *travestis* rely less on the idea of the mask and more on the sexual indecision the figure embodies. The image of the mask, I hold, still pertains in some representations of *travestis* and their metaphorical use to explain the social order; *travestis*, in some cases, continue to be engaged from a position of marginality, both in terms of their envisioned cultural space and in terms of the textual space accorded them. They are also persistently viewed in the name of spectacle, as Birkenmaier also argues.

Their cultural marginality was mirrored in the narratives that depicted them in the period before the 1980s. Mostly minor characters in these texts, homosexuals and *travestis* function as plot devices or symbols of a certain order. They are signifying others. In a wide range of texts, they function performatively to point to or embody larger issues at hand. Narrative marginality is not a precondition for them to function metaphorically, however. Even when writers install the *travesti* to a more central place in their works, they frequently maintain the symbolic function, and very little in the way of an exploration of the subjectivities of those existing outside of normative sex and gender relations is evidenced. Many of the attributions of doubleness, superficiality, frivolity, and dangerousness remain. Here I would cite the celebrated works of José Donoso, Severo Sarduy, and Manuel Puig—all from the 1960s and 1970s. Donoso and Puig give great precedence to the depiction of their *travesti* characters in *El lugar sin límites* (1966; *Place Without Limits*) and *El beso de la mujer araña* (1976; *The Kiss of the Spiderwoman*), respectively. La Manuela and Molina were breakthrough characterizations in the sense that they formed the main foci of their narratives. Never before in Latin America had same-sex desire and gender difference been visualized with such insistence. Puig's work has a noticeable investment in this visualization, since as a homosexual writer, he wished to challenge some of the prevailing notions about homosexuality in the period. He was also deeply pledged to opposing authoritarian regimes of control around all aspects of existence—libidinal, social, and political. Thus his narrative is greatly connected to such a project, as is Donoso's.[2] But since their works precede the emergence of a politicized *travesti* subjectivity, they do not entirely break free of the most stereotyped formulations of effeminate homosexuality and cross-gendered identity. Their pledge to critiquing the social order also programs the structure of their representations to the level of paradigm. As such, La Manuela and Molina operate symbolically in each work's take on social reality, and a perspective from the gender-variant or sexually different subject is largely occluded. Sarduy's controversial work, meanwhile, which incorporates a collection of so-called deviant subjects—including transsexuals and *travestis*—is disposed from the start to the use of transvestism and sex change as symbolic of historical and cultural change and the evolution of Cuban nationhood. For example, the *travestis* in his works of fiction—*De donde son los cantantes* (1967; *From Cuba with a Song*), *Cobra* (1972) and *Colibrí* (1984)—serve as themes or components in a grand baroque opera about the constitution of Cuban identity. Auxilio and Socorro, two *travestis*, move in and out of the narrative of *De donde son los cantantes*, commenting on Cuban history as it unfolds, and are directly related to its elements of African, Indian, Spanish and Chinese heritage.

While these writers are indispensable in conceiving of the lineage of representations of *locas* and *travestis* in Latin American cultural production, much has been written on them—notably by Ben Sifuentes-Jáuregui in *Transvestism, Masculinity, and Latin American Literature: Genders Share Flesh* (2001), a predecessor to this work. In this book I have therefore chosen to read texts that come from the period after the formative work of Donoso, Puig, and Sarduy. The works I examine pertain to a period of cultural emergence of sexual and gender minorities as distinct political identities—the homosexual and the *travesti*. As subjugated discourses from a minority perspective gain ground—for *travestis*, especially after 1990—one might expect some shifts in the depiction of gender-variant, visibly marginalized homosexual and trans subjects as frivolous, as sideline, as grotesque, and as signifying others. The films and novels and that I examine in this study are produced in this new period.

The Terms and Logics of Sexual Diversity and Sex and Gender Variance in Latin America

Political and cultural movements in Latin America in the name of sexual diversity, alongside a range of other social movements of difference, really only emerged onto the national proscenium in the early 1970s, most notably in Mexico and Argentina. This process occurred later in other Latin American countries still affected by right-wing dictatorship or socialist authoritarianism, where the logics of machismo precluded their earlier appearance (Green 1994, 1999; Klein 1998; Leiner 1994; Lumsden 1991; Mogrovejo 2000; Robles 1998; Sardá 1998). In Puerto Rico, Cuba, Chile, and Brazil, the processes of the sociopolitical visibilization of *travestis* and transsexuals, for example, are only really noticeable from the early to mid-nineties onward. Each geopolitical location obeys its own social and political logic in the particular ways different forms of sexual identity begin to occupy and unsettle the public imaginary: subjects identified by their sex or gender variance thus display different conditions of possibility for the emergence of their subjectivities. This book, then, addresses a crucial period in the changing perceptions of nonnormative sexualities in Latin America—1985 to 2005—a period that saw the political and cultural emergence throughout the region of subjects visible for their differences from established sexual norms. This emergence has been captured in several key cinematic and literary texts, some of which have staged sensitive and complex portrayals of nonnormative sexual identity; others bind their sex- and gender-diverse characters to scenarios of national-cultural transgression, playing with historic associations coded in stage, screen, and song, and thereby underscoring tropes of sex, gender, and nation via mythic visions. The cabaret and the musical genre of the bolero figure prominently in this regard. The texts that engage in such maneuvers tend to invoke cross-gendering chiefly in reference to the sociopolitical crises brought in train: the supposed corruption of the social order and the undermining of monolithic conceptions of identity, whether sexual, gender, or national.

The terms "sexual diversity" and "sex/gender variance," although notionally inclusive of all forms of sexual and gender expression and lived subjectivity, are most commonly used in contemporary discourse in Latin America and elsewhere to refer to subjects whose sexual practices and identities fall outside the domain of heterosexuality and whose gender expressions and identities are also contrary to what is culturally expected of them on the basis of their biological sex. "Sexual diversity" relates to persons who are lesbian, gay, bisexual, or trans, whereas "sex/gender variance" refers to those who express a mixture of genders, those who live part time or full time in social genders different to those assigned them at birth, or those who have transitioned physically from one sex to the other.

A study that does not avoid these particularities but keeps them in full view, especially given the cross-cultural and cross-linguistic nature of the texts and contexts to which it refers, must inevitably confront the issue of culturally specific concepts and terminology. Nearly two decades of work in English and other languages has been produced to date in the fields of queer and transgender studies on sexuality and sex and gender nonnormativity, their representation, and their representability. Work on specifically Latin American manifestations of the same has also been undertaken since the mid-1990s by scholars who have negotiated the intersecting but often contradictory paradigms of lesbian, gay, and queer subjectivities in "Latin America" and their representation in cultural texts.[3] Less work, however, has centered on these questions in regard to the sociopolitical emergence of subjects visible for their sex and gender transitivity. Some of the insights of scholars in the field form the backdrop to this book's explorations; others are challenged in situating the very concerns I raise here.

If the study of queer and trans representations has been a contested area, identity categories themselves have been the point of much disagreement (Alcoff 2006). In regard to the logics of sexuality, gender, and identity in Latin America, setting the terms requires not only the nuances of culturally specific readings but also a historical focus that permits the recognition that identities change over time and vary according to places and spaces of enunciation, globalizing processes, and transnational exchange, even within the conceptual framework known as "Latin America" (Altman 2001; Cantú 1999). Sexual diversity and sex and gender variance exhibit differences in Latin American locales and produce identity logics and formations distinct from those found, for instance, in the Anglophone world. But there also exist homosexualities and trans identities, and evolving discourses about the same, across the different geopolitical and national locations that make up that floating signifier, "Latin America" (Lancaster 1998). Some of these are not dissimilar to those of the Anglophone world; such convergences are increasing in an age characterized by "the dissemination of various mediated forms of culture, embodiment, and desire [that] happens at ever higher speeds and across long, striated distances in the context of reconfigurations and reconsolidations of economic, state and national power" (Povinelli and Chauncey 1999, 441).

In spite of this, certain trends for thinking about these identities are obtained both in the social world and its representations. That is to say, certain patterns of logic for organizing and recognizing identity that are unique to the region can be distinguished, which run alongside the shifting patterns of modernity, urbanization, and insertion in global networks of the different locales. Since this book examines the production, potential reinforcement, or transformation in the social imaginary of identities visible for their difference in terms of sexuality and gender, it is important to interrogate the nature of these logics, at least as they have been manifest since the rise of representations of homosexualities and other sexual subjectivities of difference.

The link between effeminacy and homosexuality, present in Europe at the birth of the concept "homosexual" and for at least a century afterward there and in the United States, is still one that structures both perceptions and lived versions of homosexuality in Latin America (Muñoz 2004).[4] Although discourses of homosexuality are also multiple in the region, such that it is possible to speak of and observe gay identities not visibly associated with ideas of femininity, sexual passivity, or gender atypicality, the logic that one is an expression of the other is still meaningful, both to those who live out lives visibly as homosexuals and to their larger cultures. Stereotypical or not, homosexualities marked for their divergence from gender norms persist as a visible cultural sign, and, in some places, as *the* sign. Taken up as a self-identified position, this form of homosexuality attracts local terms such as *loca, jota, cola,* and other variations.

What has become historically differentiated out as "transgender" in other (notably U.S.) spaces is often visualized as part of the "homosexual" in Latin American cultures.[5] Even subjects who live as another social gender and adopt feminine expressions, modes of dress, and address (*travestis*) are frequently seen to exist on a homosexual continuum. As such, "*travesti*" is much disputed and subject to different conceptual and lived elaborations, depending on the degrees of prominence of one discourse of homosexuality over another—same-sex attraction versus a desiring body marked by gender variance. In Argentina, for instance, the space for a separate *travesti* identity, different from "gay" or "homosexual," is increasingly consolidating itself. However, in northern Mexico (and other places), *travesti*, "homosexual," and "gay" are still used interchangeably. Moreover, what I am calling "*loca*" and "*travesti*" identities themselves overlap, both in terms of people's lived expressions and in terms of public perceptions of identity.

While "*travesti*" has as English cognate in the word "transvestite," its semantic field is actually far more extensive and variable than the sexological term "transvestite," which emerges out of a European discourse of sexual deviance, would suggest.[6] This has prompted some sociologists and anthropologists of sexuality to assign the Anglophone concept "transgender" to such subjects; however the term "transgender"—which can be used in at least two senses in English to refer to she or he who lives in the opposite gender role without surgery or anyone who is nonnormatively gendered, including transsexuals, transvestites, and drag queens and kings (Bornstein 1994)—is also inadequate in some important respects. The word "*transgénero*" has only entered into (specifically academic and activist) parlance in Spanish and Portuguese in the last decade. Many subjects who understand themselves as *travesti* do not use the word at all, or have notions of selfhood and desire that are not in the ambit of contemporary understandings of transgender as an expression of *gendered* difference. For *travestis* historically, the vision of themselves as (homo)sexual subjects who are feminine has organized both public and private visions of subjectivity and intersubjectivity. Their selves are as much about sexuality and desire as they are about gender, their femininity often being an expression of their desired (passive) role; in some instances, they are more concerned with sex and desire.[7]

The conceptual breadth of "*travesti*" also allows a variety of identifications in differing contexts. Some *travestis* understand themselves as women (especially, in Argentinian contexts); others as homosexuals who are like women but not female (Brazil, Chile, Mexico, and Cuba). The complexity of these identifications has been examined in much ethnographic work (Carrier 1995; Kulick 1998; Lancaster 1992; Murray 1995; Parker 1999; Prieur 1998; Núñez Noriega 1999; González Pérez 2003). Most of these studies demonstrate that, although individual *travestis* may understand and construct their subjectivities in reference to the feminine, they distinguish themselves from male-to-female *transexuales*, who identify as women and often seek sex reassignment surgery (SRS) to become that vision of themselves. Being *travesti* is thus not the same as being transgender and without SRS; it is another space and another identity outside the strictures of sex and gender normativity that is specific to Latin American sites. Although "*travesti*" has a conceptual breadth that means the term may include a diversity of subjects, just as "transgender" does in its second ascribed sense, the two terms have evolved in different locales and different languages and are not immediately commensurable. Like Rosamond S. King (2008), I am loath to use a term such as "transgender" in relation to identities and identifications that have emerged in quite different circumstances from those that have arisen in the United States. In this study I will use the Spanish and Portuguese term "*travesti*" and "trans" (which is in circulation in the region) alongside other local concepts and argot used in reference to sexualities of difference, such as *maricón*, *bicha*, *viado*, and *loca*, in an effort to catch the nuances in representation that a purely queer or transgender tradition of understanding identity could easily miss.

Although the realities of so-called trans Latin American subjects have attracted the attention of sociologists and anthropologists from within and outside the region, in Spanish-, Portuguese-, and English-language scholarship, cultural and literary critics have only recently begun to respond to the intense visibility of these trans subjects in contemporary

Latin American cultural sites. Some of this preliminary work is restricted by its limited focus on the transvestite as textual effect and the unwillingness to countenance the fact that, where sexual variance and gender crossing appear in contemporary texts, the issue of the subjectivity and subjectification of such figures in the contexts from which the texts emerge is of prime importance. In this book the relation between representations and emergent subjectivities is not ignored; rather, it is central to the discussion. As such, the book takes the reader into new terrain that challenges preconceptions about the logics of the textual inscription of sex and gender variance in contemporary instances of Latin American cultural production.

REFRAMING THEORY, REFRAMING REPRESENTATION

Loca, in its own right . . . suggests or proposes a form of hysterical identity (pathologized at the clinical level, scandalous at the popular one) constitutive of an individual lacking sanity, composure or ascription to the dominant norms: effeminate homosexuals, mad women, rebels for any cause.

—Lawrence La Fountain-Stokes,
"Queer Puerto Rican Translocalities"

In the chapters that follow, the logics of the representation of what I am terming here "*locas*" (feminine homosexuals), "*transformistas*" (drag performers), "*travestis*," and "*transexuales*" are tracked, unpacked, and foregrounded in all their of shifting discursive dimensions. Cinematic and literary texts are seen as particularly fruitful sites to explore the shifting discursive limits of the disputed textual and identity terrains of *loca* homosexuals, *travestis*, trans- and (in one instance) intersexual subjects, as in their production and critical reception one finds (re)articulated many of the central components of the dominant ways of thinking about and conceiving of sex and gender variance. This study is anchored in the understanding, expressed by Steven Seidman, that cinematic and literary texts—like other cultural texts—can be viewed as "social and political practices . . . organized by social and cultural codes, and indeed as social forces that structure identities, social norms, and power relations" (1997, 147). I am not interested in representation for representation's sake; rather, I am acutely concerned with how representations potentially impact on, refer to, and dialogue with social realities that are often, perhaps implicitly, viewed as merely outside, and therefore somehow extraneous to, the text. This book thus offers not only a study of the rhetorical limits and possibilities of the inscription of sexual identity and trans subjectivity in Latin American instances but also a kind of sociology of literature and cinema. In this way, the book asks different questions and provides different answers to those posed in previous studies, studies that I refer to at length in Chapter 1 and in successive sections of the analysis.

So why ask such questions at all? In my view, an examination of the representations of trans subjectivities and sexual identities *anywhere* is intrinsically problematic and caught up in the ethics of the politics of knowledge about minorities, as well as the creation of space for minority knowledges, that resignify and contest dominant representations. My orientation as a cultural and literary critic who has been involved at different stages of my life in queer and trans movements and who also participated in cross-cultural and bilingual activist exchange for some time, makes this a matter of course: knowledges can both restrict and liberate, and knowledges that oppress do so not simply at an intellectual, abstract level. I cannot deny my own investments in these ethical questions, and I sense that the issues of epistemological violence in reference to queer and trans subjects in the English-speaking world (I write from Sydney, Australia) and *loca, travesti*, and trans subjects in Latin America are imbricated irrevocably in the realm of everyday social and institutional violence, experienced in varying, and often alarming, degrees. I ask questions about how criticism—whether queer or not, whether Anglo or Latin American—itself is implicated in the discursive reproduction in Latin America of a reigning episteme about contemporary sexual and gendered subjects, to use Foucault's terminology. These questions matter, I believe, outside the circuits of academia.

In the first chapter, I carefully pursue what I see as the contours of this reigning episteme about effeminacy and *travestismo*, in particular. This takes us back more than a century in time to the emergence of the medico-legal framing of *inverts* in discourses of social control and public order, to racialized and sexualized others in nation discourse. Discursive formations of this tenor are also present in literary texts that figured (cross-gendered) homosexuality in the first part of the twentieth century, encompassing the vivid appearance of such figures of otherness as the prostitute, the homosexual, and the *travesti* in art, culture, and criticism in successive years. These currents of representation culminate finally in a veritable groundswell in talk and visualizations around transgressive acts and identities in the last decade of the millennium in the region. The dominant knowledge frameworks that inscribe *travestismo*, found in a diverse spectrum of texts and contexts, produce a figure that plays off a range of concerns—the carnivalesque, the performative, a vector of scandal and crisis, symbolic of national identity and its (de)construction. In this epistemological formation, *travestismo* emerges across a range of sites variously as a sign of deception, criminality, dissimulation, play, and optical illusion; consequently, to use the phrasing of the transsexual scholar to whom my account of the force and effect of metaphor in Chapter 1 is indebted, Viviane Namaste, *travestis* and transsexuals are made to appear, in such logic, as "purely *figural*—that is, literally *impossible*" in this reigning field of sense making around sex and gender variance in Latin American texts and contexts (Namaste 2000, 93; emphasis in original). Such foregrounding of knowledge and its formation is crucial to the readings of the texts that make up the corpus of this book's analysis in order to think through the ethical dimensions to their representations of *locas*, *travestis*, and transsexuals.

Chapter 2, "Grotesque Spectacles: The Janus Face of the State and Gender-Variant Bodies in Reinaldo Arenas," examines the representations of *locas*, *travestis*, and all manner of gender-crossing acts in the work of Cuban writer Reinaldo Arenas. Here I read Arenas's oeuvre in the context of the official Cuban productions of the *loca* and *travesti* as deviant, counterrevolutionary, and symbolic of corruption. Although initially recuperative of the image of the *loca*, Arenas's project is complicated by the fact that some of his articulations of gender crossers and their identities reproduce the terms used to describe such individuals by the state. They are allegorized to symbolize corruption and contradiction in the sociopolitical order. Arenas is not the first to conjoin gender crossing or sexually hybrid bodies to corruption in the sociopolitical order. This trope also pertains in other Latin American literary works of the same time period, including Colombian Jaime Manrique's *Colombian Gold* (1983) and Argentinian Luisa Valenzuela's *Cola de lagartija* (1983; *A Lizard's Tale*), as well as the later work of Arenas's compatriot, Leonardo Padura, *Máscaras* (1997; *Masks*). Although not examined here, together with Arenas's ironic allegorization of sex- and gender-variant bodies, they provide evidence of the persistence of a logic that is Latin American; that is to say, they are both molded by and obey a particular logic that has structured the representation and conceptualization of sex and gender variance in the region. While attributions of deception are often attached to trans people in, for instance, North America, as the work of Julia Serano (2007) and Talia Bettcher (2007) has shown, these are not marked by the kinds of associations of grotesquerie and criminality that, as I argue in an article on media productions (Lewis 2008), are typical of Latin American locales.

Chapter 3 pursues the contrastive possibilities of the exploration versus the metaphorization of subjectivity in relation to the depiction of *locas*, *travestis*, and drag performers (*transformistas*) in Latin American film from the 1970s onward. The figuring of gender nonnormative acts and subjects as comical or grotesque spectacles, and as minor players who embody decay or weakness, is strongly present in these cultural forms as well. They are also employed as intermediaries or narrative helpers. *Locas, travestis,* and *transformistas* are vividly associated with stage or club life in a series of *cabaretera* or *fichera* films of the period. I turn my attention strategically to a number of filmic texts—including María Novaro's *Danzón* (Mexico, 1992), Orlando Rojas's *Las noches de Constantinopla* (Cuba, 2002; *Constantinople Nights*), and Karim Aïnouz's *Madame Satã* (Brazil, 2002; *Madam Satan*), all produced in the post-1990 period, even as the different locales provide evidence of varied degrees of cultural space for the expression of sex and gender diversity. Most of the texts analyzed do not visualize their *travestis* and *transformistas* as possibilities beyond the space of the cabaret—a key site historically for imagining sexual identities—or the performative, both within the respective narrative designs of each film and their takes on gender norms and identity, although Aïnouz's text offers some surprising exceptions.

In Chapter 4, I juxtapose two novels, Pedro Juan Gutiérrez's *El Rey de La Habana* (2001; *The King of Havana*) and Mario Bellatin's *Salón de belleza* (1999; *Beauty Salon*), which in many ways are polar opposites in their narrative strategies. Both depict *travestis,* and both go some way to resisting the mere allegorization of trans bodies. In Chapter 5, the Mexican Luis Zapata's novel *La hermana secreta de Angélica María* (1989; *The Secret Sister of Angélica María*) and Puerto Rican Mayra Santos-Febres's novel *Sirena Selena, vestida de pena* (2000; *Sirena Selena*) are examined. These texts share three obsessions: the travesti and transsexual are depicted as seductive and dangerous, they are connected intimately to popular culture through song and cinema, and they have some (problematic) relationship with the idea of nation and identity. Zapata's text has elicited meager critical response. Santos-Febres's novel, in contrast, has received much critical appraisal, mostly in terms of the limits of national identity. I read both the critics and the texts because as discourses, they interact to reinforce the idea of the "*travesti*" or "transsexual" as an empty term that can only register at the level of the symbolic. I question the production of this kind of discourse around the *travesti* and the transsexual by reading against the grain in the two texts.

The final chapter considers in depth the work of Chilean *cronista* (chronicle writer) and novelist Pedro Lemebel. *La esquina es mi corazón* (1995; *The Street Corner is My Heart*) and *Loco afán: Crónicas de sidario* (1997; *Mad Undertaking: AIDS Chronicles*) are the two collections of *crónicas* selected for analysis. In *La esquina es mi corazón*, Lemebel investigates the marks the Pinochet dictatorship (1973–90) has left behind: the persistence of the fear of surveillance and repression, and the effects of the neoliberal economic model and its processes of globalization on Chile's most marginalized social sectors. In *Loco afán: Crónicas de sidario*, Lemebel depicts *locas* and *travestis*, particularly those involved in the sex trade and living with HIV/AIDS, in a variety of testimonial vignettes in post-1973 Santiago. In many ways, Lemebel offers a revalorization of these maligned figures and engages them as transgressive radicals in a way similar to certain strands of transgender theory, although their social class may be the deciding factor in their subversiveness, rather than, in a strict sense, their gender or sexuality. He thus politicizes *loca* and *travesti* subjectivity. This project continues in the novel that this chapter examines, *Tengo miedo torero* (2002; *My Tender Matador*). There he makes visible their existence; that is, not as mainstream and acceptable subjects but still endowed with experiences, stories, and engagements. Finally, the study closes with a consideration of how to the presence or absence of the inscription of subjectivity might accrue political effects for real life *locas*, *travestis*, and *transexuales*. I reflect on the previous chapters and what their implications for the process of visibilization or elision of subjectivity might be in general terms.

ISSUES OF SOCIOECONOMIC CONTEXT IN TEXTUAL REPRESENTATIONS

> *In the passage from modernity to postmodernity the grounds and frontiers of Latin American regional and national cultures, traditions and patrimonies are being opened up and transformed with an intensity and depth that have probably never been seen or experienced before . . . something is happening to the grounds and frontiers of Latin American nations. Something is happening to the underlying telos of nationhood and national identity formations.*
>
> —Gareth Williams, *The Other Side of the Popular: Neoliberalism and Subalternity in Latin America*

Changes in political and cultural economy can bring about the questioning of long-held truths and structures. Most recently, the neoliberal model, with all its claims to transcendence and inevitability, has met with a number of challenges throughout the region and the explosion of social movements contesting its exclusions, *travesti* movements among them. A wave of popular leftist parties has gained power and questioned the application of neoliberalist theories to Latin America and its pretensions to being the natural and inevitable order of things. "Special Period" Cuba in the nineties also underwent its own upheavals that have brought about major economic and social restructuring, albeit for very different reasons. While neoliberalism is challenged in a great many Latin American countries, its impact in cultural and socioeconomic terms has been undeniable. Ironically, the fragmentation of reliable "truths" that it has brought about in the cultural terrain may serve different ends and create different effects—some potentially positive (for the recognition of difference or the unexpected openings of nonstate political space), and some not so positive. Notably, the sense that neoliberalist reform has weakened state foundations and borders sometimes translates culturally as a crisis in national identity; on another point the move to vaunted transnationality augurs a heightened real and virtual sense of transition, a state of mixture and hybridity of cultural signs and norms (Canclini 1989). Figurations of *travestis*, transsexuals, and *locas* on occasion may be said to register rhetorically on all these scales as symbolic, symptomatic, or reflective of such things.

Given that the influx of neoliberalism in Latin America came about first in Chile under the Pinochet regime and elsewhere subsequent to the infamous financial crises of the 1980s in places such as Brazil and Mexico, the concomitant reshaping and rerouting of socioeconomic relations and cultural discourses of nation occur precisely in the period this book covers. This arguably accounts for the concern with a crisis in nation or at least the sense of an impending transformation in the symbolic limits of national identity. If modernity marks the period of the consolidation of the nation-state in Latin America (and, as I will argue, the modern nation-state is established, in part, via a refusal of nonnormative genders and sexualities, as well as racial and ethnic others), the postmodern moment marks the beginning of its undoing as a grand narrative. Both moments—at the dawn of the twentieth century ("modernity") and the century's end ("postmodernity" or the postnational moment)—generate anxieties that get mapped onto subjects who are seen as "anxiety producing," although the problem or crisis they are said to embody may be of different orders.

Although the much recognized condition of the erosion of the national horizon and any master narrative of national identity (which is succinctly summed up by Gareth Williams in the quote that begins this section) serves as a starting point, the distinct adjuncts of the emergence of each text examined in the coming chapters are explored in due detail. With this in mind, the proposition that those texts more recently produced should demonstrate a deeper engagement with *loca* and *travesti* lives, due to the increased visibility of these subjects (as actors among the many new social movements), is investigated, nuanced, and challenged by way of addressing each locale's particularity around questions of the place of sex and gender minorities. Distinct historical, economic, national, and sociocultural dimensions will form the backdrop of the analysis of the texts. So, too, the reshaping of (trans)national relations will be an implicit reference point in the analysis of many of the texts. Cuba of the 1960s and 1970s, and the state of affairs just before the famous Mariel boatlift, represent very different historical junctures than that found in the Special

Period Cuba of the 1990s; these differences will be taken into account in the analysis of the various Cuban texts. Karim Aïnouz's film *Madame Satã* (2002) emerges precisely at the point of a major change that beckons Brazil at the start of the twenty-first century: the death knell to neoliberal orientations and the election of Luiz Inácio Lula da Silva, whose more than decade-long struggle to occupy government via his popular leftist Workers Party comes to fruition, confirming the rise of a posthegemonic politics of pluralization in society. Likewise, the conditions manifest in dictatorial, postdictatorial, and then transitional neoliberalist Chile will form the backdrop of the analysis of Lemebel's texts. The tightening economic conditions under the *sexenio* of Carlos Salinas de Gortari (1988–94), which culminated in the signing of the North American Free Trade Agreement (NAFTA) and its much-discussed transformation of socioeconomic relations in Mexico, will be an implicit reference point in the analysis of Mexican texts of the period. The state of relations, as well, between the United States and Puerto Rico in the early years of the twenty-first century when the Puerto Rican novel *Sirena Selena vestida de pena* was released, shadows my reading of the text in Chapter 5. Different locales and junctures afford different potentialities in terms of representation and the emergence of trans subjectivities. The texts, in their capacity as mediators and shapers of social realities, need to be located in their different time frames.

The dominant episteme of effeminacy and *travestismo* that emerges in the era of modern capital (from the late 1800s onward), and its potential transformation in light of a newly changed geopolitical landscape in the region (the late twentieth century), is of necessity related to dominant ideologemes (orthodox narratives) of gender and their own ongoing transformation. Many of the reigning discourses of masculinity, femininity (machismo and marianismo), and heterosexuality find themselves under revision in the era of global culture and transnational flows. Gender roles, like other social relations, have been impacted by neoliberalism in Latin America. What this means for the place of sexual minorities like *travestis* in the region is, as yet, inconclusive. But in terms of representations, we see an interesting blend of both inherited visions and newer frameworks. Visions of gender and dominant doxa are being refigured—transfigured, so to speak—by these new representations. But it is also true that older ideologemes persist and are rearticulated in certain ways.

As such, the way gender is configured in the sites in which the texts are produced and received will be key to any analysis. Gender has a long history in Latin America, but it is specious even to talk about gender there as if a uniform set of schema could be obtained across a geopolitical space of such cultural and linguistic variation, as intimated by Lancaster (1998), and Chant and Craske (2003). However, it is patently the case that gender in Latin America does exhibit certain shared (colonial and postcolonial) histories, crossings, patterns, and flows. This is what makes it possible at all to talk about *Latin American* gender ideologemes and dominant epistemes about *travestismo*. This book endeavors to reveal the current of rhetorical employments of *travestismo* in the region that makes it possible to think of specifically Latin American ways of thinking about sex and gender variance, caught up, as they have been, in hegemonic productions.

"Effeminate" homosexuals and *travestis*, notes Guillermo Núñez Noriega, are said to have "costumbres raras" (strange customs; 1999, 97).[8] Public transgression of gender is what is considered suspect in this formulation: variously alien, exotic, and inexplicable. Individuals are exhorted to play down the public show of such "strange" behaviors, which represent "escándalo" (scandal). For Núñez Noriega, it is not transgression that is questioned as such; rather, the form in which one exhibits this transgression, when, where, and how much matters more (243). Says Núñez Noriega, "Nuestro momento histórico se caracteriza por una pugna entre diferentes actores sociales por la aplicabilidad de criterios como 'normalidad,' 'naturaleza,' 'moralidad,' 'decencia,' 'pecado,' entre otros" (34; Our historical moment is characterized by a struggle between different social actors for the applicability of categories like "normality," "nature," "morality," "decency," "sin," among others.) *Locas* and *travestis* are social actors deeply implicated in these terms, as much in the field of sexuality as in that of gender. In the powerful binaries "normalidad-anormalidad" (normality-abnormality) and "naturalidad-antinaturalidad" (naturality-antinaturality) the sets "hombre-masculinidad-heterosexualidad" (man-masculinity-heterosexuality) and "mujer-feminidad-heterosexualidad" (woman-femininity-heterosexuality) are linked to the positive descriptor: "Naturaleza rara-afeminamiento-homosexualidad" (strange nature-effeminacy-homosexuality) assumes the negative descriptor (82–83). These axes of normalization, which naturalize both heterosexuality and male and female gender norms as well as articulate themselves in the field of sexual morality as risks to the social body, are the implicit structuring logic to many past and contemporary visions of sex and gender variance as explored at length in this book.

Throughout these pages, I take up the work, then, not just of the literary and film critic but also of the analyst of culture and the textually mediated social realm. If *locas*, *travestis*, and transsexuals have been discursively inscribed as problems, an agonistic site in which other problems rhetorically play themselves out or may be broached, what room is there to visualize them otherwise and conceive of them in ways not merely metaphorical? Have recently emerged minority knowledges that accompany the homosexual and nascent trans social movements of Latin America begun to create a space where this is at all possible? Some of the texts examined in the coming chapters indicate new horizons in imagining and inscribing these subjectivities. These new horizons in visions of sex and gender variance in Latin America shake up preconceptions that (trans)figures, whenever and wherever they appear, are always already metaphorical. They reveal avenues for the textual inscription of subjectivity that, while multilayered, resonant, and dialogic, does not restrict "lo trans" (trans phenomena) to the purely figural. They mark, in this way, something new in cultural visions that require new tools of analysis; such an analysis starts from the assumption that *locas, travestis,* and transsexuals are not inherently illustrative, deconstructive movements or props of postmodern gender theory but complex sites unto themselves, experienced in the everyday world and mediated by and in cultural forms. This book thus offers a wider vision of the dynamic of representations and the construction of these subjectivities than that which has been advanced in the few previous works on the subject.

Like John Phillips, the author of *Transgender on Screen* (2006), I acknowledge that this book is principally about fictional representations of *locas, travestis,* and transsexuals, not about the various manifestations of sexual identity and trans subjectivities in real life. Although his project rejects the ethical-political in favor of the psychoanalytical, making it quite different from this book's orientation, Phillips briefly ponders about the ultimate separability of the real from its representation, citing Louis Althusser when he states that all social reality is mediated through representations. Althusser's claim underpins the purposefulness of the present study itself (Phillips 2006, 27). Representations, as Stuart Hall has shown (1997), are not reflective of reality nor can they be used as evidence to read off audience responses, and yet the rhetorical features of discourse do structure the way that readers and audiences think about phenomena represented. They also shape and are shaped by culture. They are a form of cultural action, and as such, the epistemological questions and concerns about the impact of the logics of sexual minority representation that lie at the heart of this book insist on a hearing.

Chapter 1

Thinking Figurations Otherwise

Reframing Dominant Knowledges of Sex and Gender Variance in Latin America

Of Representations and Epistemes: Some Preliminaries

In the mural *La katharsis*, which hangs in Mexico City's Palacio de Bellas Artes, the great Mexican postrevolutionary artist José Clemente Orozco depicts a nightmarish panorama of militarism, conflict, and the collapse of a sociopolitical order. The title of the painting suggests a dramatic purgation of demons away from the usual strictures of society; a hell-bent letting loose of destructive energies in a baptism by fire; the perils of war, fascism, technology, and the modern age. In a visual field devoid of any recognizable agents of such forces—the painting is crowded by repeated but anonymous dark shapes flanked suffocatingly by metal coils and armaments—the only complete face and body that appears is that of the woman sprawled naked in the foreground. Her masklike visage stares vacantly and giddily at the viewer. Pearls wrapped around her neck above bare and drooping breasts, legs wide open, she is a prostitute—one of many painted by this artist. What is she doing alongside these indisputable images of the excesses of the bourgeois order: war and imperialism? What is the link? Is the sexual image suggested by this figure symbolic of the orgy of violence indicated in the rest of the painting? Here she is not trampled on or shown as brutalized or subjected to the surrounding terror; rather, she is a surface sign of its deep corruption; the wanton girl-toy of the rich, the Whore of Babylon whose presence is a metonym of the incipient moral decline in Europe—the old dame whose felled head lies next to the prostitute in the painting—and of the excesses of the industrial era.

This study does not concern the pictorial arts, yet Orozco's mural is a useful starting place to explore some of the theoretical and epistemological dimensions to an inquiry into the representation of sexual minorities in literary and filmic production, which is the principal objective of this chapter. Like the prostitute who is invoked as a symbol of the sociopolitical panorama exposed by Orozco—who to be sure, was not alone in his metaphorical use of such figures—*locas, travestis*, and transsexuals in recent decades (1985–2005) have been engaged in many literary and filmic texts from Latin America as symbols of another order—at times represented as purveyors of apocalypse, and at others, of redemptive possibility, among other things.

Orozco's prostitute is lifeless, bereft of individuality and social context: she is a mannequin, a tragicomic exhibit, a condensation of characteristics that embody superficiality, the loss of spirit and meaning, and a hollow decadence. *Locas, travestis*, and transsexuals are at times similarly invoked and manipulated in contemporary cultural production from Latin America, with comparable consequences: the diminution of any sense of inner life, interpersonal history, or subjectivity of the figures so portrayed.

The work of Donna Guy (1991) demonstrates that in the late nineteenth and for much of the twentieth century, the female prostitute was perceived as a threat to family and nation in Argentina. Like prostitutes in Latin American and other cultural contexts, visibly gender nonconforming homosexuals, as well as cross-dressing and cross-living *travestis* and transsexuals, have long been perceived as problematic. As sexual minorities, all these persons have been subject to intensive and objectifying discursive treatments from the late nineteenth century to the end of the millennium—another fin de siècle whose competing anxieties have inspired a resurgence of representations of sex and gender diverse figures seen to transgress the moral order and its sacred divisions.

In the new millennium, recognizing the upsurge in depictions of cross-gender acts, identities, and trans subjects, several critics in Latin American studies are giving more attention to the place of *lo loca* and *lo trans* in representations of nonnormative sexualities and genders. Most of these critics work from the context of Caribbean productions and Chilean representations in art and literature and are Latin American themselves (Arroyo 2003b, the critics from the special issue of *Centro* edited by Sandoval-Sánchez 2003, Richard 1993); others are Latinos writing from the geopolitical space of the United States (Sifuentes-Jáuregui 2001). Many draw on the idea of transvestites as "natural" metaphors for the construal of the national subject. They either understand the place of the *travesti* as embodiment of national colonial identity or resistance to its imposition.[1]

Informed by the structuralism of Severo Sarduy, and later, the queer theory work of Marjorie Garber and (early) Judith Butler, all emphasize *travestismo* as a performance, suffused with varying degrees of theatricality, artificiality, and simulation. Literary critics rarely, if ever, draw on Butler's more recent ethically concerned work seen in *Undoing Gender* (2004). Her influential theories of performativity attract attention. Critics do not tie the work of representation to the real-life impacts around gender crossing that Butler has begun to explore, mostly in response to criticism directed at her earlier work. Ben Sifuentes-Jáuregui begins his study by giving a working definition of transvestism: "transvestism is a performance of gender" (2001, 2). Further, for him, transvestism's operational strategy is the "denaturalization of genders," blurring the distinctions between self and other (4). Sifuentes-Jáuregui and his Latin American colleagues are invested in the idea of *travestismo* as symptomatic or instrumental of something; they do not explore the possibilities of the textual inscription of subjectivity.[2] For these critics, the very performativity of *travestismo*—as a ground for configuring through gesture and imitation—establishes it as primordially and preeminently metaphorical in any text in which gender variant figures are present.

This book parts ways with such notions. While sex- and gender-crossing figures have historically been linked to the national sphere, and as a consequence, subject to allegorization, there is nothing "natural" to this representational treatment in culture and discourse. Such a critical determination provides little room to situate representations of *locas*, *travestis*, and transsexuals that are not preeminently disposed to metaphor and may be informed by emergent, alternative knowledges. In this chapter, and through the analysis of texts undertaken in this book, I lay bare the discursive conditions of possibility that allow *locas*, *travestis*, and transsexuals to be invoked in the name of the national, and the rhetorical mechanisms that permit them to be appropriated as a sign of change, crisis, or trouble, by engaging in a deconstructive excavation of the genealogy of dominant knowledges about sex and gender variance in the Latin American context. Such dominant knowledges, formed over time, have structured the representation and representability of past and present visions of sex and gender variance. The reigning episteme that encodes effeminacy and *travestismo* in reference to things as diverse as concealment, criminality, subversion, parody, colonial mimesis, and hybridity needs to be situated in terms of its lineage, across the range of sites in which such attributions appear. A fundamental precept of this chapter is that theories that choose sex and gender variance as the object of their inquiry, and that do not lay bare the genealogy of representations in text and culture, can themselves reproduce and prop up dominant visions. As such I include critical approaches to *lo trans* in texts and contexts within the purview of my genealogy, in order to remain alert to this danger but also as a measure that serves to situate my own, very different approach. This approach draws on understandings of the place of subjectivity, which is also addressed in depth in the current chapter. A critical genealogy of dominant frameworks about *locas*, *travestis*, and transsexuals and their representation in texts has so far not been undertaken by contemporary critics writing on the subject of the cultural representation of sex and gender variance in Latin America, and, as such, is long overdue.

Discourses of the National "Body" and Social Order: "Deviance," Crisis, and Metaphor

Literary historiography pinpoints the emergence of homosexual types in literary representations in Latin America and how they are forever linked to the social order. David William Foster, in his introduction to *Sexual Textualities: Essays on Queer/ing Latin American Writing* (1997), for instance, argues that since the appearance of what is recognized as the first modern Latin American "homosexual" novel, Adolfo Camhina's *Bom Crioulo* (Brazil, 1895; *Bom-Crioulo: The Black Man and the Cabin Boy*), there has been a greater emphasis on homoerotic acts rather than questions of individual identity in Latin American literature, especially in modernity. He notes that in this text, and subsequent texts, homosexuality is frequently related to the greater patriarchal order "rather than the emphasis one finds in American writing on questions of personal identity and internal psychological process" (1997, 2). The linking of the libidinal economy of the "passive" homosexual role to the social order lays the conceptual groundwork for the linking of *locas*, *travestis*, and transsexuals in their gender styles and positionalities to other spheres in contemporary texts.[3]

Outside Latin American literature, in both medico-legal and nationalist discourse, we see precedents of the invocation of sex– and gender–diverse acts and subjects in connection to problems in the national-cultural sphere. The dying years of the nineteenth century and the dawning of the twentieth foresaw the intense scrutiny and taxonomization of subjects in the public gaze who differed from certain standard norms in Argentina, Mexico, Nicaragua, and other Latin American nations (Fernández 2004, 25). Emergent homosexual and *travesti* subcultures were targeted by lawmakers, criminologists, and medical professionals—among other groups such as working-class itinerant laborers, prostitutes, and immigrants as well as indigenous people—as the source of a range of social "vices" that seemingly threatened bourgeois morality, its ideas of property, behavioral and bodily standards, and the safe flow of capital and control of classes.[4] Same-sex erotic practices, cross-dressing and cross-living behaviors became discursively inscribed as a sort of person—the invert—whose nature was aberrant, deviant, and cross-sexed. Further, subjects who displayed such behaviors were associated "scientifically" with crime and grouped alongside prostitutes, professional criminals, swindlers, and violent thieves (25).

The work of Jorge Salessi (2000) is especially illuminating on the discursive forms around gendered others that such codings assumed in Argentina in the period. The "patria"—a masculine, virile entity—was threatened by several perceived enemies. State authorities exhibited a real anxiety over notions of citizen-outsider, private-public, and health-contamination. Several minorities, including homosexuals, *travestis*, and so-called public women, were all visualized as the second term in these categories. A group of *higienistas*, based at the Faculty of Medicine of the University of Buenos Aires, allied with the police and with correctional facilities to criminalize, castigate, and control these "errant" flows. These groups were characterized as *maleantes*—criminals, low-lifes, or bad seeds—who threatened the order and represented forces of anarchy. Their presence and movement through space was conceived of as a form of dangerousness. The most public of these populations—those present in the various *lupanares* (brothels), soliciting while strolling in town plazas or in the port, whether public women or homosexual inverts—were considered agitative and outside "normal" work relations: their traffic and commerce was seen to disturb the healthy flows of the social corpus. Argentina—a healthy masculine body—risked bad circulation and atrophy of its "members." The *higienistas* made recommendations to prevent the spread of a social contamination of the body politic. The *higienistas'* objective was to heal and integrate this nation—in danger of contamination and seduction into deviance (brothels and homosexual cabarets were described as sites of infection). In this way, fin-de-siècle fears around deviance and (sexual) anarchy posited publicly visible same-sex erotic practices and cross-dressing as apocalyptic signs of the end of an order, the end of an era, and the destruction of the "civilized nation."[5] Such sciences of deviance and social control were replicated in Brazil, notes James Green (1999). Salessi's work is the only one to investigate these kinds of discourses in real depth. Similar archives from other countries warrant close attention (Green 1999, 9).

Race and racial mixing also figured strongly in the positivist discourse of the late nineteenth and early twentieth centuries. Of course, the question of racial and cultural heterogeneity—and how to envision a meaningful national community in the postindependence period and modernizing project—has long been one of considerable obsession for Latin American elite thinkers and politicos. The cult of cultural and racial *mestizaje*—so key to colonial consolidation, the efforts of the wars of independence, the formation of the modern nation-state and the mythic forms of *latinidad*—was suddenly radically recontoured by the fin-de-siècle concerns for racial purity that generated considerable fear and obsession and were coded in the language of contagion. In her book *The Rise and Fall of the Cosmic Race: The Cult of Mestizaje in Latin America* (2004), Marilyn Grace Miller argues that *mestizaje* and its relation to national discourse has undergone important transformations and has been used to both racist and antiracist ends. Other writers propose a four-point periodization of different ways of conceptualizing race in relation to nation in the region (Appelbaum, Macpherson, and Rosemblatt 2003). These writers hold that racial difference has been alternately "ignored, expressed, appropriated and transformed" by nationalizing processes and in nation discourse at different times (2). Although engaged in a "positive" sense in the very name of nationalism and nation building in Mexico after the revolution and in Brazil in the 1930s under Getúlio Vargas, *mestizaje* (and, it might be observed, *mulatez*) was often condemned at the turn of the nineteenth century and the first decades of the twentieth; Europeanness and whiteness, linked to progress, were the ideal. In places were *mestizaje* was not reevaluated early in the twentieth century, scientific racism informed the rejection of nonwhite groups or implicitly encoded national citizenship in masculine and white terms in the region at least till the 1940s (Graham 1990, 3). If the specter of plagues induced a sort of hysteria around sexual subjects that demanded the elimination of all "transgressive differences" to constitute and protect the "ideal national community, imagined as a strong and healthy body," *indios, negros, mestizos,* and mulattos became, perhaps more profoundly, targets of blame as imputed historical and enduring sources of sickness, weakness and "retardation" of "la raza nacional" (Nouzeilles 2003, 51–52). Disease became the symptom and metaphor for social disorder. Mechanisms of control and surveillance were recommended by positivist scientists and educators to prevent the spread of an epidemic. In the novel *Salón de belleza*, examined in Chapter 4, Mario Bellatin very craftily reroutes the vectors of a metaphorical disease coded in epidemiological terms and attached to his gender-variant characters. Given that the 1980s saw the emergence of the AIDS epidemic, which was fused in the social imaginary in many parts of the world, including Latin America, to homosexuality, it is hardly coincidental that plague metaphors and sexual others still haunt contemporary narratives. Indeed, the convergence of visions of sex and gender otherness with the moral panic around this disease, so prone to rhetorical reelaboration, is an important dimension for multiple reasons, which are revealed in forthcoming chapters. It is also not an overstatement to signal the importance of the realities of stigma and HIV for *travestis* from that time to the present day. A full elaboration of the discursive connections between marginal others and disease—in all their metaphorically gendered and racialized dimensionalities—is hence crucial.

The discourse of the Argentina's one-time president and Buenos Aires intellectual, Domingo Faustino Sarmiento, is unremitting in its racial profiling of the "barbarism" that threatens future Argentinian society. Sarmiento further plotted the cultured "city dweller" against the rural workers and frontier Pampas gauchos. The characteristic abjection, baseness, primitivism, and, tellingly, passivity and feminization, ascribed to all these racial and ethnic others in his work promulgated the archetypal views on the struggle between the superior "civilized" elements of Latin American culture and the "backward" and debilitating admixture of bad racial "blood" supposedly plaguing the nation.[6]

Jean Franco shows how the endemic "dangerous ill" said to afflict Latin American societies was persistently coded in racial terms (1970, 56–58). Darwinistic theories on the biological predispositions of the allegedly inferior stock of Indians were advanced by the Mexican Francisco Alonso de Bulnes and linked to the perils facing nationhood in *El porvenir de las naciones latinoamericanas* (1899; *The Future of the Latin American Nations*). This work was composed during the era of Porfirio Díaz, a time in which *lo indio* (Indianness) as representative of "la problemática nacional" (the national dilemma) was intensively discussed. In different parts of Latin America, such as Colombia, the Caribbean, and Brazil, blacks were attributed with a "slave mentality" and compliant attitude; Indians were identified for their inherent "resignation" and "passivity" (Franco 1970, 58). These tropes of race and their essentialist frameworks have persisted and interpellated blacks, mulattos, and *indios* as constitutive others to the so-called superior white European citizen of the civilized ideal nation. (Later, in the context of 1930s U.S.-dominated Puerto Rico, we see the repetition of some of these racial tropes and the degradation of the feminine in the nationalist discourse of Antonio S. Pedreira (1992 [1934]).

Further, in the Andean republics and in Mexico, as Jean Franco notes, the Indian was seen as an obstacle to progress and modernity (58). The Bolivian Alcides Arguedas articulated perhaps most vividly the image of the diseased nation in *Pueblo enfermo* (1909), a body stricken by its debilitated constitution and the stupor of the natural environment, both materialized in the Indian. Brazil's complicated history with the problematics of race is underwritten by the facts of slavery there, remembering that the nation was the last to outlaw it in the region. "Branqueamento" as an ideal—whitening and becoming more like the white, via breeding and custom—was prevalent as a philosophy even after the abolition of slavery. Together with Cuba, Brazil has displayed some differences in thinking race in relation to nation that are important—and different moments of mythologization in the name of the national community. In spite of this, racial and cultural difference are still nodes that structure their national elaborations.

Just as the Argentinian *higienistas* sought to heal and integrate the nation—in danger of contamination and seduction into deviance—so, too, did politicians in Argentina and elsewhere in pre–World War II Latin America promote programs to "dilute" the *mestizo* racial stock from its weakening, and feminizing, influences. Writing in the first two decades of the twentieth century, the Argentinian medico-criminologist, sociologist, and psychiatrist José Ingenieros, for instance, favored Germanic European immigration over Italian, Spanish, or French to strengthen the race from its Indio-Hispanic congenital inferiority (Terán 1986). The qualities of barbarity attributed by Sarmiento to *indios* and "mixed-breed" gauchos would be bred out under the civilizing influence of modern European immigrants. Interestingly, Sarmiento himself also warned of the *afeminamiento* (feminization) of Argentinian literature and culture, which for him represented an emasculation of the virility of the society and the nation.

Weak in their dispositions and unnatural in their passions, both racial and sexual subjects, then, were perceived as a threat to the harmony of the imagined social corpus and theorized as a contamination of the national body. Perhaps it is unsurprising to find that the metaphors of abjection and otherness used in reference to the aforementioned racial others are also deployed in reference to *locas*, *travestis*, and transsexuals. In the heat of anxieties around the possibility of anarchy, sexual minorities were positioned from this time as a source of many ills. Even when *mestizaje* as a sign of mixity was revalorized and appropriated in the name of joining potential contradictions together in state projects of national unity and common imagined histories, both racial and gendered crossings served symbolically to signify the national realm. Hence the connection between racial and gendered others is resignified but does not loosen. In fact, as we will later see in the work of contemporary cultural critics, *travestismo* is so married in Latin American thought to the processes of national identity and *mestizaje* as to create, I will argue, a kind of *travestizaje*, in which the figure of the *travesti* is advanced as a figure par excellence of the process of national identity construction. This is an element of the dominant episteme that is complexly constructed across a range of discursive sites and naturalized by much postmodern (especially queer) theory.

NATIONALIST DISCOURSE AND ITS DEFINITIONAL OTHERS

In reference to paradigmatic nationalist discourse in Latin America and elsewhere, critics such as Doris Sommer (1991), Joane Nagel (1998), Josefina Ludmer (2002), George Mosse (1985), and Andrew Parker et al. (1992) have argued that nationalism and the process of nation formation are structured in heterosexist, masculinist, and patriarchal terms; this is the only real logic behind the idea that nonmasculine males, cross-dressers, and male-to-female (MTF) transgender people—and "bad" women—serve as apt metaphors for crisis or contradiction in nation or national trouble.

In Latin America the concept of nation building has relied on naturalized notions of "male" and "female," with the first category subordinating the second. One could well agree with George Mosse's words that "nationalism had a special affinity for male society," and together with the concept of respectability, "legitimized the dominance of men over women" in Latin America (1985, 67).

Doris Sommer argues in *Foundational Fictions: The National Romances of Latin America* (1991) that the symbolic construction of nation as an imagined community is seen in Latin American romantic literature's representation of heterosexual romantic pairings that transcend the boundaries of race, class, and region to signify the unity and unification of nation. Sexual and affectional links across lines of difference diffused the possibility of a threat that always haunted—and haunts—a stable notion of nation. Sommer's thesis confirms the gender-bipolar heteronormative elements in nation discourse even if it does not explore explicitly the way other forms of difference may become sources of tension in national imaginings. In *Mexican Masculinities* (2003), Robert McKee Irwin argues, however, that as a masculinist discourse, nationalism is modeled more on relations between men, arguing that Sommer underestimates the central role of the figuring of male homosocial relationships in the image of nation building and unity. Clearly both critics see a strong link between the culture's gender conceptions, sexuality, and its concepts of national identity.

Critics such as Nira Yuval-Davis (1997) and Amy Kaminsky (1993) highlight as well the position of women within this schema of nation and national reproduction, with respect to the naturalized historical understandings of motherhood in the national project. The simultaneous deprecation of women, due to the patriarchal contents of the national project, ironically possesses a parallel elevation of the celebrated role of the mother. Women, however, see themselves confined to this role as their "good" and "proper" place. Yuval-Davis explores how national processes and national reproduction are bound up with gender codes that specify definite ideas about manhood and womanhood, wherein manhood is the structuring and ordering force (the state) and womanhood that which is subjected (the life of the nation). These motifs recur at many junctures of colonial and national expansion in many parts of the world. Kaminsky focuses on this phenomenon in Latin American texts and contexts, showing that although "patria" may mean "fatherland," it connotes on a very compelling level in feminine ways, in a move that connects the patriarchal project of the nation-state to the land, *la tierra*, conceived as feminine. "La tierra nourishes, sustains, is prior to transformation by politics, economics or technology," all fields traditionally posited as the realm of men (1993, 5). Men occupy the public and women the private: a realm supposedly untouched by commerce or the affairs of the world. Women, by their touted biological reproductive function and due to the putative facticity of sex, embody the field of *la tierra*.

The *criollo* project of nation in the new republics of Latin America in the colonial period was very much a gendered one; writers such as Yuval-Davis and Kaminsky provide necessary reflections on how nations are gendered and how genders are nationalized. In modernity, the process of nation-state formation—*forjando patria* (forging the fatherland)—also relied on gendered codes. The state was the father and the nation the mother; the citizens were the children. The phrase *madre patria*, invoked by modern constructions of nationalism, relies on a metaphor of gender complementarity, reinstalling the male image in the guise of power and government and the female in the role of nurturer, protector, and the womb from which springs the life of the nation. Idealization of motherhood was thus key to this discourse of nation, implying the drive to reproduction at all costs, which is based as an ideology on very heteronormative principles. *Locas* and *travestis*—seen as unproductive in biological and social terms and unnaturally feminine—meet a kind of double exclusion. This exclusion operates due to their perceived failure to embody proper and mutually exclusive genders, as the concept of nature dictates, and because they, at best, occupy a space similar to women, in which forms of feminine identification and sexuality that do not involve reproduction are denigrated. Only masculine, patriarchal men gain symbolic capital in this regime of nation and its scheme of hetero-masculinist triumphalism and domination.

As Benedict Anderson has indicated, "the nation is always conceived as a deep, horizontal comradeship" (1991, 5), a passionate brotherhood, or in the words, again, of Irwin, nationhood has in Latin America and other places been conceived as "a virile institution" (Irwin 2003, 15). Concomitantly, as Anderson also states, implying "some element of alterity for its definition," a nation is ineluctably "shaped by what it opposes" (1991, 6). But by the very fact that such identities depend constitutively on difference means that nations are "forever haunted by their various definitional others" (5). Historically, these various definitional others in the Latin American context include inverts and *locas* and *travestis* in contemporary terms. The notion of national unity is frequently modeled on sex and gender norms. Usurping this unity—or problematizing the idea of nation—is represented through a subversion or transgression of these norms (6). In understanding the effects of colonialism, there is an intellectual tradition from the colonial through to the modern era that advances the notion of the feminization of so-called conquered peoples by a masculine colonial master in Latin America. Such a tradition—largely advanced by elite intellectual males—offers vivid confirmation of the work of Yuval-Davis and Kaminsky. People who in the real world showed alignments with the feminine were discursively implicated in this move; the derogatively labeled effeminate homosexual, said to take the sexually passive role, constituted one such person (apart from women). The gendered understanding of colonialism in this way became entangled with individual gendered identities, roles, and choices.[7] This is key to the construction of the dominant episteme for thinking about effeminacy and *travestismo* in the twentieth century.

Apart from the discursive lineage that connects same-sex eroticism and trans practices to problems in the national sphere—as forms of threat to the nation that come from an "afuera" (Salessi 1999)—it is in the fin-de-siècle period that the effeminate or cross-dressed male is first visualized as a shamed and shameful body; as artificial, comic, and grotesque; as excessively "dressed," scandalous, and drawing attention to itself. The new century in Mexico was ushered in with the case of *Los '41*—to which Ben Sifuentes-Jáuregui devotes the first chapter of his book—when police performed a raid on a group of upper class males or *lagartijos* (fops) dancing with cross-dressed partners—and ignited the public imagination around questions of homosexuality, transvestism, and decadence.[8] Many of the attributions inaugurated at this time are still found in media discourse on *travestis* in many locales, which continues to advance the terms of falsity, depravity, criminality, and *malas costumbres* (bad custom). Legal statutes originate from the time in which criminologists determined gender-crossing and effeminate homosexuals as a criminal type; these similarly invoke the terms of *ofensas al pudor público* (offences to public modesty), *las buenas costumbres* (good custom), and the promotion of "escándalo." Inverts then, and *locas* and *travestis* now, represented and represent a rupture in the set terms for the public body in medico-legal discourse. Speaking of the contemporary period, Josefina Fernández notes that these formulations presently circulate so widely that they put limits on seeing *travesti* identity in any other way in dominant culture: they are always located socially "del lado de lo abyecto" (2004, 118; "alongside the abject").[9] In political discourse across the region, party politics and the borrowing or stealing of policies of another group are very commonly framed as "travestismo político." Intrigue and corruption at the political level are commonly married to the image of *travestis* and *travestismo*.[10]

These discursive conditions, then, have made and, to some extent, continue to make it possible to enjoin effeminacy and *travestismo* in the name of imagining crisis and corruption and to conjoin them with the problematics of national identity and its construction. In the next section, I show that, by their overreliance on the queer theory work on transvestism and transgender, contemporary criticism that treats the representation of *locas*, *travestis*, and *transexuales* in Latin American cinema and literature fails to question and in fact reenmeshes itself in the dominant views of sex- and gender-variant figures as essentially figurative and symbolic of identity composition or crisis, bypassing a deconstruction of the metaphor and a view of the possibilities of envisioning sex and gender transitivity outside its terms.

Theory Trouble: On Not Avoiding the Subject

As alluded to at the beginning of this chapter, theoretical approaches to the representation of sex and gender crossing in Latin American cultural production are inspired by three principal sources: the work of Severo Sarduy (1969; 1982), Marjorie Garber (1992), and Judith Butler (1990; 1993). Some of Sarduy's work anticipates that of the other two thinkers, although it emerged prior to queer theory. In spite of their differences of methodology and approach, in each thinker, the transvestite—as idea, as stage performer, as cultural "role," or as repertoire—is the chosen object for critical view. In virtually all extant work on the literary and cinematic representation of *travestis*, these critics function as the inescapable points of reference. And yet, on a number of counts, such a free application of theory is problematic. First, in relying on work that is largely abstract and devoid of deeper considerations as to the cultural locations of and range of perceptions around *travestis*, at best, critics risk providing generalizing readings; at worst, by uncritically employing the rhetorical turns of structuralist approaches and postmodern queer theory, they verge on celebrating and naturalizing the allegorization of such subjects in literary and cinematic texts, authorizing, via particular academic discourses, the instrumentalist view of the trans figures in texts and culture, wherein sex and gender crossing and change never obtain any status beyond the performative and symbolic. Second, the privileging of the work of, in this instance, Garber and (early) Butler becomes problematic when critics draw on these thinkers to account for representations of *travestis* in Latin American texts but do not account for the important fact that their theories evolved elsewhere and respond to debates and logics that are of U.S. origin. The inclusion of Sarduy's work on transvestites in this contemporary scholarship may, on occasion, function as a de facto attempt to connect Latin American representations to Latin American critical work on the figure of the *travesti* and yet only to the extent that Sarduy's work combines with elements from queer's deconstructive use of "transgender." Those who analyze contemporary cultural representation of *locas*, *travestis*, and *transexuales* rarely seek out work on sexual and gender subjectivities in a Latin American context; they also do not move outside the terms of *travestismo* as a performative identity vector that inevitably speaks to and embodies other concerns.

Theory's blind spot around its own enmeshment in the dominant ways of thinking about *travestismo* or sex and gender variance is what I address in this section, using the work of several scholars whose objects of analysis, as in the inquiry of Garber and Butler, are also trans people, but who themselves are trans. If queer theory has made "transgender" a key point of its theoretical deliberations, it has also patently brought about an explosion in talk—especially, but not only, in academic sites—around transvestites, transgendered, and transsexual people. And yet much of this talk has been restricted by the privileging of theories about nonnormative gender identities that do little to challenge some of the underpinnings of the trans person as performer or metaphorical figure. I highlight these things in order to situate how and why this book opts for a different approach and remains suspicious of the reifying tendencies of queer-inspired contemporary criticism.

The theories of the gay Cuban writer exiled in Paris, Severo Sarduy, elaborated in two of his crucial works, *Escrito sobre un cuerpo* (1969; *Written on a Body*) and *La simulación* (1983; *The Simulation*), have been formative in cultural and critical conceptualizations of *travestis* and *transexuales* in Latin America. Writing under the obvious influence of the French poststructuralism of Lacan and Barthes, notions of excess and artificiality are also extended in Sarduy's work on *travestis*, as well as the terms of theatricality, the baroque, and carnivalesque performance. The language of appropriation and incorporation, self and other, so central to Lacan's notions of identity formation, orient Sarduy's visions. Further, in his fictional work that depicts *travestis*, the relation to the national subject is recast; Sarduy draws on the Lacanian analysis of *travestismo* and offers implications for identity formation and its mechanisms, especially in relation to (Cuban) collective and cultural identity.

For Sarduy, *travestismo* is about the appropriation of gesture, clothing, and its extension beyond established limits. It refers to simulation and the covering up of a lack. *Travestismo* is a movement, a chain of infinitely deployed signifiers that have no fixed signified. The *travesti*[11] does not emulate women but, rather, looks at the artifactual construction of Woman and femininity and reproduces it.[12] *Travestismo* concerns a play of surfaces, a successive presentation of masks. The lack or defect to which Sarduy refers concerns castration anxiety and this drives the *travesti* to cross-dress. *Travestismo* becomes for the cross-dresser a way of gesturally identifying with the female, without actually becoming a female "himself." As "he" cross-dresses, he keeps his penis, which reminds him he is still a man. This accentuates the feeling of masculinity and compensates for the sense of psychic loss effected by the fantasy of castration. Sarduy does not hesitate to inscribe this transvestite construction of femininity as thoroughly phallic.[13]

Sarduy never visualizes the possibility of a *travesti* subject—the *travesti* is always essentially male: a male caught in the mirror phase and seduced by symbolic identification with the (m)other. He hence desires to incorporate her, for in Oedipal terms, she has stolen the phallus. *Travestismo* is a way of covering over that loss. Further, *travestismo* is clearly conceived by Sarduy as chiefly a visual effect, a copy of a copy. In these terms it constitutes the reflection in a mirror that dissolves the distinction between self and other, and is the product of a fantasy of identification, incorporation, fusing, and appropriation. This language is often central to the way many critics conceive of the function of *travestis* in literary and visual texts (see especially Richard 2003).

Garber has been formative in shaping perceptions of what transvestism and transgender might mean in culture generally. In her book *Vested Interests: Cross Dressing and Cultural Anxiety* (1992), she talks of the transvestite in culture and literature as a figure that indicates the place of category crisis, "disrupting and calling attention to cultural, social or aesthetic dissonances" (1992, 16). The transvestite for her indicates category crisis. There has been a tendency to look past the transvestite to a "crisis of elsewhere"; that is, this trans figure has been used as a sign for crises in other categories like race, class, or nationality.

Garber analyzes a wide range of texts as examples. The presence of the female-to-male (FTM) cross-dresser played by Barbra Streisand in the film *Yentl*, for instance, is for Garber an example of the use of the transvestite figure to deal with the issues of U.S. immigration and anti-Semitism, ethnic mixing, crossings of race and class, and consequential changes in national culture. These issues could be said to be the core themes of the film, then, and not the subject of gender crossing per se (79). The transvestite is too ambiguous, too anxiety producing, to be looked at directly, so much so that if he or she is figured, then it is to embody other characteristics. The transvestite is assumed by Garber to constitute a natural metaphor for such characteristics. In the Latin American context, Sifuentes-Jáuregui and others ascribe to this view, calling principally on the authority of Garber's text.

Why might the transvestite be the most classic metaphor to embody questions of crossing or crisis in race, ethnicity, or national identity? Garber's notion of transvestism as a "third space" offers an explanation for the connection between transvestism and the idea of national identity construction in a postcolonial setting.[14] The "third" is not so much a solid term as a mode of articulation, which Garber explicitly links to the Third World and identity renegotiation in the face of colonialism. Garber asserts that she does not understand the Third World as a fixed place—conceptually it paralyzes us within a homogeneous scheme that cannot account for the multiplicities and diversity contained by the term—but rather as a mode of enunciation, which has contestatory power, as the much touted Third World other is articulated back to the West in ways that exceed and trouble First World fantasies of its other.

This position has been highly influential in readings by American Latino and several Caribbean scholars (see, especially, Sandoval-Sánchez 2003). For all these critics, the *travesti*'s body can be read as metaphorical of the colonized body. *Travestismo* is posited as an even more appropriate metaphor for states of coloniality than the image of the mask used by Frantz Fanon (see especially van Haesendonck 2003, 87); the *travesti* is evaluated as a figure who collates an already projected and idealized image of an other, which is representative of what all colonial subjects do in arriving at their own identities. Both identities are performed before a dominant gaze; in the case of the *travesti*, the public whom she seductively entertains, confuses, and hoodwinks with her putatively copied femininity (see Richard 1993); in the case of colonial subjects, the hegemonic Western Self that demands these subjects represent the other according to pre-set visions of colonized peoples. For some critics, this image of otherness is always an imposition, and *travestismo* similarly derives from submission and domination (Richard 1993; and critics in Sandoval-Sánchez 2003). For others, the performance of otherness as symbolized by "transvestic gender" is a space of subversion and resistance (Sifuentes-Jáuregui 2001). As such, these critics concur with the maxim expressed by Garber that transvestism always expresses a range of "vested interests" as its troubling power maps itself into so many areas (1993, 11–13).

Two landmark texts by Butler that deploy transvestites and transsexuals in their arguments, *Gender Trouble: Feminism and the Subversion of Identity* (1990) and *Bodies That Matter: On the Discursive Limits of "Sex"* (1993), have exerted a major influence on ways of reading and writing trans figures. Although in more recent work, such as the previously mentioned *Undoing Gender*, Butler complicates her discursive foci by looking beyond the gestural and performative in regards to trans genders, these two earlier texts are still much more drawn upon by literary and cultural critics reading trans acts and identities in narrative forms. In *Gender Trouble*, Butler employs drag to illustrate the way gender and the sense of a gendered being is secured via a constant repetition that is a copy of a copy. Drag, she argues, foregrounds the imitative structure of gender acts by underlining their radical contingency. Drag is about parody: it ironically denaturalizes gender by showing its performative nature, not attempting to conceal it—realness and naturality are effects. Drag for Butler exposes the imaginary relations between sex and gender; there is no abiding core for which gender is the outcome or expression; rather the expression (the outside) constitutes the idea of an inside, which is decentered especially when drag draws attention to its construction. Drag makes conscious what all subjects do every day (1990, 137–38). Saying that gender is performed and that drag allegorizes the moment of its construction is not the same as saying that one can simply put on or cast off a gender at whim, as if it were simply a question of costume change.[15]

In spite of these qualifications, the place of transgender—both drag and transsexuality—is crucial to Butler's early theorizations. Butler's reading in *Bodies That Matter* of the life of the Latina transsexual prostitute, Venus Xtravaganza, as featured in the film *Paris Is Burning*, advances the conception that transgender can represent the ascription of norms, not simply those of gender, but also ethnicity and privilege. While Garber pegs transvestism as always symbolic of a "crisis elsewhere"—in race, class, and other categories—Butler argues in "Gender is Burning," a chapter of *Bodies That Matter*, that "in *Paris Is Burning*, becoming real, becoming a real woman . . . constitutes the site of the phantasmatic promise of rescue from poverty, homophobia, and racist delegitimation" (1993, 30). This interpretation maps transsexuality as a desire for assimilation to dominant norms of privilege and escape from one position to another. Transgender thus can be read, on occasion, claims Butler, as a vector or vehicle for transcending certain material conditions curtailed by the usual restrictions of race and one's standing. The enactment of (trans)gender thus does not merely point to the performed nature of all gender; it may serve the reconstitution of other raced and classed identities.[16]

The deployment of *travestismo* as an organizational grid that is a perfect metaphor from national and regional identity construction in Latin America—in a movement that reconstructs *mestizaje* as *travestizaje*—obtains theoretical authorization when critics cite Garber's and Butler's notions of "transgender" as a matrix of (gender, class, and race) identity construction. The parodic postcard produced by the Chilean-Australian artist, Juan Dávila, *El libertador* (1994; *The Liberator*), is frequently invoked to forward the vision of *travestismo* as conceptually in line with national and cultural identity formation. Dávila's postcard shows a Simón Bolívar atop horse sexually transformed—with both breasts and vagina—cross-dressed and cross-gendered, with putatively Indian features. Richard (1998) reminds us that Dávila's queering of this sacred figure of *latinidad*, so central to nation formation, makes conscious the elements of the subaltern that, while not always celebrated, forge the hybrid synthesis of Latin American culture in the postindependence and modern periods.

Arroyo's account of travestismo cultural, meanwhile, also describes cross-gendering as reflective of the combination of subaltern elements—raced and gendered—to produce a whole identity. While Arroyo (2003b) stresses that all subjects do this, she singles out *travestismo* to represent this process of national identification, positing a form of *travestizaje*, literalizing what Dávila's postcard evokes. This is a movement she detects in Cuban and Brazilian discourses of nation; Arroyo does not go far enough, however, to deconstruct the deep logic that fuses *travestismo* with national identity construction or with the image of the mask and play of signifiers. The lacuna in such theorizing is evident in that critics are unable to see past *travestismo* as performative vector or symbol and symptom of national and regional identity; this is not helped by the methodological issue of what forms of knowledge about *travestis* they use.

Although visions of trans performativity and allegory in particular have achieved a high level of critical authority and ubiquitousness as bibliographical sources in many studies, they have not gone unchallenged. Jay Prosser delivers a trenchant appraisal of the centrality of transgender as trope in Butler's work in his book *Second Skins: The Body Narratives of Transsexuality* (1998). Viviane Namaste (2000) reads and challenges queer theory's appropriation of transgender. She confirms Jay Prosser's thesis on the allegorization of transgender for queer's theoretical project—as seen in the early work of Butler—and also argues that when queer theorists write about transgender phenomena in a diverse range of texts and contexts, they tend to disregard or erase trans subjectivity (Namaste 2000, 2; 270–71).

Namaste posits that Butler in her early influential texts allegorizes transgender and transsexual lives and bodies to talk about the production of gender and race norms. She interrogates Butler's analysis of *Paris Is Burning* as given in *Bodies That Matter* (1993, 13) and also challenges some of the assumptions behind Garber's notion of the transvestite as deployed in *Vested Interests*. In particular, it is worth looking at her critique of Garber's approach, as this approach informs so many critical appraisals generally, to show where her own analysis differs from Garber's.

Namaste agrees with Garber that transgendered and transsexual people are frequently invoked to represent crises in nation or national identity. She differs, however, from Garber in that she does not see them as natural metaphors for this condition in any way. In doing so, she contradicts the critics so far discussed, all of whom posit the connection as logical and self-evident. A sociologist and semiotician, Namaste highlights the rhetorical processes at work that act to constitute metaphors that link transvestites, transsexuals, and other nonnormative gender subjects to other issues via the vehicle of troping. Garber never exposes the constructed nature of the metaphorization of transvestites or transsexuals to the ends of representing class, race, or national crises, perhaps because—like much queer theory—she takes their symbolic function as a given. Namaste posits that Garber fails to see the transvestite as anything other than a performative and performing figure; in seeking to explicate the anxieties in culture about the transvestite, to look at the transvestite, Garber, too, looks through the transvestite (2000, 14–15). In trying to account for the cultural energies inscribed in transvestism, she tends to generalize, as if the transvestite were always singular and symbolic. The transvestite is always a stage performer for Garber—a movement, a set of characteristics, a sartorial code switch—not a subject with a context and lived experience or subjectivity (14). This is a tendency we also observed in Sifuentes-Jáuregui's work, whose theoretical framework is based on Garber's and that of Richard (1993). Namaste claims that in Garber's examination of the transvestite in texts as diverse as the Hollywood film *The Silence of the Lambs* and the trans community magazine, *Tapestries*, "Garber never examines the social context of these representations, implying that academics can look 'at' transvestites in these texts without accounting for their material, discursive and institutional locations" (15).[17]

Namaste is interested, in contrast, in the political consequences of the rhetorical structures found in representations; she politicizes the representation of transgender subjects because, as a transsexual scholar-activist, she would agree with film critic and queer scholar Richard Dyer's point of view (in his case, about images of gay and lesbian subjects in film) that "how social groups are treated in cultural representation is part and parcel of how they are treated in life, that poverty, harassment, self-hate and discrimination . . . are shored up and instituted by representation" (1993, 1). Namaste turns to the use of metaphor in texts that link transgendered figures to crisis in national culture. She opts for philosopher Max Black's interactionist view of metaphor, which sees that "metaphor connects two subjects, one principal and one subsidiary . . . through a 'system of associated commonplaces.' This phrase refers to all associations invoked by a particular term, regardless of whether they are true. Black maintains that a principal subject is constituted through the metaphorical function of a subsidiary subject and its corresponding field of reference" (2000, 97). The key here is that metaphor does not contain two subjects that are inherently alike; the two terms are made analogous by their being placed together and by the meanings derived from the connotative field, often based on other representations. Instead of seeing transgendered people as a convenient metaphor of crisis, she argues that they are troped or appropriated to signify other things, which are often in contradiction to their self-concepts. Central to this is the assertion that, in the interactionist view of metaphor, the subsidiary subject highlights and orders how the principal subject is perceived (98).

Namaste's highly polemical thesis is that where transsexual and transgender persons are produced as figures in many mass-cultural texts, they are concomitantly erased as subjects in their own right. The point of production is the point of erasure. The textual inscription of such subjects as figures in fact empties them out, precluding the possibility of their viability as lived and hence livable subject positions in the real world. Namaste argues that this process leads to invisibilization: transgender people, made purely figurative in texts, are rendered literally impossible in the "real" (3, 98).

AGAINST ALLEGORIES, AGAINST QUEER PARADIGMS

This book's argument distances itself from the theoretical and epistemological assumption that *travestis* or transsexuals are connected to the constitution of national-cultural identity by virtue of inherently common and parallel features in both. It subscribes, instead, to Namaste's view of the metaphorization of transgendered and transsexual people. Applying her theorizations, we can see that, in several of the novels and films examined in Chapters 2, 3, and 5, two terms are placed together: *locas* and *travestis* or transsexuals in the subsidiary position, and cultural identity and nation in the first. Following Namaste, a metaphor does not contain two subjects that are inherently alike; the two terms are made analogous by their being placed together and their meanings derived from the connotative field, which are often based on other representations and influenced by patriarchal masculinist national discourse, a discourse that has also been pervasive in Latin America as we have seen. The cultural meanings or associated commonplaces, as Max Black calls them, are derived from the kinds of representations that circulate in discourse; they are then extended to order our perception of the principal subject. Common attributions made to *locas*, *travestis*, and transsexuals include the characteristics of doubleness, charade, bodily and sexual excess or grotesquerie, artificiality, simulation, and appropriation, as discussed in this chapter. Such associative commonplaces, although clearly recurrent in culture, are vigorously contested in this study. Likewise, theory that reproduces them, parsing such attributions with the language and rhetorical turns of Sarduy and queer theory—most dramatically shown in the work of Richard (1993)—is deeply embedded in the logics that this study purposely seeks to disarm. Richard, in advancing her "retoque" (retouching) theory of *travestis* as imitative figures that are symbolic of Latin American identity construction, articulates them into the realm of ritualized falsification, hyperbole, narcissism, illusion, the grotesque, criminality, concealment, and flight. The transformation of *locas*, *travestis*, and transsexuals into metaphors locks them into a circuit of meaning that hyperbolizes and undermines the possibility of imagining their lives and situatedness at the everyday level in ways that do not draw on the most abject and objectifying forms of knowledge.

While the theories of Judith Butler have contributed in a valuable fashion to accounting for the ways in which the compulsory sex and gender system is enforced, and for debunking the idea of natural genders, their close association with transgender, when taken up by critics, has restricted ways of understanding gender-variant and trans people to the purely illustrative and symbolic. This is because in many examples of queer inquiry her theories of performativity are principally applied to those who live outside normative sex and gender relations while normatively gendered men and women tend to retain constative grounding.[18] Ironically, this may not have been Butler's original project, but transgender generally has come to stand for the deconstruction of gender, as advanced in her earlier theories. As Namaste and Prosser show, the place of embodied subjectivity and social context is noticeably absent in these ways of talking about such subjects. This perhaps encourages critics—and authors or filmmakers informed by queer theory—to relegate gender-variant *locas* and *travestis* to a largely abstract conceptual arena, of interest mainly in poststructuralist debates about the impossibility of any essential ontological being or identity. To say that an identity is constructed is not to assert that it is not in evidence experientially or socially in the world or that it need be thought of as a vessel for the containment of all other identity parameters. While the identities of *locas, travestis,* and transsexuals may be shaped by other axes of race and class, as well as the general colonial situation, this is vastly different from proposing that they are simply vehicles for transformation in other categories or that they merely point to these categories. Such assertions refuse to nuance the identities of these gender-variant and trans subjects and instead see them as enabling vectors in which to read the panorama of race, ethnicity, class, and nation, thus negating *loca, travesti,* and transsexual identities as complex sites of subjectivity not reducible to these fields.

Subjectivity in the always-already allegorical account is effectively censored. Most criticism on Latin American representations is inattentive to denaturalizing or exposing the discursive lineages of the metaphorization of *locas, travestis,* and *transexuales* to embody national-cultural problems, as seen in medico-legal and national discourse in several locales, aspects of vital importance in contextualizing the use of these subjects as national metaphors. Added to this, such work tends to rely on simplistic notions, such as First World and Third World, and does not advance a dynamic view of identity constitution, intersubjective relations, and the sociopolitical realm.

This leads this critic to question the purpose of theory, critical inquiry, textual analysis, and the role of intellectuals. How do they ground representations? How do they understand their referentiality to the social world in which they are produced? Do their theories simply reframe their objects of analysis in abject and totalizing ways? As Namaste states, "Critics within queer theory write about the figural representation of transsexuals only to deny their literal referents," which she calls erasure (2000, 51). Erasure for her "designates a social context in which transsexual and transgendered people are reduced to the merely figural: rhetorical tropes and discursive levers invoked to talk about social relations of gender, nation or class that preempt the very possibility of transsexual bodies, identities and lives" (51–52). That analytical approach provides little insight into the social, institutional, and cultural locations in which such representations are produced and into what it means to be "transvestite" or "transsexual" in the cultures in which the texts are embedded, that is, in their particular sites of production and reception. These are seen as central to the present study. Moreover, by not avoiding the *subject*, this book will examine how texts might make visible or invisible a subjectivity; that is to say, the objective is to examine not simply how *locas*, *travestis*, or transsexuals perform *in* texts, but rather, how *texts* perform *locas*, *travestis*, and transsexuals.

Subjectivity and the Possibilities of Its Textual Inscription

How can texts inscribe or make visible gender-variant homosexual and trans subjectivities? How can texts make visible any subjectivity? The two questions are surely linked, and as such, the theoretical arc of this study extends not just to the representation of *locas*, *travestis*, or transsexuals but also to the representation of any subjectivity in the process of political emergence.

Several contemporary ethnographical studies investigate the self-concepts and identifications of "effeminate" male homosexuals known in different places as *bichas*, *viados*, *jotas*, *cochones* and *colas*, and cross-living *travestis* known also as *vestidas* in other places (Parker 1999; Lancaster 1992; 1998, Prieur 1998; Donoso 1990). These subjects commonly form a subset of the wider homosexual community. Dominant middle-class gays, in contrast, tend to be the more gender normative and structure their relations with one another based more on the so-called egalitarian model. They also do not differentiate these relations in terms of positionality and the related gender role styles to which *travestis* subscribe (Lancaster 1992, 1998; Lumsden 1991; Murray 1995). Much research suggests that in many parts of Latin America, these models of homosexuality exist side by side— the gender differentiated and the non–gender differentiated. The first is more aligned with the popular classes and based on the active-passive distinction (Lumsden 1991; Murray 1995; Carrier 1995).[19] In the active-passive paradigm—called pejoratively by some commentators the "antiquated model" of homoerotic relations—only the passive partner, whose gender style tends to the feminine, is understood as homosexual. The penetrating, active partner slips by the public radar that assigns gender atypicality thanks to his performance of establishment-aligned masculinity and is hence rarely labeled as homosexual. The *loca* or *travesti* who relates to this paradigm also understands her lover as nonhomosexual (Lumsden 1991; Carrier 1995; Murray 1995; Núñez Noriega 1999).

The psychic dimensions to subjectivity are also interwoven with the social, whose interface is the body. The body becomes a site through which subjectivity is constructed and difference is articulated. Annick Prieur in her study of Mexican *jotas* and *vestidas* argues that her subjects see their corporeality as a personal achievement that imbues them with sensuality and distinctiveness, a vehicle for visibility and definition, and whose gender signs are malleable. Of course, when we speak of the body, we should speak of bodies. Bodies signify, morph, and interact: they are the point of intersubjective relations, the grid work of the experience of being not just a subject among subjects but also the experience of being subjected. Many studies show the great efforts to which *travestis* resort in order to embody their *travestismo*: feminizing body modifications using industrial silicone or oil and incurring some danger in the process, pumping their breasts and hips, and ingesting female hormones scored off the streets. In some places, this feminizing process is understood by subjects as intricately tied up with their sense of sexuality and their desire to signal their availability to men. In other places, it is linked more to their vision of more closely inhabiting the feminine gender with which the subjects have always identified (Kulick 1998, Prieur 1998, Fernández 2004). In Prieur's and Josefina Fernández's studies, respondents claim to have always been *locas* or *travestis* and that only in later years were they able to fully become that vision of themselves. The work of Chilean psychologist, Claudia Espinoza Carramiñana (1999), draws a similar trajectory of *travesti* embodiment and calls the process "forjarse mariposa," that is, one's emergence from one form into another, more wondrous creation.

Although studies that center specifically on transsexual lives in Latin America are so scant as to be virtually nonexistent, *Identidad, cultura y sociedad. Un grito desde el silencio* (*Identity, Culture and Society: A Scream out of Silence*) by Peruvian lawyer and social scientist, Fiorella Cava (2004), provides some insights into Latin American transsexuals. Although *travestis* are different from transsexuals to the extent that many disavow a desire to have sex reassignment surgery (SRS), or even to claim the subjectivity of the "other sex"; both groups, however, experience overlapping forms of oppression. Cava notes the difficulties involved in coming out and then openly transitioning as a transsexual—experiences that cut close to the bone, as the author herself is transsexual. She talks of the trauma that erupts in families, in work, and in social networks, made especially challenging for Latin American transsexuals, in contrast to their Anglo-American counterparts, because of the enduring force of machismo in contemporary Latin culture, according to Cava (67).

Aside from psychic and cultural forces, one's residence in and habitual coursing through certain physical spaces also informs the shaping of subjectivity. All studies on *travestis* in contemporary times point to their commonplace involvement in prostitution, particularly street prostitution. *Travesti* culture is informed to a large degree by the type of work undertaken by its members that is socially stigmatized and open to a variety of risks—running the gamut from abusive clients to corrupt law enforcement officers and their, at times, arbitrary and discriminatory targeting of *travesti* sex workers through fines, incarceration, and sexual abuse. Prostitution, however, also serves as a means of restitution to forge new links, and new families, and to survive where no other work is available. This arises because, due to their visible difference, effeminate homosexuals and *travestis* in many places are expelled from family, school, and neighborhood environments and face grave difficulties in finding conventional forms of employment (Fernández 2004).

Connected to these material realities, the axes of class and ethnicity inform the shape subjectivity takes. Prieur's study shows clear links to her *jotas*' and *vestidas*' gendered stylings of the body and their class (1998, 150). With any subjectivity, attention to what feminists frequently call "intersectionality" is important: How do the various axes of class, race, sexuality, and gender combine and reexpress each other? If one category is simplistically used in a text to symbolize another—by virtue of substitution—what is lost from the picture? These are pivotal to the tension between *lo trans* as explored, complex phenomena and *lo trans* as a rhetorical category or vector that points to other fields in their assumed entirety and hermetic distinction—such as "race," "nation," and "global and postmodern identity."

Subjectivity constantly reconstitutes itself, and this depends to a large extent on another concept, that is, the intersubjective. This concerns the subject's insertion and elaboration alongside and within relation to others in the lifeworld. Subjectivity is facilitated through language via the constant transpositions of the body in the linguistic order. This involves the redrafting and articulating of possible narrative and speaking points by which people make sense of their surroundings and situationality. To realize oneself is to find oneself as part of a community with a common set of experiences and worldviews—or cast out, but that in itself shapes one. *Locas* and *travestis* often also find themselves sidelined in gay culture, as their *actitud escandalosa* (scandalous attitude) is said to be a source of ill repute. Forced out of one community, they form another. This is often the *ambiente*, or the space, of street prostitution: so-called marginal spaces in which one is (out)cast, as we have seen. The distinctive forms of sociolect in subcultures constitute one manifestation of subjectivity. Here one would point to the argot of a group, and specifically with respect to the way its members talk about themselves and are talked about. Such forms of speech are particularly enunciative in the case and cause of a (trans) gendered subjectivity in Spanish, with the use of gendered adjectives and pronouns. The work of Guillermo Núñez Noriega (1997) on homosexual and *travesti* subcultures in Hermosillo, Mexico, and their use of *joteadas*, or camp slang, as well as a study by César O. González Pérez on *jotas* and *gays travestidos* (2002) in Colima, Mexico, on a similar form of linguistic play called *perreos* provide examples of this. In this way, language might be said to constitute us; however, we also reconstitute language.

Studies by Cuban psychologists Janet Mesa Peña and Diley Hernández Cruz from the *Centro de Investigación y Desarrollo de la Cultura Cubana* (Center for the Research and Development of Cuban Culture) on *transformistas, travestis*, and *transexuales* in Havana (2004), Sheilla Rodríguez-Madera and José Toro-Alfonso and their pioneering work on transgender people and HIV/AIDS in Puerto Rico (2005), and Mexican Rosío Córdova Plaza on the criminalization of *travesti* sex workers in Xalapa, Veracruz (2007), sketch in considerable detail the social, cultural, and institutional factors that order the lived experiences of real-world *travestis* and transsexuals in their various locales. Such locales are pertinent to this study.

Josefina Fernández, as I have mentioned elsewhere (Lewis 2006), does not only view *lo travesti* as a personal and subjective identity but as a political identity as well, referring to its uneasy articulation in the context of discourses of deviance, control, surveillance, and juridical interpellation. Fernández understands *travestis* in their personal and sociopolitical facets, not simply as an illustration of any single theory. In one part of her study she profiles their struggle to obtain a space in the wider lesbian, gay, bisexual, and transgender (LGBT) movement in Argentina and argues for a recognition of sexual rights by the state. Although Fernández focuses on *travesti* populations in Buenos Aires, her findings extend beyond the borders of Argentina, as gender variant and trans people in Chile, Mexico, and the Caribbean have begun to organize against social and economic exclusion and have thus initiated the politicization of subjectivity. In doing so, they have been importantly involved in the generation of new knowledge frameworks about sex and gender variance and diversity.

Subjectivity does not imply a unified self nor a self that is knowable to itself. Rather, this self is radically decentered, multiple, and dispersed.

It emerges through dialogue with others, as well as through participation in visual economies of identification that are embedded in economic relations, such as in music videos, advertising, fashion, style, and other increasingly global semiotic networks that offer promises of newness, becoming, and belonging. Several studies of *travestis* pinpoint the sources of inspiration for their public personae—especially during hours of labor in prostitution—in popular cultural images of *vedettes*, for example (Prieur 1998, Fernández 2004). Subjectivity emerges in varied locations: in the context of the family, labor settings, religious institutions, law courts, recreational and leisure spaces, schools, doctors' offices, and so forth. These are also key domains for *locas, travestis*, and transsexuals as they negotiate the imperiled terrain of public visibility and intersubjective becoming as sexually and gender-diverse peoples.

All of these factors are important in evaluating to what extent a text visualizes the subjectivity of *loca, travesti*, or transsexual characters. If as readers we can state that a text has captured a sense of subjectivity, we need to be able to point to the kind of features of subjectivity mentioned above: its embodied nature, its emergence in and through the sociolinguistic order, and the self's historicity and multiple locations.

Some Final Remarks

No somos viciosas ni enfermas
No pretendemos engañar a nadie con nuestro aspecto
No estamos locas por el sexo.
[We aren't diseased or sick
We don't mean to trick anyone with our appearance
We're not just crazy about sex.]

—Traveschile (a peak Chilean *travesti* group)

In emphasizing the forces that have influenced the formation of the subjectivities and of the real-world subjects known as *locas, travestis*, and *transexuales* in Latin America, this study does not make any facile attempt, of course, to demand that textual representations be seen as mirrors of some outside reality or that literary or cinema critics, indeed, become sociologists. Instead, it serves to remind critical and cultural scholars to extend their views of the possibilities of *loca, travesti*, and transsexual figures in contemporary texts beyond performative or allegorizing paradigms that cannot account for subjectivity and its articulation and that themselves do not break away from the dominant episteme that locates *locas, travestis*, and transsexuals in certain paradigmatic ways. A view that gives countenance to sex- and gender-variant subjects in culture allows the critic to reposition depictions in relation to what is known and knowable among competing knowledges about these subjects in different locations and times, their degrees of social integration, and forms of identification and self-concepts, aspects completely lacking, as we have seen, in queer-inspired accounts in much of the work previously discussed. This is particularly fruitful for the reading of texts in which *loca, travesti,* or transsexual characters move beyond mere stereotype and where a sustained interest in representing these figures as social types is in evidence.[20] Several of the texts that this book examines pursue this line, and thus purely figural understandings of *loca, travesti,* and transsexual lives, embodiments, and emplacements are considered inadequate.

When we speak of "representations," the significance of the term in the study of literature, film, and sexual, ethnic, and other minorities cannot be underestimated. It implies a certain set of priorities, understandings about texts, and readerly orientations: what is it that texts do and make possible for reader interpretation and how might they be seen to speak about people's lives or identities, about stereotypes and cultural context? Committed poststructuralists, following thinkers such as Jacques Derrida and Paul De Man, might assert that no representation can ultimately escape metaphorization, for the very arbitrariness of the processes of signification may lend any representation to allegory. Indeed, the writer Pedro Lemebel, whose work is considered in the closing chapter of this book, reflects on such a problematic. Keeping in mind that representations are never transparent or direct but rather frequently opaque and polysemic, it is taken as axiomatic here that it is better to speak of representational effects accrued in given contexts. Just as in language where a lexical item does not simply have one meaning, and meanings are themselves constructed by the reader, rhetorical operations depend on certain features of recognition and connotative association to obtain their effects. This need not set the critic adrift for any lack of a speaking position or valid argument, however. Rather, the predominance of certain constructions of meaning and culturally embedded knowledge formulations in incessant circulation demands an intervention at this level, at the level of the signification, which in turn presents us with a politics of representation.

The work of Reinaldo Arenas, examined in Chapter 2, as well as the novel by Mario Bellatin, considered in Chapter 4, provide good examples of this point. They may not pursue realism in any documentary or faux-objective style, which is the claim of the writer Pedro Juan Gutiérrez in regard to his novel *El Rey de la Habana,* also studied in Chapter 4, but their depictions of gender-variant and trans acts and people still remit to our knowledge of real-life subjects, situations, and ways of talking about such subjects. They may themselves problematize the connection between literary practices of signification and our knowledge of the real world or real subjects—Bellatin's text certainly does this and Arenas's work plays with textual reversals and ironies, that is, the essence of the carnivalesque. Other texts—for example, the film *Las noches de Constantinopla*, studied in Chapter 3—work in the comedic vein. In one way or another, however, all these texts still deal with forms of knowledge, worldviews, discourses, and cultural meanings that form their place of production, dissemination, and reception, as well as certain aesthetic traditions in representation.

Literary and filmic texts may not be imitative of some perceived reality, but neither do they exist in isolation. The representation of *lo trans* and gender-variant homosexuality in films and literature cannot be excised from the intertextuality exhibited with other narratives, both literary and nonliterary, visual or verbal, in the culture from which the texts derive—including those outlined in the section on discursive formations about *locas, travestis*, and transsexuals. In their very narrative structure, one may perceive ways of talking that define, construct and produce objects of knowledge (Barker 2000, 390). Representations are thus never free of political import. Not only do they respond to certain knowledges, then, but they also shape them.

Although far from universally true, contemporary Latin American film and literary forms often engage gender-variant or trans acts and subjects figuratively; they may serve a particular structural function in thematic or metaphorical design. However, following Namaste, the mechanisms of the placing together of two terms in metaphor need to be addressed. Added to this, the terms that equate gender atypicality to problems at the level of nation need to be denaturalized and discursively highlighted in terms of their genealogy. The marrying of *travestismo* to *mestizaje—travestizaje—* needs interrogation. This is something that most critics do not undertake currently, as we have also seen. Figurations belong to the realm of rhetoric, which often employs metaphor or tropes; rhetoric as a field relates to the ability of a particular mode of speaking or representation to persuade and influence, but as studies have shown, rhetoric also structures discourse and ultimately the way we think about certain phenomena (Lakoff and Johnson 1980; Morgan 1986; Valverde 1991). Figures of speech, then, become figures of thought.

Critical and cultural codings that posit *locas, travestis*, and transsexuals as enigmatic sphinxes, contradictory ruses, exotic spectacles, deceptive miscreants, that which is beyond what constitutes personhood or livability, and specters of colonial alterity, anarchy, and "end times" need to be exposed as constructions and not naturalized as a priori characteristics of the subjects so described. Clearly, then, for queer theorists, the challenge lies in accounting for trans subjectivities in texts beyond the merely performative and to locate representations in their social, cultural, and institutional sites of production and reception. For postcolonial critics, the task might be to differentiate between the notion that subjectivities of all kinds are in part molded by overarching (colonial) conditions and the idea that they are simply symbolic of these conditions. The contribution to transgender studies is also valuable, providing a view of trans subjectivities in Latin America that do not always conform to Anglo-American separations between one's sexuality and one's sense of gender, as in the case of *locas* and *travestis*. The readings given here of a selection of literary and filmic texts provide the opportunity for queer, postcolonial, and transgender theorists to reconceptualize some of the common ideas around subjects who live outside normative sex and gender relations and how they are represented in cultural production.

Chapter 2

Grotesque Spectacles

The Janus Face of the State and Gender-Variant Bodies in Reinaldo Arenas

Landscape Painting

The work of the late Cuban dissident writer Reinaldo Arenas can be conceptualized as a giant tableau that seeks to portray within its multidimensional space the panorama of the sexual and sociopolitical order under which he lived, struggled, and wrote, that is, Castro's revolutionary Cuba of the 1960s and 1970s, until his flight in the Mariel boatlift in 1980. The author himself constantly emphasized the need to see his literary production as an organic whole, in spite of the perpetual revisions to each novel, short story, or poem he was forced by circumstance to make within his lifetime. Arenas conceived a unity of five novels that he wrote and named the *pentagonía*, the fourth of which, *El color del verano* (1982; *The Color of Summer*) has the secondary title *El nuevo jardín de las delicias* (Garden of Earthly Delights) named after the painting by Hieronymus Bosch, which itself is a multidimensional tableau. The other four novels, *Celestino antes del alba* (1967; *Singing from the Well*), *El palacio de las blanquísimas mofetas* (1980; *The Palace of the White Skunks*), *Otra vez el mar* (1982; *Farewell to the Sea*), and *El asalto* (1990; *The Assault*), respectively, seek to suggest this continuity at an intertextual level; episodes recur or are told with a different slant, names are recycled, characters resemble one another, titles are recouped and redistributed, and, in frequently witty asides, direct metatextual reference is often made about the existence or composition of other parts of the writer's oeuvre. This self-referentiality implies a series of textual echoes—details given in relief. Importantly, the protagonists morph into one another; the implication is, following the narrative throughout the *pentagonía*, that we are following the evolution of its hero or antihero, his multilayered existence and split self that in no small part is caused by the contradictory reality of living under a regime with a paranoid personality complex.

Arenas saw all his work in its *conjunto* as a life project. Indeed, his "life" writing and fictional writing are fused, providing together a contestatory discourse on the regime, an act of revenge, his gift to the post-Castro future. This chapter refers to Arenas's complete oeuvre. It will trace elements that recur in much of the *pentagonía* and other works that call our attention to the positions Arenas takes on the sociopolitical reality he endeavors to paint here, with inescapable reference to those most condemned by the system: *locas* and *travestis*. Both *locas* and *travestis* have gained much visibility in recent years in Cuba.¹ Arenas did not live to see the emergence of marginalized homosexual and *travesti* subjectivities in several sociocultural domains in the 1990s. His visions of cross-gender acts and *loca* or *travesti* embodiments, more than anything, are a product of their time and circumstance.

In this chapter, I will focus most particularly on four works: the novels *Arturo, la estrella más brillante* (1984; *The Brightest Star*), *El color del verano* (1991), *El asalto* (1991), and his autobiographical text *Antes que anochezca* (1998; *Before Night Falls*). In all these works we find ample depictions of differently gendered people. These representations often sound in different registers, but "cross-gendering" as an act and a reality is central to Arenas's critique of the social and sexual order for a number of reasons. Arenas goes some way in his work to recuperating *locas* and *travestis* from their position of marginal abjection under the Castro regime. Where the visualization of gender-variant bodies and persons is fused with elements of the grotesque, however, the writer marks an ambivalence toward "gender atypicality." How this ambivalence is manifested and its implications at the level of representation will be examined at length in this chapter.

Trials of Visibility: Castro's Cuba, Homosexuality, and Gender Variance

Given that Arenas's life experiences and politics as a member of a persecuted sexual minority inform his writing to such a profound degree, any consideration of the issue of ambivalence toward *locas* and *travestis* in his oeuvre must be profiled with reference to the official institutions, practices, and statements that defined the place of the gender variants and homosexuals in the historical period in question.

The persecution of homosexuals as official state policy and practice, especially in the two decades following Cuba's 1959 revolution, is now a generally accepted and well-documented fact (Leiner 1994; Lumsden 1996; Young 1981). Homosexuals could not be part of the revolution because they were considered by nature antiproductive and symbolic of the capitalist excess and corruption that had existed on the island under the Batista regime. They became enemies of the state, as Marvin Leiner points out, in the nationalistic drive toward the defense of the revolution, since "they could not fit into this ideological social unity" spearheaded by the vision of the "New Man" and "New Woman" working in tandem for the good of society, both morally and materially (1994, 28).[2] The most salient features of this tendency are evident in the testimony of homosexual men rounded up and sent to agricultural work camps set up in 1965, the ominous UMAP (Unidades Militares de Ayuda a la Producción), which were a species of concentration camps where forced labor was the order of the day.[3]

Underemphasized in the documentation of the persecution of homosexuals in this period is the fact that such policies and practices were attacks specifically on "effeminate" people and anyone who exhibited forms of gender "deviance" or transgression. The Cuban Revolution's moral agenda was not simply an assault on homosexuality as understood in Anglo-American terms but rather gender variance, which was the outward sign of sexual deviance and perversion, and a potential contamination of the body politic. As Brad Epps argues, this involved a politics of appearance. According to Epps, homosexuality was seen in Cuba (both before and after the revolution) "as a mere matter of appearance" (1995b, 232). As Epps argues in two parts of a highly elucidatory article,

> Designating less a libidinal relationship between individuals of the same gender than a particular role, position, or style of behavior, homosexuality, male homosexuality that is, primarily designates those men who exhibit "feminine" traits or otherwise show that they assume so-called passive or receptive positions in sexual intercourse. (232)
>
> Homosexuality is largely a matter of appearance, a problem of public visibility, a highly politicized question of style. The way we walk, the way we talk, the way we gesture, the way we stand; our hair, our clothing, our complexion; the music we listen to, the books we read ... all this and more ... the revolution becomes a struggle over signs, and against a codification whereby any play of difference, any arbitrariness, ambivalence, or ambiguity must be rigorously reworked: a man is a man is a man. There is not, or at least there should not be, any confusing play between or across or through surface and depth, content and form. (242–43)

In fact, such a confusing play between, across or through surface and depth was interpreted culturally as suspect and coded discursively as duplicity or contradiction. The terms of "showiness" and "extravagance" carry the cultural charge of posing, to follow Sylvia Molloy's thesis (1998), where posing equals imposture, that is, deceit and pathology.[4] "Extravagance" is further seen as "self-advertisement" that makes the spectator nervous, a kind of self-styling that not only stands in as being for "homosexuality" but also, importantly, being against something. Or, to rework Molloy's analysis in Cuban terms, not only does this way of posing and acting express a refusal of masculinity, but also a refusal of the revolutionary ideals of "man" and all that this would signify (143–48).[5]

Paul Julian Smith would no doubt agree with Brad Epps, but he names the official crackdowns on gender-variant behavior and persons as part of the regime's "trial of visibility" (1996, 77). *Locas* and *travestis* were those principally in the firing line precisely because of their visibility. Such a moral agenda developed a climate of incredibly narrow definitions of gender roles for men and women. The pseudoscientific discourse of the effeminate homosexual was thus coded in terms of betrayal and subversion—of national interests and of gender itself.

LA MARICONERÍA PLENAMENTE ASUMIDA: THE POETICS OF AUTHENTICITY AND THE POLITICS OF RESISTANCE

None of the aforementioned is lost on Arenas of course. In his work, we perceive a critique of this politics of appearance and its methods of oppression and persecution. On one level he presents the *loca* as a symbol of liberatory possibility. Ironically, on another level, he marks an ambivalence to gender-variant homosexuals and *travestis*, a kind of ambivalence that is also found in official discourse. This point will be explored later in the chapter in detail. It is important to address first how Arenas resignifies *mariconería* (queenly styles and identity) as a point of oppositional militancy principally for himself and other homosexual artists and intellectuals. He does this by interrogating the macho's claims to naturalness and authenticity, proposing instead that the much-reviled *loca* holds such promise—a radical position indeed.

Arenas speaks in the voice of the *loca* subject in his autobiography, as do many of the narrators of his fiction; in *El color del verano*, the narrative voice in fact addresses the reader on a number of occasions as a fellow *loca*: "Vaya usted a saber, mi querida loca" (1991, 88; Your guess is as good as mine, dear *loca*). The carnivalesque, parodic quality of much of Arenas's writing has been discussed at length by several critics (Epps 1995b; Ríos Avila 1998; Soto 1998). In short, it effects an irreverent approach to all identities that would lay claim to superiority, especially those deemed as natural and normal under what Eve Kosofsky Sedgwick calls "the male paranoid plot" of defensive heteronormativity (1994, 163). In Bakhtinian terms, the anarchic letting loose, inversion of categories of "official order" that carnival activity produces, is apparent in the frequent "ritual spectacles" and "comic verbal compositions" that pepper all of Arenas's texts (Vice 1997, 151). This is particularly true of *El color del verano*, where a carnival organized by the dictator Fifo in honor of his fifty years in power is hijacked by the *locas* and ultimately leads to the collapse of the state. The *loca*, whose camp humor and gender expression presents the regime with a contradiction, is a point of departure for the mobilization of a resistant politics—of pleasure, joy, debasement, "mockery," or laughter, bringing down to Earth that which is most highly esteemed and elevated. Arenas delights in the challenge that *mariconería* presents to a system that is antipleasure and seeks to patrol borders to prevent crossings, hybridity, and ambiguity in gender, sexuality, and identity. As he asserts in *Antes que anochezca*, "Toda dictadura es casta y antivital; toda manifestación de vida es en sí un enemigo de cualquier régimen dogmático. Era lógico que Fidel Castro nos persiguiera, no nos dejara fornicar, y tratara de eliminar cualquier ostentación pública de vida" (1998, 119; Every dictatorship is chaste and anti-life; any manifestation of life is in itself an enemy of any dogmatic regime. It was logical for Fidel Castro to persecute us, to not let us fornicate and to try to eliminate any public show of life). Moreover, he is strongly in favor of a *mariconería* that does not shrink from its task, that is, of being faithful to its own exigencies of personal expression and desire. These two things—personal expression and unfettered desire—are the cornerstones of Arenas's notions of authenticity in self and identity, which the regime seeks to delimit, suffocate, and eliminate. The very *mariconería* that Castrist discourse tropes as *traicionera* (treacherous) to nature and society is where Arenas seeks the development of authenticity—for himself as a writer and dissident sexual outlaw. *La mariconería plenamente asumida*, being publicly and defiantly *loca*, is a form of empowerment and resistance by which all other claims to "authenticity" should be measured and found lacking.

Arenas develops a scheme for understanding the different varieties of homosexuality on the island, which does not obey faithfully the cultural perceptions of who counts as homosexual and who does not. According to cultural dynamics as studied by Murray (1995), among others, he who is assigned the label "homosexual" is usually the passive partner or that individual who displays gender-atypical traits. The active or masculine partner remains invisible. Arenas deliberately makes conscious the axis of visibility and invisibility. *Locas* as same-sex desiring individuals who seek *hombres de verdad* ("real" men) are simply the most visible. In this way, Arenas refuses a simple homo-hetero typology and seeks to expose what is often concealed due to the very forces of homophobia so present in Cuban culture. Arenas reserves his praise for that *loca* who does not attempt to hide herself—or is even blissfully unaware of the consequences of her perceived transgressions, as intent on fulfilling her desire as she is. Arenas elevates from her position of abjection and subjugation what he terms the *loca de argolla* in both his autobiography and *El color del verano*, or the *loca atada*; the *locas* whom he most admires are these, including fellow writers Virgilio Piñera and José Lezama Lima. The four great categories of the *loca* are revealed in the autobiography and also with much more parodic detail in a speech given by one of the *loca* characters of *El color del verano* at an academic gathering. The following are taken from that novel.

The first is "La loca de argolla" (the dog collar queen):

> Es un ejemplar tan escandaloso que el sistema la ha provisto de una argolla metálica que lleva al cuello. Esa argolla puede ser visible o invisible. Cada vez que por alguna razón política, moral o económica, la loca de argolla debe ser confinada a un campo de trabajo, lo único que tienen que hacer los agentes del sistema es tirarle un garfio a la argolla. Así, este tipo de loca es recogida fácilmente. (1991, 393)
>
> [She is such a scandalous specimen that the system has furnished her with a metal ring around the neck. This ring can be visible or invisible. Every time that for some political, moral, or economic reason, the *loca* with a ring must be confined to a work camp, the only thing that the system's agents have to do is throw a hook around the ring. In this way this kind of *loca* is easily picked up.]

"La loca de argolla" always seeks out *hombres de verdad* as sexual partners, an aspect of her sexuality that is central to Arenas's vision of *la mariconería plenamente asumida*.

Next comes "La loca común": "Este tipo de loca tiene su compromiso que es otra loca común" (393) or, in other words, he maintains relationships principally with other common *locas*.

Third is "La loca tapada" (the closeted queen):

> Esa loca puede llegar a ser abogado, profesor de marxismo leninismo, militante de la Juventud Comunista, dirigente de una empresa, miembro del Partido Comunista y párroco de una iglesia católica . . . Desde luego, la loca tapada es una loca que se niega rotundamente a ser loca. Es una loca fatal, pues casi nunca puede manifestarse en su dimensión total. Vive aterrorizada temiendo que le tiendan alguna trampa fálica. No quiere saber nada de las otras locas. (393–94)
>
> [This *loca* might end up being an attorney, a teacher of Marxism Leninism, a Communist Youth militant, a business leader, member of the Communist Party, and a Catholic Church parishioner . . . Of course, the closeted *loca* is a *loca* who completely denies being one. She's a deadly *loca*, since she can really never show herself in her entirety. She lives terrified, fearing that

someone will play a phallic trick on her. She doesn't want to know anything about the other *locas*.]

Fourth, "la loca regia," a kind of officially accepted queen, who has contacts in high places and is thus protected. She is ostentatious in every sense and feels no loyalty to anyone but herself: "Es dueña de secretos insólitos, de una maldad descomunal, de un talento ilimitado y oportunista, de un pasado que la vincula a los poderes más sórdidos y permanentes. Inmune a todo descalabro o chanchullo político y moral, ella en sí misma es un secreto o un enigma estatal" (394–95; She is the owner of stunning secrets, of extraordinary evil, an unlimited opportunist talent, a past that links her to the most permanent and sordid powers. Immune to any political or moral scandal or undoing, she herself is a state secret or enigma).

The *loca tapada* is the saddest case of all; "tapada" here suggests the wearing of a mask and the leading of a double life. This *loca* is clearly a victim of the order and yet is also a persecutor. Arenas ironizes the claims to masculinity and heterosexuality of this closet queen. In doing so, he unpacks the assumption of a neat divide between homo and hetero, the appraisals and policing of the politics of appearance. His divisions of the *loca*, while heaping praise on *la loca de argolla*, problematize both sides of that binary. *Locas*, in fact, are everywhere. The most pernicious types are those who deny themselves and those who wear their guise of power, like *la loca regia*. The queer is rejected by the regime but also is part of the regime and, to some extent, may be said to embody it. How this is materialized in terms of metaphors connecting gender-variant expression to the state shall be considered further on.

Alongside his four great categories of the *loca*, Arenas develops a parallel system of categorization for the *bugarrón*, that is, the male-identified, active-role pursuer of mainly *locas* and whose homoerotic practices do not come under public scrutiny, as he never loses alignment with establishment masculinity. In fact, he overcompensates for it in his hyperperformance of masculinity in order to avoid any suspicion. Arenas exposes the enactment of this gendered identity as a kind of drag itself: a play of surfaces, gestures, and postures that is privileged culturally. He ridicules the superiority of the macho whose normative principle is a disavowal of homosexuality as it becomes read through effeminacy: "Un hombre machista tiene un concepto tan elevado de la masculinidad que su mayor placer sería que otro hombre le diera por el culo" (182; "The macho has such an elevated sense of masculinity that his greatest pleasure would be for another man to give it to him up the ass"). La Chelo, also called by the text Zebro Sardoya, a code name that playfully alludes to the writer Severo Sarduy, is the source of oracular pronouncements. This character, like several others in *El color del verano*, is duplicitous, being an agent of the dictator. Through the speech by la Chelo on the four types of *bugarrón* in *El color del verano*, Arenas implicates the macho figure in same-sex desire by tying him to the pairing with the *maricón* that publicly never sees the light of day: "Ya se sabe que sin el bugarrón no hay loca y viceversa" (207; It's well known that without the buggerer there's no *loca* and vice versa). It is worth pointing out, however, that the *bugarrón* is only condemned for his pretensions and *prepotencia*. For Arenas, as a *loca* himself, he is still the object of desire.

Arenas's ideal is of a sexual paradise that operates like rebel theatre in a repressive environment: a game of opposites wherein the effeminate, sexually "passive"[6] subject seeks to partner up with the *hombre de verdad*, the *loca* with the macho. The eroticism is found precisely in the difference in roles and gender expression between the two. Arenas clearly finds joy and cause for celebration in the dramatic materialization of difference from heteronormativity that *maricomnería* allows. He scorns the idea of the more Anglo-style gay relations, where *loca* always sleeps with *loca* or two machos or would-be machos find themselves in bed together. The passive-active paradigm and its realization through a play of gender opposites is where he posits the most radical impulse for sexual difference; anything else is boring or sanitized. In *El color del verano*, the *loca* has been exiled from this paradise, much like the original Adam and Eve, for having sinned. This paradise metaphorically relates to the utopian vision of the Cuban Revolution, from which homosexuals have been cast out. *Locas* are neither Adam, the "New Man," nor Eve, his counterpart, but rather, the sly and seductive serpent, at least from the point of view of the *Máximo Líder* (the Maximum Leader, Fidel Castro) who, like God, judges all. And yet *maricomnería*, as an ever-mobile libidinal strategy, offers the promise of the creation of alternative gardens of earthly delights. *Maricomnería* becomes the avenue for an escape from heteronormative repression, to recreate sexual paradise on Earth, which under the regime, is pure hell. The *loca* is, on a very compelling level, the symbol of the pleasure principle and of "realness" to self.

Inside/Outside: Performing Gender, Performing Abjection

In spite of the positive appraisal of *loca* identity, Arenas in many texts paints ambivalent portraits of gender-variant people. These are his fellow *locas*, both those persecuted by the system and in its jails. In his autobiography, Arenas recounts meeting other *locas* on the inside when he is sent to El Morro prison. There he describes in shocking detail the cruelty and violence committed by those higher up in the prison hierarchy against the *locas*.

Los homosexuales ocupaban las dos peores galeras del Morro; eran unas galeras subterráneas en la planta baja, que se llenaba de agua cuando subía la marea; era un sitio asfixiante y sin baño. A los homosexuales no se les trataba allí como a seres humanos, sino como bestias. Eran los últimos en salir a comer y por eso los veíamos pasar, por cualquier cosa insignificante que hicieran, los golpeaban cruelmente . . . Por supuesto nadie allí les decía homosexuales, sino maricones o en el mejor de los casos, locas. Aquella galera de las locas era, realmente, el último círculo del Infierno. (1998, 206)

[The homosexuals occupied the worst galleys of El Morro; these were underground galleys on the ground floor that filled up with water whenever the tide came in; it was a suffocating place and without a bathroom. The homosexuals there weren't treated like human beings but like beasts. They were the last in coming out to eat and so whenever we saw them pass by, for any insignificant thing they did, they would be beaten cruelly . . . Of course no one there called them "homosexuals" but "faggots" or at best "*locas*" instead. That galley of *locas* was really the last circle of Hell.]

The prison environment operates on its own principles of abuse and submission, which are an exaggeration of the kinds of conditions in Cuba on the outside. Arenas arrives there, cataloged as a CIA agent and a murderer, among other things. While in prison, he gingerly forms alliances with some of the prisoners; these are, however, always temporary, and reliant on what he can do for them and they for him. He becomes a writer of love letters for a fee and even teaches French. He does not have sexual relations, finding the prison too degrading and exposed. From the outset we see that he is not one of the *locas* he describes. He views them with some sympathy; he describes the creativity, for instance, of the *locas maleteros*, who help transport contraband items brought into the prison (cigarettes and drugs among them) by inserting them in their rectums. Interestingly, their role as go-betweens could be suggestive of their "in-betweenness" in terms of gender. Arenas also depicts the prison sisterhood of *locas*, which is often very competitive, since the *locas* vie for the attention and protection of macho inmates and are often treated as sexual goods to be bought and sold. He talks of the vicious "rencillas" (cat fights) that occur between the *locas*, and between *locas* and other prisoners. At the bottom of the rung, the *locas* invent their own means of defense called "entizados," which are made of sticks studded with razor blades, and many end up disfigured in these quarrels. Arenas also bears witness to the occasional suicide and murder of several *locas*, one of whom is a performing drag queen.

In the prison, as in Cuban culture, a convincing performance of masculinity buys symbolic capital. Indeed, the close-up view provided of the prison bears a metonymical relation to the punitive, panopticon methods of the state generally at the time. Cuba itself is like a prison: in El Morro the techniques of repression are only more intense and hidden from national and international view. The *locas*, being effeminate and nonmacho, are subject to this system of value that positions them as weak, to be sexually used (like women), and disposable. The prison economy seems to function on the basis of creating and supporting these gender differences. One is keenly aware of every movement and every gesture and its gendered implications because one is forever on show and judged. The prisoners in this sense perform gender in a compelled fashion. Arenas does not display, however, an unreserved admiration for the gender performances of the *locas*, which often take on the character of the drag show in *Antes que anochezca* and even more so in *Arturo, la estrella más brillante*. He does not seem to understand the full implications of the symbolic resistance obtained through their enactment of gender difference. For the *locas*, the intense dramatization of (cross)gender becomes a means of buying symbolic sexual capital because their cross-gendered expressions thematize their availability to their gender opposites, the machos. This is often how presenting as female, as *travesti*, in the larger culture is interpreted. In the prison environment, it becomes a question of survival, that is, the taking on of the cross-dressed role. In both the autobiography and *Arturo, la estrella más brillante*, Arenas reveals the resourcefulness of such *locas* in being able to invent something out of nothing; they use old sugar sacks and fashion them into dresses; rags become crafted into wigs, rouge from food dyes and dirt. In *Arturo, la estrella más brillante*, which is based on the experiences of a friend confined to one of the infamous UMAP camps in the 1960s, the protagonist Arturo first rebels against being forced into the role of *loca* "on show"; the prison guards see him as "maricón," but he resists following what Brad Epps calls those "scripts" that are expected of him.[7] These scripts might be framed in terms of Judith Butler's theories of performativity and citationality vis-à-vis the forced reiteration of the law (1990, 1993). The other *locas* see him as closed, snobbish "Madame Tapón." Inevitably he submerges himself in this culture in order to escape persecution and becomes one of the *locas cautivas*. He does a better job of it than anyone else. In one scene, he is crowned "Reina de las locas cautivas" ("Queen of the captive queers") (1984, 38), but it is not something with which he identifies. In this novella, as in the portraits of the other gender-liminal "in-betweens" in Arenas's work, a profound distrust is expressed about the *mariconería* of such individuals, which appears to exceed the limits established within Cuban culture. Arenas may speak in the voice of the *loca* in his autobiography and other works, but he is forever an onlooker, not really a part of the group. One gets the sense that Arenas assumes the role of the objectivist ethnographer, which is not to say that the features he profiles are inauthentic but rather, that they accrue to an external and representative standpoint. As far as his own *mariconería* and its link to his vitality as a sexual being and writer are concerned, this is something he defends to death. Often the reader gains the impression that the positive appraisal of personal authenticity accorded by the writer to himself and other *loca* writers he admires could not ever be extended to those beings who are so abject in their gender crossing and "sissy-hood" in his novels. The language of the grotesque so important to the depiction of those figures leaves the reader on slippery, ambiguous ground.

THE GROTESQUE: THE RELATIVE VALUE OF BODIES

Where the irony or campy irreverence of Arenas's portraits turns to the grotesque, the representation of gender-variant individuals veers off course. His project of decentering the hierarchy that privileges the macho over the effeminate or gender-variant subject seems precariously disrupted by this ambivalence. In this section, I will look at how this hierarchy is in fact reinstalled by Arenas and some of the implications of this.

As Sue Vice posits in her book *Introducing Bakhtin*, "degradation" is a typical and important operation of the grotesque. Its central trait is an ambivalent act (1997, 155). The grotesque realism that typifies much of Arenas's work is a complement and extension at one level of the carnivalesque mentioned before. As Brad Epps states in another article, this time juxtaposing Arenas with Montaigne, "if the grotesque is strange, even monstrous, it is in part because it styles the self as twisted round and shot through with otherness" (1995a, 41). Part of Arenas's vision of *locas* as being located by discourse as noncitizens seeks to reflect this abject status by recourse to the grotesque. But the grotesque does have other implications, especially since so much discourse on homosexuality in Cuba is bound up in its metaphors. As Epps argues further on, "the grotesque does in fact recall the excrescences of a cave, the superfluous, if subterranean, surgings of the natural world. At the same time it is tied to artifice and adornment, or even more, to a counterfeiting and outrageous reworking of nature" (42). This is in fact how the *locas cautivas*, and many of the other *locas* on Fifo's prison island in *El color del verano*, are coded. In spite of the critique of poseur masculinity, masculine bodies are those that are sexy, "authentic," healthy, and strong—never coded as grotesque. That is reserved for the *loca* body. Many *locas* are described as sick, deformed, ugly, and monstrous. Tomasito La Goyesca, a monstrous hypersexualized dwarf, is a case in point, as is Tedevoro (also known as Teodoro Tapón). So are the *locas* La Maléfica, La Supersatánica, Oscar, and many other *pájaros* in the course of this particular novel. The chapter "Oscar vuela de noche" in *El color del verano* illustrates Arenas's deployment of some of the very physically abject characteristics of the grotesque in his description of Oscar as "una loca de dientes gigantescos, cabeza calva y redonda, cuerpo nudoso y encorvado, como el de un murciélago . . . Y Oscar bate sus inmensas alas de murciélago, escruta con sus enormes ojos saltones y rojos, y su desproporcionada cabeza baja en picada" (1991, 98; "a *loca* with gigantic teeth, round and bald head, sinewy and bent over body, like that of a bat . . . And Oscar flaps his immense bat wings, scrutinizes with his huge red popping eyes, and with his oversized head looks downward"). Other *locas* include Hiram Pratt, whom the narrator dubs as "La Reina de las Arañas" (114; The Queen of the Spiders). We also meet a *loca* called Oliente Churre—Smelly Filth. Tedevoro ("I devour you") suffers a fate associated literally with this kind of toilet humor: stigma sticks to him. In one incident, this *loca*—always desperate to engage in sexual acts with any masculine male that he chances upon—enters into a giant urinal provisionally set up for the carnival revelers. Customarily rejected, to his surprise in the urinal he finds himself surrounded by eroticized men, who touch him all over, or so he imagines, licking him with their tongues. Emerging from the urinal he discovers he has in fact been covered in feces, and, smelling to high heaven, the laughingstock of the crowd, he sprints to the ocean and swims out to sea to wash himself clean.

La Ogresa is another portrait of a *loca* with HIV, which similarly wallows in the kind of pathologizing treatment accorded effeminate homosexuals and *travestis* by the regime: as sources of shame, disease, infection, of deformity of body and soul, and, as we will see later, of a suspect duplicity (170). There is no room for the erotic here. That is not to say that Arenas's use of grotesque realism does a disservice to the description of the reality of HIV/AIDS in a system ill equipped to manage the pandemic, both in terms of economy and sexual health programs. The images seem to gravitate to the same center: grotesque and abject, with HIV or not, these *locas* are ridiculed and routinely described as balding, squat, lecherous, pustular, superficial, and untrustworthy. They are characterized as insects, abhorred creatures of the night, hybrid and genetically mutated, and bodies without health or sexual power.

Of course, this is camp at its most darkly comic and ironic.[8] Perhaps camp always borders on the grotesque. However, why is it that effeminate homosexuals and cross-dressers only get this treatment? It seems to repeat the pathologizing gaze of the state that inscribes the masculine and manly body as fit, virile, and praiseworthy, and the effeminate one as suspect, weak, diseased, and perversely at odds with nature. This perhaps preempts the onslaught of such grotesque codings in the era of AIDS, an irony certainly not unapparent to Arenas. Arenas may resignify *mariconería* for his own purposes as Suzanne Kaebnick suggests (1997, 104), but his unremitting use of the grotesque for fellow *locas* is often reiterative of the discourses he attempts to challenge. Or perhaps such grotesquerie is "symbolic of death and renewal," the "Janus-face of the grotesque," two-sided, and a kind of ambivalence at once praised and condemned, as Vice would have it (1997, 171). The grotesque realism reaches its fever pitch in the last novel of the *pentagonía*, *El asalto*. Although all the subjects of the regime in this postapocalyptic nightmare of a novel are debased animals, the prime monster of the piece is the dictator and mother figure who is double gendered. The populace itself is too nonhuman to be properly differentiated by gender.

Arenas's deployment of the grotesque manifests his ambivalence toward gender-variant acts and identifications in no uncertain terms, reinforcing the hierarchy that attributes positive values only to those bodies that achieve the ideals of the masculinist culture and discourse of Castro's Cuba. The irony is hence double. Arenas may serve a blow to the concepts of the naturalness and ascendancy of hypermasculinity by dressing it down, but his critique stops short of a radical reappraisal of the relative set of values assigned to bodies that do not fulfill national-political and gender-bipolar aspirations. In proudly vindicating the eroticism experienced by *locas* such as himself for the masculine male, Arenas articulates a parallel devaluing and antieroticization of the *loca* or gender-variant body. The atypical gender performance and embodiments of *locas* and *travestis* are seen as a kind of grotesquerie. Hybrid, diseased, and perverse, in Arenas's use of the grotesque, they are not just abject but also representative of "a counterfeiting and outrageous re-working of nature" (Epps 1995a, 42). This simply repeats the codings of official culture. How this grotesquerie is deployed through troping gender variance as symbolic of the state will be explored in the following sections.

Surface versus Hidden Identity: The Dualities of the State and the Gender-Variant Body

All my novels pose a constant and contradictory duality, which is characteristic of every human being.

—Reinaldo Arenas in interview in Soto's *Reinaldo Arenas*

All identities are equidistant from sham and deception.

—Roger Lancaster, "Transgenderism in Latin America"

As described in Chapter 1, in much recent literary and filmic production from Latin America, gender-variant or trans subjects function as mere tropes. Metonymically representing the crisis in other categories and political spheres, they are sometimes made to embody ambivalence or corruption in the social order. The work of Viviane Namaste (2000) in examining the troping of transgender subjects to stand in for crisis in national culture is central here. As Namaste and others, such as Yuval-Davis (1997) and Kaminsky (1993), argue, concepts of nation, national identity, and nation formation very often partake of masculinist and patriarchal definitions of history and culture. Stability of national culture is symbolically guaranteed by the reinforcement of traditional gender norms. Such bodies do not conform to the vision of national subject; nor are they faithful to the masculinity proposed as the basic precondition to the formation of nation. Although they embody the femininity, which, in the incarnation of the nation as mother is praiseworthy, theirs is a femininity of a different order. The *loca*'s gender expression is posited as evidence of perversion, of subversion of gender, and of a negation of productivity. Historically, as we have seen, this was related in Cuban cultural discourse to the touted "nonreproductivity" of homosexuality, remembering that *locas* in Cuba in the 1960s and 1970s were also deemed "antiwork." They represented the threat of the other, always located "outside" self and nation, a threat said to undermine the order and its continuance. This continuance relies on masculinist visions of the place of men, the place of women, and the naturality of gender norms in reference to both. *Locas* become the glitch in the apparatus of social and sexual (re)production.

While Arenas appears conscious of the inadmissibility of the *loca* as national subject, the ambivalence toward his gender-atypical characters is always tied to the terms of a duality between surface identity and hidden identity. This section explores the writer's obsession with the dualities present in his social world and shows how the dualities depicted as dualities of the system run parallel to the dualities manifest in his descriptions of *locas*, *travestis*, and other gender-variant acts and embodiments. Troping of such subjects is often sustained by visualizing them as dualities. It is important to keep in mind that this visualization of gender variance is not neutral, as if it had existence as a true or faithful rendering a priori. In looking at the way any writer represents subjects in texts, it is crucial not to lose sight of the fact that she or he chooses from an array of possible codings. As a reader, I remain suspicious of the extent to which Arenas applies his dictum that duality is a characteristic of every human being. Just as masculine or gender-normative people escape the mark of ambivalence in Arenas's work, so, too, do they escape being as thoroughly coded in terms of duality, betrayal, and deception as do his poorly treated gender-variant characters. In considering the rhetorics of the trope that links cross-gendered subjects to crises at a national or political level, it is necessary to explore further what Arenas pursues in mapping the dualities he sees, and what emphasis he assigns them.

As much as the concept of authenticity is crucial in understanding Arenas's appraisal of *mariconería*, he is also very conscious of having to wear, to perform, various identities in different settings. There are macro- and microsocial pressures at hand that make all the more difficult the endless pursuit of authenticity that obsesses the writer. He makes the point that this is the double bind for Cubans—especially homosexual Cubans—under the Castro regime. This is textually communicated in the constant *desdoblamientos* (unravelings) of each of the narrators in the *pentagonía*'s novels. As Soto demonstrates, in *Celestino antes del alba*, the child narrator and the adult poet Celestino are fused; in *El palacio de las blanquísimas mofetas*, we see the doubling of Fortunato and Adolfina; in *Otra vez el mar*, Héctor and his wife are one person, "a double, an alter ego, in order to survive in a repressive environment" (Soto 1998, 53); in *El color del verano*, both Reinaldo Arenas and Gabriel/Reinaldo/the Tétrica Mofeta are the writers of a novel called *El color del verano* (the novel within a novel or mise en abîme). The splitting is explained early on: "No soy una persona, sino dos o tres a la vez. Para ti sigo siendo Gabriel, para aquellos que leen lo que escribo y que casi nunca puedo publicar soy Reinaldo, para el resto de mis amigos con los cuales de vez en cuando me escapo para ser yo totalmente, soy la Tétrica Mofeta" (1991, 101; I'm not one person, but two or three at the same time. For you I'm still Gabriel, for those that read what I write but almost never publish, I'm Reinaldo, for the rest of my friends with whom I escape once in a while, I'm the Skunk in a Funk).

The challenge of Arenas's writing is first and foremost that it makes homosexuality public, which was forbidden in Castro's Cuba at the time of the composition of his works. The homosexual, as we have seen, is expected to cover himself, just as the *loca tapada* discussed earlier. Sometimes this is literal—the forging or appropriation of identity papers in order to escape punishment or the assumption of another's identity. In all his work, Arenas's *loca* characters are people in flight—from one place to another, from one identity to another, with names exchanged and accumulated out of necessity—in order to dodge the authorities once one has been figuratively burned, or *quemado*, to flee the constant surveillance and suspicion of the neighborhood committees, to ensure cover, and to be able to survive and move freely, if only for a time. Oliente Churre's thesis in *El color del verano* on *pájaros*, literally "birds" but also a euphemism for homosexuals, gives a poetic explanation of the term and the peripatetic life of the visible homosexual in Cuba:

> Las aves migratorias, los pájaros, en su perenne afán de encontrar el clima adecuado, el nido, el árbol, el gajo donde quedaron los recuerdos. Un homosexual es un ser aéreo, desasido, sin sitio fijo o propio que anhela de

alguna manera retornar a no se sabe exactamente qué lugar. Estamos siempre buscando un sitio que al parecer no existe. (390)[9]

[Migratory birds, these queens, in their perennial quest to find the suitable climate, the nest, the tree, the crevice where their memories are stored. The homosexual is an airy creature, untethered, without a fixed place of his own that one way or another he longs to return to without knowing where it is. We are always looking for a place that, it seems, doesn't exist.]

In this climate, the *loca* never knows who her friends are; in fact, they may be friends and informers simultaneously. One consequence of this that can be seen in the relations between characters in Arenas's work is that no one ever truly knows, or trusts, one another. The double life of the Cuban *loca* is doubly complex; there is a sense of having to perform constantly, of having to move incessantly, adrift and further from one's original identity. This implies the need to become a virtuoso of disguise, movement, and impersonation. In this myriad of identity changes and doublings of personality, the reality of the country itself is implicated in dualities and layered superimpositions, possessing, in effect, two faces: one "real" and hidden, the other, the surface face of the system, a grotesque or counterfeit parody of the "original." In *El color del verano*, we are told of the existence of two countries in one—the country and the countercountry: "Porque cada país, como todas las cosas en el mundo, tienen su contrario; y lo contrario a un país es su contrapaís, las fuerzas oscuras que tratan de que sólo perdure la superficialidad y el horror, y que todo lo noble, hermoso, valiente, vital (el verdadero país) desaparezcan" (131; "Because every country, like everything in the world, has its opposite; and the opposite of a country is its countercountry, the dark forces that only want superficiality and horror to survive, that wish to make all that's noble, valiant and vital disappear (the true country)").

One of the chapters of *El color del verano* is entitled "La Dualidad de Fifo" (The Duality of Fifo), Fifo being the dictator (411).[10] Similarly, in *El asalto*, the totalitarian face of reality institutes a duality suggested by the phrases deployed in the novel, "nonoche," "noparque," and "contrasiesta." This duality points to a world inflected by the negative of what it was (whose terms were positive), all memory of which is wiped and eradicated from speech. The official world is one led by the Counterwhisperers; the whisperers are those common folk laid siege by this order that negates everything, destroying its "other side" in the process, and suppressing it. The nameless protagonist of this novel, unlike those of Arenas's previous works, is the persecutor, not the persecuted. He is an agent of the Counterwhisperers, in search of those who would talk badly in hushed undertones of the regime. The narrative follows his endless search for his mother with the aim of destroying her. He fears he will become her, and in order to avert this fate, he must obliterate her. Critics have commented on Arenas's deliberate assailing of the mother figure, one of the most revered figures in Cuban and other Hispanophone societies (Soto 1998, 65). The president himself is the *Reprimero*, in charge of the repression of another reality, one that is more authentic, real, honest, below the surface, and underground. The official face of the state (its discourse of national reality and identity) is grotesque and monstrous. Even night, the other face of day, has been banished, since it represents inactivity and a waste of energy that should be channeled into productivity; it suggests another order separate from "day," or the eternal summer that Cuba suffers in *El color del verano* that is also an imposition or artificial creation at the hands of the dictator, Fifo. In his autobiography, Arenas constantly alludes to the excessive theatricality of Fidel Castro's public appearances and the political trials he organizes. Under the scopic drive of the panopticon state, everything is orchestrated as spectacle: lifeless, rehearsed, and artificial. In *El asalto*, language and the reality it constructs have effected an inversion. What one says becomes the opposite of what one means, or it must be inverted to conform to the official reality under pain of death. How one acts may or may not have anything to do with one's real intentions; phrases are uttered for the purpose of showing support of the system. They are repeated endlessly as citations of the order and its authority, as if scripted.

Arenas passionately advocates the stripping away of this reality, this script, to find that which is authentic, real, and the original self/country— in other words, to reveal "lo diverso, luminoso, misterioso y festivo . . . de una identidad y de una fe" (1991, 131; what's diverse, luminous, mysterious and festive . . . in an identity and belief).

The authentic self and country proves that the alter ego is no identity at all; it is, instead, a mask, a front, a facade, and a counterfeit reality that chokes and deadens, tying the subject ever more to the strictures of the order, precluding its liberation, obliterating its individuality, and dehumanizing and enslaving its spirit. In this way, he writes against the grain of duality, seeking to find forever an almost romanticist source of authenticity, occluded by the culture of surveillance, double meaning, and suspicion around him. This is no doubt an accurate rendering of the experience of being a sexual and political refugee in one's own country, of being harassed, constantly monitored, on display, imprisoned, forced to obey to save one's life and sanity (and that of others), pledge allegiance to empty platitudes and politics one doesn't believe in, make retractions, and deny one's very own erotic desires and experiences. It also follows the tradition of several great works critical of despotic regimes—such as George Orwell's *1984*—that depict the cognitive estrangement brought about by highly restricting propagandist governments, whose official reality is, at best, an invention and, at worst, a complete reversal of truth. *El asalto* keenly depicts a society wherein the function of language is to defer meaning endlessly and to scramble, distort, and restructure reality. A new veneer of appearances papers over reality, illiciting an implicit set of binaries: the created utopian world and its shadow, the glorious nation of the people and an order of individuals subjected to terror, a duality founded in fact. This split, this dualism, is evidenced at macro and micro levels. In this way, Arenas offers a keen depiction of the way power operates in regimes like that evidenced in Castro's Cuba in the 1960s and 1970s. His instinct to look to the side of the dualism negated by official discourse is something with which the reader is sympathetic.

The power of his testimony is not at issue here. What is at issue for me is the way the metaphor of the mask or disguise and its implied dualism (imposed surface versus subterranean depth) is often extended through the *loca* or gender-crossing figures and the language Arenas constantly uses to describe these individuals, that is, as inauthentic. They too are depicted dualistically: male-bodied effeminate homosexuals who put on masks, who perform across gender, and in doing so, negate themselves, play into the system, and mirror its deceptive superficiality (a false reality) in the process. This dualism of deep essence versus surface, which the mask constitutes here, turns on the opposition between biological gender ("true" gender, the "truth" of the body) and transvestic gender (counterfeit, superficial, distorting, illusory, and constructed through vestment, attire, and gestural impersonation). The trope of the transvestite (and cross-gendered people in general) as symbolic of contradiction and hence expressive of other contradictions entails the image of a public mask or disguise imposed on a private, divergent inner reality. This may seem at first glance a logical allegory for the official impositions and cover-ups or distortions imposed on a "true" (hidden) reality, but it is one that restricts and debases the term "trans" in the comparison and so needs to be interrogated.

In *El asalto*, this duality is revealed in the climactic scene of the unmasking of the Reprimero, the grand dictator, who is in fact the protagonist's mother in disguise! Critics, such as Biron (2000), Ríos Avila (1998), and Soto (1998), have pointed to the dimension of the monstrous feminine at work in the grotesque realism of *El asalto*. The mother is abject in her female genitalia and menstrual flow, which disgusts the protagonist. The scene where he comes upon the dictator, recognizes his own mother, and strips away her armory and sexually violates her has been examined as an Oedipal fantasy of insecure masculinity (Soto 1998; Biron 2000). I do not contest this interpretation. But I would argue that as a monstrous other, the dual-gender aspect, the two in one, the description of her hairy body and menstrual flow, and the hybrid images that combine spider, rat, and toad push the margin of excess. These descriptions from

El asalto—which extend upon the grotesque figuring of the *loca* body in the same tenor—are found in several parts of the text:

> Las orejas de mi madre son largas, ásperas y anchas como las de un murciélago grande, ratón, perro o elefante o qué coño de bicho, siempre alerta; sus ojos redondos, giratorios y saltones, como de rata o sapo, o qué carajo. Su nariz es como un pico de pájaro furioso, su hocico, su trompa, es alargada y a la vez redonda, con mucho de perro o de boa o de quién carajo podrá decirlo. Su cuello es corto y giratorio, cuello de búho o de garza aplastada o sabrá el diablo de qué rara bestia. En cuanto a su cuerpo, que cada vez que lo descubro me ha parecido que se inflaba más . . . es voluminoso, potente, barrigudo, ventrudo, abultado, vasto, hediondo, peludo por algunos lados, blancuzco por otros, y totalmente desfachatado. (1984, 41)
>
> [My mother's ears are long, rough, and wide, like those of a large bat, dog, or elephant or who knows what bloody beast, always on alert. Her round eyes, swiveling and popping, like a rat's or toad's or who the hell knows what. Her nose is like the beak of a furious bird, her snout, her trunk, is elongated and round at the same time, with something of a dog or boa constrictor about it, or lord knows what strange creature. As for her body, which each time I look at it appears to swell even more . . . it's voluminous, powerful, pot bellied, bulky, vast, smelly, hairy all over, whitish in other parts, completely brazen.]

And, later,

> Ella está allí, ella está cerca, ella viene. Se planta ante mí. Abre sus inmensas patas descomunales y orina. El chorro me empapa, y corro, asfixiándome en ese olor a miao [*sic*]. Corro, pero la yegua, plantándose ante mí, abre otra vez sus inmensas patas, y otra vez me lanza el chorro. Miro hacia arriba, y he ahí la pelambrera gigante, siempre sobre mí, como una araña monstruosa, engullendo, retorciéndose. (126)
>
> [There she is, she's nearby, she's coming. She sets down before me. Se lifts her immense extraordinary legs and urinates. The stream soaks me and I run, suffocated in the smell of pee. I run, but the mare, setting down in front of me, lifts her immense legs, and again lashes out a stream on me. I look down, and there's the gigantic mass of hair, always over me, like a monstrous spider, gulping down, twisting itself.]

The image of Big Brother as Big Mother in fact echoes such a portrait found in the second canto of *Otra vez el mar*. Soto characterizes the figure depicted in *Otra vez el mar* as a "diabolical mother, malevolent, forever vigilant" who is shown as "cupping her testicles" (1998, 66). In *El asalto*, the Big Mother figure is similar and, although the testicles are not mentioned this time, she is still phallic. Another critic says of the final rape scene, "By killing the phallic couple embodied in the mother as *Reprimerísimo*, Arenas enacts the fantasy of overcoming the source of his abjection, the possibility of killing the ambiguous objects of desire" (Ríos Avila 1998, 114).[11] The protagonist is also a persecutor of homosexuals; this is primarily what Ríos Avila is suggesting here. But I would go further—gender atypicality, seen as a source of pure corruption, is also being eradicated here. He wants to destroy the possibility of becoming mother or becoming woman himself, which would fragment his very conception of self. Moreover, the incorporation of the mother in its grotesque aspect as representative of Big Brother—the national-political horizon—obtains complexly parodic aspects that resonate with the elements of patriarchal logics that link motherhood to nation, and the patriarchal father to the state. I will return to this point in discussing the climactic scene of *El asalto* in the next section.

Skirting the Trope: The Queer in the Regime and the Regime in the Queer

In *El asalto*, movement and flux in gender describe a switch in the gradient of power; when the dictator is exposed as the narrator's mother, he loses (phallic) power. Nevertheless, the two in one is clearly monstrous, unnatural, and supernatural. That the regime should be figured this way is a point of major interest. Arenas spends so much time and space in other works depicting the aggressive masculinity of the state that seeks to subjugate effeminacy. He picks apart its precepts and posturing toward authority and superiority; he complicates gender. Here, in the heart of the workings of power, gender crossing reappears. Given the apocalyptic vision of the novel, could this blending of sexes and genders point to the end of history that is painted here? Critic Rita Felski (1996) cites a link between the sense of the end of history and the postmodern obsession with the transgender motif in writers as diverse as Jean Baudrillard (1993), Donna Haraway (1991; 1992), and Italian philosopher Gianni Vattimo (1988). The notions of the end of an era and a crisis in political order and sexual and gender blurring were seen at the turn of the nineteenth century. In fact, that fin de siècle in all its touted anarchy and decadence repeats at the end of the twentieth century, although in quite a different set of conditions, that is, in postmodernity. Baudrillard sees the supposed "loss of desire" in the postmodern moment as linked to the disappearance of sexual difference. For him, we have become "indifferent and undifferentiated beings, androgynous and hermaphroditic" (1993, 25). The citizens of *El asalto* fit very much this mold.

Transsexuality, as Felski notes in reference to the work of Sandy Stone, "inspires a multiplicity of claims and counterclaims regarding its liberatory or catastrophic meanings" (1996, 342). Gender-variant and sexually hybrid bodies are clearly catastrophic for Arenas and equated to reversals or concealments of "meaning" or "truth." This linking of trans to apocalypse has also been noted by Peruvian transsexual lawyer and social scientist Fiorella Cava: "Se afirma que somos seres desviados . . . mutantes, degenerados, imperfectos, productos al final de los tiempos, entes apocalípticos" (2004, 124–25; It is claimed that we are deviant beings . . . mutants, degenerates, imperfect, products of the end of ages, apocalyptic creatures). This surely provides evidence of Arenas's own enlistment of the metaphors of Cuban anti*loca* discourse and his co-option into cultural ideas about gender-different subjects. Yet it could simply signal a restatement of Arenas's complex recognition that while *lo queer* is rejected by the regime, it is also part of the regime. Or perhaps it functions as a mode of mimicking parodically the terms of the Hispanophone nation—*la madre patria*, which formally contains a dual sex aspect, both mother and father—in the most monstrous ways.

Following the move that conjoins cross-gender embodiments to this mother-father duality of nation in *El asalto*, Arenas seems to provide a darkly ironic comment on "national reality" via a queering or transsexing of the terms of nation and state. The monstrous dual-sexed mother is an embodiment of the crisis of nation and the nation in crisis: an aberrant mutation that refuses to stay in the bounds of the natural. Does Arenas marry the grotesque to cross-gender embodiment, which also suffuses his images of *locas* and *travestis* in other texts, to forge a reverse discourse on the subject of nation and (re)productivity? Reverse discourses, in their contestatory force, cite the terms of hegemonic production in articulating a response to the established regimes of power-knowledge, as Foucault would have it (1978, 4). Here it could be argued that to make his critique of state and nation, Arenas makes such a citation in a chain that links monstrous motherhood to queer and trans bodies, the latter especially understood as "antiproductive" and grotesque in homo- and travestophobic Cuban discourse of the period. And yet the consequences of such a link are not fully thought through. After all, is the trans motif here really an accurate semblance of the duplicity of the guises of power? Does gender crossing equal aberrant duplicity and hence the opposite of Arenas's concept of authenticity? And why invoke gender crossing and sexual hybridity in monstrous terms?

Haraway may appreciate the "promises of monsters" (1991, 295) and conceptualize a hybrid cyborg creature that contains trans elements and crossings of all kinds—human, animal, and machine as well as sexual difference—but she, unlike Arenas, explores transgender as a site of redemptive possibility rather than some "nightmarish catastrophe," as Felski notes (1996, 342). Arenas's visions do not inscribe such possibilities; nor do they invoke *loca* and *travesti* "monstrousness"—occupying culturally the position of "the abject"—in any final gesture of liberation.

As Susan Stryker, in her groundbreaking essay "My Words to Victor Frankenstein above the Village of Chamounix: Performing Transgender Rage," observes, "the attribution of monstrosity remains a palpable characteristic of most lesbian and gay representations of transsexuality, displaying in unnerving detail the anxious, fearful underside of the current cultural fascination with transgenderism" (2006b, 245). Arenas, as a gay writer, seems caught up in this relation of disgust and fascination around gender crossing and gender atypicality. He appears paralyzed by the "contradiction" that cross-gendered behavior or embodiment presents to the regime in the discursive world of its own productions. His imagination is in thrall to such modes of thinking that are ultimately phobic to (and condemning of) gender difference. He is not on the side of the "monsters."

Further, I would argue, after Epps, that Arenas is caught in a double bind: how to conceive of an identity beyond the terms through which the subject is interpellated or called into being by discourse? How can one be, finally, authentic? Arenas identifies with the *loca* when it suits him but disowns her gender atypicality because he sees the taking up of the term to be fraught with baggage, a cargo he is not prepared to carry because of the extreme stigma of gender-atypical behavior for "biological" males in Cuba. He invariably reads *locas* and *travestis* as interpellated as gender and sexual others. In his attempt to renegotiate a position for himself, he reattaches stigma to these identities, which he sees as excessive, theatrical, and, in Brad Epps's vocabulary, "scripted." Yet, following Butler, are not all identities scripted? An identity clearly implies a process of identification and is never entirely free floating or conjured up by the subject's will. The subject comes into being through such scripts and identifications with the styles, acts, and forms of being and acting that correspond with them. This is what makes all gender (and gendered identities) performative. Arenas gets lost in the pursuit of authenticity, assuming a sort of superiority or removal from other *locas* and their gendered abjection. His position is dictated more by an erotics of the imagination whose object of desire cannot be the *loca*. This is his double bind. This is amply illustrated by the thematics of his novella, *Arturo, la estrella más brillante*, of which the hallmark feature is the search for an identity and erotic object who is simultaneously the desired other and self (*él*) in the context of the most pronounced subjection. This demonstrates that Arenas may be incapable of thinking outside the binaries established by the discursive productions of his own culture. At the sexual-artistic level, his attractions and desires force a positive appraisal of the macho body even as he may question at times its ascendancy as natural. His object of desire is always the masculine male: an ideal, an endpoint in an endless pursuit wavering between poles of auto-generated selfhood and group-associated identification. Clearly masculinity—as desirable, as ideal—is reinstalled in the status as authentic because it is differentiated from and resistant to the "excesses" of femininity. Arenas, in relying on the fiction of an authentic self (and what is this premised on? being the "enlightened" writer?), buys back into the binaries he parodies initially because he cannot overturn his system of value that makes *maricionería* gender expression inevitably abject and more artificial than the natural or primordial masculinity he desires and to which he ascribes.

Returning to the depictions of the *locas cautivas* in *Arturo, la estrella más brillante*, we see that, as in his autobiography, these *locas* occupy the lowest rung of the camp's hierarchy. According to the third-person-omniscient narrative voice in *Arturo*, the prisoners are divided into "'ellos,' 'los otros' y 'los demás'" ("them, the others, and the rest"; 1984, 10). This is how "ellos" (or, better said, "ellas") are described in one section:

> Ellos, con sus infinitas conversaciones inútiles, ellos con sus gestos excesivamente afeminados, artificiales, grotescos, ellos rebajándolo todo, corrompiéndolo todo, hasta la auténtica furia del que padece el terror, hasta el abusado ritual de las patadas, los culatazos en las nalgas, las bofetadas; hasta la ceremonia de un fusilamiento se convertía, se transformaba, para ellos en un ajetreo de palabras rebuscadas, de poses y chistes de ocasión; . . . ellos pintándose el rostro con lo que apareciese, improvisando pelucas con flecos de yagua y hojas de maguey, remedando minifaldas con sacos de yute hábilmente substraídos de los almacenes custodiados, y en la noche confundiendo sus insatisfacciones, chillando, soltando su estúpida jeringonza, sus estúpidos ademanes exhibicionistas, sus máscaras que de tanto usarlas habían pasado a ser sus propios rostros. (12–13)
>
> [Them, with their infinite useless conversations, them, with their excessively effeminate gestures, artificial, grotesque, them, putting everything down, corrupting everything, even the authentic fury of he who suffers terror, even the abused ritual of the kick in the behind, knife blades in the buttocks, blows; even the ceremony of the firing squad would become, transform itself for them, into a flurry of pretentious words, poses, throwaway lines; . . . them, painting their faces with anything around, improvising wigs with palm and maguey leaves, patching together miniskirts out of jute bags skillfully taken from guarded warehouses, and at night, muddying their disappointments, shrieking, letting loose their stupid slang, their stupid exhibitionist movements, their masks, that from having worn them so often had become their own faces.]

Reading these deeply ambivalent codings of the trans figures in Arenas's work, it is not difficult to see how they textually resonate with the terms of ambivalence of the national reality explored in this instance. Both suggest the image of the surface artificiality. If we apply Viviane Namaste's deployment of Max Black's interactionist view of metaphor, that is, that "metaphor connects two subjects, one principal and one subsidiary . . . through a 'system of associated commonplaces'" (2000, 97) and that the subsidiary subject highlights and orders how the principle subject is perceived (98), the urgency of unpacking the trope becomes apparent in its ethical dimensions. The use of trans figures by Arenas for tropological ends places "the state" in the position as principal subject and "drag performer," "the gender ambiguous," or "the travesti" variously in the subordinate term. The status of the trans performer subject and all the associated common places evoked by this term in culture are extended to the principal term "the state" or more specifically, the dictator. These associated commonplaces ironically draw on the very discourses of sexual and gender deviance articulated by the Castro regime that Arenas on a more conscious level endeavors to contest, summed up by Sylvia Molloy's model of the pose: the *loca* as traitorous, deceitful, and false. On a subtextual level, however, those elements such as "artificiality," "surface," "ruse," and "duplicity," which appear as traces in the description of trans figures in Arenas's oeuvre, activate the connotative and intertextual meanings of gender crossing in the cultural site of production and the intratextual connections spelled out in parallel dualisms mentioned previously to signify political corruption, masquerade, and deception. The transfiguration of the grotesque (in the corporeal and vestimentary styles of the performing *locas, travestis,* and dual-sexed persons) is expressive of the grotesque, deceptive face of the regime; it highlights and orders the other dualisms deployed in Arenas's more general political critique of the system. These terms form a kind of tropic unity that appears incontestable, since it is primarily the principal subject that is in view. Aspects of the subsidiary term that are not materialized in the text, or alternative characteristics from outside the connotative field that would not fit the metaphorical chain, are under erasure here, such is the force of the analogy.

The use of cross- and transgendered acts, behaviors, and figures as motifs for crisis in national culture, or as symbols of perversion and official corruption, features persistently in Arenas's vision. As the following chapters will illustrate, Arenas is not alone in using the figures of the *loca*, the *travesti*, and the *transformista* performer in this way. However, this use is not without political implications, as we have seen in this chapter. The ubiquity of these figures in many texts, it should be stated, does not therefore grant them the status of a logical or natural association or a poetic, incidental feature of genre.

Furthermore, the figuring that we perceive in Arenas's work of gender-variant subjectivities and performance in terms of the most deceptive duality, marked by one reality that contradicts or betrays another hidden one ("a counterfeiting and outrageous re-working of nature" [Epps 1995a, 42]), is overdetermined, as it relies on the idea that certain identities are more artificial than others. The proposition that installs the masculine male as the less artificial, more authentic gendered identity and degrades as grotesque and excessive what gender bipolar mindsets label as "deviantly effeminate" or a betrayal to one's sex is both phobic to gender difference and sexist. The proposition views masculinity as the raw, the natural, and the basic, and anything else as adornment, extravagant, and a perversion of an original state. Femininity in women or men has often been figured as frivolous, superficial, devious, and deceptive. Arenas goes some way to upsetting this paradigm of an ascendant masculinity as a privileged term. His experience as a persecuted artist and homosexual under a state that constantly derides the feminine in favor of the discourse of the triumphant revolutionary virility as embodied by the New Man gives him a unique and ironic vantage point from which to judge such hypocrisy. Yet Arenas's avowal of *mariconería* for personal and political ends reaches its limits where his own bipolar notions of gender and "natural" gender are tested. His disturbance of the hierarchy is, therefore, limited. Arenas's radical project veers off course when he attempts to articulate his own eroticism, which is beset by an uneven distribution of the values of sexual attractiveness, health, beauty, and authenticity, in a schema that favors the macho. This leads, as I have argued, to a reinstallation of the hierarchy of identities suggested by the notion that some identities (here, trans ones) are more artificial than others. The ambivalence Arenas expresses is therefore a kind of gut reaction dictated by his erotic horizons. It is also structured by the hierarchies of value that underwrote the social meanings of gender in the masculinist revolutionary Cuban state of the 1960s and 1970s.

For this reader, this ambivalence presents greatest concern when it is coded through the grotesque: an often opaque and highly figurative form that is riddled with ambivalence and contradictory impulses. Perhaps the genre itself binds Arenas to his binaries; an aesthetically radical premise for the artist in search of himself has his texts teeter on the edge of a highly conservative, gender-polarity-affirming view of trans subjects and their social world. In this way, Arenas occludes his view and prevents a rigorous, throughgoing interrogation of the terms of masculinity, privilege, and gender "naturalness." His grotesque realism draws upon the selfsame lexicon of abjection and stigma assigned to gender "deviant" behavior by the system he attempts to expose. The move from comic irreverence to dark apocalyptic visions that is seen in the cycle of the *pentagonía* suggests that Arenas, while endeavoring to offer an increasingly mordant and serious view of dictatorship, was more and more susceptible to the kinds of formulations in mainstream discourse about those who take gender beyond the pale. As suggested by my analysis, he clearly envisions such subjects as posing an equivalence in their identities and "contradictory" bodies to that national monster, that enigmatic Sphinx, that Janus face of the state, that haunted him as a writer and activist right to his end. The abject codings of gender variance discussed thus far as duplicitous surface posing (*Arturo, la estrella más brillante*), as suspect and degraded (*El color del verano* and *Antes que anochezca*), together with the visualization of the dictator in all his hybrid-sexed embodiment (*El asalto*), offer convincing evidence for such a reading.

As mentioned in the introduction to this book, the inscription of sexually ambiguous bodies with connotations of the grotesque and their symbolic use to represent national or statist corruption is found not only in the work of isolated writers like Arenas but also in that of several contemporaries. The demoniacal character of El Brujo en Luisa Valenzuela's *Cola de lagartija* (1983) is an example; El Brujo is very much like the Dictator in *El asalto* and the images associated with his physicality resonate with those associated with Fifo-the Mother in Arenas's novel. Like the Mother-Dictator in *El asalto*, El Brujo is mysterious, powerful, mutant, phallic, and yet also hybrid in form. Written in a kind of neobaroque style as a critique of *la eminencia gris* (the power behind the throne), of the military-led repression against supposed civilian subversives in the "Dirty War" (1976–1983) in her country, at one point in her novel Valenzuela makes the link between trans bodies and corruption explicit in the following delirious line: "Brujo travesti, transexual, puto, reputo, brujo de meras transformaciones hormonales, brujo de confusas gónadas" (276; "*Travesti* warlock, transsexual, fag, wizard of hormonal transformations, warlock of confused gonads"). Similarly, the presence of cross-gendered acts, behaviors, and figures as motifs for perversion and official corruption are abundant in Jaime Manrique's *Colombian Gold* (1983). The cover of the book asserts its legitimacy confidently as "a novel of power and corruption": a genre-conscious take on Colombia's corrupt tradition of political oligarchy, combining the thriller with melodrama. The novel paints a picture of Colombia—particularly Barranquilla's high society—as a corrupt, stratified system of patriarchal privilege. Its protagonist reasserts this through a series of transgressions: including male-on-male rape, the sexual abuse of a servant, and cross-dressing. So, too, the crime novel *Máscaras* (1997) by Leonardo Padura plots a *travesti* at the center of an intrigue of multiple dimensions. The *travesti* in question, recently murdered, turns out to be the son of a diplomat. Her death is associated with religious mysticism, especially with the Transfiguration of Jesus. Metaphors of mystery and the mask strongly connote with this figure, who plays off a series of questions that unravel with the investigation of the political culture on which the work centers. Padura makes his debt to Sarduy and the formulations made by this author about *travestismo* clear by direct citation from *La simulación* and by dedicating his book to Sarduy. Indeed, the invocation of gender crossing and sexual excess in the name of the dark side of political culture and black magic is found in all these works, which rest on very Freudian constructs, of the kind also found in *El asalto*, as we have seen. Finally, their positions on identity and its (de)formation come directly from Lacan, a thinker with whom Valenzuela, for one, has long been associated.

The linking of cross-gender acts and *loca* or *travesti* embodiments to the national-cultural sphere, and to the associations of artificiality, contradiction, and theatrical excess, in all their Sarduyan and Lacanian sophistry, is not restricted to literary productions, however. The tradition that makes use of gender crossing as symbol or symptom of other issues, particularly in connection to the social order, is also found in the cinematic production that first began to feature *locas* and *travestis* in the 1970s in Latin America. The next chapter foregrounds this tradition and undertakes an exploration of three filmic texts, all of which clearly fall within a period that Arenas do not himself live to see: the political emergence of marginalized homosexual and *travesti* subjectivities in several domains in the 1990s. Arenas's feverish writing, his subsequent personal and cultural dislocation, and his suicide in 1990 after a lengthy AIDS-related illness prevented him from visualizing the lives and embodiments of his gender-variant characters in all but the most ambivalent and allegorizing ways; his visions, more than anything, are a product of their time and circumstance. The next three texts to be analyzed offer some glimpses into the circumvention of this discourse on *locas* and *travestis* as conflictual and grotesque in a period where new knowledges about these subjects begin to gain ground. How far the texts move beyond *lo trans* as metaphor or subjectivity is the principal question pursued in the chapter that follows.

Chapter 3

Life Is (More than) a Cabaret

Gender Crossing and "Trans" Signification in Contemporary Cinema from Latin America

If queer and trans people in Euro-American contexts have historically been associated with spectacles of the theater and the stage, then sex- and gender-diverse subjects in Latin American contexts have likewise been linked to performing arts and spaces, in particular, the space of the cabaret. Allusions to the Weimar Republic and sexual subversion aside, the cabaret, and on occasion, the brothel, is no mere space for the provision of entertainment and the satisfaction of desire. Ana López has called the cabaret as depicted in Mexican cinema a liminal space where what is usually contained by the moral order of the day is given full rein (1991, 43). Sergio de la Mora says that throughout the history of Mexican cinema, the cabaret "has been the privileged space for articulating gender/sexual identities" (1992–93, 83). Importantly, the cabaret (along with the brothel in other films) has also been a site for negotiating issues of changes in nation and identity.

Although many of such examples of cinematic visualizations of sex and gender variance are found in Mexican cultural productions, other "national" cultures have also framed *locas* and *travestis* in terms of sexual excess and theatricality in works of literature and film. This current in thinking about nonnormative sexuality, particularly homosexuality and effeminacy, was strong in both pre- and postrevolutionary Cuba as we saw in the last chapter, where around the time of the emergence of Castro's oppositional guerrilla movement, homosexuals were associated with the seedy world of bars, nightlife, and commercial pleasure, symbolic, in the revolutionary mindset, of colonialism and capitalist corruption of Cuban culture. In Brazil, the association of gender-crossing homosexuals and *travestis* with carnival is indelible, so much so that *travestis*—understood as symbols of the carnivalesque—are frequently proffered as archetypal of a kind of Brazilianness. The carnival, and the ritualized cross-gendering that it permits within the constraints of a once-a-year ephemeral spectacle, is posited as a quintessentially Brazilian celebration of openness and tolerance toward all forms of cultural mixing, but especially, of the nation's sexual minorities. This is, of course, the product for a form of myth making that displaces the realities of lived sex and gender variance in Brazilian culture, which is subject to degrees of stigmatization and socioeconomic exclusion that are also found in other parts of the region, as Kulick (1998) points out.

The influence of the framing of sex and gender variance in terms of performance and excess cannot be underestimated, however. In spite of national differences, the cinemas of the three countries from which the films that this chapter analyzes come all share this framework of conceptualizing and situating gender crossing and sexual identity. Likewise, by situating their *locas, transformistas,* and *travestis* within the worlds of the brothel-cabaret, a consideration of the extent to which they use these types and locales to broach issues of nation and cultural identity is of acute relevance, not merely because this topic constitutes the main concern of the present book, but also because cinematic productions, in their visual imaginings, so powerfully shape and mold the possibilities and limits of contemporary representation.

Although the focus of this chapter is on contemporary filmic production, centering the attention, as it does, on María Novaro's *Danzón* (Mexico, 1991), Orlando Rojas's *Las noches de Constantinopla* (Cuba, 2001; *Constantinople Nights*), and Karim Aïnouz's *Madame Satã* (Brazil, 2002; *Madame Satan*), previous filmic visions of homosexuality and gender crossing from these places are necessary to foreground. To this end, I will give both the texture and background that an analysis of contemporary productions requires before examining each film in detail. The films for analysis need to be considered in light of the traditions they inherit and potentially contest. Consideration of extant critical perspectives that would account for their representations is hence also relevant and will be included before examining the films. The chapter engages in a comparative look at productions that span the period that the entire book encompasses, namely the period that has seen the emergence of sex- and gender-diversity activism in the region and the articulation of trans and homosexual political subjectivities, providing sociohistorical detail around each film to nuance the analysis.

Images That Matter:
The History of Homosexual and
Gender-Variant Types in Cinema

While in recent years several critics have begun to focus attention specifically on *locas* and *travestis* in Latin American literary productions, as outlined in Chapter 1, fewer have examined their representation in cinema in the region. Antonio Moreno's *A personagem homossexual no cinema brasileiro* (2001; *The Figure of the Homosexual in Brazilian Cinema*) looks at images of homosexuals in Brazilian film from 1923 to 1996. David William Foster's study *Queer Issues in Contemporary Latin American Cinema* (2003) offers an overview of the representation of homosexuality in Latin American film. Sergio de la Mora's recent work *Cinemachismo: Masculinities and Sexuality in Mexican Film* (2006) examines the representation of masculinities and sexualities in Mexican cinema from 1950 to 2004, mapping the relationship of these to national identity.

De la Mora's study is particularly useful in considering gender-variant characters in film. He draws on the work of queer film critic Richard Dyer who, in turn, has devised a four-point description of the most common stereotypes deployed in the representation of homosexuality in English-language cinema. Traditionally, cinema has pursued a representation of homosexuality in the name of elucidating the construction of sexual identities in general and more specifically in terms of gender and the depiction of psychosexual dispositions in men and women. Dyer's four cinematic "homosexual types" include the "In-between," the Macho, the Sad Young Man, and the Lesbian Feminist (1993, 42).

Drawing on Dyer's observations, de la Mora looks at films in the *fichera* genre, which abound in homosexual characters that always fulfill the in-between stereotype.[1] *Fichera* films were the most common genre of films in Mexico from the early 1970s to the mid-1980s. These films borrow themes from the *cabaretera* films of the 1940s, which explored urban nightlife and featured musical numbers, and in so doing consistently featured a queen archetype (2006, 109) *Fichera* films invariably depicted a strongly macho character alongside the queen. The queen, de la Mora argues, was a point of deviancy used to fix and naturalize heterosexual masculinity as normal: "the inclusion of the scandalous difference of the queen, the sign of an in-between gender, neither man nor woman but a 'failure' to be either" (113). De la Mora provides the following films as examples and points to their recurrent use of the queen type: the first *fichera* film *Bellas de noche* (Miguel M. Delgado, 1975; *Night Beauties*); *Zona roja* (Emilio Fernández, 1975; *Red Light District*), which deploys the typical mythic victimized-prostitute narrative; *Salón México* (an antecedent to the *fichera* genre, Emilio Fernández, 1949); *El día del compadre* (Carlos Vassallo, 1983; *Buddies' Day*); *Noches de cabaret* (Rafael

Portillo, 1977; *Cabaret Nights*), in which a man falls for a *travesti* who is actually a woman;[2] and *Muñecas de media noche* (Portillo, 1978; *Midnight Dolls*), whose protagonists must dress in drag in one sequence in order to escape the mafia. As in other films in the Hollywood tradition studied by Vito Russo in *The Celluloid Closet* (1981), homosexuality in Mexican cinema is signaled only in terms of gender variance, that is, in the guise of the sissy, the "effeminate" man and effete queen, or the *loca*. These in-between characters were narratively marginal to the main "straight" characters.

Mexican academic Mario Muñoz confirms such figurations. Muñoz's interest is mainly literary, and yet he includes some substantive comments on Latin American filmic productions of the time that have shaped the public imaginary around the possibilities of homosexuality and gender-crossing characters in contemporary narrative. In the cinema of the 1970s and 1980s, the topic of gender crossing or effeminacy in men was a point of spectacle, slapstick, irony, and caricature, according to this critic (Muñoz 1996, 12). *Locas* and *travestis* assume a marginal position relative to other characters, says Muñoz. In fulfilling roles as waiters, confidantes, go-betweens, hairdressers, or servants, their function is to act as mere mediators between hookers and their clients, or between an elite ruling class and their subalterns (12). They are an indispensable feature of gay show-business life, humorous and exaggerated on stage, victimized and submissive off stage. Relegated to the poor barrios and brothels, they exist on the borders between the acceptable and the illicit. Commonly they are the target of ridicule, manhandled by aggressive men, and depicted as superficial and inferior in comparison to the main protagonists—normative men and women. Their presence serves to illustrate the operation of machismo in patriarchal society, and they are inevitably symbolic in some way: a tabula rasa on which are inscribed the forces of co-option and violence. Like de la Mora, Muñoz refers principally to Mexican films; and yet Moreno's observations in regard to Brazilian cinema also tally with this picture. In a series of films such as *A lira do delirio* (1978; *Lyre of Delirium*), *Amor bandido* (1979; *Bandit Love*), *Ópera do malandro* (1986; *Malandro*), *O anjo nasceu* (1969; *The Angel Was Born*), *Navalha na carne* (1969; *Razor in the Flesh*), *O casamento* (1975; *The Marriage*), and *A casa assassinada* (1971; *The Murdered House*), the homosexual is always depicted as a *travesti* with a low level of education, living in squalor and violence, characterized as false, vengeful, and treacherous, and frequently she meets a disastrous end. Her difference is marked by effeminate gestures, carnivalesque wardrobe, and a dissimulating demeanor that signifies pretence.

These depictions in cinema have regulated the public image of gender nonconforming individuals in a profound way, and as archetypes they are immediately familiar. In positive terms, they may be cheeky, burlesque, and wanton. In negative terms, they are visualized as all exterior and theatrical surface. Some common mise-en-scène facets of this cinematic stereotype include the use of a high-pitched voice, excessive pancake makeup, colored hair, scandalous costumes, obscene throwaway lines, and extremely effeminate gestures. For Muñoz, expunged of humanity in all their marginality and attributed inferiority and compliance, they appear mere circus freaks, symbols of weakness, deviance, and cultural deformation. They have no inner life, no depth beyond the cultivated mask and pose (12–13).

Moreno's, De la Mora's, and Muñoz's observations notwithstanding, some films have attempted to go beyond the jaded image of *locas*, *travestis*, and gender-crossing acts in order to explore such characters with more seriousness. Arturo Ripstein's 1977 film *El lugar sin límites* (*The Place Without Limits*), based on the Chilean novel of the same name by José Donoso, attempts just that. Also alluding to the *fichera* or *cabaretera* films that take place in brothels or nightclubs, its *travesti* character forms the center of the film's exploration of issues of eroticism, machismo, and the patriarchal order. De la Mora considers this film in detail. La Manuela, a *travesti* brothel madam, is not the comic figure of the previous tradition and is, instead, treated with a great deal of sympathy. In spite of this, the film does not shatter completely the mold of the *loca* or *travesti* described previously, as La Manuela is still a victim. She is depicted as passive and masochistic, showy and flawed. Strains of the grotesque adhere to her. Her depiction is a pointedly enabling one: she is used to broach other issues. Notwithstanding its limitations, the film stands out from other features of the period that merely sustain the comedic role of the gender crosser in their approach.

Alternative images of *locas* and *travestis* as part of the social landscape, resistant with their own voice and presence and a particular catalogue of experiences, desires, and objectives, as mentioned in the introduction to this book, have only begun to emerge in the 1990s, with the rise of sexual- and gender-minority activism in Latin America. This has seen *travesti* people emerge as protagonists and agents in the contested domain of the media, in the law courts and academic inquiry and in civil society. This is a very different climate from that which dominated in previous years, when the image of *locas* and *travestis* was much less complex and governed more by received popular imagery, and when their voices were rarely, if ever, heard. The previously mentioned films can only be judged in terms of their particular time and place. Their reticence to move beyond the paradigm of gender crosser as symbolic, theatrical, comic, or tragic is a reflection of the general ignorance about homosexual and trans lives at the time. Speaking with the benefit of at least fifteen years of increased visibility around the issues of working-class effeminate homosexuality and *travestismo*, it would be perhaps unfair to cast judgment on these productions based on our own contemporary visions.

In spite of the recent emergence of homosexual and trans subjects in all their multivocality, the pressures of cultural normativity around gender and sexuality have not vanished overnight. Mass forms—particularly the cinema, as De Lauretis (1987) reminds us—play a chief role in the perpetuation and dissemination of the normalizing project. Two recent films not analyzed here but that feature very briefly *travesti* characters—*Crónica de un desayuno* (Mexico, 2000; *A Breakfast Chronicle*) and *La Perrera* (Uruguay, 2006; *The Dog Pound*)—illustrate this. Not only are their *travesti* characters violently assaulted as soon as they make an appearance visually, but their presence serves merely to illustrate the forces of machismo and thus mark a spectral and fleeting "gender otherness."

The three films selected for close analysis are perhaps more complex, and yet they are not immune to entanglements with issues of national identity, cultural change, and gender. The space of the cabaret is notable in all three films, suggesting the possibility of metaphorical uses of the trans figure. The three films provide a litmus test to gauge whether, given the contemporary visibility of *travesti* and *loca* lives, recent filmmaking has managed to move beyond the terms of *travesti* and drag queen as archetype or symbolic stage creature and thus explore more deeply the subjectivities of their protagonists. By looking at these texts in this way, we might reveal the changing place of *travestis* and *locas* in the cultural imaginary and evaluate whether the tendency toward troping is maintained or minimized.

Maria Novaro's *DANZÓN*

Maria Novaro emerged in the 1980s in an industry primarily dominated by men whose depictions of women in their films reinforced an established tradition of female stereotypes in Mexican cinema, the kind that the *cabaretera* and *fichera* genres themselves deployed. These stereotypes concerned dualistic representations of women: good, saintly, sacrificial types and bad women, often prostitutes. In the 1980s the Mexican state initiated projects to encourage the participation of women in the industry as filmmakers. From the beginning, Novaro's films broached "women's issues" and attempted to break down the traditional stereotypes. In *Lola* (1989), a middle-class woman struggles to overcome particular class attitudes by striking out independently and raising a young daughter on her own. *El jardín del Edén* (1994; *The Garden of Eden*), set in Tijuana, explores the friendships of four very different women: an Anglo-American tourist, a Chicana art collector, an indigenous woman, and a widowed mother of three. Another film, *Sin dejar huella* (2000; *Without a*

Trace), also centers on women, one a university-educated art dealer and the other a working-class young mother, both of whom are on the run from authorities. In all these films, two-dimensional preconceptions of bad women are exposed, as the characters' motives are shown as complex. Novaro is consistently preoccupied with exploring motherhood as well. All these themes are present in the film *Danzón*.

According to Romy Sutherland (2002), there has been much debate as to whether *Danzón* is a feminist film and, indeed, as to whether Novaro herself is a feminist filmmaker. The director defines herself as a feminist personally but insists that her films do not follow any deliberate feminist project. She believes her work should not be restricted to a fixed ideological stance, and she is more concerned with exploring human relationships. To compound matters, the actress who played the role of the protagonist Julia in *Danzón*, the famous María Rojo, insists that it is a feminist text. Others assert that it is more feminine than feminist. Suffice it to say, the film is concerned with a woman liberating herself—as Novaro's other films are—although it is a matter of interpretation whether Julia in this instance is liberating herself from the confining gender ideology that women in Mexican culture face or whether she is coming to terms with it. In describing the film as feminist or not, critics seek to evaluate its sexual politics as either progressive (pinned to a women's liberation project) or retrograde. This tension shadows my analysis, which will look more particularly at the place of *travestismo* in the film in the context of its larger explorations of gender ideology and the state of gender relations at the time it was made. Whether Novaro or her detractors would prefer to call the film feminist or not, it is deeply concerned with gender ideology, lived or actual gender, as visualized in past and contemporary modes.

In this film dominated by women, the few men who appear are not agents of control over women's lives. Patriarchy is not embodied in people or even concretely institutionalized. There are no fathers or authorities that might impede the decisions or movements of the protagonist, Julia. Rather, a disembodied traditional gender idealism structures her life, and a more abstract system of economic relations divides her world into the domestic and the public.

Julia, a forty-something telephone operator from Mexico City with a fourteen-year-old daughter, embraces a kind of gender traditionalism that belies her current circumstances. This is symbolized by her obsession with *danzón*, a slow, stately dance that entered Mexico in the 1930s via Cuba. Julia is a paradigmatical late-1980s, incipient-1990s, lower-middle-class woman. In the time period in which the story takes place, *danzón* has the exotic appeal of a far-off nostalgic world where men were *galanes* (genteel but strong lovers) and women their dedicated partners, the latter's looks containing a subdued and feminine eroticism that paired with their partners' guiding suave macho grace. The film is structured by this kind of slow movement, opening with scenes of silver-slippered feet gliding over the dance floor, returning at intervals to this dance even as the film progresses and changes are observed, and closing again with Julia in the dance hall. This structuring device hints at an ideological panorama that at the micro level does not reflect the everyday but is referred to as a point of reference, an inheritance, and a set of principles. The *danzón* form encompasses an idealized version of heterosexuality: men and women have their allotted roles. As Claudia Schaefer states, "the two partners must never, ever look at one another in the eye but instead focus on an imaginary point somewhere beyond the 'real', which is what imbues it with romance: the impossible" (2003, 60). But Julia is a firm believer in this idealized heterosexuality where the woman does not lose her honor. That she ascribes so willingly to its norms suggests that women are as much involved in the social reproduction of the status quo in regards to sex-role differentiation as men.

Novaro thus creates the historical backdrop against which her updated story of a woman's quest is set. This quest narrative seeks to explore the changes that have occurred in past and present manifestations of gender norms as seen in the relations between men and women in Mexico. Novaro wants to prod gently our expectations as formed by Mexican cinema, cultural history, and the story of women's participation in society. To illustrate this, a little information on plot and characterization is necessary.

The *danzón* for Julia is not just a pastime; it is an escape from her dreary world of work and her lack of romantic prospects, a voyage from reality into fantasy. Her circle of friends are her other female workmates. Her dance partner, Carmelo, is her quintessential nostalgic vision of what men should be for women: aloof, masculine, older, authoritative, but gentlemanly. She will dance with no other.

One night Julia and her work friend Silvia are at one of the *danzón* clubs in the city. Julia is restless because Carmelo has failed to show up, which is very uncharacteristic of him. Julia gets word that he has disappeared after being accused of stealing money from the bar at which he works. Increasingly moody, directionless, and unable to trace her beau, acting on the rumor that Carmelo has gone to Veracruz, Julia takes time off work and, after cashing in some of her retirement fund, embarks on a five-hour train trip to that city of tropical dreams of Mexican cinema, Veracruz, but ends up finding a lot more than Carmelo awaiting her. This is not quite the Veracruz as traditionally depicted in Mexican golden age cinema. To be certain, the usual gallery of characters are there—the abandoned mother who runs the hotel at which Julia arrives, the prostitute Colorada and her pimp, the cabaret drag artistes who inhabit the shadows of this near-mythical town, the sailors and itinerants who trawl the waterfront, and the boleros invoking love lost and betrayal. But they are its modern incarnation, and hence the abandoned mother is not so suffering. Colorada the working girl is not tragic or dominated by her pimp, and Susy the *travesti* and her fellow performing friends Yadira and Karla are treated sympathetically—not as artificial or inferior personalities. This is testament to Novaro's intent to pursue more nuanced portrayals that overturn the traditionally maligned visions of woman and femininity. But as depictions they also serve as contrasts to Julia's treasured principles of a past gendered traditionalism—partially constructed by the popular imagination—and thus to underline the changes in women's affectional possibilities, identities, and alliances. The *travesti* nightclub performer Susy—portrayed by veteran gay drag personality Tito Vasconcelos—functions to point to these alternative versions of gender and its (re)construction. It is imperative to examine first, however, the ideological dimensions to the different versions of "woman" and femininity as available in Mexico culture and investigate the changes in gender relations to which the film primarily responds, in its drive to portray the state of Mexican national culture. As the film deals with competing versions of woman and femininity, we need to grasp how these historically distinct trends emerged.

Julia, on meeting Susy, is encouraged by her to accentuate her femininity, but Julia fears this will make her appear as a whore. In accordance with her firmly held principles of gender traditionalism, Julia seeks to transmit the norms of virtue and goodness to her daughter, who seems more interested in rock music and skimpy clothing. Julia sees in *danzón* a useful guide to navigate her daughter through the rocky terrain of the "dangers" of stepping outside the female role in relation to men. However, her daughter seems uninterested in the dance, as she is part of a new generation that follows the kinds of changes the film profiles. Julia's daughter is not beholden to her mother's more antiquated ideals of femininity.

Julia preserves these notions because of her enculturated sense of vulnerability as a woman. As a mother, she shows the desire to oversee the reproduction of certain norms that to her appear unquestionable. The mother's role in this cultural reproduction is hence foregrounded by the film. Such norms represent the "known" to Julia, who feels that it is only her natural place to pass them on to her daughter, lest she be exposed to the trouble of the unknown.

Concomitant with the kinds of norms manifest in *danzón*'s traditional gender schema, there is a pervasive ideology that dictates the terms of social respectability and women's standing. To be without a man in the house, to be a single woman, one needs to prove one's virtue, for to live alone, in Mexican terms, "without a suitable man as guardian of her virtue . . . would be tantamount to being publicly available, that is, a prostitute" according to this traditional model (Melhuus 1996, 245).

This dichotomy of the virgin (the respectable woman and the chaste mother) and the whore conceptually challenges Julia. She has been raised on moral codes that posit women's sexuality as an ambivalent source of virtue. This virtue must be maintained at all costs, not simply for an individual woman's sense of propriety, but also for the continuance of a cultural state of affairs in which it is women who are assumed to be the protectors of virtue and men who are unable to rein in their impulses. Such ideas derive from the interplay of the discourses of *marianismo* and *machismo* in Mexican culture. These discourses underwrite social relations. For the sake of the social order, then, women tread the line between respectability and public notoriety. The loss of respectability and descent into notoriety is intimately connected to norms of gender and sexuality and potentially implicates other women. Julia is expected to function as a role model for her daughter and for the community: to lurch in the other direction risks crisis. As Marit Melhuus states, "On the one hand, the ideal of her moral rectitude is stressed and expressed through the symbolic value of virginity. . . . On the other hand, motherhood is the epitome of womanhood" (1996, 244). It is this set of norms that Julia idealizes but is forced to confront—both in Veracruz and in her everyday life where she is not regarded as a "perfect" woman. She straddles the public and private sphere by necessity: she goes out to work, that is, she implicitly breaches and traverses the borders between the so-called feminine domestic or private sphere and the public space said to belong to men. *Danzón* thus disperses and at the same time attempts to dispense with notions of "decent" versus "indecent" women. Novaro characterizes Julia as an emergent modern woman caught between the traditional and the pragmatic notions of women and their place in the world. Novaro's film, then, rhetorically reinstates the position of women as responsible for cultural reproduction and spars with the patriarchal logics that insist on the femininity of motherhood—in all its "asexuality" and "passivity"—as the grounds for maintaining the social order.

In regard to this, the question of women's position in the family became an "issue" on the radar, culturally, when in the years preceding the film's release (1985–90), sociologists claimed to have "discovered" that women were now increasingly the heads of households in Mexico. As Elizabeth Dore explains in her article "The Holy Family," "In the 1980s, sociologists discovered a high proportion of female-headed households in Latin America. With the prevailing stereotype of the family, they concluded that such households were a new phenomenon. This research attracted the attention of politicians searching for a simple explanation of crime and poverty. As in the United States and Europe, Latin American policymakers cast the blame for an array of social ills on female-headed households, stigmatised as 'non-traditional'" (1997, 102). Of course, as Dore is at pains to clarify, the picture of dependency of women and their inferior status in the affairs of the household was more an ideological invention than a historical truth. The point is that Mexican culture had been so regulated by dichotomous notions of women, motherhood, and virtue that it had concealed the true circumstances of women's (unacknowledged) position in many families over a long period of time and thus maintained the purity of the notion of "family." Diversity in family relations (single parent, female led, nonmatrimonial, or adoptive arrangements, to name a few) has always existed, in spite of the ideological persistence of the paradigm of the patriarchal unit and the male as the breadwinner. The dawning realization of women as active agents in familial and economic relations, and in their own destinies, as we see from the previous quote, provoked a kind of cultural crisis. The emergence in the workforce of ever greater numbers of women—in spite of the cultural prohibitions—added to this crisis. The injunction that men are supposed to be the breadwinners "exerting complete authority over their wives and children" (Smith 1997, 125) was of little value in the *sexenio* of Carlos Salinas de Gortari (1988–94). This period was typified by the neoliberalist policy that came to its head in the signing of the North American Free Trade Agreement (NAFTA), but it also witnessed changes in mass consumption and employment that reshaped the more traditional notions of the place of men and women.[3] Seemingly impractical at this point in time, the male-as-breadwinner injunction still retained its ideological authority and hence the perceived crisis in men's and women's roles came to the forefront of media and public discussion. Novaro's film struggles with these contrasts between the ideal and traditional, and lived and actual gender relations, responding to the symbolic crisis around women's independence, changing notions of women's virtue and worth, and so on. Julia's idealization of the *danzón* is a cultural relic that for Novaro needs some kind of confrontation or mediation, both in terms of current ideological operations and the nostalgic visions of the past.

As intimated earlier, Susy points to the crisis and questioning of gender norms in the national horizon, but this assertion needs to be unpacked and profiled in terms of how the film's narrative progresses and how Susy is visualized and situated within this narrative. Within her own habitual social circles, which limit contact to anyone but other women like herself, it is perhaps unlikely that Julia should befriend someone so different from her ideas of "men" and "women," a drag artiste and female-identifying *travesti*, at that. But then that is what the change of location provides the protagonist: new horizons. After checking into the hotel and being comforted on her plight by the proprietress with the words that "men are all the same," she converses with the working girl, La Colorada, who, considerably more seasoned in the world of sex and relationships, advises her on how to go looking for her man. She dines out in the plaza, noticeably relaxing in her new locale with its open atmosphere. She relinquishes her usual modest guardedness and reserve (typical of women socialized into ideals of decent behavior for their sex) by coquettishly parlaying with a random Russian tourist. She hopes to chance upon Carmelo, without luck. Back at the hotel, La Colorada tells her to look for him where the *danzón habitués* gather nightly. Julia sets off but does not find Carmelo. Instead, she finds Susy. The two chat and become immediate friends. Julia realizes there is something remarkably "different" about her newfound friend, and her interest is piqued. Susy promises to assist Julia in her search for Carmelo but also invites her to her show, where she performs "El Coquero" (The Coconut Vendor).

This scene provides much semiotic detail. The camera pans, taking in the forms of big-breasted women sculpted into the walls. It then proceeds to frame the lip-synched performance of Susy, big hipped and sensual as any *bailadora jarocha* (traditional dancer from Veracruz). After the show, we are taken into the privacy of her dressing room, where the previous performance is effectively deconstructed into its working parts: the camera catches sight of a pair of falsies; Susy is removing her makeup and taking to Julia. We see the wig and cosmetics: all the appurtenances of the artifactual construction of woman. Susy suggests to Julia that she try the wig and cosmetics on. A woman reconstructing herself as woman? That is precisely Susy's point. Susy is an *artista*, but offstage, as well, she considers herself a woman. Rather than being a disguise, these appurtenances are a vehicle to reveal what lies within, to bring it to the surface, so to speak. A sexy, prepossessed version of femininity is reclaimed by these actions.

This scene is not the first time the film broaches the construction of femininity. Susy's pronounced and expressive femininity contrasts to the more demure versions Julia that has come to believe. She is a challenge to Julia's beliefs around gender at so many levels. When Susy makes her up, Julia voices the fear that people will think she is a prostitute. She asks "¿No crees que sea excesiva?" (You don't think it's over the top?), but bracing herself—and with Susy's reassurances—she goes for a walk on the *malecón (pier)*, searching for Carmelo in one of the ships.

Julia does not end up finding Carmelo in Veracruz, in spite of her and Susy's better efforts. She does, however, find a completely different world that does not observe the ordinary social rules. These new and freer possibilities are found in Veracruz, in La Colorada's independent, sassy, working-girl attitude and in the fluid gender performativity of Susy. Wide eyed to these developments, Julia is herself transformed—both physically and inwardly—under Susy's influence. Susy, as a trans person and performer, questions the rather staid cultural codes that dictate the roles of men and women, principles so cherished by Julia in her vision of the *danzón*. The *danzón* and its allotted roles are given a literal reversal in another telling scene. The *danzón* form encompasses an idealized version of heterosexuality: men and women have differentiated and complementary, and always fixed, functions to fulfill in relation to each other. Back at her apartment, intoning boleros (a genre, as Chapters 5 and 6 show, often linked to *travestis* in film and literature), Susy pleads with Julia to teach her the female part of the *danzón*. This throws her into a queer terrain of cognitive disorientation. Up to now, Julia has enjoyed the free play of gender around her. Moreover, she has taken on its performative precepts and embraced them in others. The *danzón* for her still represents that last sacred formation of hetero and gender normativity, which Susy as a cross-gendered "other" (masculine body performing female) brings into check. Despite Susy's insistence on performing female in the *danzón* (since it comes more naturally to her), Julia obstinately tries to anchor the heteronormative maneuvers underwritten in the dance in the body: male-bodied individuals should take the male role, females the female one.

JULIA: Agárrame como un hombre.
SUSY: Enséñame de mujer.
JULIA: Tú tienes los hombros muy anchos.
[JULIA: Hold onto me like a man.
SUSY: Teach me the woman's part.
JULIA: You have very broad shoulders.]

She relents, and it finally dawns on her—and the Mexican audience seeing things from her point of view—that the world of gender, roles, and relationships may be more complex than they seem.

Only when Julia has passed through this process is she able to transcend herself in her relations with men. She takes on a younger male lover—Rubén, the long-haired sailor—and discovers the potentiality for giving her sexuality free rein. She is not struck by lightning or found in some alleyway for violating norms. Novaro thus signals that such a woman—single mother, working outside the home—can and does operate in a space free of the traditional judgments associated with Julia's and previous generations. The soft and tender Rubén also embodies these "new" norms, which loosen the more conventional demands made on men and women.

Susy—like many other *locas* and *travestis* in film history—fulfills, then, the role of confidante, go-between, and helper. Moreover, her very gender variance is a metaphorical representation of the freeing up of gender norms in contemporary Mexican society—partly feared and maligned, but recast by Novaro through Susy. She embodies the whole gamut of

Mexican versions of femininity—retrieved and reactivated from the world of nostalgia: the bolero and the *cabaretera*. As a figure she operates to deconstruct and renegotiate the axes of decency and indecency, public and private: as *travesti* and cabaret performer, her realm is the night. By day, she dresses *en homme* and remains at home. By night, in feminine mode she violates the principle that public space is restricted to the movement of men. Her link to the cabaret is also crucial to her representative function. The stress on her performativeness links her perpetually to the stage of the cabaret. If we recall both López's and de la Mora's concepts of the central place of the cabaret in national-identity imagery—sexuality and gender identity forming its constitutive heart—it is unsurprising that she functions in the film as a point of manifestation for the changes in gender and national-cultural norms with which the film is centrally concerned. Susy is always shown acting, even when off the stage. Ultimately, however, Susy's story is eclipsed by the main one—that of the heterosexual protagonist, Julia. Beyond the gestural and metaphorical, very little in the way of a clear picture of Susy's day-to-day life is shown. When Julia decides to return to Mexico City, she leaves a note at the hotel and abandons not only Susy but also the world of liberation that she has come to know.

Many critics have attacked the conventional ending, which seems to communicate a conservative message and prompts viewers to see the film as hardly feminist (McAlister 1993; Rashkin 2001; Córtez 1998). Julia returns to Mexico City with a visible warm glow as a changed woman. She also returns to the *danzón* halls, with a renewed determination, and in a moment of cinematic closure, which confirms the centrality of heteronormativity in this narrative, finds Carmelo awaiting her again, just where she left him. This seems to undermine the kind of pledge to the reinscription of gender roles and sexuality pursued in the quest Julia has undertaken. When Julia returns to Mexico City, the free-gendered world of Veracruz becomes a postcard memory, whereas Mexico City is the reality. Men, women, work, and the romance of the *danzón* with its fixed, defined roles are reinstated. The physical journey from center (the country's capital) to the margins (coastal Veracruz) parallels Julia's journey from the grasp of dominant gender ideology to a kind of sex and gender *terra incognita*—the Oz that lies beyond Kansas and reality.

The film received ecstatic approval outside Mexico.[4] Its positive tone of acceptance for open sexuality and gender difference surely played a part in this reception but this belies the reality that the sexually diverse face in a culture that does not wholly embrace them. The director seems to acknowledge that there has been a change in sex roles and norms since the cherished old days and that this is a new age of gender unconventionality and transformation in the roles expected of men and of women (especially for the younger generation). Maria Novaro's *travesti* characters—Susy and her friends Karla and Yadira, who play a more minor role—seem to point symbolically to those concerns and to stand in for those changes. That Novaro treats them sympathetically is beyond doubt. Such a free world is perhaps Mexico's future. But locationally and pragmatically—for Julia's existence and that of women like her—as figures they are peripheral and separated from the strictures of heteronormativity observed in the aspirations of Julia and the *danzón*. Susy, her *travesti compañeras* (friends), and the prostitute Colorada are left behind, as expendable narrative helpers who move the plot and thematic concerns. To put it another way, they function as purely performative figures on a distant stage in an unreal setting. Everyday middle-class heterosexual life in Mexico City is the "real world" off the stage that stays with us once we have left the cinema. The movement from center to margin back to center again is completed by Julia's reunion with Carmelo, a reunion whose normativity is ultimately given precedence over the "exotic" other world of *travestismo* and free love in Veracruz. The symbolic crisis in gender concerning women as active social agents, and the implication this might have for change in relations between men and women, is resolved by an appeal to appease the public with the security of normative closure. As *travesti* characters, Yadira, Karla, and especially Susy are important to the rhetorical design of the film; they add color and they come to constitute folkloric figures in the blandishments of the text's final nostalgic compromise. They are performative in various senses; they literally perform in the film's twilight cabaret world, they perform a function for Julia (transmitting information, advice, and securing contacts); and they perform in the sense of the film's entire ideological project. They are choral devices that ring in the terms of cultural change, whose potential threat is forestalled by the film's too easy denouement.

Orlando Rojas's *Las noches de Constantinopla*

Danzón, then, is demonstrably inattentive to the realities of trans lives as they are lived and incognizant of the cultural emergence of *travestis* as social actors. The film employs them chiefly as rhetorical devices. It is useful to consider the film alongside another, this time a Cuban production made ten years later in 2002, in order to see whether this tendency has changed in Latin American filmmaking. Isolated from some of the social and political developments seen in the rest of Latin America, Cuba has nevertheless for a long time been a front-runner in the depictions in many media of gender crossers and crossing. This study returns at several points to consider Cuba and its cultural productions of sexual and gender variance at different junctures of time. As mentioned in the last chapter, due to state sanctions against the formation of independent political-interest groups, Cuba has not witnessed the emergence of an openly politicized *travesti* subjectivity. And yet, *travesti* and *transformista* lives are very much on the radar if we recall Lizette Vila's documentary work *Y hembra es el alma mía* (1992; *My Soul is a Woman*) and the more recent *Sexualidad: un derecho a la vida* (2004; *Sexuality: A Right to Life*). *Mariposas en el andamio* (*Butterflies on the Scaffold*) also paved the way to shattering some of the myths about gay drag artists and *travestis*, insisting on their viable role in society. All these productions have visibilized *loca* and *travesti* lives and experiences without resorting to trivialization or judgment of their subjects.

Orlando Rojas's film *Las noches de Constantinopla* emerges in this context. A former member of the Instituto Cubano del Arte e Industria Cinematográficos (ICAIC, the Cuban Institute for Art and Cinema), Rojas has an impressive filmography to date and has worked on numerous short and full-length films as both scriptwriter and director. As with Novaro, in all his work there are certain recurrent themes, mainly revolving around the individual and the social order. His career has not been without its reverses, as the state closure of production of two of his films, *El cerco de la pasión* (*Wall of Passion*) and (the doubly ironic titled) *Cerrado por reformas* (*Closed for Reforms*), would suggest. Rojas claims—as Fabiola Santiago relates in an article from the *Miami Herald* included online at *Cubanet*—that Castro continues to make statements about counter-revolutionary artists and directors. Interviewed by Santiago, Rojas further explains that this has created an untenable situation where completion of projects is jeopardized, a situation only worsened by the economic crisis, named by Castro the "Special Period."[5] In order to make films in Cuba, it is necessary to engage in a kind of *camuflaje* (camouflage), according to this director, a point to which we will return shortly (Santiago 2003). After the production of *Las noches de Constantinopla*, Rojas defected to the United States. His most well-known works are *Una novia para David* (1985; *A Girlfriend for David*), *Papeles secundarios* (1989; *Minor Parts*), and *Las noches de Constantinopla* (2002). The first deals with David, a high school student, who overcomes prejudice—and his friends' endless jokes—and asks out an overweight and less than conventionally attractive classmate. The second film follows the on- and offstage activities of a group of professional stage actors who are rehearsing a play. With ironic commentary on the nature of acting and real life, the film discusses the need to overcome prejudice and question tradition. These aspects are also present in *Las noches de Constantinopla*: the blur between stage and real life, and the need to be open to the new.

A film like *Las noches de Constantinopla*, which some might view as an argument for the need for sexual freedoms, openness, and the celebration of diversity in all its forms—queer and straight—is almost unimaginable without the precedent of Tomás Gutiérrez Alea's *Fresa y chocolate* (1994; *Strawberry and Chocolate*). This taboo-breaking historical redress of the persecution of *locas* as visible homosexuals marked a moment of permission for filmmakers to turn a critical eye on the regime, but via softer tactics pleading for humanism and tolerance of difference. In an interview with Columba Vértiz, Rojas signals that Gutiérrez Alea's work forms an important source of inspiration for his film. Structurally, the films have much in common (Vértiz 2000). Both are comedic dramas that tackle serious matters. Paul Julian Smith has discussed *Fresa y chocolate*'s blatant heterocentric form, wherein homosexuality is effectively relegated to a second plane and viewed and inspected by the primordial point of view of the main straight character, David (1996, 85). Heterosexual eroticism is constantly affirmed and made visible; and homosexuality is obscured and continues to be referred to in terms of its unmentionability (91). This statement could equally be applied to Rojas's film, as *Las noches* similarly possesses a hetero center. The dominant point of view of the main straight character, Hernán, is established visually from the beginning, as Hernán observes the clandestine rehearsal of a drag show. Hernán continues to be the one who looks at many points of the film. The viewer follows Hernán's sight line and is thus enjoined to take up his position. The main erotic relationship that develops is heterosexual, and the *locas* and performing *transformistas* work at the margins of the film—both in its visual space, as we shall see, and at the level of diegesis, that is, "plot space." The commonality that we can perceive between the two films is not accidental. Rojas is a great admirer of *Fresa y chocolate* and, like Gutiérrez Alea, is a heterosexual filmmaker who, with this film, ventured to depict queer and gender-variant figures for the first time.

The film is a lighthearted drama about an aristocratic family, los Arrascal, whose estate and fortunes have fallen on hard times. It has a rather mythic or hypnotic quality, assisted by a scattering of surreal dream sequences (again, from the point of view of Hernán), carnivalesque performances, and symbolic elements that place the film firmly in the comedic realm.[6] The performing *locas* and *transformistas* are key to its tenor and pace and remind the viewer of the history of representations of such persons, which the beginning of this chapter outlined. That is not to say that they are depicted negatively. Rather, their theatricality, buffoonery, and general "excess" are emphasized. The absence of grotesque associations or attribution of inferiority and victimhood provides evidence of a shift in thinking about gender crossers and crossing, as was also the case of the depiction of Susy in *Danzón*. In this sense, we perceive a progression from the earlier, abject portraits—a response, perhaps, to the affirmation by *travestis* of themselves as people in recent years. To ascertain if *Las noches de Constantinopla* breaks away from the representation of *travestis* and cross-dressing *locas* as signifying others, it is first necessary to profile the plot and characters.

Nominally set in the Cuba of the new millennium, the film's main location is the multistoried mansion, Villa Florida, which is ruled by an ailing but iron-fisted matriarch, Doña Eugenia. She is approaching eighty and is practically penniless and on the verge of ruin, in spite of her illustrious heritage as a descendant of one of Cuba's first families and her ownership of the most valuable paintings of Cuban art. Living in a partial dream world of persecution—at the start of the film she feverishly complains of her vision of the entire household as cannibals out to eat up her patrimony and herself—Eugenia is haughty and proud. The gendered dimensions of patrimony—or *patrimonio* as it is spoken of in the film—are important. *Patrimonio* is connected to *patria* and might be described as the visible and concrete manifestations of the fatherland, the property of a masculinist and statist tradition. This patriarchal heritage accumulated through successive generations is placed on sale. In spite of innumerable offers to purchase her patrimony and refinance the troubled estate, Eugenia resolutely refuses to capitulate. Hernán is her grandson. A timid but well-meaning virgin who also happens to be a closet pornographer, he has written an erotic novel called "Las noches de Constantinopla" (Constantinople nights), which provides the film's title. Hernán's saucy and liberated singer sister, Cristiana, has—unbeknown to Hernán—submitted his novel to an international best erotica competition, under a pseudonym. Hernán's manuscript wins and Radio Amsterdam announces the Cuban success on its airwaves. Eugenia is less than impressed, commenting, "Un pornógrafo . . . lo único que le faltaba a este país" ("A pornographer . . . just what this country needed"). Her familial jurisdiction is hence also a moral one. The mansion's multistory dimensions spatially plot the hierarchy of relations, as Eugenia reigns over all, and the servants—Celeste, the black maid, and Pachi, her illegitimate mulatto son—dwell in the lower regions of the house, scurrying to attend to Eugenia's whims at the ring of a bell. Pachi is the head of a performance troupe of *transformistas*—Fresa, Vainilla, and Chocolate—a not-so-subtle reference to Gutiérrez Alea's film and effectively a reinscription of queer subjectivities in tune with that film's premises. They rehearse in the *orillas* (edges) of the mansion. Their queerly gendered presence is shot through with the sociocultural terms of marginality manifest in class, race, and *lo loca* (*loca*ness).

This setting allows Rojas to pass off his film as politically correct in socialist Cuban terms—as a cursory reading would prompt one to take stock of its critique of class elitism, racism, aristocratic repression, and snobbery. Even Castro and his inner circle may find its hypothetical depiction of an all-but-banished aristocracy and its preciousness comic and inoffensive. On the most literal level, we observe the story of a paradigmatical white racist matriarch of prerevolutionary times and the dotty manias of the long-dead ruling class.

The film, in this way, posits a historical recuperation of cultural memory for laughs in the present day. Given this, the film would seem to pose little threat. Ostensibly the film is the story of a clash of generations: one moribund and antiquated, the other modern, adventurous, and *en plena flor (in full bloom)*. Remembering Rojas's techniques of *camuflaje (camouflage)*, it would be ingenuous to stop there, however. Given the shutting down of his previous and more obviously political film, Rojas indeed engages in *camuflaje* in *Las noches de Constantinopla*. With all the sound, fury, and feathers that the film in its *barroquismo* (baroque style) flaunts, the narrative invites other readings via references and reversals that might otherwise go unnoticed amid all the color. This *camuflaje* entails a kind of perverse coding of opposites. Villa Florida is not representative of rightwing Cuba in exile, but rather, of Castro's Cuba. The soon-to-be octogenarian matriarch is, in fact, Castro, the patriarch who at the time of the film's release was nearing eighty (and is as paranoid as Eugenia is). La Doña's heritage signals a sly poke at Castro's.[7] Eugenia's sexual repressiveness can be read as Castro's historically verifiable political and moral repressiveness. When Eugenia falls into a coma on discovering that her "innocent" grandson is the author of the pornographic novel, her death is predicted. And yet she rallies, succumbs again, and regains consciousness by the film's end. This could be read in terms of Castro's public fainting while giving a speech at an event in June 2001 and the rumor of incipient death or that he has Parkinson's (Castro "Faints" During Speech 2001).[8] Following the metaphorical line of reasoning, the mansion represents Cuban society, still stratified and yet proud of its national heritage, which it holds on to in spite of impending poverty and starvation. Celeste makes broth that contains shreds of potato. There is no money in the coffers to buy things, and the family resorts to cooking shrubs. With Eugenia dispatched to the hospital, the pressures to sell off her patrimony increase. Hernán is resistant, not wishing to betray his grandmother's wishes, but there are many eager clients for the purchase of this patrimony, most of whom are foreign specialists and investors. The sale of the estate's assets—and Cuba's—seems vital to the survival of the household and, hence, to the Cuban people, all of whom are represented by this microcosm. We have the mestizo-dominant family made up of Uncle Jorge, the somnambulist Aunt Greta, as well as the new generation—Hernán and Cristiana. Pachi is the unrecognized son of Jorge and Celeste. The lack of a recognized father and his mulatto status demote him in the Cuban patriarchal scheme of things. A subversive reference made by Pachi historicizes and anchors in revolutionary time the seeming atemporality of the film's imaginative (and camouflaged) location. He interrupts his Afro-Cuban mother who is cleaning and chastises her for her submissiveness: "Te han explotado por toda la vida mamá y nada nos toca. Hace cuarenta años que hay una revolución socialista en este país . . . No soy tú, porque tú tienes alma de esclava ("They've exploited you your whole life ma and we haven't got anything out of it. Forty years ago there was a revolution in this country . . . I'm not you, because you have the soul of a slave"). The implication is that the marginal and unrecognized segments of society still suffer under a kind of repression and penury in Cuba, in spite of its revolutionary aims. Further, as in the rest of the film, we see that the whole household feels the impact of economic scarcity, and all levels of society are affected, albeit in different ways.

The mansion (that is, Cuba) is in a period of transition—from an old kingdom to a new, seemingly anarchic state of affairs, long suppressed. This transition is both economic and libidinal. Cristiana tells Hernán that it is high time he lose his virginity, a hackneyed and heterocentric view of Cuba as a young man who must pass through a rite of passage to mature in the world. This is significant: Hernán is the author—the creative force—of "Las noches de Constantinopla" as well as the point of focalization and epicenter of the narrative. Hernán's relationship with the female variety performer, Manón, is the one most explicitly shown and constitutes the main thread that conducts the viewer through the diverse array of desires, motivations, and identities that emerge into the open when the matriarch is away. The younger generation—in the name of liberty of all kinds—is prepared to perform for money, to sell itself. This is a reflection of Cuba at its present crossroads, surviving the Special Period, where the entertainment industry and tourist economy supplies the goods and sells Cuba to foreigners—to liberalize the economy from the grip of the state that represents the inherited antiquated order. Hernán is caught between the desire to hold on to the strictures of the old order for the sake of his *abuela*—who is literally the (grand)mother and therefore protector of the nation—and the desire for new freedoms. Such might be the kind of dilemma faced by the young now, who maintain their loyalty to Castro and his revolution and yet see the marketing of Cuba and its opening into informal capitalism as a necessary step to break out of the island's economic crisis.

Cristiana and Manón—against Hernán's wishes—clandestinely execute the slow sell-off of the paintings. At the least expected moment, Eugenia begins to recover. Hernán then finds out that the patrimony has all but disappeared, and in order to avert the disgrace of Eugenia finding out, he strikes a deal with an art expert to create replicas of the sold paintings so the matriarch may never know. They have seven days to raise the funds to finance this.[9] So they set up a venue called "Cabaret

Constantinopla." Cristiana arrives with her band and they try to attract the public by playing Cuban songs. This is not enough, however, and due to a dearth of stage performers or dancers, the show lacks flavor. Finally Hernán relents to Pachi's aggressive insistence that Fresa, Vainilla, and Chocolate headline the proceedings at the mansion, with the cooperation of Manón, arguing, "Tú tienes las bailarinas aquí y en definitiva, sólo son apariencias y las apariencias engañan" (You have your dancers here, and at the end of the day it's just appearances and appearances can deceive). Who needs women dressed as women when you have *transformistas*? Like the vaunted expert copies of the original priceless *cuadros*, who will be able to tell the difference? With the addition of the drag revue, the event is a roaring success, and the replicas are easily financed with money to spare. A connection is thus clearly made between the simulation of Cuban national heritage (patrimony) for profit and *transformismo*. Drag performance and identities are implicated in the framework of a market-driven reproduction of Cubanness, and this is underlined by the folkloric flavor of the numbers they perform: faux-virtuous Eve-like *criollo* women, a futuristic cha-cha line, and so forth. The performance of drag is linked to the performance of national identities in a very deliberate way. Rojas plays off the terms of real and false, actual and staged, constantly, until they turn in on themselves.

When the matriarch finally resumes her throne, she does a volte-face; she decides she was wrong and will sell off the artworks after all, unaware of the deception. Hernán, Celeste, and the gang insist that she retain them, knowing full well that the originals have already been sold and Eugenia would simply be selling fakes, which might damage her authority and standing and expose their initial lie. Eugenia is not to be deterred and presses on with the idea of an auction. Her family can only follow suit, and they pledge (conspiring among themselves) to realize a fake auction of the fakes, and again, the cross-dressed performers are present, this time dressed as society women. This signposts a ruse: they make bids as if it were the real thing, but it is really playacting. Again we see the implicit equation between *transformismo* and theatre, drag and falsification, in a false version of an already-falsified cultural heritage, that is, in the patrimony of the *cuadros*. Cuba is posited, then, as a nation in drag. The *transformistas* embody both national crisis and, ironically, its solution. But their "reproduction" is an empty one: a copy of a copy of a copy. The "theater" of the auction undoes itself, and Hernán and Cristiana confess. At this point, one of the cross-dressed "society women" asks rhetorically, "Is it all over?" and proceeds to undress, revealing a male body. The revelation of the copied nature of the replicas of the national artwork is juxtaposed with the revealing of the performative nature of the drag impersonation of the society woman. This suggests a simulation of national heritage very removed from the terms of the heteronormative coupling of the mother (nation) with the father (state) found in nation discourse. Authenticity and continuity of nation obtain no guarantee in this context, and *transformista* forms of "production" signify depthless illusion according to the film's logic.

While Joel del Río (2001) suggests in an online review in *La Jiribilla* that the cross-dressing in this film pays tribute to Billy Wilder's *Some Like It Hot*, I would argue that *Las noches de Constantinopla* is more in the tradition of the productions featuring effeminate homosexuals and cross-dressers that began to emerge in the 1970s in Latin America, as profiled by Muñoz (1996, 12–13). The inherent structure of the film, which places heterosexuality and naturalized gender acts at the center and the queerly gendered on the margins and confined to the stage, means that the *transformistas* are propelled into a space where they can only be signifying others and mediators in a crisis. Like the *travestis* in *Danzón*, they have a performative function in the film's larger concerns. These concerns in Rojas's film cover libidinal awakening, libertinism, and the "dressing up" of national culture for commercial purposes, here in the context of the Cuban Special Period and its increased reliance on tourism and the entertainment industry for dollars, via the refunctionalization of national cultural symbols for consumption. This may be a conscious or unconscious move on the part of the director. Disaffected by the regime and its restrictions, it is obvious that Rojas advances a camouflaged critique. Whether or not he deliberately positions *transformismo* and drag identities as indicative of the move for the cultural repackaging, reproduction, and marketing of Cubanness remains to be seen. Out of costume and offstage, they do not obtain a clear kind of space or meaning. There is but one moment in the film in which it is suggested that existing as a cross-dresser can be personally dangerous. This happens when the police turn up at Villa Florida just when things get worked up and Chocolate and Vainilla are *en persona*—full wig and make up. The two duck under the trestle tables on the estate's lawns and hastily remove their wigs. It is a fleeting moment used mainly for comic effect and thus does not stand out or contradict the fundamental place of drag in the film—as spectacle, as outrageousness, and as a reflection of the disingenuous recycling of Cuban culture for profit. Had it been elaborated on—or indeed, had the queer characters of Pachi and his friends been explored more fully—the chain that links cross-dressing to false imitation of cultural heritage may have been broken up or problematized.

Karim Aïnouz's *Madame Satã*

Madame Satã, the first feature film of the young Brazilian director Karim Aïnouz, is a treatment of the legendary life of João Francisco dos Santos, the notorious drag and capoeira performer born of slaves in Northeastern Brazil in 1900. There have been many treatments of dos Santos's infamous career. Aïnouz, however, focuses on his subject's life before the coming of the myth, and the film's main events take place in 1930s Rio de Janeiro and then culminate after his release from imprisonment and subsequent crowning as queen of the cabaret scene in 1943, when dos Santos was popularly baptized "Madame Satã."

The film begins with a sequence of mug shots of dos Santos subsequent to his arrest. A voice-over informs us of the criminal perversity of the subject we behold, now made object, and places him in the domain of the sexually marginal, a source of vice, a member of the lumpen, and a danger to society. The language is taken directly from a real arrest transcript from the time and is reminiscent in its abject interpellation of any number of documents that figured those outside normative social and work relations, as mentioned in Chapter 1. Like the *higienistas* in Argentina immersed in fears of race and sexual contamination, Brazil's equivalents, at the time in which the film's events take place, wrote in their studies of "passive pederasts" who represented "social problems" to be combated vigorously. As Magali Gouveia Engel observes, "It was only in the 1920s and 1930s that the debate on homosexuality was to be consolidated in the fields of medicine and criminology . . . [which were] marked by the perspective that linked 'mental disturbances' to the endocrinological characteristics of individuals. This focus, based especially on the studies of Gregório Marañón, professor of medicine at Madrid University, was broadly reflected in the concepts put forward by other important specialists, including Afrânio Peixoto (fev. 1933), Leonídio Ribeiro (1938) and Estácio de Lima (1935)" (2008, 178). Although the voice-over at the beginning of *Madame Satã*, and the police file on which it is based, do not name the criminal subject racially, the criminal world to which we are then introduced is marked and marginalized in terms of race, and this vector—where class, race, and sexuality meet—is one that structured the figuring by positivists who pathologized difference for the sake of social control. As Gouvea Engel further states, "a complex interplay between race, social class and homosexuality permeated in the medical and legal concepts and practices seeking to criminalize and give psychiatric connotations to male sexualities diagnosed as abnormal" (178). Race, sexuality, gender, and class: these are the main concerns of the film. And yet none is treated didactically or metaphorically, although it is important that the protagonist incarnates struggles in each of these categories and emerges from the confluence of multiple oppressions based on them. The film is set in the period just before the arrival of Getúlio Vargas's *Estado Novo* when race begins to be revalorized and the myth of racial democracy, intellectually authorized by Gilberto Freyre, begins. Importantly, however, *Madame Satã* was produced and released in the neoliberal-questioning and newly democratizing Brazilian state led by Luiz Inácio Lula da Silva. It uses the well-known life of dos Santos but tells the story in alignment with a more contemporary politics, spearheaded by the new social movements in the country.

Madame Satã is a visually and musically lush work, replete with mythic allusions, especially as they concern blackness and performance, the black body, and the performance of gender and sexuality, key features that I will explore here. The lead title protagonist is a deliberate collage of genders: by turns feminine and extremely masculine, he encapsulates the high and the low, the radical and the radically conventional (being the father of a child), the gentleman and scoundrel. He faces entrapment and desires escape. Aïnouz engages, in the representation of dos Santos, the legend of the *malandro* in a bid to trace the contradictions and contours of both Brazilian identity—as a national foundational myth consolidated in the decades to come—and an African identity. The place of samba is also important here, as is, too, the space of the cabaret, a feature that links this film to the two discussed previously, as well as the fact that the protagonist is a *transformista*.

I have chosen this third film—the most recent of those studied in the present chapter—in order to explore how, mythic maneuvers aside, cinematic representations of cross-gendered sexual diversity can move beyond the metaphorical. As seductively suggestive as *Madame Satã* is, drawing us in with its exquisite eroticism and its traumatic violence, the thoroughly embodied realization of the protagonist by Lazaro Ramos, and the intimacy of the camera's proximity to his body, pulls the viewer out of the lull of gesture and symbol into cascading physicality.

In a commentary online, Aïnouz very consciously frames the importance of a nonfolkloric and nonstereotypical representation of his subject:

> De cara, eu não queria construir un personagem folclorico, estereotipado. Quando você folcloriza, você se distancia, trivializa, banaliza. Isso não me interessava. Me interessava olhar as filigranas por tras desse mito, como era o seu cotidiano, a manera como ele dançava, comia, vivia, transava, andava na rua. (Aïnouz 2003)
>
> [From the beginning, I didn't want to construct a folkloric, stereotyped character. When you make something folkloric, you distance it, trivialize it, make it banal. That's not what interested me. I was interested in tracing the filigree behind that myth, what he was like in the everyday, the way he danced, ate, lived, moved, and walked the street.]

The delirium of the film's imagery moves from us the cabaret to the streets of Lapa and the people who populate these spaces: prostitutes, their clients, *negros*, mulattos, would-be white diva songstresses, gays, straights, and men on the make. The darkened streets of this poor Rio district accrue textures of everyday life: a lyrical cacophony of passions and conflict. Dos Santos moves through this landscape, embodying all its intensities in one person: from understudy to the racist white diva who performs as Scheherazade in *A Thousand and One Nights* but mocks him, to street-hustler-turned-pimp and thief. Lover of the *mestizo* Renatinho whom he dubs "my Indian Prince," dos Santos exhibits feminine wiles but is dominant in bed; his tenderness toward Renatinho and his fellow *bicha*—Brazilian slang for effeminate homosexual—easily turns into rage, demonstrating that this *viado* (faggot) is also *louca*, in the two senses described by LaFountain Stokes, as quoted in this book's Introduction. These two senses ascribed to the *loca* or *louca*—which means literally crazy woman—refer to a subversive form of public display and also a kind of personal-political unpredictability. The complexity of Ramos's performance reveals a personage torn by demons.

Dos Santos is the *malandro* but is heroic precisely because he is also a *viado* and proud. The *malandro* is a hedonistic figure that shirks the productivity of the body in formal work relations in favor of a life of roguery and adventure—productivity for pleasure. He is a "representante da população marginalizada que inventa sus próprias estratégias de construção da ordem social" (Cerqueira and Da Silva 2007, 7; representative of the marginalized population that invents its own strategies of constructing the social order). The *malandro* is also a symbol of masculinity, linked to aggressive street life. Dos Santos, as depicted in the film, is certainly that: patriarch of his own house and street, he rules and lords it over Laurita, fellow prostitute and mother of his child, and Tabú, sissy soul sister of Dos Santos, whom he treats like a younger sibling, constantly denigrating her, often violently. The diabolical character of the protagonist displays his struggles with the confines of a socially circumscribed identity.

Aïnouz's cinematography registers the rippling tensions and momentary flights and releases of this body in great detail. As Lisa Shaw states, "his body is . . . privileged cinematically, with the texture of his skin highlighted by the processing of the negative, and a succession of extreme close-ups of individual parts of his body, such as his back or armpits, forcing the audience to identify with him as a human being rather than a mythical figure" (2007, 89–90). And yet this body—in all of its emphasized Africanness—recalls the history of the enslaved body, a set of schema for a contorted subjectivity under siege, of the kind described by Fanon in *Black Skin, White Masks* (1950). The unexpected recontouring of femininity on this taut body—unexpected because of the weight of feared black male sexuality that burdens the figure of the "negão" (Carvalho 1996) in Brazilian culture and more so given the status of the *malandro*—provides a space of liberation from an earthbound body whose every muscle and sinew pulls and retracts under the force of a triple oppression: as black, poor, and homosexual.

Alongside the much-mythologized figure of the *malandro* the film usesfragments of samba—also "elevated" from its subaltern origins to the status as a sign of Brazilianness. However, what Aïnouz advances in his film is not a recasting of Brazil, but, rather, a focus on discourses of *negritud* and their reworking. This is important to foreground in order to zero in on the degree to which the film does not deploy bodily and cultural signs in the service of national metaphor. This is made possible given the era in which the film was created—an era in which it is more much possible to invoke subject positions previously appropriated and allegorized for national purposes, both in film and political culture.

Brazil exhibits a tumultuous economic, social, and political history, one that is full of ups and downs, replete with promises of liberation and change, from financial "miracles" and periodic "democratic" openings to the rule of dictatorship. The First Republic, founded in the wake of the abolition of slavery, espoused liberal ideals of citizenship that still ironically excluded and made invisible blacks. Vargas's *Estado Novo*, begun in 1937 and lasting until 1945, encouraged cultural expression of difference but merely for the state's purposes; in actuality the formation of a politicized Afro-Brazilian identity had to wait till after World War II, when the myth of "racial democracy" began to be interrogated among critical intellectuals but persisted in popular circles (Warren and Winndance Twine 2002). The 1950s economic boom give way to collapse and a subsequent two-decade (1964–85) military control of the country. Hardline forms of oppression and control only galvanized increasingly radical sectors, notable for their guerilla tactics. The military rulers promoted economic growth and development based on international credit, which came crashing down as the country reneged on its loan repayments. At this point Brazil became subject to a wave of austerity programs designed by the International Monetary Fund, instituting simultaneously an era of economic liberalization and an unraveling of military control, as dictatorship ceded to a form of democratization in the 1980s. Neoliberalism paradoxically provided the space for the emergence of groups around particular interests but also further deepened the economic exclusion that marks racism in the country.

The resurgence of Afro-Brazilian identity as a community-rooted cultural and political project occurred in this climate, where the very terms of nationalism, as forged by the modern Brazilian state, increasingly frayed at the edges. There certainly was a black movement before then. The late 1970s simply saw a firmer articulation of politicized Afro-Brazilian identity. By the 1990s, militancy had achieved a much more mainstream influence as adherents began to question racism at all levels of Brazilian society and entered major political parties. So, too, at the same time that Afro-Brazilian identity was in reemergence politically in the 1980s, sexual minorities were establishing a political presence in alignment with feminists and the radical left. A gay and lesbian publication *Lampião da Esquina* (*Street Corner Lantern*) was launched and an advocacy group, SOMOS: Grupo de Afirmação Homossexual (WE ARE: Homosexual Affirmation Group), was formed and worked in a semiclandestine fashion in coordination with black and women's groups (Green 1994). Although they had in common the goal of ending the dictatorship, many saw the dominant leftist opposition as narrow in its class analysis. It was only with the formation of Lula's Workers Party that deeper sympathies around sexuality, gender, and race began to coalesce. Later, in the 1990s, *travesti* activism and the struggles of those most marginalized among the sexually diverse began to register in the public domain, as individuals organized around sex work, HIV/AIDS, police violence, and also murders of *travestis*, in conjunction with national and international nongovernmental organizations. A lot of public attention, especially in the last fifteen years, has been gained, "as violence and the difficult living conditions faced by many Brazilians have been the focus of significant collective reflection on the part of the media, the public and politicians" (Klein 1998, 338). The struggles of groups such as the Movimento dos Trabalhadores Rurais Sem Terra (MST) and *favelados* (shantytown dwellers) are two more widespread manifestations of these new actors, but they are not the only ones.

These are significant historical developments that would seem to account for the contrasts between prior depictions of the queen and *travesti* character of former Brazilian cinema, particularly from the popular cinema of the 1960s (not part of the Cinema Novo movement), and the kind demonstrated by *Madame Satã*. Tatiana Signorelli Heise (2006) contrasts the two periods of 1964 to 1974 and 1994 to 2004 to show the shift in trends in the representation of social marginality. The films of the 1960s and 1970s, she argues, provided diagnostics of Brazilian society and dictatorship. Films of the latter period, in contrast, are more nuanced, telling particular and localized stories, even as they may retain a concern with the microrealities of the country. Using *Rainha Diaba* (Antonio Carlos da Fontoura, 1974; *The Devil Queen*) as an example (among other films from the period), Signorelli Heise shows how "effeminate" homosexuals and *travestis* were frequently emblematized in film from the earlier period in the name of the sociopolitical sphere, underlining that "En quanto filmes do período 1968 a 1974 centralizam a narrativa no personagem transgressor para utilizá-lo como emblema de una cojuntura política e social contaminada" (2006, 75; Films from the 1968 to 1974 period center on a narrative whose transgressive character is used as an emblem of the contaminated social and political juncture in question). In *Rainha Diaba*, all the characters possess exaggeratedly comic features and theatrical gestures that make the viewer see them as fictions, not as real people. The *travesti* or queen character, in particular, far from signifying complexity or profundity of character, embodies an ambiguity that contributes to the impression of allegory. This is perhaps unsurprising given the then lack of counterdiscourses around homosexuality, which did not reach mainstream potential until under the second period of filmic representations of gender-variant homosexuality pinpointed by Signorelli Heise, that is, the 1990s. In films like *Rainha Diaba*, the queen is a two-faced character. Effeminate, dressed up as if in carnival costume, full of airs, graces, and emotional crises, she is "alguém que simula ser o que não é" (76; someone who pretends to be what they aren't). In this way, in *Rainha Diaba* and similar films of the period, argues Signorelli Heise, the queen or *travesti* "aproximá-la das características do governo militar. Afinal, a ditadura militar no Brasil tambiém simulava ser o que não era: vestia um país pobre e periferio com a fantasia de país desenvolvido," its project of a fake modernity hiding a reality of poverty (76; approximates the characteristics of the military government. By its end, the military dictatorship in Brazil also pretended to be what it wasn't: it dressed up a poor and peripheral country in the fantasy of a developed one). Where films from the 1960s and 1970s tended to confront Brazilian national reality via allegory, films of the 1990s and new millennium, among them *Madame Satã*, argues Signorelli Heise, tell individual stories that are not metaphorical. The social context and political juncture appear as background to individual stories.

In the case of *Madame Satã*, some nuancing to the previous account is in order. While the film certainly does trace an individual life and paints a portrait that does not merely lend itself to national metaphor, the mythic gestures do enable a reading to locate the film's subject in relation to an assertion of Afrocentric identity. This is the particular and localized that can now be enunciated away from the utterance of the national, disarticulated from former appropriative representations of blackness. The fact that nearly two decades of the resurgence of Afro-Brazilian politics predates its making, and black and *travesti* subjects have achieved a visibility and presence especially in the last ten years, would account for the specificity of its identifying citations, which were not possible in the past era. The stage becomes a focal point of the extrapolation of such identifying elements, but in *Madame Satã*, this space is not used to stage any story of the nation as such, unlike in the films previously discussed.

In contrast, all the citations and gestures of the film's cabaret moments refer principally to black icons—from the Afro-Brazilian religion, *candomblé*, and also from the filmic and burlesque pantheon. It is no accident that *candomblé* is a source of inspiration for dos Santos's personae. As Parker notes, in this belief systems "there is also a socially constructed place for the *bicha* . . . Any number of studies have pointed to the importance of effeminate *bichas* in the structure of Afro-Brazilian religious cults" (1999, 35). Such persons are regarded as a "bridge of the spirits," may be *pai de santos* (priests), and are commonly known as "adé" (special conduits of the divine). Their artistic flair and dramatism are seen as propitious for the rituals involved (Conner and Hatfield Sparks 2004, 99; 102). Many *bicha* practitioners are aligned with gender-complex *orixá* (the deities of candomblé). Iansan, referenced in *Madame Satã*, is one of them. Iansan is female but with potent, rageful qualities representing the wind, hurricanes, and similar forces of nature. Dos Santos also invokes Ogún, a masculine, fiery entity who is also syncretized to Saint Sebastian, patron of homosexuals, and especially associated with the poor and marginalized (Mott 1996). Added to the magico-religious world of *candomblé*, the film gestures to invented Africanesque goddesses, with names like "a negra de Bulacoche" (the Negra of Bulacoche) and "Jamacy, a rainha da floresta" (Jamacy, the Queen of the Forest). Here the self-tropicalized exoticism of a black femininity is melded with masculine energy: "She would run among plants and fly through the hills. And so, Jamacy turned into a golden jaguar, with a soft face and a delightful countenance." The mulata figure is another point of identification for dos Santos in his wild, hypnotic, and incantatory scenes both at the Blue Danube and Cabaret Lux, where he regularly performs at different moments of the film. The mulata is referenced also in the scenes where Dos Santos seductively invites his white lover, Renatinho, to "taste these thighs," calling himself a "morena mala" who will provide his beloved a "mother's love." Although the mulata, as Natasha Pravaz demonstrates, is a central "figure . . . in the constitution of Brazilian discourses of national identity" (2000, 48), here and in the cabaret scenes, Dos Santos consciously toys with but subverts such images. Historically as a figure "in Brazilian culture, she represents the concrete and symbolic synthesis of sexual intercourse between a white master and his black slave" (48). However, such a configuration is pointedly reversed in the very act of appropriation: dos Santos is in power—being the active pursuer—subduing his white lover. Moreover, the expected *bicha* passivity is contradicted to reveal rapacious desire. These staged incarnations of a raced and tropicalized sexuality, something pursued in more detail in the next chapter in reference to a Cuban novel that similarly invokes Afro-diasporic religion and *mulatez* (in a perhaps more profound way), culminate in a transcultural borrowing of black femininity in a Francophone context, as dos Santos takes from another myth, identifying with the legendary Josephine Baker, herself both a symbol of sensuality and maternal love.

In her article "The Diva Politics of Reception," Jeanne Scheper (2007) looks at the invocation of the figure of Baker in different transnational cultural texts and contexts. While Baker has been seen by many critics as the purveyor of the image of the fetishized, objectified, primitivized black body in her performances, her embodiment of cultural myths and prototypes of a fantasized blackness (for the metropole) has also been viewed as enabling and ironic. Baker famously portrayed a whole gamut of personae on the stage and screen but also in her very public life. Scheper underlines the use of these potentialities by dos Santos—an avowed "disciple" of his muse who at one point is shown watching one of her films, *Tam Tam*—in his performances in *Madame Satã*, "Dos Santos sees himself not as a fan but as an initiate of la Baker. For him, Baker has something divine to teach. Through Baker he can gain a measure of freedom by manifesting her performance and authorship of glamor, celebrity, and female stardom. In short, he is given license to inhabit cultural spaces that have excluded his body" (2007, 89). In these spiritually imbued scenes (where blackness connects to femininity, sexuality, and the African diaspora simultaneously, in tune with *candomblé*), the bonds of the oppressed body, so overlain with meanings, are broken. The performative space of the cabaret allows a "transing" of identities—which meld both blackness and *bicha* femininity—breaking the usual routines of accepted and acceptable (national) identities, to forge new ones. This "transing" is of the order of transcendence made possible also for the *travesti* character, Sandra, and her participation in santería in the Cuban novel examined in the next chapter. Scheper, drawing on the work of José Esteban Muñoz, locates this identificatory "transing" in the matrix of disidentifications. In *Disidentifications: Queers of Color and Performance of Politics* (1999) Muñoz looks at the camp performance art of Carmelita Tropicana and Ela Troyano, among other performers of color. He connects the work of *choteos* in their ironic mockery to the ambivalence marginalized subjects—in particular those of color—express toward dominant forms, styles, and regimes of identity. This ambivalence can be expressed through imitation that also rejects those norms—derides them—and subversively appropriates them at the same time. Muñoz labels this strategy "disidentification," one that is very political. Dos Santos's invoking of *mulatez* and sexualized black femininity is best viewed as an appropriation of potentially essentialistic and colonial discourses to different ends of liberation and empowerment.

The fact that the film is so intimately concerned with the telling of the interweaving of a black and *bicha* identity can be related to the very presence of sexual subalterns and their location in the everyday in contemporary Brazil. Although the film does not refer explicitly to the period demarcated by Signorelli Heise as the period where new stories are told in a democratizing and neoliberal Brazil, in which national stories have weakened and new social actors have emerged in contestation, namely the turn of the twentieth century and the beginning of the twenty first, it nevertheless responds to the emergence in the contemporary panorama of new presences and new narratives of subjectivity. And it is unsurprising that the figure of dos Santos was chosen to articulate these in the film. Academic studies and journalist accounts provide testament to the importance of Afro-Brazilian religion and culture among *bichas* and *travestis* and to the fact that large numbers of them, given their supremely marginalized status, occupy the dual-subject position of both *negras* and *bichas* (Conner and Hatfield Sparks 2004; Kulick 1998). Such subjects do ford spaces of racialized and gendered marginality as they become reproduced in social and sexual relations, and as such, the connection to a bygone rogue antihero from decades past is logical. Many *travestis* themselves speak a Yoruba-based dialect, *pajubá*, as a sociolect that is particular to their population and also allows them to communicate among themselves and avoid both civil and police surveillance (Wolfe 2006). This argot, tellingly, is becoming popular among those who celebrate the revival of a regional and Afro-centered identity discourse, one that is not enmeshed in Brazilianness but in the experiences of marginalized sectors and those who confront criminalization in day-to-day existence (Rojas 2008).

Although Gustavo Subero in a recent article called "Fear of the Trannies" (2008) claims that Latin American cinema, in contrast to literature, has been ill disposed to exploring the subjectivities and embodiments of gender-crossing subjects, citing a form of filmic heteronormativity that disallows its visual representation, *Madame Satã* would seem to prove otherwise. Its inclusion of the cabaret links it to other cinematic traditions of figuring homosexuality and transitivity of gender; and yet, unlike in the other two films that this chapter has explored, the gender-crossing figure is not merely a stage animal; nor is the stage an enabling vehicle to broach temporarily "displaced" concerns about crises or changes in the national-cultural horizon, which is the case with the use of this space and its associated *travestis* and *transformistas* in *Danzón* and *Las noches de Constantinopla*. Subero, I think, mistakes the lack of transsexual embodiment for a disinterest or, indeed, a rejection, of transspecific bodies. I would argue, however, that this fails to account not only for the culturally specific limits and possibilities in envisioning sexual identity and gender movement, remembering that the *travesti* is not immediately able to be compared to either transvestite or transsexual in Latino/a contexts, but also for the nuances in the relationality and ironic textures on display in films like *Madame Satã*. Subero looks for "transgender" in films that are primarily about Latin American forms of gendered homoeroticism and finds them lacking, arguing that, apart from those that he examines, few exist in the history of Latin American cinema. And yet as the introduction to this chapter detailed, cinema from the region positively abounds in such characterizations, characterizations important to bear in mind when assessing contemporary representations.

The three texts I have discussed in this chapter manage to avoid reproducing the unremittingly jaded images of performing *locas* and *travestis* familiar from the kinds of productions of the 1970s and 1980s, that is, as seen in the clichéd image of the "queen" stereotype. The drag queens and full-time trans characters who inhabit these narratives are not the inferior, degraded, and passive victims of former mass-cultural portrayals. They are not the targets of ridicule and excessive violence. Nor are they symbols of weakness or perversion. The first two films I discussed, however, do not depart radically from some of the features of earlier representations. The *transformistas* and *travestis* of *Danzón* and *Las noches de Constantinopla* continue to work within the bounds of gender crossing as spectacle, purely located on the stage, in a marginal site that comments on the main thread of each production's concerns. Both films' use of trans acts and lives functions from the sidelines; Fresa, Vainilla, and Chocolate from *Las noches* are not "in-betweens" but still they are go-betweens, working at solving a crisis for the sake of an elite family, flitting between the members of a lower socially ranked sector and an aristocracy. Susy from *Danzón* is also a mediator in the journey of the film's main character, Julia—providing information, linking her to the man she seeks, and acting as confidante and enabler. As *transformistas* and *travestis*, they are variously cheeky, wanton, and burlesque. Clearly some shift can be perceived in the depictions of gender crossing and crossers in these films. *Locas* and *travestis* are now no longer used to illustrate the forces of machismo as they are in the person of La Manuela in *El lugar sin límites*. But they are still illustrative of something very removed from the ontological realities of being gender different in culture. *Danzón* and *Las noches de Constantinopla* for all their "positivity" do not articulate anything about trans subjectivity. The possibility of speaking from a *travesti* or nonnormative gender position is diminished because both films deploy signifiers of "transness" in the name of other issues. These issues may not concern male dominance in the social order, but they still evoke certain textual parallels that explore other aspects of that social order.

Aïnouz's film is qualitatively different in this regard. *Madame Satã* works at the edges of acceptable identities and reworks identity logics and spaces that have been co-opted in the name of the national, breaking them down to reveal the specificities of the raced and gendered subjectivities so often erased in the elite discourses of Brazilianness. Aïnouz thus returns us to the stage and the mythic realms of the cinematic imagination, but in order to refract these images through a different optic, with a different cast and angle, separating out the contrasting hues of a heroic legend who becomes representative of the new marginalized actors emerging from the blinding light of whiteness and nation. The tones and articulations of the central body in the film—dos Santos reborn at the narrative's end as Madame Satã in one triumphant shout—keep the eye trained perpetually on the complexly morphing protagonist.

In connection to this corporeal storytelling, in the next chapter, two novels from the mid-1990s are juxtaposed. In very different ways they offer a compelling revisualization of subjectivity—one centered primarily on the body. To what extent that visualization may play with and unpack mythic productions, as *Madame Satã* surely does, and to what extent it might rarify what are so often inscribed as "exotic" phenomena serve as central axes of the analysis.

Chapter 4

Authorizing Subjectivity

Eroticism, Epidemia, and the (In)validation of Bodies in Pedro Juan Gutiérrez's *El Rey de La Habana* and Mario Bellatin's *Salón de belleza*

Bodies and Subjectivities

The body in all its glory or decadence is a central concern for many writers who visualize sex and gender variance in Latin American contexts. Through the body, *locas* and *travestis* enact their difference: they corporealize their desiring selves and gender identification through a series of visible signs that express femininity as it is understood and constructed culturally and mediated through elements of class, race, and other factors. This process of embodying subjectivity is never entirely straightforward for such individuals whose sex and gender variance represents in heteronormative culture an ambiguity and incoherence between "biological" sex and the gender they cultivate and perform in everyday life.

It appears that the *travesti* body, to borrow Sandy Stone's reflection on productions of the transsexual body, is "a hotly contested site of cultural inscription" (1991, 294). While all kinds of bodies emerge through, and are subject to, cultural inscriptions, some *are* more intensely marked than others.[1] When *loca* and *travesti* embodiments provoke anxiety for the writer or director, their very corporeality can assume the dimensions of the monstrous, perverse, and contradictory, as we have seen in the work of Arenas. They are manipulated textually to become symbolic of something, not infrequently the social or political state of the nation. This involves a kind of semiotic overloading or overdetermination, a fixing of the gender expression of *locas* and *travestis* in deterministic language: they are all surface posing and artifice, with nothing underneath. Similarly, representations in which the *travesti* body is simply performative, showing up or contrasting with so called nonstaged (that is, "natural") identities, rely on overdeterminations, constructing the *travesti* body as all performance, a symbolic unto itself. This was the case of the films *Danzón* and *Las noches de Constantinopla*, discussed in the last chapter.

In many of the texts examined so far, the *travesti* body is indeed a hotly contested site for the "ongoing struggles over beliefs and practices" of the culture about men and women, sexuality, and national change (Stone 1991, 294). Very few of the *locas* or *travestis* discussed so far are imagined as individuals furnished with a living, breathing inner life, a set of personal motivations and desires or even a culturally located place. Moving beyond the terms of theatrical "staged" identity or the stereotypically grotesque, in this chapter we look at two texts, Pedro Juan Gutiérrez's *El Rey de La Habana* (*The King of Havana*) and Mario Bellatin's *Salón de belleza* (*Beauty Salon*), both of which continue this fervent obsession with the body.

The novels to be examined were published within a year of each other: Bellatin's *Salón de belleza* in 1994 and Gutiérrez's *El Rey de La Habana* outside the writer's country of origin, Cuba, in 1995. Both feature significant *travesti* characters. *El Rey de La Habana* depicts the larger-than-life Sandra as one of a range of women with whom its eponymous protagonist becomes involved, while in *Salón de belleza* the *travesti* voice and gaze is given centrality as the first-person narrator of the novel's world. Both novels provide provocative reappraisals of sex and gender-variant subjectivity, and how it is mapped culturally, but they do this in differing ways. In these two works Gutiérrez and Bellatin give pride of place to the body, its fashioning, and the meanings it accrues in the social realm. In its third-person omniscient narrative mode, *El Rey de La Habana* reveals an interest in all kinds of "marginal" bodies, how they interact, how they define against one another, how they gender themselves, and how they become sites of eroticism. As such, Gutiérrez's novel goes beyond the scope of the *travesti* or gender-variant body, which is the primary focus of *Salón de belleza*. In the latter, the narrator becomes the caregiver of a great quantity of bodies all afflicted with the same mysterious desexualizing disease, bodies that belong to subjects who are united by this desexualizing condition and their status as sexual and gender outlaws. Bellatin's work is technically and thematically the flipside of Gutiérrez's, so it will be useful to examine both texts to illuminate the implications of these contrasting inscriptions of the body, what they express about trans subjectivity, and the place accorded such lived difference in culture. This chapter also measures how they bypass or reinscribe the central problem of the troping of trans subjects to be symbolic of some national characteristic or representative of cultural change.

El Rey de La Habana: Genre and Narrative Point of View

Marketed and identified by its author as a dirty realist novel, *El Rey de La Habana* displays all the characteristics of this genre: the dark side of life, the "underbelly" of society's underrepresented factions, a world stripped bare and probed with an unsentimental eye. Originally a U.S. genre in the tradition of Henry Miller and Charles Bukowski, dirty realism as a mode is unrelenting in its often jaded depiction of the unheroic, the crude, raw, and disillusioned facets of postindustrial urban (street) life. It also seeks to uncover a reality that is presumed to be automatically other: the domain of the dirt, the cast aside, and the much maligned and marginalized. In interviews, Gutiérrez has avowed the preeminently realist impulse behind this book (and others), written during Cuba's euphemistically named Special Period, mentioned in the previous chapter. In an interview with Stephen J. Clark, Gutiérrez relates that this novel is written for those without a voice, drawn from "real life" and based on "real people" observed by him close hand during about five years eking out his existence as a writer in central Havana (Clark 2001). Gutiérrez's formative influences include Tom Wolfe, Truman Capote, and Ernest Hemingway—all writers known for their reportage style. Gutiérrez himself has worked in Cuba as a journalist. Lest we ready ourselves to brand his particular species of dirty realism sensationalistic or tabloid, Gutiérrez and his supporters point out that—unlike in other Latin American countries—in Cuba the *nota roja* (tabloid) style of journalism is nonexistent and therefore not sellable: the public is not familiar with such a genre and this is not the author's intention (Gutiérrez 2001b). The author dissuades the reader from the temptation to make that kind of intertexual inference, pointing outside to his North American inspirations, which are transferred to a peculiarly Cuban juncture of the present, the way life is lived now for the unacknowledged majority of Cubans facing economic exile (Clark 2001). The text's saturation with sexual imagery and language, and its incessant depictions of violence and bodily states of hunger, homelessness, deprivation, and isolation and yet also momentary pleasure are not, Gutiérrez suggests, inventions, but the facts of existence for Cuba's forgotten people. The novel was published outside Cuba by Spain's Editorial Anagrama, as with his first work *Trilogía sucia de La Habana* (*Dirty Havana Trilogy*). The first was offered publication in Cuba, subject to substantial revisions, which Gutiérrez refused (Clark 2001). Both works are permitted circulation in Cuba (contrary to their more or less implied criticism of the economic policies of the regime), but short of publication on Cuban soil, they are principally read outside the island by a Spanish- and English-reading public. The primary sites of his novels' publication and their readerships will be taken up later in accounting for the kinds of depictions of Cuban "marginality" contained in the book, most centrally where the *travesti* Sandra is depicted.

The "dirty" takes on new proportions in *El Rey de La Habana*. We can see this in the unparalleled and unconventional erotic encounters that take place in a seemingly endless range of bourgeois nose-turning environments in the novel. Gutiérrez's narrator is witness to all this in its barest physicality and remains equanimously nonjudgmental. It is debatable whether or not the narrator's no-holds-barred bird's eye view of this panorama qualifies him as a voyeur, for where he holds back on judgment, he exhibits a tone of lustful exhilaration in the adventures and misadventures of his protagonist, Reynaldo, or Rey for short. Most of the narration is focalized through Rey's eyes, although the narrator frequently editorializes on events, people, and locations in a way that exceeds the protagonist's point of view: as narrator he knows more than his teenage antihero can. So, contrary to the author's protestations about the documentary-like honesty of his text, we see as readers that it is a recreation, one not unaware of the role of narrative distance and location, the location of the reader, irony, literary influences, and cultural associations.

In his study of masculinity as represented in four Latin American novels, Pedro Koo notes the ironic recycling of the picaresque in *El Rey de La Habana* (2003, 219). Rey, violently orphaned at the beginning of the novel at the mere age of thirteen, erroneously pursued as culpable by authorities, and incarcerated in a juvenile correctional facility for three years, escapes and proceeds to lead the life of an itinerant *pícaro* variously as beggar, thief, gravedigger, stevedore, peanut seller, and drug courier, all under the care and jurisdiction not of a series of *amos* (owners), but rather a collection of *amas*. Not only do they secure him employment on occasion, but often they provide exclusively for him, both financially and sexually. These women—differentiated by age, occupation, femininity, physical attractiveness, and level of dissoluteness—compose part of the gallery of characters who populate the novel and who fall under the narrative gaze. Arguably, the most significant women for Rey in terms of erotic fulfillment and affection are Magdalena, also referred to in the text as Magda, and Sandra.

Although the novel could be seen as an open-ended, free-wheeling tour of the full stretch of sexual roles, appetites, and the gender rainbow, this world in all its unbound "marginality" still holds, at least nominally, to normative principles. Magda is, importantly, the spokesperson of many of the gender norms presented in the novel. Magda rebukes Rey on a number of occasions for his inattention: "¿Tú? Que eres mi marido y me tienes que cuidar" (Gutiérrez 2001a, 146; "You? You're my husband and you have to look after me"). She compares him to her lover on the side, who provides for her every need: "Eso sí es un hombre! Con mucho billete" (200; "Now *that's* a man! Someone with lots of cash!"). Other characters also voice similar norms, and they are things to which Rey—with some degree of naïveté—aspires. Rey is obsessed with meeting the ideals of masculinity that elude him, and he constantly fends off the possibility of being feminized.[2]

Into this setting emerges Sandra, the *travesti*. *Travestis* are first mentioned in passing on page 40 of the novel as "esa fauna no agresiva pero pícara y convincente" ("that nonaggressive but cheeky and convincing street fauna"). As Ena Lucía Portela notes, referring to *El Rey de La Habana* in a critical article, they are depicted as part of a subculture whose members include

> jineteras y pingueros, proxenetas, vividores, pícaros, traficantes de todo lo traficable, borrachos, drogadictos, balseros, tipos agresivos y feroces con el cuchillo entre los dientes, veteranos de la guerra en África que perdieron la chaveta, locos arrebatados, ex presidiarios, y también otros que quizás en otras sociedades no serían marginales, o al menos no tanto, como los travestis, las lesbianas, los enfermos de sida y los santeros. (Portela 2003)
>
> [*jineteras* and *pingueros*, pimps, hustlers, picaros, traffickers of anything traffickable, drunkards, drug addicts, rafters, aggressive and ferocious guys with blades between their teeth, stark raving madmen, ex-cons, and others as well that perhaps in other societies wouldn't be marginal, or at least not as much, like *travestis*, lesbians, those ill with AIDS, and *santero* priests.]

All come under narrative scrutiny in very bodily ways. The body in the novel, among other things, is a vehicle for economic mobility. *Muchachos* and *muchachas* market their bodies to tourists by night in the elite sections of the island in pursuit of U.S. dollars. (The period in which the novel was written, that is, the Special Period, clearly shapes these realities.) Bodies are raced, classed, and gendered in various ways by the narrator. Subjectivity is explored via the body's exterior manifestation. This is in large part an operation of the third-person narrator, who, loath to enter the thoughts of anyone but the protagonist, visualizes and distinguishes the cohorts and conspirators of this world corporally. Sexuality is also written on the body and understood as a consequence of biology or natural disposition. The bourgeois notions of public and private are increasingly voided in this context of commercialized sex and scopophilic sexual display by young men on the docks masturbating themselves into a frenzy in front of lovemaking couples and passersby. The implication is that for the poor, in crowded and compromised conditions, very little remains private, and the body, the most basic thing one possesses, represents perhaps the sole avenue for empowerment, self-actualization, and influence.

The (Extraordinary) Body in the Text: Exploring *Travesti* Subjectivity

The place of the body, and how it becomes readable in terms of sexuality, race, class, and as a site of interpersonal transformation, is crucial in considering the representation of the *travesti*, Sandra. For the narrator, this body in the text is an extraordinary body. Gutiérrez is to be praised that, genre pressures aside, his novel's manifestation of *travesti* subjectivity does not simply end up as the dead body in the text—as is all too often the case. In crime novels or television detective series, we usually first meet trans characters in the morgue. But Gutiérrez opts for a more challenging maneuver and depicts her as a focal point of energy and life, sexuality and allure, at once perplexing to the young Rey and deeply fascinating. Our first view of her retains the traditional terms of contradiction and ambiguity, but these are fused with an eroticism that piques the reader's interest and confronts any preconceptions. The cultural equation between homosexuality and transvestism is deeply embedded in this encounter: we are seeing from Rey's point of view, formed by the attitudes around him that say men are men and women are women and any "male" who transgresses this tenet is a *maricón* or deceiving through masquerade. Uncommon in literature, this is subtly conveyed in the novel without infusing Sandra's body with images of the grotesque. Sandra attempts to pleasure him while he sleeps on her stoop. Rey's initial reaction is one of violence, but curiosity overtakes him:

> Rey lo agarró por el pescuezo y lo iba a lanzar escaleras abajo, cuando vio que estaba disfrazado de mujer. Tenía una cara lindísima y una peluca rubia. Y se contuvo. Se miraron de frente. Era preciosa. Una mujer limpia, con cutis delicado, perfumada. Con una falda corta. Se quedaron en silencio mirándose. (Gutiérrez 2001a, 62)
> [Rey grabbed him by the lapel and threw him downstairs, when he saw that he was disguised as a woman. He had a beautiful face and a blonde wig. Rey pulled himself together. They looked at each other face to face. She was beautiful. A clean woman, perfumed, with a delicate complexion. In a short skirt. They stood in silence staring at one another.]

This marks the moment of encounter with a great unknown, another way of being that textually requires a certain degree of linguistic acrobatics: masculine and feminine subject and object pronouns become slippery and change places when Sandra is mentioned. The scopic vacillation over this "extraordinary" body is akin to the eye's inability to perceive the vase and the two linked faces in the famous diagram simultaneously, even though they are both there. The desire to see both is subverted by the restriction of only being able to perceive one at a time the vase or the faces: "Rey lo miró bien, ahora en la luz. Le había golpeado duro. Tenía un par de moretones en las mejillas. Y lindo. ¿O linda? Era precioso, en realidad. Parecía una mujer bellísima, pero al mismo tiempo parecía un hombre bellísimo. Rey nunca había visto algo parecido" (63; Rey looked at him, under the light now. He had struck her hard. She had a couple of bruises on her cheeks. And handsome. Or pretty? Precious anyway. She looked like a beautiful woman, but at the same time a beautiful man. Rey had never seen such a thing before). Sandra immediately contrasts with Magda; with her ideals of refinement and her cleanliness, she outstrips Magda in terms of womanliness and class. Even though we are told that her small breasts were achieved by hormone pills, they are "originales. Nada de silicona" (65; "Original. No silicone"). When Magda all but abandons Rey, Sandra supersedes her with her feminine charms and maternal attitude. Sandra holds nothing but disdain for Magda, for whom she is simply "esa mujer, pelandruja, churriosa, puta, muertadehambre, chismosa y bretera" (64; "that woman, bedraggled hair, smelly, whore, street trash, tattle-tale gossip"). Sandra asks, "¿Qué tiene ella que no tenga yo? Yo por lo menos me baño todos los días y cuando tengo un hombre lo cuido como si fuera príncipe. Y no le falta nada. Nada. Yo sí cuido a mis hombres" (64; "What's she got that I haven't? At least I bathe every day and when I've got a man I look after him like a prince. And he doesn't need a thing. Nothing. *I* look after my men").

In considering Sandra's ideals, Koo singles out this character for her conservative gender notions, which he claims are those of a middle-class woman (2003, 246). He sees her *travestismo* as proceeding from a sort of false gender consciousness, arguing this with reference to her dream of marrying a millionaire. Koo ignores the fact that so many of the other born-female women characters express a similar sentiment—and also the desire to protect Rey. Katia and Yunisleidi, whom Rey meets later in the novel, express a similar desire for servitude to their man, and Yunisleidi also expresses the hope of being rescued from destitution by that rich *güiro* (white) tourist. In fact, what all these women have in common is their involvement in sex work as a creative solution to their dire economic circumstances. That would seem to be the main motivation for such fantasies. The gender norms any woman is expected to live up to should also be taken into account here. As we have seen, in many Latin American contexts, women's sexuality and destiny is assumed to be organized around men. That is to say, one gains respect culturally by complying with the demands of heterosexuality, matrimony, and dependency on a man. A woman who strikes out on her own can be perceived as selfish, ambitious, and going against her "natural" role. Social expectations—which to be sure differ according to class—plot the path a woman is supposed to take.

In Bourdieu's terms, they shape her habitus. Bourdieu refers to the habitus in *Logic of Practice* as composed of the "common schemes of perception, conception and action" belonging to and expressed by a particular group or social class (1990, 60). It is made up of "durable, transposable dispositions" that are shaped by and shape the possibilities of being in the social world, one's mobility, values, and aspirations (53). All the women in the novel express the gender doxa of their culture (to use another term from Bourdieu, this time from *Language and Symbolic Power*), even if their intersocial behavior differs on this count. Doxa refers to the statements or value expressions that people make that remain unquestioned and taken for granted. They depend, however, on specific worldviews and orthodox assumptions that are particular to one's social and material conditions of existence (1991, 55–56).

In this way, Sandra's construction of femininity is very much linked to her prostitute identity: a highly *femme*, sexualized construction, which the novel demonstrates requires time, patience, imagination, and talent. Ironically, as the narrator focalizes through Rey's eyes and hence visually roams and inspects the surface of Sandra's body, the act of transformation in dressing up for a night of work convinces the young *pícaro* Rey that this, truly, is a woman: "hecha y derecha" ("through and through"):

> Sandra, en blúmers y con las teticas al aire, comenzó a maquillarse. Primero se rasuró bien la cara, las axilas, las piernas. Cremas suavizadoras, bases, polvos, pintura de labios, peluca rubia, sombra en los ojos, pestañas postizas, uñas postizas. Le llevó más de una hora. Aquel mulato hermoso, andrógino, bello, fue mutando lentamente en una mulata especialmente atractiva, con un fuerte magnetismo sexual. (Gutiérrez 2001a, 77)
>
> [Sandra, in bloomers and tits in the air, began to make herself up. First she shaved her face, armpits, legs. Softening creams, foundation, powder, lipstick, blonde wig, eye shadow, fake eyelashes, fake nails. It took more than an hour. That handsome, androgynous, beautiful mulatto was morphing slowly into an especially attractive mulatta, with a strong dose of sexual magnetism.]

This is far from being a mask, or hiding a "divergent reality" as the *travestis* are depicted in the work of Arenas. It is a becoming, reminding the reader of Simone de Beauvoir's truism "one is not born a woman, but, rather, becomes one" (1973, 301). For Sandra, Molloy's "very visible self-fashioning" incorporates her sense of gendered self; the outside expresses the inside, as with any other claim to identity (1998, 147). This inside is perceived in equally congenital ways as a male-born-male or female-born-female's sense of gender is perceived: it is something inside that one is born with. Sandra says, "Siempre he sido loca. Loca arrebatá. Desde que nací" (Gutiérrez 2001a, 69; "I've always been a *loca*. Unabashedly *loca*. Since I was born").

Sociologists such as Carlos Basilio Muñoz (2004) and Stephen O. Murray (1995) argue that although binary notions of men, women, male sexuality, and female sexuality have a strong hold in Latin American settings, there also exists the idea that some males are "born" unable to live up to norms of masculinity and that they may show this disposition very early.[3] Effeminacy is seen culturally as a signpost of homosexuality but is often recalled by many *travestis* themselves as the first evidence of a gender difference that distinguishes them from *los gays*. *Los gays*, some *travesti* respondents in sociological studies have reported, are reserved and avoid any open feminine identification. They may feel attraction to other males but only express sexual interest discreetly or much later in life (Fernández 2004, 78). *Travestis*, in contrast, show their femininity very early in life, before puberty and before many are even conscious of any sexual attraction for males. Other people call them homosexual before they even express such inclinations. For these *travestis*, something about their "core" identity shows through in spite of the forbidding environment that monitors and punishes deviance from gender norms. It is only when they find the right space in the outer world as adults that they are able to fully embody what they have always felt themselves to be (78–80).

Gutiérrez's text is rich in this regard, since it avoids both stigmatizing Sandra as a *travesti* and is able to demonstrate her complexity visually and through dialogue. The stylization and iconography seen in the crumbling living quarters Sandra has beautified represent an extension of her embodied subjectivity. Similarly self-conscious, multiple, and layered, they point to a recreation of life within poverty, a care of self that defies Magda and Rey, and an overt association with Cuban tradition and its transcultured contemporary setting:

> Cuando Rey entró al cuarto se quedó asombrado. ¡Allí dentro había de todo! Desde luz eléctrica hasta televisor, refrigerador, cortinas de encajes, una cama amplia con muñecos de peluche encima, una coqueta cubierta de frascos de cremas y perfumes. Todo limpio, inmaculado, sin una mota de polvo, las paredes pintadas de blanco, adornadas con grandes pósters en colores de bellísimas mujeres desnudas. En un rincón un altar presidido por un crucifijo y la triada inevitable en Cuba: San Lázaro, la Virgen de la Caridad del Cobre y Santa Bárbara. Y flores, muchas flores. Muñequitos de plástico y de vidrio por todas partes. Pequeñas budas, elefantes, chinas, bailarinas de mambo, indios de yeso. Todo mezclado. El kitsch elevado a su máxima expresión. (Gutiérrez 2001a, 63)
> [When Rey entered the room he was stunned. Everything was there! From electric light to television, refrigerator, lace curtains, a wide bed with fluffy toys on top, a dresser covered with creams and perfumes. All clean, immaculate, without a speck of dust, white painted walls, decorated with

giant posters of very beautiful naked women. And in the corner, an altar presided over by a crucifix and the inevitable Cuban triptych: San Lázaro, the Virgen de la Caridad del Cobre and Santa Bárbara. And flowers, many flowers. Little plastic and crystal dolls everywhere. All mixed together. Kitsch elevated to its maximum expression.]

It is this connection to Cuban tradition, as signaled by the collection of religious and popular culture objects mentioned in the above quote, and Sandra's embodiment of it, which are textually extended when we learn of her devotion to santería. For Sandra, her practice of this religion, a relative to the Afro-Brazilian *candomblé* discussed in the previous chapter, underlines her place in a counter-Catholic orthodox world of identity flux and flow and allows her to participate in rites of bodily transformation otherwise denied in the day-to-day realm. The significance of Gutiérrez's placement of Sandra in the context of santería is explored in greater depth in the subsequent section. First, however, as a preliminary to a full discussion of the connection between *travesti* subjectivity and the practice of santería, I examine how the text elucidates Sandra's sense of bodily ego and how this operates in her and others' perceptions of her identity.

The term "bodily ego" was coined by Freud, who posits that "the ego is ultimately derived from bodily sensations, chiefly from those springing from the surface of the body. It may thus be regarded as a mental projection of the surface of the body, besides . . . representing the superficies of the mental apparatus" (1989, 20). For Freud, our sense of self is intimately tied up with our internal image of the body's surfaces, its limits, and differences from other bodies. Not only do we "have" a body, but also an introjected image of the body, accumulated through sensations and experiences from life. The bodily ego's map of the external body may or may not conform to the body's present state. Moreover, the bodily ego is an idealization of the body. Butler adds that the psychic component interacts with the cultural and that the bodily ego's projection or idealization is also formed by cultural norms and not just formative bodily sensations (Butler 1998). This offers a very dynamic conception of embodied subjectivity in the world. It also accounts for Sandra's sense of being in the wrong body: bodily ego mismatches the physical fact, which, somewhat painfully for Sandra, risks being revealed when she is naked. Jay Prosser powerfully invokes the concept of "bodily ego" to explain why many transsexuals, for one, have the sense of "wrong embodiment" (Prosser 1998, 69). Employing the work, furthermore, of Didier Anzieu and Oliver Sacks, Prosser argues that the sense of one's body is not ocular, that is, based on sight (77–78). Rather, it is based on sensations that are anchored in the skin, which is the membrane between self and world. Sacks speaks of "body agnosia" in a series of case histories of individuals who experience a severe disjuncture with certain body parts and their sense of themselves: people who experience their limbs as foreign objects and those who continue to experience a part that is no longer there. Sacks names the sense by which the body knows itself "propioception" (Prosser 1998, 78). It has a neurological basis. The neurological perception of the body does not always coincide with the body's present material state. Likewise, one's subjective experience of the body is not the same as the way it appears to an outsider in Anzieu's account. One's experience of self relates to the comfort one has in one's own skin, whose status as the ground of perception is primary to Anzieu. The actual state of one's genitals here constitutes a blind spot of feeling (propioception) for many (preoperative) transpeople (77–78). Like the person who feels a limb to be foreign, individuals like Sandra cannot "feel" their sex as it is embodied in its present state; rather, they feel it to be other.

The subjective sense of her body is maintained in collaboration with Rey, by the deferment of attaching meaning to her male genitals or touching them in any way. Interestingly, the narrator is more than willing to "go there" in a very filmic manner. The novel is littered with references to her "falo erecto," which Rey avoids observing but on which the text teases the reader to focus. Whenever they have sex, the meaning of her male genitals is constantly deferred. This protects Sandra's sense of femaleness. As Prosser explicates, "This dis-ownership of sex, the untouchability of the body, maintains the integrity of the alternatively gendered imaginary" (77). Such a tactic is clearly in evidence in Sandra's nakedness. In this way, even if the "ocular-centric" (Prosser's term) narrative point of view reveals Sandra's male genital morphology, the subjective perspective of psychic sex and bodily ego is suggestively communicated.

Not only does the "dis-ownership of sex" displace the discomforting sense of "wrong embodiment" that Sandra experiences, but it also pulls Rey back from the cognitive abyss of being confronted by the possibility of risking his own sense of intact heterosexuality. For Rey, the maintenance of strict bodily controls in their interaction allows him to protect his notion of masculinity when engaging sexually with this fully unimagined other. He forbids Sandra from touching his buttocks, as this might reply a reversal to the passive role, and mark him as homosexual according to cultural logics and undo the suspension of psychically introjected gender roles being performed between them, only to moor it again in the physical fact of Sandra's genitalia. However, the matter of Rey's attraction to Sandra is more complex than it seems. He indeed views her as a woman "hecha y derecha," he defers fixing male gender notions to her genital morphology, but he is also excited by the tension between these possibilities. The roaming over the body of Sandra, the mapping the "contradictions" between how she animates the body based on her conception of self and what she has between her legs, is pornographically investigated.

In private moments, then, he experiences a kind of discreet jouissance at this *chica* and the evidence of her body:

> Se deseaban. Lo hicieron en todas las posiciones imaginables. Sandra era una experta, aunque jamás había leído el Kama Sutra. Rey evitó que Sandra le tocara las nalgas y él no lo tocó ni miró, al menos no directamente, el falo erecto de Sandra.
> —Yo soy hombre. No me toques las nalgas— le dijo.
> Sandra estaba acostumbrada a eso, Se puso más femenina aún y lo sacó de las casillas . . . Se vistió vaporosa y provocativamente con unas braguitas de encaje y una blusa transparente y mínima. Todo en blanco. En las braguitas tan delicadas resaltaba la bola formada por sus huevos y su gran tolete. Aquello originaba una sensualidad brutal. Rey lo miró y se excitó muchísimo con aquel contraste tan atractivo, pero al instante comprendió que tenía que dominarse, y rechazó la idea:
> <<Yo soy un hombre, cojones>>, pensó. (Gutiérrez 2001a, 90)
> [They desired one another. They did it in every imaginable position. Sandra was an expert, even though she had never read the Kama Sutra. Rey didn't let Sandra touch his buttocks and he didn't touch or look, at least not directly, at Sandra's erect penis.
> —I'm a man. Don't touch my buttocks— he said.
> Sandra was used to that. She made herself even more feminine and drove him crazy . . . She dressed airily and provocatively in lace garters and a see-through mini blouse. All in white. Through the delicate little garters the lump shaped by her balls and shaft stood out. Rey looked at it and became very turned on by the exciting contrast, but immediately he understood that he had to control himself and he rejected the idea:
> <<I'm a man, damn it>>, he thought.]

For Sandra her embodiment is incomplete. In spite of what she views as Magda's ineptitude at performing the role of "woman," Sandra still expresses envy toward her for what she does not yet possess: female genitals. Sandra is perhaps unusual in this regard. Many *travestis* dissociate themselves from the model of operative transsexuality that sees sex-reassignment surgery (SRS) as the ultimate step for complete transformation into womanhood. Moreover, commonly they frame their gender identity as being "like women" but not trying to "be" women, as discussed in Chapter 1. Retaining male genitalia may be desirable to themselves as a source of pleasure, and to their clients in prostitution who are often attracted to the idea of the *travestis* being both male and female at the same time or in between. Sandra dreams of being complete. In this sense she is more like a transsexual. Sandra longs for a transformation so alchemical that it would simultaneously right this "wrong" body and bestow her with the power of maternity denied by her partially male physiology.

En un repentino exabrupto, Sandra se puso de pie, se agarró su masacote de pinga y huevos con las manos, por encima de las braguitas de encajes blancos. Se las remeneó como un *macho* y le dijo:
—Por esto, mira, por esto. Si yo pudiera, me los cortaba. ¡No quiero ser hombre! Lo que más quiero en la vida es ser mujer. Una mujer normal. Con todo. Con una vágina húmeda y olorosa y dos pechos grandes y hermosos y un buen culón, y tener un marido que me quiera y me cuide, y me preñe, y parirle tres o cuatro hijos . . . Pero mira lo que tengo: este pingón y estos huevos. (91)
[With a sudden change of tone, Sandra stood up, grabbed her dick and balls in her hands through the white garters. She thrust them out like a macho and told him:
—Because of this, look. If I could, I'd cut them off. I don't want to be a man! What I want most in this life is to be a woman. A normal woman. With everything. A wet smelly pussy and two beautiful big breasts and a big ass, and a husband that loves and cares for me, who'll get me pregnant with three or four kids . . . But look what I've got: this big dick and these balls.]

Locating *Travesti* Identity in Culture: The Transformative Practices of Santería

Denied her sex by biology, Sandra finds the powers of spiritual transformation in gender in santería, a transcultural religious practice with Catholic elements. Yet santería, unlike Western religious and philosophical traditions that maintain the spirit and the flesh as distinct, melds the two, as its ritual practices invoke the spiritual in the physical realm: the spirits have physical needs, they are sated with rum and cigars, and they frequently possess the bodies of their devotees. Sandra is a unique portal for such forces, as she is open and receptive. The fact that she already physically occupies male and female or stands outside them, and that psychically she is female identified, makes her an especially propitious candidate.

Santería—more officially known in Cuba as *Regla de Ocha* or *Isin Orishás*, or "the way of the *orishás*"—is one manifestation of the various African diasporic religions that came to the Caribbean and Brazil, notably including the already cited *candomblé*, with the arrival of slaves from the Yoruba and other tribes from the mid-sixteenth century onward. As noted in the introduction to *Cassell's Encyclopedia of Queer Myth, Symbol and Spirit: Gay, Lesbian, Bisexual, and Transgender Lore*, Yoruba religions have a special niche for same-sex-loving and gender-variant individuals, possessing more than twenty-five terms for such people (Conner, Hatfield Sparks, and Sparks 1997, 3). Many practitioners are homosexually oriented or gender variant. Santería holds to the belief in a Supreme Being, from which all other *orishás* emanate. These *orishás* are sometimes called *santos* and those guided and channeled by them, *santeros* and *santeras*. Outwardly this may take forms of a variant on Catholic iconography, but as the editors of the encyclopedia note, the history of Yoruba traditions and their adaptation to new circumstances in Cuba must be remembered: "While they were forced to outwardly adopt Christianity, many continued to worship their gods, albeit in the guise of Catholic saints, and to hold their ancient celebrations, albeit on the feast days of the saints" (2). Ancestor spirits as well as the *orishás* that usually represent natural forces provide guidance and spiritual energy called *ashé*. This *ashé* is experienced by states of altered consciousness, "achieved through drumming, chanting, dancing, and other 'techniques of ecstasy'" (2). Sacrifices or offerings may be made to appease and seek blessings from *orishás*. Men and women initiates are considered the spiritual "sons" or "daughters" of a "father" or "mother" *orishá*. Gender-variant males usually have a female *orishá* as mother. As the editors point out, "*Orishá* who are considered patrons of such persons include: OBATALA, OSHUN, YEMAYA, OLOKUN, YEWA, OYA, INLE, LOGUNEDE, OSHUMARE, and ORUNMILA." (3) Many of these deities have an androgynous or gender-variant history. As such, Conner, Hatfield Sparks, and Sparks note, "The religion may appeal to gender variant, homosexual/lesbian, and bisexual persons because they discover within it deities who will defend them and whose sacred tales mirror their own. The religion may also appeal to them because it allows for, indeed often demands, the expression of behavior regarded as gender variant. Temples of the religion may also serve as sanctuaries for those who have been forced out of their homes by intolerant family members. Temples may serve as meeting places for those seeking community among like-minded individuals" (4). But gender variants and passive homosexuals are also considered apt for the priestly medium role—rather like that of a shaman—for their expressiveness and receptivity. Alongside women, they can be "mounted" by the deities. From the religion's roots back in Africa, the relationship between the god and the priest is visualized in masculine-feminine terms: women make better mediums because they can be receptive to being possessed or penetrated by the god, hence effeminate males and *travestis* can as well (5).

But it goes further than this. In the previously discussed Brazilian manifestation of Yoruba diasporic religion—*candomblé*—gender-variant people stand outside male and female and are uniquely close to the supernatural. In Brazil, *bichas*—the equivalent of the *loca* or *travesti*—tend to be feared, appreciated, and respected. Supernatural power is often attributed to them "because, in deviating from the prescribed gender and sexual roles, they are envisioned as inhabiting quasi-mystical 'regions of the cosmos which are defined as outside society'" (4). This may also be the case in Cuba and certainly in the novel, where santería is held in awe and respect among the poor, even if Rey does not quite understand it. Of course caution would dictate that santería should not simply be idealized in a salvational narrative of inclusiveness for sexual diversity, even as chief motifs among its practices and iconography do not strictly fall in line with "Western" binary notions of sex and gender. Salvador Vidal-Ortiz (2008) speaks of the tendency among researchers to either view santería practitioners as phobic toward homosexual and trans participants or completely tolerant and accepting. In reality, the religion may include examples of homophobia and also tolerance among its adherents; a nuanced view that allows that cultural discourses interpenetrate religious forms and their contexts, just as in other spheres of social existence, is in order. That said, in the world painted by Gutiérrez, the idealized view seems to pertain more: Sandra's condition as supernatural third term because of her "transness" is recognized by those around her. Before a tussle between Magda and Sandra for ownership over their man, Magda instructs Rey to stop eating the food that Sandra prepares because "eso tiene brujería" (Gutiérrez 2001a, 98; it's bewitched).

This is where Gutiérrez locates Sandra—in a culturally ordained, shamanic third space—in his evocative portrayal of her being "mounted" by the spirit Tomasa:

> Sandra se puso un poco histérica y empezó a temblar. Con pequeños ronquidos, como bufando, con los ojos cerrados. Rey quedó azorado. Sandra abrió los ojos. Los tenía en blanco y convulsionaba. Rey nunca había visto a alguien pasando un muerto. Las convulsiones se incrementaron y Sandra cayó al piso. Su muerto era una negra conga, muy sabrosona. Sandra se transformó en una vieja, pero con una cara dulce y simpática. Hablando en español enredado y en congo, casi ininteligible, pidió aguardiente y tabaco. Estiraba la bemba y hacía gesto de chupar: <<chup-chup-chup-chup>> . . . Se dirigió hasta el pequeño altar de Sandra. Allí había una botella de aguardiente y dos puros. Bebió. Encendió el tabaco con mano temblorosa. Fumó. Aspiró al fondo. Bebió otro buche largo, y dijo:
> —Tomasa va a hablá pa'ti. (91)
>
> [Sandra turned slightly hysterical and started to tremble. With a couple of snorts, panting like an animal, her eyes closed. Rey was stunned. Sandra opened her eyes. They were rolled back in their sockets and she was shaking. Rey had never seen someone possessed by the dead. The convulsions grew and Sandra fell to the floor. Her spirit was a black Congo woman, very sensual. Sandra turned into an old woman, but one with a sweet and friendly face. Speaking in Spanish mixed with Congonese, nearly unintelligible, she asked for *aguardiente* and tobacco.[4] She stuck out her lip and gestured to suck <<chup-chup-chup-chup>> . . . She turned toward Sandra's small altar. There was a bottle of *aguardiente* and two cigars there. She lit the cigars with a trembling hand. She smoked. Inhaled deeply. She took another long swig and said:
> —Tomasa will speak for you.]

Specific reference is also made to her spiritual mothers Yemayá and Ochún a little later in the passage. Sandra makes plain her connection with Ochún in particular: "Yo soy hija de Ochún y conmigo vas a adelantar mucho" (80; I'm the daughter of Ochún and you'll go far with me). Ochún is, in the pantheon of deities, "the *orishá* of rivers and lakes, sensuality, and the fine arts. Christianized as Our Lady of Caridad del Cobre" (Conner, Hatfield Sparks, and Sparks 1997, 258). These are aspects associated with Sandra in the novel, too: fluidity, eroticism, refinement, and skill, as we have seen. She is, to say the least, a very memorable character, and the foregoing passage represents an unusually memorable scene in Cuban literature. One wonders if there is any other quite like it; the fusion of both Afro-Cuban elements and her transness makes for an unparalleled eroticism and exoticism. To be sure, santería has been used by resident and expatriate Cuban and Puerto Rican writers before and since. In an article on historical and literary representations of santería, M. T. Marrero raises an interesting question in relation to this: "Is it possible to incorporate vital elements of a West African tribal, pantheistic religion without 'exoticizing' ourselves?" (1997, 142). Gutiérrez's novel treads this line—surely the idealization of santería is part of this—and in doing so, risks entering the realm of reductive tropes of both *travestismo* and *cubanidad*, a point that the next section explores.

Cuba pobre pero exótica: Another Tropical Fiction?

The slippage facilitated by Sandra's fluid gender-variant body provides Gutiérrez with a site for a range of inscriptions, which are outlined in this chapter. Many of them point to a sexualized and prototypical construction of *cubanidad*, as discussed earlier. Gutiérrez clearly demonstrates that Sandra occupies a social-sexual place in contemporary Cuba as a prostitute and as an extraordinary and respected practitioner of santería. Some readers may find it all too extraordinary. After all, if Sandra, along with Rey and other characters, are real people, individuals that we might expect to come across in the world, how would we characterize their humanity? And if they are sorely underrepresented in Cuban letters, why the mythic gestures? Gutiérrez risks overstating the case. The text contains very little in the way of evidence of social stigma toward Sandra or her prostitute friends. Only Magda ever expresses any strong antipathy toward her. While the position of sexual minorities has arguably improved since the period outlined in the chapter on Arenas, and *travestis* in particular have been more openly celebrated in the country and overseas—*Mariposas en el andamio* covers well this shift—Cuban culture is still mediated by bipolar gender-normative notions and sanctions against those seen to deviate sex and sexuality terms, as is the case elsewhere in Latin America (Chant and Craske 2003, 141).

How far are Sandra and other characters embraced as social types or to what extent are they picaresque updates of former literary antiheroes and rogues, updates that proffer a revamped and "darkly" attractive version of Cuba for the reader, predominantly located outside Cuba, as was highlighted at the beginning of this chapter? The eroticization and exoticization of identity for a group of subjects, which in their marginalized status in the real world have been excluded from the realm of the subject itself, might be seen as fetishistic and opportunist by some readers and at odds with the novel's avowed realist impulse. The novel—whose colloquial use of Cuban *jerga* (slang) and scenarios supports its verisimilitude—stretches belief that this is simply a narrative in which the names of the real people have simply been changed, as Gutiérrez suggests to one interviewer, the U.S. scholar Stephen Clark.[5] The reader may be wont to ask if Gutiérrez can play it both ways, and to whom is he playing this tune. After all, whether we as readers ought to be disturbed by the degrading and soul-destroying conditions of impoverishment that the author is at pains to portray here, or titillated by the pornographic framings of any and every woman and man in the novel, are valid points of contention. Some readers, in spite of the complexity in representation of characters like Sandra, may be tempted to see Gutiérrez's Cuba (the other Cuba, the Cuba outside the "área dólar") as yet another tropical fiction for Anglo-American and European consumption. Of course, remembering Gutiérrez's pledge to realism, and the small number of U.S. citizens who visit the island due to the continued embargo on trade and travel, U.S. readers may be inclined to take the novel's representations on authority. Remembering also that Gutiérrez's books circulate mainly in North America, I believe there is an argument to be made here about his awareness of that readership and its preconceived tropical images of the island. Gutiérrez does pay due attention to laying bare the presence of tourists and the privileges they enjoy in the newly emergent market Cuba, which is unavailable to most Cubans except through various forms of serving-class labor. However, the narrative gaze—variously individuating bodies on the basis of class, sex, and race—nevertheless imbues its "marginals" with an always available and salacious sexuality, occasionally confirming dominant narratives of *machista* sexuality and, by recourse to *hembrismo*, a classed, raced, "untamed" sexual voraciousness in the female characters. The extensively detailed orgy scene with three willing "mulatas" suggests this (Gutiérrez 2001a, 125). Black men are inevitably imposing and aggressive, animalistic: "Los negros, desarmados, daban voltíos como tigres en la selva" (185; The blacks, unarmed, leapt in the air like tigers in the jungle). Tropicalizations, as Frances Aparicio and Susana Chávez-Silverman suggest in their introduction to *Tropicalizations: Transcultural Representations of Latinidad*, are not "the exclusive domain of First World Writers" but "also evident in the representation of subaltern subjects who write about and 'other' those with even less power and social status" (1997, 10).[6] Further, to tropicalize, for these critics, "means to trope, to imbue a particular space, geography, group or nation with a set of traits, images and values. These intersecting discourses are distributed among official texts, history, literature, and the media" (8). These issues have a real affinity with my argument. And yet here I do not want to be reductive and state this is the only possible way of viewing *El Rey de Habana* and its deployment of *travesti* and other "marginal" figures. Gutiérrez may indeed push the envelope, as his *travesti* character Sandra is a fusion of so many strands of Cubanness: she is exotic in her *travestismo*, but she is also a *mulata*, a prostitute, highly sexualized, and a mover between so many categories of sex and class, between the world of disempowered *Cuba pobre* and *indigente* and the world of the *orishás*. Is she somehow an articulation of the author's vision of contemporary Cuba? Sandra is, to be sure, only one of a gallery of "marginal" characters, any of which could arguably be advanced as exemplary of the side of Cuban life explored in the novel. She is not the main character, and although she does not die miserably at the hands of some killer, she ends up in prison on drug charges approximately halfway through the novel (Gutiérrez 2001a, 112). While the narrative does tread the line between prototypes and social types in its not unproblematic dirty realist mode, it would be difficult to state categorically that *travestismo* itself is troped to signify at the level of nation, for instance. Given the absence on behalf of this narrator of the kind of unanalyzed and culturally received stigma evident in Arenas's texts, I do not think Gutiérrez pursues this line in his depiction of Sandra. Arenas uses the bodily signs of his *loca* and *travesti* characters and imbues them with artificiality and the grotesque; these bodily signs themselves become metaphorical of the state. He empties out their subjectivity and tropes them as symbols for the national-political order. Gutiérrez does not employ Sandra in this way. However, the issues of tropicalization and the construction of national fictions are linked and therefore any depictions that express a degree of tropicality may implicitly participate in the projection of the image of a nation or group. A fuller discussion of the fictional figuration of *travestismo* in relation to the projection of the national-cultural situation will be developed after analyzing the second novel, *Salón de belleza*, in order to tease out the contrasts between the two and the dialectic of tropicalizations and their reinscriptions.

Salón de belleza: Genre and Narrative Point of View

If *El Rey de La Habana* is marked by its realist orientation, the work of Mario Bellatin does the opposite. It prioritizes style over naturalism, investing its energies in linguistic play and association, relying on the powers of self-referentiality from one novel or story to the next in the writer's oeuvre. In an interview with Daniel Flores Bueno (2001), Bellatin dismisses the kind of literature that pretends to paint portraits of reality. For him, reality is reality—best represented in news bulletins or on the Internet—and literature is about effect and metalinguistic creation. That reality may parallel events or characterizations in his work is purely coincidental or intertextual. He is interested in structuring spaces in which to explore ideas. In this sense, his work could not be more different from that of Gutiérrez. One gets the sense from reading his work that if Bellatin had not chosen to be a fiction writer he would have been a poet. Perhaps he already is, since the novelist's usual designs—plot, detailed characterizations, and explorations of relationships—are less important to him. Bellatin is more obsessed with tone, voice, and image.

In 2005, Alfaguara released Bellatin's *Obra reunida (Collected Works)*, bringing together *Salón de belleza* (1994) with other short works including *Efecto invernadero* (1992; *Greenhouse Effect*), *Damas chinas* (1995; *Chinese Ladies*), *El jardín de la señora Murakami* (2000; *The Garden of Mrs Murakami*), *La escuela del dolor humano de Sechuán* (2001; *The Szechuan School of Pain*), *Jacobo el mutante* (2002; *Jacob the Mutant*), and *Perros héroes* (2003; *Dog Heroes*), *Flores* (2004; *Flowers*), among others. Here I have no intention of rendering a literal interpretation of *Salón de belleza*, unlike Paolo de Lima in his article "Peces enclaustrados, cuerpos putrefactos y espacios simbólicos marginales en una novela latinoamericana de fin de siglo" (2004; "Cloistered Fish, Putrid Bodies, and Marginal Symbolic Spaces in the End-of-Century Latin American Novel"), which provides an example of the dumbfounded critic's desire to tie the novel's scattered references down to a particular time and place and hence anchor its ambiguity into something "verifiable," a response that could equally be titled "Desperately seeking national fictions." Bellatin in interviews avoids identifying himself as Peruvian, even though he was raised in Peru. Currently living in Mexico City, his place of birth, he also attests to the sensation of not possessing a defined nationality.[7] Identifying Bellatin as Peruvian-Mexican may provide a way of entry into the text's suggestive references. However, Bellatin is rather fond of interspersing all his texts with Latin American, Asian, Middle Eastern, and European references, occasionally giving the impression that he knows each place firsthand. His elaborate deployment of Japanese signifiers in other novels is a case in point.[8]

Bellatin's work is very suggestive and difficult to locate in that Latin American tradition of fiction that frames its importance in terms of exploring national reality, history, or time and place. Latin American writing is so often called upon to be representative of such things.[9] Much work on *Salón de belleza* does not move beyond the national-realist frame: as a representation of the deterioration of contemporary society (Huamán 2000), the emergence of the homosexual subject in Peru (Reisz 2001; Ugarteche 1997), and so on.

Rather than attempting to anchor the ambiguity of Bellatin's work into something "verifiable," the second part of this chapter explores how the novel's chief images and symbolic articulations reverberate with certain discursive formations around questions of contagious disease, gender-variant identity, and the body. The central node is, of course, the narrative voice that carries these elements through the evolving but detached consciousness and view of the cross-dressing protagonist-narrator. Bellatin's work is clarifying, rather than mystifying, precisely because of its meta- and intertextual style, which allows the reader many entry points and continues to resonate long after the first reading. It is perhaps ironic that such resonance is achieved in greater rhetorical detail in this novel than in Gutiérrez's work, which is not to underrate the latter; instead I mean to signal that realist works do not necessarily lead to clarification, but can further mystify their subjects. For all *El Rey de La Habana*'s positive and detailed exploration of "marginal" identity and existence, the possibility that the writer overexoticizes his characters with his third-person observer realist mode is a valid critique. If realism with its attempts at seamless representation of "the world" can serve to offer a particular reading via the strategy of verisimilitude, antirealist enterprises with their rhetorical sweep offer the potential to deconstruct elements of narrative form and provide the reader with clues to its operations. This strategy is at the heart of *Salón de belleza*. Narrating the succumbing of a group of sexual "marginals" to an epidemic in a typically indirect, clinical but visceral way, this novel imbricates itself with other narratives about plagues, both literary and cultural: here, most notably, HIV/AIDS. This is achieved via a series of montages or vignettes that center on the bodies of the novel's dying young men and its cross-dressing protagonist, and more obliquely, his tropical fish. The montage of references and elements coalesce around issues of the body in health, the body in decline, the beautified body and the stark, diseased body in mourning, and thus permits me to continue the exploration of corporeality discussed at the beginning of this chapter. Bellatin offers this feast of images to the work of deconstruction. As such, my approach takes the form of an examination of the novel's rhetorical designs, specified in reference to the construction of the *loca* or *travesti* body as a text besieged by discourses.

In terms of narrative voice and point of view, Bellatin's text is enunciated in the first person by a hairdresser who lives in an unnamed suburb of ill repute in an unnamed town. He tells the story in the present, so his view of unfolding events is never superior to ours or to other characters in the novel, except, of course, when relating aspects of his own past. The present matters most here, as the mysterious disease referred to by the narrator throughout the novel as "el mal" (the illness) or "la peste" (the plague) slowly takes over certain inhabitants of the city who turn up in great numbers to his beauty salon to seek refuge and treatment. The beauty salon is renowned for its careful attention to the care and presentation of its loyal clientele. Moreover, it is a focal point for those who do not fit into normative society. Its proprietor is well known as an eccentric and flamboyant personage in town, whose establishment does not turn away individuals because of their attributed marginality. It is one of the few "safe" places for such people. And yet, those struck with the "mal" begin to outnumber the usual clients. The beauty salon is turned inadvertently into a *moridero* (a dying house), and its former glory descends into darkness and debilitation. But the past is important, too; from this narrator we learn of the halcyon days before the plague struck. The illness alters the salon as dramatically as it does the bodies of those under its throes, eventually claiming its proprietor. The contrasting temporal forays—analepsis and present-time narration—are pivotal, since they provide two versions of the body.

Remembrance of Things Past: Youth, Health, Risk, and the Trans-Erotic Body

The narrator, forced out of home at the tender age of fifteen for not fulfilling his mother's dreams of being the "niño recto" (good boy) of the family (1999, 45) is taken under the wing of the owner of a disco, who becomes something of a parental figure, and runs a male-only hotel where the narrator begins to work. He schools him in the art of frugality and personal care, advising foremost on the value of youth and its ephemerality. This guidance enables him to establish the salon a few years later, when he returns to the capital and forges an independent, adult life.

The salon represents a project of beautification wherein the proprietor practices the art of transformation: rejuvenating and reconstructing the femininity of the female clients who come to the premises, which are similarly carefully adorned so as to raise the aura of class and style. With the foundation of the salon he finds himself financially stable but spiritually empty. His passions are tied up in the care of others, not of himself. The only sense of life and liberty he derives are in the three days a week he dedicates to cross-dressing publicly in the streets and looking for men for sex. His cross-dressing is similarly associated in the text with the adornment of the salon. He and his colleagues then begin to *travestirse* in the salon itself—which extends upon the aesthetic of the premises and makes the female customers feel even more at home, so that they can be more intimate, feel respected, and confide their secrets.

Travestismo as an act of personal care and erotic becoming is linked to this nostalgic era of unfettered youth and risk. The flashbacks make possible a glimpse of homoerotic cross-gendered identity under precarious conditions before the illness strikes the town. The body in health is only conceivable in contrast to the body diseased; it is something lost and not to be regained and knowable only by comparison. The narrator's dispassionate tone when addressing the present does not disrupt the evocation of this golden age or utopia of the body, but rather intensifies it.

So what does this suggest about gender-atypical identity? The *travesti* narrator is not a *travesti* in exactly the same way Sandra is.[10] That is why the male descriptors are used. He spends only some of his time in female persona, recreationally and in the context of street prostitution. Sandra's day-to-day identification and embodiment of the feminine persona is much more constant; she considers herself a woman but for her genitals, and she is largely considered this way by those around her.

In contrast to Sandra's cross-gendering in everyday life and in the context of sex work, in *Salón de belleza* the narrator's cross-dressing escapades occur always at night: furtively, in localized zones of the city, outside the realm of nine-to-five "normality." They are recalled as episodes of hedonistic celebration and are always tempered and circumscribed by the agents of the law and therefore inscribed with meanings of trespass as well as transformation, geographically, sexually, and culturally. *Travestismo* as an act and a reality is intimately linked by the narrative to illicitness, marginality, and prostitute identity. Dressing up and going public, he and his *travesti* friends must beware the neo-nazi gangs who pick on queers and gender variants. The text alludes to a "Banda de Matacabros" (15; an antigay gang) and also to police raids and abuse, an unfortunate reality for many *travestis* who work in prostitution in Latin America. This facet is not notable for its realist tendency; rather, it helps nuance the sociocultural setting in which the protagonist's subjectivity as *travesti* becomes apparent. The narrator says that he and his *compañeros* would avoid the glare of the general public's gaze on their gender-subversive rituals by taking their clothes with them to those areas known for sexual commerce. This can be seen in the following two quotations: "Porque la transformación se tiene que hacer en ese lugar y furtivamente" (20–21; Because we had to do the transformation there and furtively) and "No podíamos viajar vestidos de mujer, pues en más de una ocasión habíamos pasado por peligrosas situaciones" (24; We couldn't travel dressed as women as more than once we had gotten into dangerous situations"). The narrator mentions the "puntos de contacto que se establecen en las grandes avenidas" (20; points of contact forged in the long avenues). The subversion and transgression of space and identity culturally and nationally is intimated also by the ironic reference to hiding the suitcases that held their feminine attire inside an alcove in the one of the Monuments to the Heroes of the Fatherland.

All these clues establish two axes to his *travesti* identity: the one seen by day and conforming to the rules of social propriety, and the other, *cual mariposa de noche*, in the tradition of vampire figures, only permitted life in the dark, obeying other rules and dictated by passion and unstoppable effervescence. In fact, even the censure and abuse by the police is associated with attraction, exploring the borderline between phobia and eroticism. The narrator mentions a *travesti* friend who liked to dress exotically, that "siempre usaba plumas, guantes y abalorios de ese tipo" (18; always wore feathers, gloves, and other accessories like that). She is surprised one evening to find herself ignored by passing cars, incapable of drawing with her erotic style even the police who would normally be tempted to take her for a ride.

The street, then, is the space for the *escenificación* of this gender performance, which faithfully obeys the precepts of *vedettismo* and all the highly sexualized glamour it requires. Vujosevich, Giménez, Moreira, and others (1998) call *vedettismo* (starlet quality) "una feminidad exacerbada" (an overdone femininity) and argue that the practice of street prostitution provides a space for its manifestation (9). This is the case in the depiction of Sandra in *El Rey de La Habana*, and the text even explicitly refers to her as "toda una vedette" (a real starlet) when she dresses up for a night of working in Havana (Gutiérrez 2001a, 52). Josefina Fernández (2004) devotes considerable theoretical consideration to the construction of this femininity as seen among her *travesti* respondents who work the streets in Buenos Aires. She does this in nonstigmatizing ways. She agrees with the basic tenet that the street provides the setting for the construction of *travesti* identity, but she does not use terms such as "exaggeration" or "hyperintensification." She posits that women and *travestis* involved in prostitution rely on different models for their construction of gender presentation:

> [La] prostitución es para las travestis la oportunidad para la presentación de sí mismas y de su trabajo como espectáculo. Y el espectáculo se arma con un vestido y una apariencia física que son diferentes para mujeres y travestis en prostitución porque responden a modelos femeninos distintos . . . Porque la mujer se crió con el estereotipo de una mujer y la travesti con el de prostituta . . . la imagen referencial de ellas es la prostituta o, en todo caso, una vedette que se conoce a través de los medios de comunicación o de espectáculos artísticos diversos. De manera contraria, las mujeres en prostitución

han tenido a sus madres como fuente identitaria y esta diferencia da como resultado dos maneras diferentes de ver el mundo y de llevarlo a cuestas. (2004, 100–101)

[For *travestis* prostitution is the opportunity to present themselves and their work as a spectacle. And the spectacle is put together with a dress and a physical appearance that is different for women and *travestis* in prostitution because they respond to different models of femininity . . . This is because women grow up with the stereotype of the woman and *travestis* with that of the prostitute . . . the image of reference for them is the prostitute, or at least the starlet, whom they come to know via the media or show business. In contrast women in prostitution have their mothers as a source of identity constructs and this difference has as a result two different ways of seeing the world and taking it on.]

Having been shunted out of home early, *travestis* often do not have the kind of constant contact with the image of femininity that women have with their mothers. Such is the case of the narrator and his broken relationship with his own mother in *Salón de belleza*. Fernández's account sheds considerable light on those aspects intimated in the narration about *travesti* gender identity and the socially negotiated sense of self.

When not working the streets, the narrator and his *travesti* friends frequent soft-porn movie theatres to pass the time. The celebration of nonnormative gender and sexuality found in the youthful body, the body in health (he notes later, in illness, that he lacks the strength for such things now) is also apparent in the frequent encounters in the saunas the narrator visits. He goes to these saunas strictly dressed *en homme*. Leaving behind the vedette persona that serves so well to make one stand out, he is swallowed into the anonymity of the sauna, where bodies confuse themselves and become diffuse as the mist that envelopes them. Here, says the narrator, "cualquier cosa puede ocurrir" (Bellatin 1999, 19; anything could happen). While through *travestismo* the body is made, cultivated, accentuated, eroticized, and public, in the private space of the sauna, naked like all the other male bodies, it is unmade, melded, and dissolved into others homoerotically. Both *travestismo* and homoeroticism in the text hinge on the valorization of the youthful and healthy body, which starkly and ominously is stripped of humanity, sexual potential, and life in disease. The body in health, for this narrator, is the site of the inscription of self-aware and expressive individuality, sensuality, trespass, and crossing. It is a fluid space, multivalent and open to manipulation. It is the *materia prima* with which its *estilista* (stylist) works: part visionary, part other, but always disposed to change and renewal. The sauna, with its mists of creation and recreation, is compared at one point to the inside of the aquariums the protagonist collects to decorate the salon. The fish within—exotic, showy—mirror cross-dressing identity, and are bringers of life and color, but also, eventually, bad luck. Glory and shame exist side by side; the transerotic body is a heightened artefactual construction of beauty that is tinged by the stigmas of society and its patrolling of borders. As we shall see, the fish and aquarium metaphor inaugurates a discursive level in *Salón de belleza* that relates rhetorically to the fates of the narrator and the young sex and gender outlaws he takes in, something explored by Romeo Grompone (1999) in his narratological analysis that separates the elements of discourse and story. The aquariums' increasingly murky waters portend another future that will enwrap the bodies formerly characterized by their health, beauty, pride, individuality, and vigor in a miasma of negative productions.

THE BODY IN DISEASE: EMBODYING THE (OB)SCENE

Pero aquellos son tiempos idos que no volverán.
[Those times are gone and they won't come back.]

—Mario Bellatin, *Salón de belleza*

With the plague, the salon and the life of the narrator become the negative of what they once were. The change is presaged in the succumbing of the fish—the *Carpas doradas* (goldfish) and guppies—to fungus and other strange infections and deformations of the gills and a perceptible change in odor in the salon's surrounds. The illness comes from outside and colonizes the environment. Its exact etiology is unknown, but the signs are always indelible: a slow but multiplying procession of weeping wounds on the face and body that are immune to treatment and represent stigmata or the mark of doom for those who manifest them in the body's exterior, as well as a loss of weight and a listlessness. As the waters of the aquariums take on a green, opaque appearance, so, too, the salon is subsumed in a murky cloud of pestilence that repels passersby, eliciting "muecas de asco" (23; grimaces of disgust). This keeps all but those struck by the illness away from the salon's doors. Even local residents from a "moral-majority" group incensed by the presence of "perversion" in their district engage in a kind of *charivari* to demand the closing of the salon, now *moridero*. However, they are fearful of entering because of the strong stench emanating from its enclosure and the implication of contagion. Far from the life and vibrancy of earlier days, the salon is inhabited by a mournful lethargy. The narrator adjusts to this change and becomes the chief observer of its decline with the same removed fascination by which he notes the competitive and sometimes carnivorous behavior of some of his fish and the various diseases contracted by others. In contrast to the previous multicolored tropical fish, which in their exoticism are linked to *travestismo*, the carnivorous fish are like the protestors and attack the former. The increasingly sick fish that were preyed upon but now scare off their predators are like the *locas* struck by the plague. Such echoes between the fish world and the outer world structure the narration and provide ironic commentary. The deadpan voice of the narrator imbues the text with irony, too. He observes, wryly, "No sé de dónde me viene la terquedad de llevar yo solo la conducción del establecimiento" (31; I don't know where the tenacity to keep this establishment going by myself came from).

The plague heralds a new era of apocalypse; the disease is a dramatization of death in life, the extinction of individuality and identity. It entails a rapid *envilecimiento (degradation)*, which goes hand in hand with an unstoppable *envejecimiento (aging)*, as if caught by a time-lapse camera. The terms in Spanish are telling here because of their morphological similarity and because more than the words' connotations of debasement and aging, they imply the embodiment of these processes, which work actively to transform the once wondrous, youthful, and multivarious gender-transgressive body into something obscene, low grade, and horrifying. The body of those suffering from the disease is seen as the blank, the tabula rasa or a passive site on which these articulations are made. The narrator himself relinquishes the control to write his own body; his only control is to continue overseeing the salon in its new phase as a medieval dying house. There the victims and the disease are sequestered from public view, for the body in disease is obscene and hence offstage, not the site of public performance or celebration.[11] It is a source of shame and must be hidden. Furthermore, it is the receptacle of all that which is denied, vilified, and exiled into abjection. For the narrator, then, all resistance is futile and all efforts at creation or rejuvenation must be negated. There is, after all, no space for such considerations. Implicit here is that the forces previously referenced in the novel, which proscribe gender-variant identity and "deviant" sexuality, have generalized and extended themselves to such a point that the salon is the last place where such people—maligned by society—can go. But it is too late: the paradigms of abject identity have colonized their very bodies.

The narrator makes a clear break personally between the celebration of *travesti* identity and its mourning and passing with the advent of the plague on his own body:

> Al descubrir las heridas en la mejilla las cosas acabaron de golpe. Llevé los vestidos, las plumas y las lentejuelas al patio donde está el excusado e hice una gran pira . . . Recuerdo que bailaba alrededor del fuego mientras cantaba una canción que ahora no recuerdo. Me imaginaba a mí mismo bailando en la discoteca con esas ropas femeninas y con la cara y el cuello totalmente cubiertos de llagas. Mi intención era caer también en el fuego.

Ser envuelto en las llamas y desaparecer antes de que la lenta agonía fuera apoderándose de mi cuerpo. (54–55)

[On discovering the sores on my cheek everything ended suddenly. I took the dresses, the feather boas and the sequins out to the patio where the outhouse is and I made a big funeral pyre . . . I remember dancing around the fire while singing a song that I have forgotten now. I imagined myself dancing in a disco in those female clothes and with my face and neck all covered with sores. I wanted to fall into that fire. To be wrapped in its flames and to disappear before the slow, agonizing death took over my body.]

He dispenses with these female clothes because dressing up—a celebration of self, liberty, and eroticism—is now incompatible with the body diseased. He can only treat this body aseptically and at a distance. No love, affection, or desire is permitted to intrude in the closed circuit of the disease. No gesture other than mourning is permitted. He realizes this very early in the text. Only once does he show feeling toward and assist a dying patient—to no end, he decides, since they all succumb, and special care and attention produces but a prolongation. He ceases to frequent the sauna because "actualmente mi cuerpo esquelético, invadido de llagas y ampollas, me impide seguir frecuentando ese lugar" (20; "right now my skeletal body, invaded by sores and boils prevents me from frequenting that place"). Further, he notes that "se acabaron las aventuras callejeras, las noches pasadas en celdas durante las redadas, las peleas a pico de botella" with a kind of unsentimental nostalgia (45; "the street capers are over, the nights spent in a jail cell during police raids, the arguments over the sharp edge of a bottle"). The disease indeed takes over or "possesses" the body so that it becomes erotically illegible—deeroticized, unintelligible but for the marks of the illness. This vision of the body is in stark contrast to the body in health as a site of beauty. The narrative becomes a kind of elegy to the former body: "a los jóvenes fuertes, a los que alguna vez fueron reinas de belleza que desaparecieran con los cuerpos torturados y sin amparo alguno" (56; to the strong young men, those who were once beauty queens and would disappear with tortured bodies and no one to come to their aid). This nest of associations and images prompts the reader to connect to narratives of epidemia in the form of AIDS of the last two decades of the twentieth century. Indeed, the previous passage could have been written by a survivor of that particular holocaust of negative meaning production and sexual hysteria, to which many journals of gay people living with the onset of what was initially known as "the gay plague" attest.[12]

Identity-Constituting and Identity-Fracturing Discourses: An Epidemic of Signification

That the illness comes from outside, that it swarms as if it is a miasma, and that its exact etiology is unknown makes it more metaphorical than biological. The fear it produces is just as unnamable; basal disgust, a desire to flee, to rid oneself of possible contamination—these are the classic operations of abjection. The illness has many guises: it signifies in various ways. It is untreatable with scientific or folk remedies. It always claims victims, who are united by the condition and their status as sex and gender outlaws. If their former scandalous conduct marked them as socially other, the disease marks them as abject pariahs, as indicated in the following references: "de cuando en cuando alguna institución se acuerda de nuestra existencia" (21; "whenever one institution or another remembered our existence"); "De los que no tienen nadie en el mundo, yo mismo tengo que ocuparme" (22; "For those who have no one in the world, that's who I'm here for"); "Buscaba evitar que esas personas perecieran como perros en medio de la calle" (50; "I sought to prevent those people from dying like dogs in the middle of the street"). This is why the *moridero* exists. The medieval inferences from the use of the word "*moridero*" link its articulation to a time of ignorance, darkness, and superstition associated with the bubonic plague, as well as to literary figurations seen most notably in Daniel Defoe's *A Journal of the Plague Year* (1722) and Albert Camus's *L'Étranger* (1942).

It is important to note, too, other Latin American literary depictions that link plague and sexual others, as well as a whole series of racial others. Mario Vargas Llosa's *Historia de Mayta* (1984), for instance, features a character named Mayta who is known to the reader in several versions. One of these versions of Mayta is homosexual. In this novel, the sick state of the Peruvian nation, imagined as a diseased body, is linked to the "effeminacy" and abject queerness of the homosexual Mayta, as Paul Allatson notes (1998, 518). Allatson further observes that the very name Mayta, which is of indigenous Quechua rather than Spanish origin, connotes his abject queer body as also racially other (520). In the novel, sexual and (leftist) political "perversions" are inextricably connected, and Mayta is the shadowy figure that embodies and articulates both forms of perversion. Plague metaphors in reference to imagined communities and nations are, as we have seen, historically widespread in Latin America and elsewhere. Moreover, *machista* homophobic discourse, which sees femininity and homosexuality as toxic to its perpetuation, exiles to the zone of the grotesque and unlivable those behaviors and identifications that appear to threaten the patriarchal order and the claims to the primacy and naturalness of heterosexual masculinity. The paranoid and reactive dimensions of defensive patriarchal masculinity have clearly structured nation discourse in many locales. Ambiguity and difference in patriarchal and statist terms are inadmissible. When a heterosexual writer such as Vargas Llosa attempted a supposedly sympathetic portrayal of "homosexuality," he made recourse in his novel to unreconstructed and unquestioned paradigms of sexual otherness and otherness in general that had already circulated for centuries in Peru and elsewhere. Bellatin's *Salón de belleza*, in contrast, is minutely aware of the construction of otherness in terms of abjection and disease and does the work of deconstruction and reconstruction that fails a writer like Vargas Llosa.

Another notable difference is that in *Salón de belleza* the plague is not inscribed in racial terms. While the plague imagery may remind the reader of representations of nation, race, and otherness already in circulation in literature and culture, it does not feature references to the "abject Indian"; nor does Bellatin's novel restrict itself to a national location or seek to diagnose the ill or perverted state of the nation, unlike the cited Vargas Llosa text. The plague's manifestation in the bodies of sexual and gender transgressors make it indisputably modern and readable as an intertext to AIDS. Bellatin as a queer writer is also far more attuned to the ramifications of plague imagery and productions of sexual otherness than Vargas Llosa or other writers who engage queer or trans bodies to represent national problems.

Susan Sontag's study *Illness as Metaphor*, later republished with a second part, *AIDS and its Metaphors* (1991), is helpful in explaining the commonalities between the plague as depicted in *Salón de belleza* and AIDS as a narrative in culture. An epidemic, as a major event, also anticipates a crisis in signification. AIDS, like other epidemics, is no exception. Like the plague in Bellatin's novel, it has various imputed origins (none proven or provable) and manifestations. It is ripe for figuration, drawing on deep-seated cultural understandings and moral formulations. For Sontag, nothing is more punitive than giving a disease a moral meaning, which is what happens with AIDS and the "mal" of the novel under discussion (1991, 17). This is what drives Sontag to unpack the elements in AIDS as a rhetorical discourse whose effects fan out socially, politically, and culturally and thus outstrip any notions of a basic, objective knowledge of its presence in the body. In the well-known narratives around the illness, a series of mysterious conditions appear, any of which could point to AIDS. AIDS, like the plague in Bellatin's novel, is "the Great Masquerader," staggered in stages of time like a dramatic performance, with a long and lengthening roster of symptoms, fevers, weight loss, fungal infections, and swollen lymph glands (Sontag 1991, 106). Sontag began her study in the 1970s on the subject of the metaphorical use of cancer, providing a cultural epidemiological history of the narrativizing of disease.

AIDS and cancer are distinct from tuberculosis, for instance, because they refuse romanticization. They are not aesthetically pleasing or erotically enhancing. On the contrary, they strip the body of possible sexual allure, autonomy, and identity. AIDS is distinct from cancer because of the associated imputation of guilt. As Sontag reads its meaning trajectory, "The unsafe behavior that produces AIDS is judged to be more than weakness. It is indulgence, delinquency—addictions to chemicals that are illegal and to sex regarded as deviant . . . AIDS is regarded as disease not only of sexual excess but also perversity" (111).

The disease writes bodies in this way in the novel. The lesions are hieroglyphs of perversion, surface signs of inner corruption, which reschematize possible positive, "identity-constituting" narratives of its sexual others into discourses that "fracture" identity. These terms are from Eve Kosofsky Sedgwick's *Tendencies*, where she interrogates the ways in which queer identity is made and unmade along different rhetorical axes (1993, 8–9). AIDS is certainly one of them, simultaneously investing and divesting the individual with certain identity markers, as Robert McRuer argues using Sedgwick's language (2002, 223). As overseer of the *moridero*, the narrator only admits patients whose bodies have become unrecognizable from their former state, that is, when they signify along the plague's own circuit. He also only admits males, one assumes, who are both *escandalosa* in their identity and public face. The patients, who in their former gender atypicality were like the *axolotls* the narrator collects with their "hibridez rara," that is, mixity, gender interstitiality, *rareza*, become indistinguishable from each other.[13] Postmortem, everyone receives a "fosa común" (common grave), with no wake or ceremony (Bellatin 1999, 44). This represents for the narrator a kind of mute order (45). With the plague, the disease and its narratives become the identity.

Bellatin's text teases the reader to look for these parallels, and his images are deconstructive of the narrativizing moments of epidemia. As such, like Sontag's work, *Salón de belleza* can be read as a deeply ethical enterprise. That Bellatin is interested in bodies in all states, as Palaversich suggests (2003, 36), without imposing unthinking frames of judgment on them, allows him in this text to think through and about those very frames, a conscious work that agrees very much with his proposal that each novel or story provides a space for the exploration of ideas and the construction and deconstruction of metaphor. Bellatin is not didactic; he allows the textual clues to carry the weight of this semiosis of bodies, states, and diseases and to suggest that all three are only knowable by the ways in which we talk about them. This is what allows the novel to be both postmodern and ethical simultaneously. The juxtaposition of two views of the body—from the position of the subject invested with autonomy and then the same subject later colonized by an illness, its meanings, and therefore dehumanized or stripped of full admission to subjecthood—displays a critical thinking of the modes of representation of otherness. This narrative juxtaposition also reveals how narrativized epidemics, like AIDS, structure significations about biologically active illnesses. His text explodes with signification (multirhetorically), something very fitting given its subject.

In the article "Biomedical Discourse: An Epidemic of Signification" featured in the landmark anthology *AIDS: Cultural Analysis, Cultural Activism*, Paula Treichler states that AIDS "is simultaneously an epidemic of a transmissible lethal disease and an epidemic of meanings or signification" (1989, 32). Furthermore, for Treichler, like Sontag, AIDS is "a story or multiple stories, read to a surprising extent from a text that does not exist: the body of the male homosexual" (1991, 42). *Salón de belleza* is fundamentally invested in this body at its most culturally challenging, visible, and borderline—the body of the *loca* or *travesti* in the Latin American cultural imaginary. The time-lapse pictures of this body, exposed to an epidemic of signification, allow the reader to see a more morbid transformation occurring than that initially visualized as workaday magic in the former incarnation of the *moridero* as a beauty salon. Bellatin is highly conscious of the uses and misuses of "marginal" bodies, from their textuality to how they are circulated, read, rewritten, and concomitantly authorized or deauthorized. The stripping of humanity produced by the plague is connected to cultural-discursive processes of invalidation, in both senses of the word: making both invalid and *in*valid certain bodies. Such a project gives centrality to the work of normalization. This spins on the axes of identity construction and identity fracturing. The *campañas de desprestigio* (hate campaigns), the social exile, and the being forgotten as part of the human race—all elements emphasized in the text in relation to the disease—suggest the lines of disempowering narrativization that also accompanied AIDS as a social text in many parts of the world. In the novel, one is led to wonder what truly destroys those inflicted, as the physical facts of the disease are inseparable from their cultural import and patina of meanings. Treichler again provides clues to how this functions with AIDS:

> The epidemic of signification that surround AIDS is neither simple nor under control. AIDS exists at a point where many entrenched narratives intersect, each with its own problematic and context in which AIDS acquires meaning. It is extremely difficult to resist the lure, familiarity, and ubiquitousness of these discourses. The AIDS virus enters the cell and integrates with its genetic code, establishing a disinformation campaign at the highest level and ensuring the replication and dissemination will be systemic. We inherit a series of discursive dichotomies; the discourse of AIDS attaches itself to these other systems of difference and plays itself out there:

- Self and not-self
- The one and the other
- Homosexual and heterosexual
- Homosexual and "the general population"
- Active and passive, guilty and innocent, perpetrator and victim
- Vice and virtue, us and them . . .
- Addiction and abstention, contamination and cleanliness
- Contagion and containment, life and death . . .

In placing the cross-dressing narrator at the novel's center, making the ordinary strange and the strange ordinary through the detached enunciation of the text and its constellation of images, Bellatin critically engages with the terms of these binaries and their production through disease as narrative, from the point of view of those affected. He shows that this narrativization is a historically and discursively tied process and project, contingent on who wields social power. In *Salón de belleza*, this is the "moral majority" whose influence rules the outside world, the virtuous parents who endeavor to insulate their sons or daughters from the salon's "vices," the perpetrators of trans and homophobic violence, the "general population," and the predatory fish that eventually scare off their infected fish prey, in a parallel symbolic movement from the aquarium (the salon) to the outer world. The vision of the halcyon days of the protagonist's *loca* or *travesti* body provides a counterpoint to the mordant web of identity fracturing significations that the event of the disease brings. This may not have been possible via a third-person perspective explaining "marginal" existence in external realist mode.

The text is simple yet dense, but it does not exoticize *travestis* like Gutiérrez's, as we have seen, since the disease offers no possibility of romanticism. In a suggestive but by no means literal way, *Salón de belleza* evokes a world in which discourses have progressively broken down and delimited nonnormative identities and bodies in the most sinister way possible, through the stigma-enabling vehicle of epidemia. This circumvents the persistence and cultural survival of a world that would reconstruct gender in noncanonical ways, to follow the line of reasoning advanced by Mary Louise Pratt (2002). This threat to survival and persistence of a subculture mirrors the concerns that *cronistas* like Lemebel have about the social erasure and extinction of *travestismo* and *loca* homosexuality, an erasure facilitated in the persistent neoliberalist (but not unchallenged) setting in several Latin American nations, which is explored in Chapter 6. Roger Zapata is one critic who has pursued such an analysis in relation to the novel (Visiting Scholars 2003–4). Such considerations are extratextual, and yet at the same time, they add to the urgency of the ethics at play in the novel. Reading *Salón de belleza*, the reality of the fundamental mismanagement of the AIDS crisis in Latin America, the way the disease has been used to stigmatize as God's divine retribution, and the consequential further socioeconomic ghettoization of sexual minorities in the region are never far from one's mind.[14] Although Paolo de Lima endeavors to fix the setting in Peru or Mexico depending on perceptions of some of the novel's geographical or linguistic references, Bellatin's own dual national identification (Mexican Peruvian), and the lack of precise naming allows the novel to read multilocationally, which is likely closer to the writer's objective. The epigraph attributed to Yasunari Kawabata at the beginning of the novel, "Cualquier clase de inhumanidad se convierte, con el tiempo, en humana" (Any type of inhumanity becomes human in time), reinforces that the dehumanization of sex and gender minorities via the disease is particular to a discursive setting, and not necessarily to a country, and that nothing is inevitable, eternal, or natural about its productions.

Both *El Rey de La Habana* and *Salón de belleza* offer provocative appraisals of gender-variant or *travesti* subjectivity. The first differences between the texts that the reader will note are generic: the former pledges itself to a realist project of representing people marginalized in 1990s Cuba, that is, the avowedly poor and ordinary people forced by new circumstances to scrape by—as does the main character of the novel, Rey—in whichever way they can. Gutiérrez furnishes his text with language and scenarios immediately recognizable to anyone who has witnessed Cuba in its Special Period—a Cuba split down the middle and divided into two versions of itself: the tourist image of Cuba, open only to those with money—the elite and *extranjeros* (foreigners)—and the other Cuba not advertised in the travel brochures, but growing in numbers. This is the Cuba faithfully rendered by the narrator, composed of a floating collection of down and outs, drunkards, palm readers, peanut sellers, *pingueros* and *jineteras* (male and female sex workers), local *machos*, *maricones* and *lesbianas*, *santeros* and *santeras*, old and young, white and black, male and female, and, of course, *travesti*. The novel by Bellatin is equally effusive in its articulation but not bound to a physical location or the enterprise of painting portraits of an identifiable national reality. Bellatin playfully hints at elements of "a real world" but does not bow to realism.

In spite of this, certain culturally specific elements in the exploration of the sexual and discursive landscape in *Salón de belleza* can be deduced—for instance, the presence of the Church, the involvement of *travestis* in prostitution, the laws that prohibit this, and the occurrence of police mistreatment. There are some overlapping elements to the depiction of gender variance in the two novels. In both, *travestismo* points to a care of self and an erotic becoming. Its public expression is linked to prostitute identity in both novels that rely on codes identified with *vedettismo*. In both novels, *travesti* identity occupies a marginal space but is still part of the cultural panorama: cohering life-affirming qualities in its practice and a good measure of sexual autonomy and individuality. *Travestismo* in both novels also transcends limits—of expected sex role and of class—either literally in the case of gender crossing, or symbolically in terms of the associated ideals of class standing for Sandra and the salon's *peluquero (hairdresser)*. But it is in the differences between their figurations where some of the more compelling elements lie.

Through Gutiérrez's third-person onlooker mode, trans identity is more exoticized and pornographically investigated than in Bellatin's novel. Of course, Sandra is not the only character subject to this eroticizing and exoticizing gaze, but the narrator, focalizing through the young Rey, seems especially fascinated by the dissonances between the signs that sex the body and its *travesti*'s sense of gender self—the trans body is after all the most extraordinary body in this text. Roaming this body, we are given a view as to just how far Sandra has corporealized her gender identification, and this serves to authorize her as simultaneously female-like and other: a third gender, neither completely female nor completely male. I phrase this in terms of authorization, because the text does not deny her subjectivity; it in fact furthers it and endeavors to locate it in relation to Cuban tradition, most notably, in santería. This serves to legitimize her *travesti* identity as a fully lived option. Sandra is no impostor, unlike in other figurations of *travestis*, and she has a cultural place. Moving along the scale of gendered identification, Bellatin's vision of *travestismo* is engaged at the nexus between erotic pastime and the beautification of the body. His vision of *travestismo* is more comparable with (homosexual) transvestism or occasional cross-dressing and geared toward the expression of individuality and also commercial-erotic encounter. This gender identification may not be skin deep, but the kinds of discourse around it are, and, as such, *travestismo* in *Salón de belleza* emphasizes particularly the transgressive aspects of such lived practices, from the glorious to the stigmatized.

Both texts explore the body, but in a postmodern turn Bellatin invests more in how the trans body as text is constructed and deconstructed discursively, in different moments and settings. The latter are not particular to a geographical location but rather are the metanarratives of sexual and gender otherness. Bodies in Gutiérrez's text bear the marks of their subject's lives and experiences—for instance, malnutrition, and state of hygiene—and are also expressive of their inner person: reflecting *macho* or *hembrista* sexuality, dispositions, identifications, and inclinations. For Gutiérrez, in general terms, the body is the register of identity; unlike Arenas, he does not privilege concepts of natural above artificial because such terms do not exist for his vision of a postindustrial Cuba of the present, where bodies relate, interact, become, and perform according to the needs of the current setting and to gain mobility. One gets the sense in this novel that the body is the beginning and end of the store; it is the only really knowable quantity for its narrator—the physical facts of existence—and its potential. In contrast, bodies are not teleological in Bellatin; they are, in great measure, effects. Materiality is an effect of discourse, hence the embodiment of *loca* and *travesti* subjectivities is tied up in the struggle over the meaning of the sexually "marginal" body and transgressive bodily practices. Bellatin is involved in an ethical enterprise to chart what modulations this subjectivity has assumed under the discursive field of "sexual epidemia." In *Salón de belleza*, as we have seen, this meaning field is the plague whose intertext is AIDS. Concomitantly, Bellatin investigates how the normativizing processes of eroticization and deeroticization, and validation and invalidation operate in the struggle for power over meaning in disease. In stark contrast to the eroticization and exoticization of the gender-transgressive body in *El Rey de La Habana*, *Salón de belleza* embarks on the reverse, such is its deconstructive maneuver in unpacking the axes of what is deemed human in identity and what is not.

Bellatin's text can be read in terms of the neoliberalist setting that has imperiled the lives and livelihoods of persons economically and socially marginalized in Latin America—*locas* and *travestis*—but its power lies in its capacity to sit as a text wherever disease narratives like AIDS have impinged on the world scene—as indeed they have—and undermined the place of those vilified and excluded from the mainstream. His antirealism allows it this flexibility. Gutiérrez text implicates itself in the problematic of representation of national reality and "national fictions" by its very unanalyzed claims to realism. It is very much a question of reader positionality to the text. What is Cuban reality? Is Cuba a text that can be read and reproduced? Further, how can the critic assert that this is not a valid representation, when on some levels, we can find credence to support the placing of Sandra in the context of santería? And yet, on what authority can its narrator and implied author speak on behalf of those without a voice, the "Cuba of today," without playing into some prototypical or even stereotypical constructions of class, gender, sexuality, and national identity? On balance, the tendency toward troping trans identity to symbolize issues of national change or crisis is not a major feature here, just as it is patently absent in Bellatin's text. However, perhaps, as Aparicio and Chávez-Silverman might argue, there is a kind of troping going on in *El Rey de La Habana*, a more general kind: the attribution of particular characteristics to this group of people representative of *Cuba pobre* that mythologize and play on preconceived ideas of *cubanidad*, as often circulated in non-Cuban contexts.

The allegorization of *travestis* and transsexuals is brought sharply into focus in the next chapter. Although, as we have seen, the troping of gender crossing as purely representative of a national-cultural panorama or problem is far from universal in the contemporary setting, its persistence requires detailed theoretical inspection. This is undertaken by way of an analysis of two more novels, as well as of the critical discourse on gender crossing that operates within and around them.

CHAPTER 5

TRANS BODIES, POPULAR CULTURE, AND (NATIONAL) IDENTITY IN CRISIS

LUIS ZAPATA'S *LA HERMANA SECRETA DE ANGÉLICA MARÍA* AND MAYRA SANTOS-FEBRES'S *SIRENA SELENA VESTIDA DE PENA*

This chapter analyzes two texts: Luis Zapata's novel *La hermana secreta de Angélica María* (1989; *The Secret Sister of Angélica María*) from Mexico and Mayra Santos-Febres's novel *Sirena Selena vestida de pena* (2000; *Sirena Selena*) from Puerto Rico. These texts have three obsessions in common: the notion of the *travesti* and transsexual as seductive and dangerous, their intimate connection to popular culture through (musical) performance, and their problematic relationship with the idea of nation and identity. The highly celebrated novel by Santos-Febres has garnered much debate about the limits of national identity. Zapata's text has elicited a more meager critical response but can be seen as a precursor to Santos-Febres's work in its use of the notion of gender as performance through its tripartite deployment of the intersex, *travesti*, and transsexual subject in its main protagonist.

It is instructive to bring these texts together for their shared concerns in order to understand better the frames of reference that have persistently been used in visualizing gender-variant acts and persons. What brings the texts analyzed in this chapter so closely together is that both use the idea of trans or intersex bodies to theorize on the nature of identity. Santos-Febres's novel has been claimed critically for all kinds of agendas, in part suggested by the author herself in the context of Puerto Rico's current colonial status, and Zapata's novel inspires a set of theoretical considerations that overlap with some of those found in the Puerto Rican novel.

As I have argued in this book, chief among the frames of reference used in depicting *locas, travestis,* and other gender-variant acts and identities is the construction of the nation and the national subject. The allegorization of gender atypicality at the national level has its specific discursive antecedents in Puerto Rico. Mayra Santos-Febres's *Sirena Selena vestida de pena* could be understood as inheriting and responding to such discursive maneuvers. Luis Zapata's *La hermana secreta de Angélica María,* meanwhile, does not implicate the *travesti* or transsexual figure profoundly in the condition of the political state of nation or coloniality, as Mexico's own struggle for independence occurred in the early 1800s and its definition of "nationness" exhibits marked differences from that of Puerto Rico.

Mexico's most defining characteristics of "nationness" followed the 1910 revolution, and this remained relatively unchanged for almost seventy years under the ruling party, el Partido Revolucionario Institucional (PRI), the successor to the foundational Partido Nacional Revolucionario (PNR). The years between World War I and World War II were important in terms of cinema's projection of a dream of shared national and cultural characteristics.[1] The relatively unproblematized status of this dream ensued until a major break in the cultural imaginary following the 1968 Tlatelolco massacre. This was preceded by the beginnings of a student and youth movement that had started to question traditional values in the 1960s. In spite of the different status in terms of colonial history and distance in time from the complicated condition of cultural-political sovereignty between the two countries, Zapata's text still raises issues connected to cultural norms, their ossification, and their reification, especially in reference to gender ideals, as seen in popular song and the cinema, which are also constitutive of notions of "Mexicanness" in the pre-1960s period.

Santos-Febres's text responds to a very different set of conditions in Puerto Rico. The island has yet to obtain true independence or release from its colonial status with the United States. Colonial time past is also colonial time present. Puerto Ricans live both with the history of some 110 years of imperial domination by the United States (and several hundred more by the Spanish), as well as the ongoing nature of that domination. In this way, the island territory, which is not yet a sovereign nation, but, rather, an unofficial state of the United States, marks an exceptional case with respect to the geopolitical sites of production examined in this book. At a time when critics commonly invoke the concept of "post-coloniality," the "afterlife" of colonialism, Puerto Rican subjects still daily confront and negotiate the realities of historical colonialism as well as states of neocolonialism.[2] The discourse of nation thus figures much more prominently in Santos-Febres's text than in Zapata's text. This discourse has also morphed and taken on different shades in response to specific historical circumstances, circumstances that will be outlined at greater length later in this chapter.

The present chapter reads the texts with the view to interrogate the propositions that have given rise to these representations and that predispose the texts to the metaphorization of gender variance. It examines the forms of discourse that precede the texts historically and that might be seen to circulate in them, as well as the discourse produced around them in the wake of their dissemination as literary works.

Decentering Identity, Performing the Symbolic: Cinema as Script and Guide in *La hermana secreta de Angélica María*

The obsession with performance and decentering identity is a major hallmark of Luis Zapata's *La hermana secreta de Angélica María* (1989). The novel was written just over a decade before *Sirena Selena vestida de pena* and as such could be said to anticipate the lines of inquiry around transgender subjects as illustrative of the performative nature of gender that becomes so central to queer theory's project.[3] Zapata inherits the vision of Manuel Puig in his cinematic, campy, and popular-culture-referenced narratives. In Puig's *La traición de Rita Hayworth* (*Betrayed by Rita Hayworth*) and *El beso de la mujer araña* (*Kiss of the Spiderwoman*), the link between the inclusion of popular song, cinema, soap opera, and the construction of identity is clearly present. This is also true of Zapata's novel, and as Alejandro Herrero-Olaizola demonstrates in his article "Homosexuales en escena: identidad y *performance* en la narrativa de Luis Zapata," it is a recurrent feature in all the Mexican writer's works (1999–2000, 249–61). A further feature that advances the notion of identity as performed is the structuring of many of Zapata's texts as pure dialogues, as if they were play or film scripts. This is another element that Zapata has taken from Puig. However, the notion of identity as performance in *La hermana secreta de Angélica María* is tied more to the stage and screen and less indicated by the text's placement on the page. Rather, its highly parodic take on identity is reinforced by the presence of an omniscient narrator, noticeably absent in those works that take the form of a dialogue, *En jirones* (1985; *In Shreds*), *Melodrama* (1983), and *¿Por qué mejor no nos vamos?* (1992; *Wouldn't It Be Best to Leave?*) among them.

In *La hermana secreta de Angélica María*, this narrator has a superior, knowing, and mocking voice that frames our reading of the story and of the central character, who is composed of three aspects: Álvaro, the gender-different youth on the brink of adolescence; Alba, the young, nervous debutante singer, on tour with a caravan of other musicians; and Alexina, the transsexual cabaret performer. They are aspects of one another in a temporal sense—isolated in the different time frames that coalesce in the narrative. Alba María is the stage name assumed by Álvaro in a process of identification with an idolized heroine of popular song and Mexican cinema, Angélica María, *la Novia de México*. This identification occurs after Álvaro's own physical change at puberty; born with mixed genital morphology but birth-assigned as male, s/he begins to menstruate and develop breasts. Although the word is never used in the text (or by critics, who prefer to opt for the term hermaphrodite), Álvaro is recognizable as intersex. Álvaro begins to live as Alba, presenting a female identity while remaining very guarded about her foregoing and rather more complex gender history. It is here that the text begins its trajectory into the realm of *travestismo*, and ultimately, transsexuality, when Alba finally becomes Alexina.

This transformation into a sublime and demonic version of Woman has resonances with Angela Carter's 1977 novel *The Passion of the New Eve*, which also connects images of femininity to the cinema. In Carter's novel, a male-to-female transformation occurs, inspired in part by the personage of Tristessa, the ghost of Hollywood past. Tristessa is a paragon of feminine charm, seductiveness, and sensuality but turns out to be transsexual herself. The idealized object, taken from the realm of cinema, is itself a reconstruction. Similar tensions are at play in Zapata's novel. The naming of the final embodiment of the process of idealization through which Álvaro travels, becoming first Alba María (in homage to the great Angélica) and then Alexina, also echoes the sometime name of the real-life nineteenth-century French intersexual Hérculine Barbin, whose life Foucault brought to public attention on the discovery of her memoirs. Barbin was born with a small opening in the groin area, which was regarded as a vagina, and thus raised as a girl. At adolescence, she began to masculinize, and it was later determined that she had internal testicles. She continued with her female assignment, adopting the name Alexina. Only in adulthood for legal reasons was she reassigned as male, taking the name Abel (Rudacille 2005, 6–7). The novel reverses this movement. Álvaro becomes Alba, then Alexina. As such, it imbricates itself in the earliest known modern narrative of an intersexual, supremely aware of its own status as inscribing sex and gender variance in its many forms—intersexuality, *travestismo*, and transsexuality. The ascription of feminine gender identity to the gender-complex protagonist occurs in a similar manner to Carter's novel, wherein gender identity construction is linked to cinema images. The style of address of the protagonist him/herself by the third-person narrator and much of the tonality of the narrative is also similar to that found in *Sirena Selena vestida de pena*. The principal and important difference in *La hermana secreta de Angélica María* is that these images come from another popular imaginary that is resolutely Mexican, not U.S. American or Puerto Rican.

The presence of popular films and song accompanies the reader throughout the text. From a very early age, Álvaro is captivated by cinema. His grandmother takes him to the movies. This is where he takes cues for the secretly desired identity he will later assume. At home his *abuela* is his audience: "Álvaro le relata pormenorizadamente la historia; repite los diálogos significativos; le describe los vestidos; las escenografías; mima los gestos e imita las voces de los actores" (Zapata 1989, 23; "Álvaro tells the story in great detail; he repeats the meaningful dialogue; he describes the dresses; the props; he mimes the gestures and imitates the voices of the actors"). Where other children begin to structure their gendered styles from those around them, and are openly encouraged to adopt mannerisms and interests "appropriate" to their designated sex, Álvaro's only space of permission and identification is the darkened space of the movie theater. His first audience is his grandmother, but then he begins to "perform" his identification before schoolmates, again scripting it from cinema. As the text relates,

> En el cine, Álvaro ha aprendido actitudes y comportamientos diferentes de los de la mayoría de la gente que lo rodea, lo cual en muchas ocasiones le ha acarreado la burla de sus compañeros. Sabe cómo demostrar enojo con una simple mirada, indiferencia dando bruscamente la espalda a quien no merece una respuesta, altivez elevando la barbilla, languidez entrecerrando los ojos, sorpresa enarcando una ceja, displicencia mirando hacia un lado y frunciendo apenas la boca. Pocas actitudes le resultan tan elocuentes como las de Lilian Prado y Mary Esquivel. (24)
> [From cinema, Álvaro has learned attitudes and behaviors different from those of the majority of people around him, which has often brought about the mockery of his classmates. He knows how to show anger with a simple glance, indifference brusquely turning his back on anyone who doesn't deserve a response, haughtiness lifting his chin, languidness half-closing his eyes, surprise lifting an eyebrow, diffidence looking to one side and just curling his mouth. Few attitudes have held such eloquence as those of Lilian Prado and Mary Esquivel.]

The other significant source of this gender modeling as citation comes in the person of Angélica María, whom Álvaro first hears singing on the radio and later sees on the big screen. A sickly and lonely child with no friends, he records all her songs off the radio and cuts out newspaper clippings featuring her photos, gluing them into a scrapbook. He cannot relate to any of the male-oriented induction rituals of his peers. When he becomes Alba, the collected visions of Angélica María are central to his construction of a public identity. Performing in both real life and as a *ranchera* singer on stage, the narrator makes clear how Angélica María as a distant, disembodied cinematic ideal is appropriated by Alba and how conscious she is of gender and identity as performance:

> La imita: recuerda los parlamentos de sus películas, tantas veces vistas, y los repite en voz alta cuando nadie lo observa, tratando de reproducir los tonos y las inflexiones de su voz; canta sus canciones acompañado por la música y la voz provenientes del tocadiscos, o bien solo, camino a la escuela, cuando se imagina, como Ella, protagonista de películas y programas de televisión: obviamente una hipotética cámara lo sigue. (54)
>
> [He imitates her: he recalls all the lines from her films, seen so many times, and repeats them out loud when no one is looking, trying to reproduce the tones and inflections of her voice; he sings her songs accompanied by the music and voice issuing from the record player, or alone, on his way to school, when he imagines himself as Her, protagonist of films and television programs: obviously a hypothetical camera follows him.]

Angélica María began her career in Mexico at the age of six as a child actress. She then moved on to become known as a teen idol in soap operas, musicals, and *lucha libre* films in the 1950s. As her star rose, reporters began to refer to her as "la novia de la juventud" (youth's sweetheart), and then, simply, as "la Novia de México" (Mexico's Sweetheart). She became a paradigmatic role model for an era.[4]

Álvaro's fantasy realm, which is visualized in the everyday through cinema and song, is the *guión* by which Alba's self is publicly actualized and privately constructed through a series of citations or repetitions of idealized norms, with the world as her audience. I use the Spanish term "guión" as it conveys the idea of both script and guide. More than merely a role played by the protagonist, the *guión* of cinematic and popular song forms the direction and shape his/her identity takes, in the movement from Álvaro to Alba. As we shall see is the case in *Sirena Selena vestida de pena*, the notion that all identity is performance, which is constantly linked to "transgender," is emphasized by the use of song. The veteran—now has-been—performer who travels with the musical troupe, Amanda Murillo, observes "la caprichosa vida, como dice la canción . . . es dura" ("this capricious life, as the song says . . . is hard"), thus furthering the connection between life and popular song (59). She also makes clear the novel's suggestive cinematic scripting of life: "Sí, la vida es como una película, chula" (59; "Yes, life is like a film, sweetheart"). Alba undergoes a crisis of sorts when she is unable to find a cue from the *guión* of film and song to act as a person in the world. Or to put it another way, she cannot construct a self without reference to the films and ballads of Angélica María. Similarly, she cannot construct herself without reference to a scripted gender norm. Something in her emulation exceeds the mold, as the real Angélica, so obsessed over by the youthful Álvaro, has aged and moved on. The novel clearly frames the time period as the mid-to-late 1960s. No longer beholden to the 1950s' mores of femininity and norms of male-female relations that Alba so idealizes, Mexico itself has moved on. This is a version of chaste womanhood, unaffected by the heady throes of the incipient sexual revolution. When Betto, from the rock-and-roll group Amok, which is representative of the new wave of rebellion, starts pursuing her, she is evasive and adopts the poses of Angélica from one of her movies. She is unable to execute any move without reference to the image of the decent, virginal Catholic girl, which her grandmother so extols in the person of Angélica. That is, the most jaded, old-fashioned, precountercultural and presexual revolution notions of "woman," as seen in the films of the 1950s. The limits of the known for Álvaro-Alba are structured by cinema—there is nothing else. Moving outside these limits implies a loss of self, as there is no script, and a concomitant descent into madness. Alba in fact suffers from a kind of hysteria and neurosis, especially around sexual matters. When the tour arrives in Acapulco, the place is nothing like the town depicted in Angélica María's film *Buenos días, Acapulco* (*Hello Acapulco*). She screams and demands to leave. Unlike her idol, fortune does not shine on her; she finds herself without the promised extra gigs or the stardom. She continues to write her *cartitas a abuelita* (letters to grandma), feigning success and happiness and creating a character in the process. In spite of this, she increasingly experiences bodily instability and depersonalization (55–56). This comes after she is briefly implicated in the murder of Betto from Amok, who is found dead, face down in a fountain. Alba, in fact, is responsible for murdering Betto, but only after he makes an overtly sexual pass at her, pressing his erect penis into her while they embrace. This makes Alba spiral out of control and the scripting of her identity veers in another direction: that of murderess. She escapes suspicion, however, as his death is blamed on the performing *charro* (a Mexican incarnation of the cowboy), said to resent Betto for his long hair, taken as a sign of homosexuality.

The key ingredient here that constantly threatens Alba is the possibility of the public discovery of her intersexuality. Her intersexuality is a source of personal confusion and dismay, and her mixed genitalia comprise a set of (culturally) mixed messages upon which she is seemingly incapable of basing an identity. Intersexuality is spoken of in highly euphemistic and abject terms in the novel and is the central node around which issues of identity and its "baselessness" are explored. Álvaro's-Alba's "sexo de los ángeles" (113; sex of the angels) is also "el Problema Insoluble" (119; irresolvable problem). Historically, the debate about the sex of the angels pursued the question of whether they were male or female. It was a question of utmost philosophical and theological import to Rome during the mid-fifteenth century in the dying years of the Byzantine Empire. Bodies seen to be neither or both—intersex bodies—have been the subjects of diverse treatment over time and in different cultures. In some cultures, they are at the center of an epistemological crossroads; if identity materializes itself via a stable sex, that is, male or female, what then of those who very corporeality provides no (seemingly) solid referent? They may be either angelic or monstrous in the novel's terms. This is an epistemological crux that neither Álvaro nor his grandmother is willing to confront. Intersex is configured here as the lack of a stable bodily referent—the body exceeding the terms that dictate that bodies are either male or female and genders mimetically reflect this "fact." As such, the revelation of Álvaro's-Alba's mixed genitalia deploys the devices of abject horror. The first public discovery of these mixed genitalia is by a childhood friend, Toño:

> Álvaro se sorprende al ver el pene de su amigo: le parece más grande de lo normal. Toño reacciona de la misma manera, pero en su sorpresa hay además miedo, como si entrara en contacto con algo desconocido, algo, quizás, demoniaco, inexplicable.
> —¿Qué tienes ahí?— pregunta Toño.
> —Nada, nada— contesta Álvaro, que, asustado por la expresión de su amigo, intenta cubrirse de nuevo.
> —A ver, déjame ver.
> —¡No, no quiero!
> —¡Que me dejes ver, te digo!
> Toño lo empuja: los pantalones bajados hasta los tobillos le impiden cualquier movimiento y cae. Toño puede entonces separar las piernas de Álvaro y observar detenidamente su sexo, con una mezcla de repugnancia y curiosidad: bajo la verga, aún no desarrollada del todo, y donde deberían estar los testículos, hay una rajada como las de las mujeres de las fotos, rodeada por un vello incipiente. Como si estuviera ante un animal asqueroso. (87)
>
> [Álvaro is surprised on seeing his friend's penis: it seems bigger than normal. Toño reacts the same way, but in his surprise there's also fear, as if he had entered in contact with something unknown, something, perhaps, demonic, inexplicable.
> —What have you got down there?— Toño asks.
> —Nothing, nothing— answers Álvaro, who, frightened by his friend's expression, tries to cover himself again.
> —Hey, let's see.
> —No, I don't want you to.
> —Let me see I said!
> Toño pushes him: his pants pulled down to his ankles stop any movement and he falls. Toño then parts Álvaro's legs and stares carefully at his sex, with a mixture of disgust and curiosity: under his cock, there's a crack like those of women in the photos, surrounded by the beginnings of pubic hair. As if he were looking at a revolting animal.]

In her article "El femenino monstruoso," Diana Palaversich addresses the use of horror conventions in the novel by reference to Julia Kristeva's theories of horror and their reelaboration by Barbara Creed in her book on the monstrous feminine (1999–2000, 237). Abject bodies in horror films are tied up with the notions of the normal and abnormal, masculine and feminine, good and bad. Bodies that trespass or threaten to trespass these limits are abject, and this is key to the construction of the monstrous in this genre of film. For Palaversich, the feminization aspect is most clearly linked to the monstrous here: the presence of a vagina under the penis, which reveals itself again when Álvaro begins to menstruate (238).[5] Kristeva's thesis that the abject provokes both repulsion and attraction is present in Toño's response. It is unsurprising that Zapata fuses intersexuality to the terms of these cinematic codes of abject corporeality, since cinema frames the way that identity is constructed in the novel. The links between intersexed bodies, cinema, and the performance of the feminine also find their source in the nexus of the monstrous and the feminine—as excess, as overextended, and as phantasmagoric fantasy. The fantasy is scripted through the vehicle of "transsexuality," as we shall see.

The intersex body as a body with no solid sex referent, on which the feminine is scripted, becomes illustrative of the processes of all gendering. Intersexuality functions to demonstrate, for Zapata, that bodily life is not prior to gender identity. That is, gender is entirely a production or a projection, based on other productions and projections, without any previously established and reliable sexed materiality. If Álvaro-Alba is neither male or female, or both, or even a third sex, then the femininity that s/he constructs in the process of creating an identity does not have any direct basis in the body. This is very much in line with poststructuralist accounts of the materialization of gender, as typified by the queer theory of Butler: the body does not stand outside of discourse and "having a sex" cannot be separated from "gendering" or being gendered. There is no essence written in the body, no interior truth, no core gender identity, of which gendered expressions could be said to be a natural outcome. Thus, for the novel, there is no self to precede its enactment or scripting. The novel hence anticipates some key concepts that would prove fundamental to the work of queer theory.

The threat of exposure of the lack of a solid referent for Alba's gender risks plunging her into the realm of nonsubjecthood, however. Culturally recognized gender relies on the assumption that one is sexed in definite ways, with male or female morphology expressing male or female gender. Butler terms this "the metaphysics of substance" (Butler 1993, 10). As the abject attributions suggest, the lack of this substance is also a source of deep private shame. This is common to many accounts of growing up intersex in contemporary times; culturally, divergence from a "recognizable" anatomical sex is seen as highly anomalous and shameful, something to be hidden from view and not directly addressed (Kessler 1998; Chase 1999). Furthermore, in a clinical setting, it is seen as something to be corrected if the child is to attain a coherent sense of identity (Kessler 1998). This understanding is applied to those born intersexed in both Latin America and the English-speaking world (Cabral 2003; Cava 2004). In the medical management of intersex conditions, a clear physical sex reassignment is a matter of top priority, and parents are encouraged to downplay the fact of their child's difference (Preves 2003). This may shroud the child's intersex history in mystery, stigma, and silence.

Álvaro's intersexuality is shrouded in secret, just as his/her birth, origins, and parentage are. Álvaro's grandmother invents myriad stories to explain the absence of any mother or father in his/her life: that they died in the flood of 1952, that they took off with a circus; an incurable illness struck them down, a trailer ran them over on a highway and Álvaro was not with them because s/he had the mumps, God took them, s/he was really born in Brazil and his/her father had a diamond mine, his/her parents died in a plane crash and only s/he survived in the jungle, and so on (Zapata 1989, 119–20). Only when she is dying does *abuelita* reveal the real reason behind their disappearance—Álvaro's intersexuality. Addressing Álvaro as *mi hijito* and *mi hijita*, she relates that because of the "Problema Insoluble," they grew ashamed and abandoned Álvaro and traveled with his/her older sister (119–20).

Álvaro-Alba experiences that mark of shame typical of the intersex subject whose condition becomes an elaborately managed secret—the product of lies, stories, and avoidance. This shame, mainly sublimated in the novel, causes Álvaro-Alba to perceive other bodies and their sexed nature as a threat, a reminder, and a return of the repressed. Álvaro's-Alba's ascription to suffocating notions of feminine *pudor* (modesty) derives from a denial of the body—others' and his/her own. Early on, the novel contains a scene in a school change room where Álvaro watches the other boys' naked bodies and is forced to confront the possibility of displaying his own, but cannot, and vomits (80–81). Bodily fluids—or the hint of them—also cause similar reactions. This is itself a typical reaction in the presence of the abject. As a boy and young virginal woman, the protagonist reminds us, in another cinematic reference, of the psychotic and melodramatic character played by Catherine Deneuve in *Repulsion*.[6]

Álvaro-Alba also undergoes the other classic dilemma experienced by many intersexuals—given much attention in the Preves study—that is, the desire to know others like him/herself in spite of the perceived dangers of self-revelation (Preves 2003, 45). Ironically, this is what the "secret sisterhood" referred to in the novel is ultimately about; the need for connection to others like him/her, at first, the much-fantasized Angélica

María (whom she sees as "her sister"), and then, the *travestis* whom Alba meets in Tijuana. For it is on arrival in Tijuana that Alba begins to identify herself with others who similarly aspire to assume a gender seemingly without basis in their genital morphology (according to cultural logics). Zapata at this point paints a brief portrait of *travesti* club culture in Tijuana—an underground of subjects who seek alignment with the feminine and an eroticized identity attractive to men. These *travestis* exist in the world of the *farándula*: shows, sex, and bodily modifications obtained clandestinely. When Alba seeks cohesion for her identity via a stable bodily referent, one of the *travesti* women gives Alba the address of a clinic where she can get "help." The lack of cohesiveness continues to plague her, especially when a star reporter, Alberto Muñiz, attempts to seduce her and discovers, like Toño earlier, her secret. Alba incarnates, in another fit of madness, off scene and without script, the murderess, in a telling sequence where she kills Alberto and cuts off his penis. Her desire for sex reassignment surgery (SRS) is then equated by Zapata with this act of castration.

Curiously the medicalization of intersex lives is not something the novel deals with in any degree—Álvaro undergoes no surgery or genital reassignment as a child or adolescent and in fact only opts to have surgery as an adult. This might be explained by the fact that Zapata is more interested in deploying intersexuality for symbolic or theoretical, not lived, concerns. Moreover, the third-person narrator does not express much empathy for the protagonist, but relates his/her life in a ludic, if fascinated, way. Zapata's narrator does not show any empathy for the predicament of the intersex subject who, zealously desirous of a stable identity because of cultural imperatives of "recognizability," will, at times and with great deliberation, attempt to be convincing, pass, and not be "found out" (Preves 2003, 82–83). Instead, for Zapata, Alba's entry into the medicalized world of transsexual transition is an excessive imposition on a body that refuses containment. The narrative voice constantly mocks every stage of its protagonist's evolution, dramatizing it in terms of melodrama, or as Palaversich notes, by reference to B-grade or pulp conventions (1999–2000, 237).[7] Transsexual transition becomes the most conservative reification of the logic of sexed body (as referent) and gender norms (as signifier). In this novel, it involves an adherence to a specified script—as primordial feminine, Carter's "New Eve," the object of men's desire, the first woman on the face of the Earth, and the femme fatale of cinema:

> Tal vez en lo que ha gastado más energías sea en la construcción de una personalidad coherente: día tras día . . . ha pensado en la persona que quisiera llegar a ser, en su lenguaje, sus gestos, su voz, su manera de caminar, su mirada, la forma en que ha de enfrentar el mundo. De la inicial ausencia de

identidad ha pasado a convertirse no solo en una mujer hecha y derecha, sino en una mujer con una personalidad arrolladora. (Zapata 1989, 138)
[Perhaps what she has spent most energy on is in the construction of a coherent personality: day by day . . . she has thought of the person she wanted to be, her language, gestures, voice, gait, gaze, the way of facing the world. From her initial absence of identity she has gone on to become not only a woman through and through, but a woman with a devastating personality.]

The surgeon, Angel Morán, provides the medical narrative of transsexuality through which she can become that out-and-out woman with a devastating, seductive femininity. He and Alba's newfound trans friends state that she was always, *en el fondo*, a "true" woman, with a true "core gender identity" that should be uncovered with the scalpel. As soon as Alba steps into Dr. Morán's consultation room, she engages with this discourse. The realization of SRS itself becomes yet one more stage for a performance of another identity, this time, anchored in the body by way of surgical reassignment. Alba imagines herself at her "reveal" in the operating theater (note both meanings) as an actress receiving an Ariel award (the Mexican equivalent of the Oscars) for her "actuación" (acting). She must always take her cue from some cinematic diva. Indeed, she cannot proceed without such a cue (126).

Lleva la mano hasta los pechos, ahora voluminosos y redondos, y hasta la entrepierna, donde nada empaña ya su condición femenina: precisamente por esa carencia, ahora sí es una mujer completa: se gesta en ella la Verdadera, la Mujer de Lava y Fuego, la que enloquecerá de pasión a todos los hombres. (126–27)
[She lifts her hand to her breasts, now full and round, and to her inner thighs, where nothing can mire her feminine condition: precisely for that absence, now she is a complete woman: in her gestates the True One, the Woman of Lava and Fire, she who will drive every man mad with passion.]

Dr. Morán is the most enthusiastic audience member of this particular performance: the fulfillment of the mythical Feminine, a creation faithful to his own medicalized script of sex and gender. Moreover, this script is utilized for the performance of another kind of stereotypical femininity in Mexican culture, that of the *ramera*, the whore, or the hypersexualized feminine. If Alba represents the virgin in the virgin-whore dichotomy, then Alexina is the other side of the equation:

Alexina, la sensualidad encarnada, la exuberancia hecha mujer, la de las piernas de oro, la de la cabellera de fuego, la de la boca carmesí; Alexina toloache de los hombres, digitalina de los ancianos, yombina de los jóvenes, la que causa emisiones involuntarias de semen en los adolescentes: Alexina . . . receptáculo de fantasias eróticas, pañuelo de sueños mojados. (29)

[Alexina, sensuality incarnate, exuberance made woman, she of the golden legs, she of the fiery mane, she of the carmine red lips; Alexina, hallucinogen of men, heart tonic for the aged, aphrodisiac of young boys, she who causes involuntary nocturnal emissions among teens: Alexina . . . receptacle of erotic fantasies, handcloth of wet dreams.]

However, as things transpire, her body rebels, and the fantasy of gender identity (and sexed embodiment) that Alexina craves fails to live up to reality. The bars in which Alexina performs are tawdry and anything but glamorous. The myth Alexina so literally tries to embody proves to be little more than a flickering image on a screen—Plato's reflections in the cave. The irony is double given the constant framing of life and identity in cinematic terms. "Does gender have a reality outside of its construction and performance?" Zapata wants to ask. These ideal forms come from somewhere, but they do not inhabit any prediscursive material realm, and their materialization is secured by imitation, by performance, which serves to mask its constructedness. Álvaro-Alba makes no distinction between the screen and life or between fantasy and reality, and thus psychologically inhabits a liminal place, suggestive of insanity and instability.[8] His/her return to bodily "in-betweenness" (as the body rebels against surgery) ultimately becomes a reflection of this status.

TRANS AND INTERSEX BODIES AS SYMBOLIC CONSTRUCTS OF THEORY: SOME IMPLICATIONS

Politically, the use of both intersexuality and transsexuality to map the novel's issues has some significant consequences. Zapata may anticipate elements of queer theory's deployment of the transgender figure as illustrative of gender and its construction, but he is also susceptible to psychoanalytic takes on the feminine, on hysteria, and on transsexuality. In *Horsexe: Essay on Transsexuality*, which was originally published in French in 1983, Catherine Millot, a French psychoanalyst, engages Lacan and claims that transsexuals make demands on the Real for its adjustment (1991, 22). Connecting the Real to sexual difference,[9] for Millot, transsexuals wish to erase bodily limits, which in some accounts of sexual difference, are judged as simply natural facts.[10] Again for Zapata, the body may represent the Real—intersexed or not—and any intervention to naturalize femaleness or maleness by recourse to the body is a kind of excessive demand on that Real, the product of intense fantasy, and a projection that draws on and is reflected in the shared language of cinema and popular song—the Symbolic. Binding transsexuality to these terms and linking intersex to psychosis may make for interesting parody and theoretical musings, but it also does nothing to destigmatize or depathologize those who live as intersexual or transsexual in the real world, the latter especially charged with living in a fantasy world. The theoretical takes on intersex and transsexuality as either examples of gender (de)construction or as forms of psychotic liminality and fantasy, which come from social constructionist and psychoanalytic accounts, respectively, are patently very influential in *La hermana secreta de Angélica María*. The appearance of theoretical sophistication may encourage the reader to reinforce the image of intersexuality, transvestism, and transsexuality as paradigmatic of identity construction and dissolution. They are, at best, props for the staging of theories of identity and identification in this supremely genre-aware text. However, just as the characters who never develop any depth should not be taken for "real" people—intersex, *travesti*, or transsexual—neither should the reader look to the novel's framings of intersexuality and transsexuality as accounts of livable and lived subjectivities. One would be mistaken for believing that the novel explores the life of an intersex or transgender individual. Instead, Zapata's novel is steeped in an array of postulations on gender production and ascription, and anything resembling a subjectivity is forestalled and perhaps even disappears under the weight of the novel's style and the irony of its rhetorics. Intersex and transgender cannot mean anything in *La hermana secreta de Angélica María* except in connection to ideas of identity, their performance, and the reification of gender norms.

Much has been written on the way medical protocols defining who counts and does not count as a "true transsexual" take the form of a prescriptive set of models, which reflect the most heterosexist and bipolar of gender ideals (Raymond 1980; Hausman 1995). Transitioners who wish to have access to medical assistance and surgeries, some writers have argued, adapt their particular life histories to suit this script (Hausman 1995; Stone 1991; Stryker 2006). Similarly, transsexuality in Zapata's novel is only understood in these particular terms. In becoming Alexina, the subject-in-crisis Alba is written into a recognized and valorized version of femininity available to heterosexual men and as mirrored in the cinema of the 1940s and 1950s. The text does not visualize the possibility of being transsexual and not submitting to some preordained script. It understands transsexuality as fully produced in those terms and thus forecloses other potential scenarios in which the subject experiencing gender dysphoria may stylize their identity in the clinical setting yet understand and live their transsexuality in a very different way outside the consultation room, aware of the disjuncture between that version of self presented to doctors and that presented in intersocial relations away from the medical discourse.

Palaversich argues that Zapata's novel anticipates but also extends upon the Butlerian celebration of transgender as a subversive exposure of gender constructedness by showing that such theoretically assumed subversion can have dire consequences in the real world. She rightly admonishes the lack of investigation beyond the purely figural in understanding the implications of transgender subjectivities (1999–2000, 234). She cites the failure of Alexina's transsexual trajectory of gender cohesiveness as evidence of this limited "figurative" approach and argues that Zapata endeavors to portray the potential perils of gender crossing in the real world (234). Given its parodic tone, I would suggest that the novel does not give the real world much profile. To be sure, the tragic end of its protagonist and her increasing isolation and descent into madness may provide a picture of marginalization and psychic exile—effects produced by the societal stigma of intersex and gender-crossing subjects in the real world. However, because of the distancing effect produced by the third-person omniscient, mocking narrative voice, little in Alba-Alexina's world can be taken seriously, and her suffering is revealed as just as theatrical as her attempts at securing a stable gender via a recognizable script. We are meant to laugh at her; her experiences are trivialized. Our sympathy as readers is not summoned by this ironic narrative framing. None of the avowed social and institutional exclusions experienced by transgender people in the real world are mentioned. In fact, the reverse is true. Alba María is the aggressor in the novel. In the real world, most commonly it is *travesti* and transsexual subjects who are found murdered or battered by police and civilians alike because of their (perceived) transgression. The reversal here suggests that Alba's difference—first referenced to the "monstrosity" of his/her intersexuality, then later to *travestismo*—is an inherent cause of violence and instability, a threat in itself. This is a common depiction in novels and films from many parts of the world—the trans figure as mad, murderous, and criminally insane. Society's sex-gender rigidity is never the murderous force.

In the novel, transsexual transition is also spoken of in reference to advances in technology (Zapata 1989, 116). This "idea of the transsexual" views transsexuals and transsexuality as purely a post–World War II medical phenomenon whose prescriptive models of gender identity reify the era's norms (Raymond 1980; Hausman 1995). Such an idea has a lineage within feminism and sociological analyses of the medical and psychiatric production of illness (Raymond 1980; Hausman 1995; Billings and Urban 1982). As Prosser states, this work tends to "isolate medical discourses to the exclusion of subjective accounts and to emphasize the transsexual's construction by the medical establishment. The transsexual appears as medicine's passive effect, a kind of unwilling technological product: transsexual subject only because subject to medical technology"

(1998, 7). Raymond claims that transsexuality is an embodiment of sexist stereotypes and relations of medicine (1980, 70), while for Hausman, all transsexuals are "dupes of gender" (1995, 140). In *La hermana secreta de Angélica María*, the protagonist in all his/her three aspects—Álvaro, Alba, and Alexina—is that passive product of the most reiterative norms of gender that have no place in contemporary life—Mexican culture having moved on somewhat from the dichotomous notions of women and men found in pre-1960s representations—and no real place in a body, which ultimately refuses its inscriptions.[11]

Claudia Schaefer suggests that the novel presents Alba María as the ultimate queer reader of hegemonic mass forms, giving her an active agency in her appropriations of ideals and norms of cinema and popular song (2003, 126–27). I argue, however, that the seeming inevitable downfall of this character would suggest the opposite, and in this sense I agree with Palaversich when she surmises that Schaefer exhibits wishful thinking in making this assertion (1999–2000, 240). The text encourages the reader to view transsexuality in the same terms as the mass cultural products of a bygone age that instate hegemonic gender norms, that is, as cultural dinosaurs. The transsexual subject is about as real as the image on the screen so parodically replayed. The third-person narrator and parodic style forecloses both our potential empathy with the intersex and trans figure deployed and the possibility of a subjective account of the intersexuality and transgenderism depicted in the novel. Realism is not the novel's point, but as a representation of intersexuality and transsexuality—one of the few to do both—it necessitates consideration in this political light.[12] Intersex and transgenderism in this novel function to talk about gender, culture, and its mechanisms of reproduction. Moreover, they are the butt of an intellectual in-joke: figural, mad, spectral, and B-grade, never able to achieve constative grounding, and ultimately, therefore, impossible as viable subjectivities.

Dressing the Nation, Redressing Colonialism: Mayra Santos-Febres's Account of *Travestismo* and Caribbean Identity

A key recent text that features a *travesti* as its protagonist is *Sirena Selena vestida de pena*, by Mayra Santos-Febres. Unlike Luis Zapata's novel, Santos-Febres's evocative text introduces the reader to a fictionalized community of Puerto Rican street and stage *dragas* and *vestidas*, that is, performing drag queens and full-time trans subjects. This work is one of the most discussed in the contemporary period and has attained both popular and critical prominence. Born in 1966, Santos-Febres is the author of four collections of poetry—*Anamú y manigua* (1991a; *Anamú and manigua*), *El orden escapado* (1991b; *The Escaped Order*), *Boat People* (2005a), and *Tercer mundo* (1999; *Third World*)—and two collections of short stories, *Pez de vidrio* (1994; *Glass Fish*) and *El cuerpo correcto* (1996; *The Correct Body*). She has written two other novels, *Cualquier miércoles soy tuya* (2004; *Any Wednesday I'm Yours*) and *Nuestra señora de la noche* (2006; *Our Lady of the Night*), and a collection of essays, *Sobre piel y papel* (2005b; *On Skin and Paper*), apart from *Sirena Selena vestida de pena*. She studied literary theory and has a PhD in Arts and Letters from Cornell University. For the past eight years she has taught in this field at the University of Puerto Rico, focusing in particular on African and Afro-Caribbean literatures and feminist theory. Given this background, it can be reasonably assumed that Santos-Febres has been cognizant of the emergence of queer theory and its impact on understandings in gender studies. Her work exhibits a postmodernist style mixed with an interest in political questions. When considering what binds all her texts together in an interview with Marcia Morgado, she states,

> Me imagino que lo que sí las une (porque es eterna pasión mía) es una preocupación por la experiencia urbana caribeña. Me obsesiona cómo se vive en las ciudades del Caribe, ese pegote de infraestructura primermundista, visión alterada por los sueños "civilizados" de las naciones que nos colonizaron. (Morgado 2000)
> [I guess that what links these works (as it's an eternal passion of mine) is the concern with Caribbean urban experience. How people live in the cities of the Caribbean obsesses me, that lacquer of First World infrastructure, the altered vision of the "civilized" dreams of the nations that colonized us.]

This places her firmly in the tradition of that political literature that seeks to understand questions of cultural identity and critique the realities of historical and present-day colonialism in Puerto Rico and the Caribbean in general. In her work we witness a concern, then, not simply for Puerto Rican national identity, but also a Pan-Caribbean one. *Sirena Selena vestida de pena* in fact takes place in two national locales—Puerto Rico and the Dominican Republic. It explores, in part, the complex political relationship between those two places, the kind of secondary form of domination that Puerto Rico exerts on the other as a consequence of the wider conditions of globalization and coloniality. Santos-Febres does, however, write from the position of a Puerto Rican black woman, and both implicitly and explicitly her work is driven by the events of Puerto Rican history, its past and present-day relationship with that manifestation of the "First World" whose presence is so keenly felt in Puerto Rico, the United States.

Santos-Febres has also stated that her experience as a black woman allows her to understand "marginality" in a particular way, to relate to a set of marginalities across categories, as her identity itself is moveable and subjective (Morgado 2000).[13] *Sirena Selena vestida de pena* might be seen, then, as an exploration of "marginality," chiefly through the *travesti* protagonist performer of the title, Sirena, and her mentor, the transsexual Martha Divine. And yet the novel purposely introjects itself into debates on national reality and sociocultural norms, if comments by the author on her use of *travestismo* in the novel are to be taken into account:

> Utilizo al personaje de *Sirena*, un travestí, de dos maneras, una metafórica y otra social. El concepto de travestismo me ayuda a pensar en cómo está organizada la sociedad en el Caribe y en América Latina: sus ciudades son travestis que se visten de Primer Mundo, adoptan los usos y las maneras que nos les corresponden a fin de "escapar" de su realidad y acercarse a lo que cada día se ve más lejos: el progreso y la civilización. (Güemes 2000, 57–58)
> [I use the character, Sirena, a travesti, in two ways: one metaphorical and the other social. The concept of *travestismo* helps me to think about how society in the Caribbean and Latin America is organized: their cities are *travestis* who dress up as the First World, who adopt uses and ways that don't correspond to them in order to "escape" their reality and to get closer to what every day edges further away: progress and civilization.]

In this statement, we can see a dense marrying of the idea of *travestis* with the notion of a Caribbean and Latin American contemporary reality. It understands *travestis* as individuals who appropriate something that does not correspond to them: feminine attire "incongruent" with their birth-assigned sex. An essentialist statement, it metaphorizes a taken-for-granted tension (bodily sex vs. performed gender) and extends its terms to Caribbean and Latin American "reality." Present on an implicit level is the couple First and Third World, with the latter embodying an essence that is dressed up with the norms of a superficial, external culture, the First World, in what amounts to a strange imposition motivated by the pressure for disguise and flight. This "dressing" represents a betrayal of an original self, an illusory and ideologically duped mimesis.

All these linkages are of crucial significance in the politics of representation that this study has endeavored to put into question. They are important axes to the ways in which the novel has been read. The majority of critics either gloss over or ignore the so-called social dimension to Santos-Febres's depiction of *travestismo* in the novel, which is all the more strange considering that this writer is seen as part of a new generation of postmodern writers that resists the tradition to read everything in terms of nation and national discourse. While issues of colonialism and identity may still be in range, binaristic notions of national essences—the colonized versus the colonizer—have given way to more complex treatments. For many years the nation, as a singularity and an ideal to be defended, was the assumed point of reference through which many phenomena were read. As Jorge Duany states in his study *The Puerto Rican Nation on the Move: Identities on the Island and in the United States*, "the search for the essence of the nation has continued unabated throughout the twentieth century, especially among colonized peoples such as Puerto Ricans" (2002, 12). This has been all the more urgent given the "ambiguity" around the question of the relationship between the United States and Puerto Rico, which politically is considered a unofficial state of the union—a so-called Estado Libre Asociado (ELA) of the United States or a member of the U.S. Commonwealth. The relationship is "ambiguous" because Puerto Rico is defined neither as a full state nor as an independent nation, and both options have been points of political organizing. The independence cause has adopted a nationalist stance in this context, seeking to understand the "national essence" in the face of cultural and political domination by the United States. Further, as Duany points out, "local intellectuals—especially college professors, scholars, and writers—have played a role in the construction of a nationalist discourse disproportionate to their numbers. Here as elsewhere, the local intelligentsia has helped to define and consolidate a national culture against what it perceives as a foreign invasion" (2002, 26). Both Antonio S. Pedreira and René Marqués, two chief architects of Puerto Rican nationalist discourse, easily fit this mold. In their work Pedreira (1930s) and Marqués (1950s and 1960s) established the paradigmatic national discourse around the concept of *la gran familia puertorriqueña* (the great Puerto Rican family), a dispersed mix of racial and ethnic groups including Africans, Spanish, and Taíno Indians, forever presided over by a patriarch who needed to control his "children," who require development toward an independent nation or notion of unity. Pedreira's *Insularismo* (1934) reads Puerto Rican history, commencing at the point just before the invasion of U.S. forces, as the story of a child becoming a teenager who suffers from a developmental disorder and never properly matures into the man he is meant to become; he is thus forever in a transitional phase or hybrid state. In the patriarchal logic of Pedreira's work, the development of the nation is depicted in male terms; the influence of women and femininity risk this development. Although, as Ben Heller points out, the origin of the nation is associated with the feminine, springing forth from the sinuous and "subdued" landscape of the island, this feminine character represents an impediment and a source of submission for Pedreira, which, combined with the "mixed races" that make up Puerto Rican ancestral heritage, are seen as causes of laxity, torpor, and retardation (Heller 1996, 394).

Pedreira thus diagnosed his countrymen and women as submissive and as victims of the "feminine nature" of the environment they inhabited. The relative isolation of the island and its very geography hindered, according to Pedreira, the active assumption of responsibility for the nation's destiny, quashing any real efforts toward fighting for and achieving autonomy. The feminine was conceived by Pedreira as both the ground of Puerto Rican culture but also its chief obstacle. Or as Heller relates, the maternal matter of the *tierra* needs domination from above (Heller 1996, 395), echoing Kaminsky's observations as noted in Chapter 1. Pedreira urges "la expansión vertical . . . para cultivar ideas y sentimientos viriles" (Pedreira 1992, 61; "vertical expansion . . . to cultivate virile ideas and feelings").[14] This involves the mastery of (linear) masculine, rational intellect over the primordial, instinctive, fluid, and "unpredictable" feminine, qualities also attributed by Pedreira, as we have seen, to Puerto Rico's African heritage. By turns both racially and biologically deterministic, Pedreira sees the feminine—with its overwhelming and enervating potential of *feminization*—as a risk to the youth of his time. Assuming the pose of José Enrique Rodó, famed writer of the earlier *Ariel*, he seeks to avert this perceived doom, that is, the state of betwixt and between (Heller 1996, 396).[15] Diagnosing "indefinition" and "passivity" not simply in terms of racial mix but also in terms of the confusion of languages (English and Spanish) in which all Puerto Ricans become interpreters or go-betweens between the United States and the island, Pedreira likens the experience of U.S. colonization to being "mounted" (Pedreira 1992, 177); for the generation of youth in the 1930s, this could only lead, argues Pedreira, to an incrementation in the number of "muchachos serviles" (servile young men), "indulgentes" (indulgent), that is, of "afeminados, insufribles hasta la vulgaridad" (effeminate men, insufferable in their vulgarity) who are already ubiquitous on the island (177–78). Such a turn of events would further impede the development of nation and a firm national identity and purpose. The island, to fulfill its destiny, must leave behind the feminine and "mature" into a man.

Marqués wrote some two and a half decades after Pedreira but under changed historical conditions related to the increasing divide between urban and rural centers on the island and waves of migration of workers to the United States, a phenomenon that produced something of an economic underclass of Puerto Ricans in cities like New York. This generation of Puerto Ricans became identified with the realities of dislocation, penury, and urban squalor of a displaced population in an Anglo-dominant U.S. context. In this setting, Marqués draws inspiration from his predecessor in charging that Puerto Ricans suffer from a kind of inferiority complex made worse by their inherent "docility." In his essay "El puertorriqueño dócil" (1966; "The Docile Puerto Rican"), Marqués charges that Puerto Ricans have lost their sense of masculine honor and become swamped by a new model of matriarchy, derived from the colonial power, the United States (1966, 170–71). Like Pedreira before him, who charged that the increase of women in teaching positions was detrimental to the nation's youth (Pedreira 1992, 118–20), implicitly positing a dangerous feminization of the island, Marqués's aversion toward women translates into a disdain toward so-called weak and timid men (Marqués 1966, 203). Marqués, writing in the face of some fifty years of colonial domination by the United States, viewed the problem of Puerto Rican national identity in equally binaristic ways. In a context in which the already ambiguous nature of Puerto Rican-U.S. relations became even more confounded by the definition of Puerto Rico as an ELA, the presence of economic imperialism seemed unlikely to draw to a close. An essayist and short-story writer who formed part of the "Generation of the 1950s," Marqués witnessed firsthand the haphazard and polarizing changes effected by "Operation Bootstrap," a program designed to "modernize" and industrialize the island's economic base. This program, while overcoming to some extent the monoculture of sugar, resulted in the massive displacement of many Puerto Ricans from the countryside to urban areas on the island, as well as the mentioned migration to the United States.

In this context, U.S. might became increasingly gendered as masculine and the *isla colonizada* gendered as feminine in the literature of Marqués and several of his contemporaries (Vega 2007). Marqués's work, like Pedreira's, notably deploys binaries of masculine and feminine, aggressive and docile, and active and passive in describing what he sees as Puerto Ricans' inability to overcome their colonial circumstances. The wavering or lack of definition he describes is related, in Marqués's view, to the Puerto Rican tendency to seek escapism, sweeten the bitter pill of reality, and understand things euphemistically and thus not name them "as they are" (1966, 188). They are also, for Marqués, the typical signs of the weak, submissive man. This discourse in its particular Puerto Rican manifestation foreshadows the construction of *locas* and *travestis* as symbols of national-colonial problematics in Santos-Febres's novel, *Sirena Selena, vestida de pena*. This is perhaps unexpected in the case of a writer both female and of color, given the misogynistic and racist overtones of the Pedreira-Marqués discourse.

Santos-Febres, writing at the end of the twentieth and beginning of the twenty-first centuries, forms part of the island's present-day intelligentsia, although she might be said to fit a different mold than the type implicit in the patriarchal values of the discourse of Pedreira and Marqués. Her work, however, like that of Marqués, exhibits a concern with the transformation of urban environments, "outside" influences, and the vagaries of national and regional cultural identity. Yet, added to this, she is pinpointed by many as part of the new generation, less concerned with the either-or national argument for the island's colonial status or its autonomy.[16] This new generation, as Duany understands it, is composed of "those postmodernist writers [that] have charged that the nationalist discourse [the notion of the unity of the nation] tends to obscure the multiple fissures and fragments within Puerto Rican society, including class, race, gender and sexual orientation" (Duany 2002, 23). For many of these writers, nationalism can be as exclusionary and oppressive as colonialism. Hence, a key intellectual and political issue within contemporary Puerto Rico is the characterization of national identity as homogeneous or hybrid (2002, 23).

Ostensibly, the social dimensions to her choice of *travestismo* to center her novel open the space of culture and social relations as imagined textually to expose the "multiple fissures and fragments within Puerto Rican society," most pointedly with respect to gender and sexual orientation. Or in the words of Arnaldo Cruz-Malavé, who interrogates the notion of "national culture" as a discourse through which the bourgeoisie, heirs to the nineteenth-century *hacendado*, sought and gained hegemony for its model of capitalist modernization, we might assume that *Sirena Selena vestida de pena* offers an example of "writing from the margins of modernization, either from the perspective of those who had been marginalized within 'the nation' or from the vantage point of those that had been literally excised from it" (1995, 140). Like other marginalized groups who have achieved more recognition historically, *travestis* and transsexuals of many ethnic backgrounds have also occupied a subaltern position in Puerto Rico.[17] Given their historical exclusion from the very notion of "citizen" in many Latin American zones, the ironies of the framing of *locas* and *travestis* in terms of nation are notable. Santos-Febres's positioning of the *travesti* at the heart of the problematics of national culture, imperialist influence, and urban change seems to echo the former historical emblematization of the feminized or passive subject—ambiguous in his/her mixity—in nationalist discourse. In the quote by the author about her dual use of *travestismo*, cited previously, Santos-Febres suggests that this metaphorization also functions in her novel to narrate the specific social realities of her subjects. And yet how can the use of *travestismo* as a socially embedded reality and a metaphorical representation work together, especially when that metaphorization misapprehends and even maligns *travestismo*? Does not one cancel out the other? In speaking symbolically in the name of the colonized national subject, can one also speak to the lives of subjects so often misrecognized culturally? How complete is the intent to paint the social dimensions of *travesti* lives and how has the text become refunctionalized to use *travestismo* as pure allegory vis-à-vis the author's own avowals and the repeated claims of many critics? These questions are central to the present discussion. The connection to former nationalist and patriarchal discourse would appear uncanny, working as it does manifestly against the interests of those sectors—mulatto, black, female, and queer—most rejected from the terms of the unified and masterly nation. As a precursor to an exploration of the use of *travestis* as metaphor and whether this dominates the reception of the text, a consideration of the social dimensions to the novel's portrayal of *travestismo* is required to clarify the issue.

THE SOCIAL REALITY OF *SIRENA SELENA VESTIDA DE PENA*

Santos-Febres's novel begins with a view of Sirena, the protagonist, as a young street kid, before he was transformed into a bolero nightclub performer by Martha Divine. Martha runs a local drag club, El Danubio Azul, and is dumbstruck by this homeless, androgynous being whom she finds singing like some otherworldly creature among the rubbish cans and ruins of San Juan and whom she "rescues" from a life of penury. Although the novel is clearly not a biography, this scene was one witnessed by the author herself in the extratextual, real San Juan. Both the world of the street *dragas* (drag queens) in whose circles Sirena moves and the *travesti* and transsexual *ambiente* the novel depicts are based on Santos-Febres's experiences as the author relates in interview (Morgado 2000).

It is reasonable, therefore, to assume that the social aspects of stage and street *travesti* life depart from the author's own stated knowledge of this community. The novel in fact initially imparts much data on this community, providing details of police monitoring of the *chicas* working the street and outside El Danubio Azul, a real place that provides a focus for the community. The story evolves from a third-person extradiegetic narrative point of view, which occasionally focalizes through the minds of its main characters: Martha, Sirena, Solange, and Hugo Graubel. A parallel story told by the third-person narrator focalizes through the characters Leocadio and his grandmother, who live in the Dominican Republic. The novel provides a historical view of the Puerto Rican *travesti* scene, especially during the decade of the 1980s with the arrival of the AIDS pandemic on the island. It paints a scene-specific typology of days gone by, including *las chicas del jet set*, who emulated Bianca Jagger and Margot Hemingway, and the performers or *transformistas* who produced shows that paid homage to Diana Ross, lip-synching to the divas of the 1970s (Santos-Febres 2000, 32). These girls came down with HIV/AIDS and died in droves. Police violence, as the novel reveals, was more severe in those times (35–36). Hence the text provides, by passing references, a glimpse of the perils of being a street *draga* in Puerto Rico, in the past and present day.

The parts of the text focalized through Martha shed light on the scene prior to Sirena's emergence, that is, in the 1980s. Martha recalls again her days working the streets and makes wry comments about Puerto Rican family men and the family unit (70). The greatest level of "data," however, comes from the third-person-omniscient telling of Sirenito's life. In the novel, the name "Sirenito" (in masculine form) is used to refer to Sirena before s/he becomes fully immersed in *travesti* life. Thereafter the text refers to "Sirena" or "Sirenita." Sirenito first becomes homeless after his maternal grandmother—his sole protector—dies. A minor, he is left with no one and is at the mercy of the state and social workers, who treat him badly because of his "difference." Valentina Frenesí, a transsexual street prostitute who becomes his guardian angel, sister, and first (substitute) mother, helps him escape the social workers' clutches and teaches him how to work as a "she" and what to charge on the streets. Sirenito begins not only to work but also to live as a she. Valentina encourages her, praising Sirenito for her beauty. Valentina takes Sirenito in to live with her, as she has been living under bridges, breaking into houses, and avoiding the authorities. When they begin to work as a duo, life starts to turn around, and Sirenito no longer wanders the streets nor sleeps outside. In spite of this, she still has to work to keep a roof over Valentina's head. One night, a white gentleman in a Mercedes offers a considerable amount of money to either Sirena or Valentina, but not both. Sirena goes with him and is missing until after dawn. Valentina goes looking for her and then discovers her bloodied and wounded, having been raped, and sobbing among pieces of rubbish in a dumpster. Valentina takes Sirenito to a clinic where she must stay for five days; social services gets hold of her again and sends out a departmental worker who reactivates her file and puts her in state custody again. After escaping once more, Valentina promises Sirenito safe harbor in her house on the condition that she no longer works the streets. She works double to pay for Sirenito's medicines, to nurse her, like a sister or mother would. Sirenito's grief from lack of maternal love, or the love of anyone, and from the abuses of the street, is compensated by this friendship. However, Valentina's increasingly obvious coke habit, which eats up considerable amounts of money, obliges Sirenito to work. Supporting each other, Valentina covers for Sirenito, writing down the car number plates of every *pargo*—San Juan slang for client—that she sees (79–92).

We can conclude, then, that Santos-Febres's portrayal of these aspects of the street-working *draga* and transsexual's life is nuanced and by no means cursory, at least in the first part of the novel. It conveys some detail of the social and institutional dimensions of the lives of the gender-variant and trans subjects it depicts.[18] The focalization through the minds of Martha and Sirena also gives the reader the sense of their consciousness and subjective dimensionality. This also occurs with Leocadio, a young boy from the Dominican Republic. Like Sirena before him, he is a preadolescent gender-variant boy who cleans rich people's houses with his beloved *abuela*. Leocadio has a real eye for details in clothing—a sign of future vestimentary virtuosity. He has a beautiful, heavenly singing voice, too (40). The text links them in such a way as to suggest they are versions of each other, separated by geography and age. We witness the early trans ideation of Leocadio: staring at his little sister, Yesenia, he cannot help thinking that those facial features should be his and that they are caught in the wrong bodies, which thus gives a view into childhood gender subjectivity and historicizes Sirena's own trajectory via parallel (54). Leocadio, like Sirena, awakens the desire of men and has been gender "in-between" or gender different since birth (57).

Later, on reaching adolescence, Leocadio is unsure of how a "boy" turns into a "man." Forced to work when his *abuela* dies, he obtains a job at the Hotel Conquistador that hosts gay nights with international patrons, where he befriends Migueles, an older and more experienced waiter. Sirena, who is also still too young to be contracted due to labor laws in Puerto Rico, is taken to the Dominican Republic so that Martha can exploit the absence of labor laws to put Sirena to work. Martha is a businesswoman, and yet this trip will also guarantee the last payment on her hospital stay for SRS surgery to become a "complete" woman. Martha glimpses Leocadio, who is on a dishwashing shift the night of her visit to the Hotel Conquistador with Hugo Graubel and an Italian impresario. Graubel is the entrepreneur who becomes fascinated by Sirena and wishes to have her perform at a function he will organize, which is part of a ploy to make her become his lover. Martha capitalizes on this interest. She, too, is a hard-nosed manageress. The night of her brush with Leocadio, she immediately sees his promise, like that of Sirenito before him. The implication in the text is that Leocadio will have to decide whether to become a *travesti* and the object of men's desires or seize agency and express his homosexuality in ways that are not predestined and fixed in active-passive roles. The terms of capitalist interests, the negotiation of the rules of sale, the marketplace, and the uneven distribution of power, are all implicated in the notion of the *travesti* and the potentiality of the active-passive axis.

This latter axis becomes an important feature for reading the possibilities of *travestismo* and homosexuality in the Caribbean context and as a grid to map economic relations and questions of colonization and resistance as well. An entire section in the novel frames these questions in terms of regional and imperialistic avenues of domination allowed via tourism—and North American gay tourism is no exception.[19] These important themes are drawn out more in the symbolic value of *travestismo* promoted by the writer and her critics, particularly those who contributed to *A Queer Dossier: Mayra Santos-Febres' "Sirena Selena vestida de pena"* a special issue of *Centro* devoted to the novel (Sandoval-Sánchez 2003).

Travestismo as Metaphor in *Sirena Selena vestida de pena*

The critics who read *Sirena Selena vestida de pena* in *A Queer Dossier: Mayra Santos-Febres' "Sirena Selena vestida de pena"* read it principally with the following question in mind: how does the *travesti* perform in the text? This comes as no surprise given the major emphasis on performance, linked to the bolero, that the novel itself demonstrates. This is evident even in the first section of the novel, in a vignette evoking tropicality, song, seduction, and Caribbean divas of the stage and screen, and thus Sirena Selena herself:

> Cáscara de coco, contento de jirimilla azul, por los dioses di, azucarada selena, suculenta sirena de las playas alumbradas, bajo un spotlight confiésate, lunática. Tú conoces los deseos desatados por las noches urbanas. Tú eres el recuerdo de remotos orgasmos reducidos a ensayos de recording. Tú y tus siete monos desalmados como un ave selenita, como ave fotoconductora de electrodes insolentes. Eres quien eres, Sirena Selena . . . y sales de tu luna de papel a cantar canciones viejas de Lucy Favery, de Sylvia Rexach, de la Lupe sibarita, vestida y adorada por los seguidores de tu rastro. (Santos-Febres 2000, 7)
>
> [Coconut shell, content in your blue shimmering, by the gods given, sweet Selena, succulent siren of the glimmering beaches; confess, beneath the spotlight, moonstruck. You know the desires unleashed by urban nights. You are the memory of distant orgasms reduced to recording sessions. You and your seven soulless braids like a selenita bird, like a bird of lightning with your insolent magnetism. You are who you are, Sirena Selena . . . and you emerge from your paper moon to sing the old songs of Lucy Favery, Sylvia Rexach, La Lupe, sybarite, dressed and adored by those who worship your path.]

Already our expectations are set up to perceive this vision of desire and androgyny as a consummate performer who relies on theatrical tradition and quotation as her source references. Sirenito, transformed by a transsexual old hand, Ms. Martha Divine, into Sirena, is quite literally a performer. And Martha Divine's comments on gender styles and expressions as productions underpin the notions of identity that circulate in the novel, both on the stage and off, as performance, that is, as Butler's highly circulated terms of gender being a reiteration of certain norms, which congeal over time to provide the "illusion" of a "natural" or "real" identity (1990, 140). Martha advises a friend who seeks help in securing gainful employment, "Billy, recuerda siempre que todo está en la imagen. Si te ves como un profesional, eres un profesional. Lo demás es coreografía y actuación" (Santos-Febres 2000, 23; Billy, remember that it's all about image. If you look like a professional, you are a professional. The rest is choreography and acting). Martha's thoughts emphasize how everyday life is a performance, a passing. She is a distinguished woman because she dresses as a distinguished woman.

This makes the reader think of the balls organized by the drag "houses" in black and Latino Harlem, New York City, as documented in Jennie Livingston's film *Paris Is Burning* (1991). The balls are contests organized to perform down to the last detail, the "illusion" of being wealthy, white, fashionable, a Wall Street banker, a supermodel, or a soldier in the military, among other personalities. Contestants are judged on the "realness" of their reproduction. A few participants remark that identity is all in the "passing"—the belief that s/he who dresses in particular way, for instance, as a professional, white, rich person, simply "is." This is said with a good measure of irony, as all the contestants come from backgrounds and present socioeconomic positions far from approximating this ideal. As Karen McCarthy-Brown argues in "Mimesis in the Face of Fear: Femme Queens, Butch Queens, and Gender Play in the Houses of Greater Newark" (2001), the ball performances might be seen not simply as a reproduction of gender norms but also as a way of performing—and thereby releasing—anger. McCarthy-Brown submits that the shows in the balls represent "ways of strengthening and protecting a vulnerable community by ritualizing, and thereby containing and redirecting, a range of potentially negative energies such as anger, fear, frustration, competition, and conflict" (McCarthy-Brown 2001, 209–10).

And yet the aforementioned sentiment of doing and becoming, the performance of gender, and the outer assumption of mobility, is echoed by Martha in the *Sirena Selena vestida de pena*. She remembers with horror the days she was "dressed" as a young Pentecostal man; she refers to it as "una producción masculina" (a masculine production), which required its own choreography particular to a kind of gender that is now unfamiliar to her (Santos-Febres 2000, 117). She recalls making the switch and having to learn minutely elements of a new production or choreography—drawing inspiration from the *patrones* (models) of the movie star and femme ingenue (117).

As Martha and Sirena pass through customs on arrival in the Dominican Republic where they have gone to put on a show for elite guests at the Hotel Colón in Santo Domingo, they fear being "read," which means having their gender interpreted as "less than real," and therefore not passing. "Realness" in gender becomes a sort of cultural passport. The enactment of gender as a form of passing is made all the more conscious in reference to Martha's transsexuality (she is preoperative) and Sirena's *travestismo*; both evoke realness, but the performed nature of this realness is put into check by the need for attention to detail, so that any "gender production" does not reveal its constructedness, lest Martha's and Sirena's performed gender be revealed as at odds with morphological sex.

This adds another dimension to the theory of the performativity of gender. This relates to the notion of any gender performance as dependent on a public gallery, the point of all legitimization and intelligibility through which a gender can be said to be real or authentic, subject to controls and approvals around identity. Such mechanisms may be found in customs, when crossing from one place to the next, hence the novel's suggestive parallel as the main characters pass through customs. Such a conceptualization is present, it will be recalled, in Butler's own formulation of gender as performance. Butler uses J. L. Austin's speech acts theory to demonstrate that gender acts, like speech acts, are legitimated as real only by reference to the established and commonly agreed-upon set of symbols, codes, norms, and procedures already installed and given authoritative status and that constitute this realness. Like performatives in speech, gender performatives only have an authoritative force that allows the enactment of "realness" because of the underlying agreed-upon terms. Moreover, every performance of gender is an approximation of an ideal. Martha is conscious of this because of the need to pass in everyday life, as failing to do so could incur punishments, but perhaps also because she is the manageress of a drag bar, where nightly gender expressions are very literally performed on the stage for entertainment purposes.

There are, of course, many styles of drag that should be distinguished here: drag that draws attention to the constructed and imitative nature of gender acts; drag that seeks to combine genders ("gender fuck") or secure an androgynous or erotic style; and drag that seeks to produce gender realness, that is, the kind of drag sometimes termed female impersonation or gender illusionism. With Sirena, Martha coproduces in her understudy a kind of gender illusionism. These are the terms with which Sirena as performer is described. Offstage, Sirena is described as a curious mix of voluptuous male-female adolescent innocence, and her cross-gendered identity clearly pertains: "La deseó así, tan chiquita, tan nenito callejero. La reconoció como la mujer de sus sueños" (59–60; He wanted her like that, so small, so like a street urchin). On stage in the Dominican Republic at the Hotel Colón, Sirena, the text relates, is an illusion, a secret that does not appear as an illusion, and therefore is a double illusion. Yet her gender expressions have a source, like Martha's, derived from the idealized glamour of superstars and vedettes (starlets). Her look is replete with "perversas inocencias" ("perverse innocence") and "vulnerabilidad asesina" (44; "killer vulnerability"); she is an adolescent playing a woman—a femme fatale with a deadly angelic gaze that will both scare and seduce her audience. Even off the stage, more in love with the idea of glamour than fame, she internalizes the precepts that Martha in her thoughts makes obvious: gender and identity are theater and superproduction. She imagines herself a movie star; she rehearses her every pose for maximum effect. Comparisons to Zapata's text are obvious here.

As if to generalize the connection between identity, gender, and performativity, Santos-Febres's depiction of the wannabe upper-class wife of the businessman, Hugo Graubel, for whom Sirena performs in Santo Domingo, is equally measured. Solange herself is intimately aware that her "society woman" identity is one that she performs. Her origins are, in fact, more common: "No cabe duda. Ella es la señora Solange Graubel, dama célebre de la alta sociedad que sonríe y da un golpe seco de talones para alejarse de la puerta que entreabrió, luego de dar su orden" (167; "There is no doubt. She is Mrs. Solange Graubel, the celebrated lady of high society who smiles and gives a sharp clap of her heels on leaving through the half-opened door, after giving her orders.") For Solange, hers is a sort of "class transvestism," in the book's terms:

> A cuántas veladas tuvo que arrastrar los pies sin ganas, para estudiar la sutil coreografía de gestos, saludos y costumbres de sobremesa? . . . Lo que en verdad revela la clase es la minuciosa, estudiada y constante puesta en escena de la elegancia. Su elegancia la salva de preguntas insidiosas sobre el estado actual de su familia, su formación profesional. (215)
>
> [To how many soirées did she have to drag herself unwillingly, to study the subtle choreography of gestures, greetings, dinner party manners? . . . What shows one's class is the detailed, studied, and constant mise-en-scene of elegance. Her elegance saves her from insidious questions about the current status of her family, her professional background.]

Solange is like a reflection of Sirena, her competitor and rival, in more ways than one. She is, the text says, "una chamaquita vestida de mujer" (168; a little girl dressed as a woman). Her own performance of identity is therefore posited, by metaphorical extension, as another kind of transvestism. And yet she is also like Martha, with pretensions to be something she is not.

This is one of the shades of meaning acquired by *travestismo*: the idea of putting on a mask, imitating and copying gestures, in order to hide an essential lack. The fact that both Martha and Solange, in their studied femininity, seek to portray themselves as above their class, is important to this configuration. Sirena herself ends up idealizing this image; she begins to look down on the "rabble" around her while she is being escorted to Graubel and swears never to return to the street (64–65). And both Martha's and Solange's dressing up as "something they aren't" contains racial dimensions. Martha seeks to be *rubia* (blonde) and pale, so she stands out among so many *prietos* (dark skinned). She talks about her plastic surgery and how she wanted to refine her features (especially her nose) so that it would allow her to look like "una nenita de bien, hija de senadores . . . yendo a una gala en el Caribe Hilton con mi novio acabado de graduar de universidad gringa" (72; a girl of class, daughter of senators . . . going to a gala at the Caribbean Hilton with my boyfriend just out of graduating from a gringa university). She makes up Sirena to have a "tez pálida y aceitunada de criolla de los años cuarenta," (pale olive complexion of a forties Creole woman) when she is really a mulata (110). However, both Sirena and Solange are destined to suffer, as the title *Sirena Selena vestida de pena* indicates. "Vestida" is a name for *travestis* and also means "dressed." Combined with "pena", the second part of the title of the novel forms an allusion to the fact that Sirena's cross-dressing brings her sorrow, and is a type of mourning, in a Lacanian sense, for a lack, for the failed dream of incorporation. Both can only approximate the thing they so desire to become or incorporate, thereby endeavoring to emulate a vision of otherness. This is shown as a construction that is shot through with class and race ambitions.

The novel hones this point via Ms. Divine's reference to performance, *travestismo*, and transsexuality as ways to "disimular la vida" (hoodwinking life). Through the voice of Martha, gender crossing is posited in the novel as a means of identity displacement and appropriation quite particular to the Caribbean experience: "así es la vida en este caldo de islas sancochadas por el hambre y por las ganas de vivir de acuerdo con otra realidad" (261; that's what life is in this beef-and-bones broth of islands soaked in hunger and the desire to live according to another reality). Furthermore, she states, "No mi amor, sin bases y sin tacas, sin trucos y sin traición la vida no es vida" (261; No my love, without foundation and heels, without tricks and deceit this life isn't life). Interestingly, this conception of Puerto Rican and Caribbean subjects as susceptible to coating the bitter pill of reality and inclined to the techniques of euphemism and escape echoes the diagnosis that Marqués provides in "El puertorriqueño dócil." These statements come at the end of the novel and hence frame the entire configuration of *travestismo* as a form of escapism and an emulation of an idealized image that is born of the desire to flee the conditions of impoverishment by taking on the outward appearances of a economically mobile identity. That is, it comprises a betrayal or depthless fantasy of wealth and class, at odds with "reality."

Again, this brings the reader back to *Paris Is Burning*, and the reading of it made by Butler. Butler's reading has been influential, particularly as the release of her first treatise on gender as performance, *Gender Trouble*, with its emphasis on drag, coincided with the release of the Jennie Livingston film. Both texts have been read alongside one another in queer studies syllabi, as Jay Prosser notes (1998, 45), and Butler's use of the film in her following book, *Bodies That Matter*, sealed the union of this landmark strand of queer theory and the documentary. It is highly probable that Santos-Febres, as a cultural studies and literary theorist, drew inspiration from Butler's analysis. *Sirena Selena vestida de pena* provides stylistic and theoretical nods to the film's configurations and Butler's take on drag and transsexuality in *Bodies That Matter*, an influential interpretation that was noted in Chapter 1. As Butler says of the drag performers who imitate wealthy white women in their famous balls, and of some of the transsexuals who desire SRS, particularly Venus Xtravaganza, "in *Paris Is Burning*, becoming real, becoming a real woman . . . constitutes the site of the phantasmatic promise of rescue from poverty, homophobia, and racist delegitimation" (1993, 130).

For Santos-Febres, like Butler, transgender identities and performances enact gender norms that are not simply marked by race and class but can become "the vehicle for the phantasmatic transformation of that nexus of race and class, the site of its articulation" (Butler 1993, 130). *Travestismo* thus functions as a mode not just of becoming woman but also of crossing to other categories, such as race. In the context of Santos-Febres's novel, this implies the assumption of capitalist gringo ideals and the emulation of the urban middle-class "sophisticate." Transgender thus gains the extension of being an example of performed gender that allows and even pursues the production of other types of identities, via the miming of regulatory norms of whiteness and privilege. This interpretation of transgender maps it as a desire for assimilation to dominant norms of privilege and escape from one position to another—by copying the hegemonic.[20]

Reading the much-cited case of the balls contextually, McCarthy-Brown observes that the claims of critics like Butler, and even bell hooks, remain at a "level of abstraction . . . [that] has tended to prevent a fuller picture from emerging" (2001, 215).[21] Thus the kind of theorizations advanced by Butler, in particular, need to be set in relief with the reminder that the transgender performances in the film and also in everyday life cannot be simply reduced to the dynamics of repetition or subversion of cultural norms. I would argue, along with McCarthy-Brown, that in both instances—in the film and real life—the matter is of greater complexity.

In spite of this caveat, the novel's marrying of the notion of gender crossing in *travestismo* to the attempt to pass as another for the sake of privilege—taking on facets of the dominant—is surely discursively linked to this visualization of transgender, and transsexuality in particular, as (at times) a nonsubversive aping that betrays another kind of desire, as seen in Butler's work. This is crucial in understanding how Santos-Febres arrives at her use of *travestis* to metaphorize what she holds that Caribbean and Latin American culture does in its attempt to deny conditions of poverty and coloniality—aping the hegemonic. Or, in the face of colonialism for Puerto Ricans, the imitation of values attached to Anglo whiteness, privilege, and possibility. In offering her critical interpretation of *travestismo* and extending it to Caribbean and Latin American culture, Santos-Febres seeks to attack this tendency to imitate middle-class, white norms of privilege that she views as currently affecting the region.

Nelly Richard, the Chilean critic mentioned in Chapter 1, understands *travestis* as individuals who recycle poses, styles, and fashions of the First World in their own gender expressions to become a secondhand North America. In what can only count as the most poeticized, loaded, and disembodied conception of *travestis* and everyday life, she inscribes them as taking something that is "not theirs" and imitating the "First World." She also attributes "falseness" to them (Richard 1993). This paradigm of appropriation, taking what "isn't theirs," is also surely echoed in Santos-Febres's perception of the metaphorical value of *travestismo*.

Much more can be said about the attributions made in the name of performance, *travestismo*, and identity, especially in terms of how the place of the bolero works in the novel. As well as a *travesti*, Sirena is also a *bolerista* (bolero singer). The novel is developed around the structure of the bolero. As critics are right to point out, drawing on the study by Iris Zavala (2000), the bolero forms a central metaphor of Caribbean reality. Sirena performs "gender," performs "race," performs bolero, and, therefore, performs "Caribbeanness." It is unsurprising, then, that the critics in *A Queer Dossier: Mayra Santos-Febres' "Sirena Selena vestida de pena"* further argue that in the novel *travestismo* serves as a metaphor for Caribbean reality, and the interconnectedness of the place of the bolero and the emphasis on performativity are surely crucial here. The bolero itself forms a kind of script for masculine and feminine identities, and for the staging of desire, in an urban setting. This is taken to its most performed level in the short story by fellow Puerto Rican Manuel Ramos Otero called "Loca la de la locura" (1987). Ramos Otero is cited by Santos-Febres as a major literary influence. In "Loca la de la locura" ("Loca, the Mad One") we meet a *travesti* nightclub performer, called simply "Loca," who has just murdered her perfidious lover, Nene Lindo. She lives in the world of fantasy and unfulfilled desire, typical of the bolero. She occupies the usually passive woman's role also typical to the bolero—long suffering and wronged by her man. She is connected textually to Sara Montiel and other stage and screen divas, just like Sirena. The bolero as a kind of gender script is made clear in this text, too, a text that can be queered and regendered, whose interpellating calls of the "I" who sings and the "you" who listens can be inverted (Zavala 2000, 108–15). Traditionally, in the bolero a male sings to a "signified absence," his woman (Aparicio 1998, 125). In Santos-Febres's novel, this has interesting implications, for the movement of the bolero is implicated in what she might see as the movement of *travestismo*: a changing of places, and an assumption of mythical, scripted roles in a confusion of (reversed) idealized identities,[22] in which the *travesti* possibly becomes the purveyor of an image of surface (urban[e]) sophistication, a scripted fantasy of desire, Caribbean exoticism, and seductive myth.

NATIONAL-CULTURAL ALLEGORY

The tradition of the national-cultural allegory and its inscription in "non-Western" literary production finds its best proponent in Fredric Jameson. In his article "Third World Literature in the Age of Multinational Capitalism" (1986), Jameson insists that novels from the Third World are always about a national situation or collective story. An individual history told is inevitably metaphorical of (and less important than) this perceived larger scheme of things (1986, 69). Moreover, libidinal investments are always read and readable in primarily political and social terms. For Jameson, "First World" texts do not demonstrate this allegorization. First World texts center themselves on "placeless individuality," "psychologism," and "projections of private subjectivity" (85). Further, as he claims, "all of this is denied to third-world culture, where the telling of the individual story and the individual experience cannot but ultimately involve the whole laborious telling of collectivity itself" (85–86).

Although José Delgado-Costa expresses the desire to undermine the totalizing gesture that proposes the inevitability of the individual story as allegory of a national collective, he and the other critics from *A Queer Dossier: Mayra Santos-Febres' "Sirena Selena vestida de pena"* do not fundamentally challenge Jameson's dictum of reading and writing praxis for so-called Third World texts (Delgado-Costa 2003, 72). In essence, their own assumptions confirm those of Jameson. As will be seen, their interpretations of the "meaning" of *travestismo* both in the novel and in the social text provide evidence of this.

Commentary on the way libidinal investments are articulated through the active-passive paradigm is also key to the promotion of the inevitability of allegory and its "naturalness." The reader will recall that early in the novel Sirena is raped by a rich, white male client. This incident finds Sirena at the lowest point of her life. She is only empowered by the help of Valentina Frenesí. She remembers the face of the rapist and the promise she made to Valentina not to let a man penetrate her again (Santos-Febres 2000, 235). Later, on the verge of her public fame and prior to her heart-stopping performance before guests in the Dominican Republic, Sirena is assailed by the designs of Hugo Graubel, another rich man. Graubel displays U.S. capitalist-allied economic interests. And yet it is Sirena who seduces him, not the reverse. Further, the turning of the tables of dominator-dominated is articulated by the fact that Graubel desires to take the passive role and is attracted to the idea of Sirena in all her "phallic" glory as *travesti*. Much emphasis is made in this part of the text on the unveiling of her penis: it is unusually large. Sirena takes the active role with Hugo, and because he increasingly calls her by the masculine, she flickers between personalities (the distant, the diva, the vulnerable, the young boy). She scratches his anus with her sharp nails and takes him from behind. Sirena is then left in a breach of identity. What will she be? What will she (un)become? But she decides to leave, taking Hugo's clothes with her (255–56). That Santos-Febres chooses to map these issues onto bodies both feminine and feminized, and mulatto and black, thereby reinvoking the terms of confounding colonial liminality and developmental error as outlined by Pedreira, is of interest. The active-passive sexual distinction is associated with relations of dominance and power, as well as gradients of gender and race hierarchies. Such relations are arrogated to the axes of sexual roles and the turning of these for several of the critics of *A Queer Dossier*, José Delgado-Costa (2003), Jossianna Arroyo (2003a), Efraín Barradas (2003), and Kristian van Haesendonck (2003) among them. These critics also equate the "dressing" of *travestismo* to relations of power and dominance in the colonial setting.

The linking of the notion of colonial dominance to the sexual act has been prevalent for centuries in Latin America, as was mentioned in Chapter 1. The most classic materialization of this is the Mexican figure of *la chingada*, literally, the penetrated one, that is, Malinche. In Mexico the product of conquest—*mestizaje*—mythically means that "todos somos hijos de la Chingada"[23] (we're all children of the Chingada). Similarly, the idea of sexual passivity (and the inextricable association of being "feminized") in males becomes a paradigm for explaining imperial domination elsewhere—certainly in Puerto Rico if the national discourse of Pedreira is any indication. For Kristian van Haesendonck, the denouement of the novel that questions the notion of who is the master and who is the slave, who is the colonizer and who is the colonized, is perfectly rendered along the active-passive reversal and the moment of *travestismo* itself (2003, 90). *Travestismo* might be the point, then, of both the reinscription of colonial relations and the possible subversion or flight from the same. When Sirena flees to an uncertain fate with Graubel's clothing—after having penetrated him—this is left unanswered. Sexual acts and libidinal practices hence resonate in ways, following Jameson, that signify allegorically about the state of the (Third World) nation. That all of this takes place alternately at the Hotel Colón and Hotel Conquistador—the hotel names explicitly placing the events in (historical) colonial terms—only reinforces the process of arrogating this individual story to the story of collective colonial realities in the novel.

Travestismo itself, as we have seen, becomes an all-encompassing field pointing to the assumption of a desired and impossible identity. This desired identity is differently raced and classed, a movement that draws on and confirms Marjorie Garber's thesis that transvestism conceals such relations through "vested interests." *Travestismo* combines through the scripting of the bolero—so paradigmatically Caribbean—to metaphorize the contemporary unstable assumption of a surface national-cultural identity projected (and performed) outward. The critics take up the baton that Santos-Febres passes them and run with it, which has something of a snowball effect, with *travestismo* coming to represent many things: an intermediate space of negotiation and agency, where identificatory gestures are figured—gestures that construct national identities (Arroyo 2003a); a metaphor for the pressures of tourism wherein *travestismo* represents the process through which *caribeños* go to present themselves as exotic others (Barradas 2003); Puerto Rico's ambiguous definition as an ELA, or the island's movement from plain old colonialism, to a newer "capitalismo lite" that plays on concepts of novelty and exotic appeal in a system of economic relations embodied by the novel's *travesti* (van Haesendonck 2003).

Van Haesendonck makes visible the other critics' only tacit approval of *travestis* and *travestismo* as being "natural" metaphors for all these things when he labels *travestismo* as an even more appropriate metaphor for states of coloniality than the image of the mask; the subaltern apes the colonizer via mimesis or selling an exotic image to the colonizer, in what amounts to an imposition of a false face on an original. In spite of the evidence of the novel's relation to the real San Juan *travesti* and transsexual world of drag bars and the street sex trade, critics like Kristian van Haesendonck discard the usefulness of such evidence and assume that in Puerto Rico there are few, if any, real *travestis*. Therefore the novel can only bear a symbolic reading of *travestismo* (2003, 80).[24]

How different are these formulations from the discourse on *locas* and *travestis* as symptoms and symbols of cultural equivocalness, colonial passivity and instability in the constitution of nation, which writers such as René Marqués and Antonio S. Pedreira invoke? Both intellectuals connected the feminine and "feminized" to the problematics of national-cultural definition and destiny. They inaugurated the allegorization of nonmale and nonmasculine subjects in nation discourse wherein, as Cruz-Malavé reminds us, "the abject, feminized, monstrous body" represented conditions of colonial backwardness, impotence and failure (1995, 141). A set of racial others, including mulattos and blacks, were also linked in this conceptual chain of passivity and "retarded" development to the problem of nation. As in *Insularismo*, in *Sirena Selena vestida de pena* we are presented with two stories of adolescents not yet matured into an adults: Sirena herself and the slightly younger Leocadio, as Puerto Rico and the Dominican Republican respectively, both nonmasculine and both nonwhite. While Santos-Febres does not frame them as having a "developmental disorder"—in the two senses of the word—their gender atypicality and the potential to change into one type of subject or another as suggested by *travestismo* and their assumption or not of the associated "passive" role functions in its place. This repeats the problematic place of feminine and *afeminado* subjects in historical national discourse. Both are faced with a dilemma and here must decide their destiny and tactics in the midst of a range of encroaching interests; that is, how to define themselves, whether to become or unbecome, perform or unperform, via *travestismo* and passive libidinality as possibilities, before they may "mature" into their future selves and as future nations, and eventually reach manhood.

There is, then, evidence to suggest that the national-cultural allegorization of the specter of "effeminacy" is reengaged in the novel. It is also of note that she uncannily reengages the so-called problem of feminization as it appears conjoined with racial mixity in nationalist discourse, given Sirena is also mulata. Any challenging new inscriptions of the possibilities of trans subjectivity thus are left by the wayside. What is of most concern, however, is that *travestis*, in the novel's terms and those of its critics, remain as performative exercises that never arrive at an identity but rather instead encapsulate subject movement, confusion, flight, and colonial hybridity. In critical interpretations of the work, such a discourse remains largely unchallenged, which risks instituting these attributions about *travestis* as a priori inherent and "natural" facts. The interlocking of the perspectives both of the academic-author and her critics accrues a level of "truth effects" for the theories they advance on *travestismo* and coloniality, theories that are deeply entrenched in certain cultural and critical ways of thinking about *travestis* as subjects that this book has sought to challenge.

CHALLENGING THE PARADIGMS OF REINSCRIPTION

In the novels I have discussed in this chapter, *travestismo* and transsexuality are assumed to constitute a reproduction of gender norms. This is coded by both texts in terms that reference the notions of gender performativity found in queer theory and anticipated by writers such as Manuel Puig and Severo Sarduy in Latin America. Furthermore, there is a strong component of fantasy in these configurations of trans figures as exemplifying gender performativity. That is, not only are the central characters of *La hermana secreta de Angélica María* and *Sirena Selena vestida de pena* made to be illustrative of gender and its iterative production—the citation of idealized norms—but also, their performance of these norms is equated to escapism, delusion, and co-option.

This we can ascertain in the comments by Santos-Febres about how she uses *travestis* as metaphorical; she locates their gender presentation and the reality of *travestismo* itself into the sphere of escapism and flight from reality. In connecting *travestis* to her take on the contemporary trend for Latin American and Caribbean cultures to imitate styles and norms that "do not belong to them," she implicates both in the realm of deception, sham, and inauthenticity. By claiming that the norms and styles intimated are First World illusions of "progress" and "civilization," she understands, first, *travestis* as imitators of the hegemonic and, second, Caribbean and Latin American urban culture as mimetic of the same.

Similarly, Zapata's novel is steeped in this kind of paradigm. The lack of a more nuanced understanding of intersex and trans lives and identities—beyond the performative and hegemonic—could at least be explained by the novel's earlier publication date. Published on the eve of the emergence of queer theory as a separate discipline, most discourse that dealt with transsexuality was largely circumspect, if not downright condemnatory, about the worth and validity of transsexual identity and debated its status as hegemonic reproduction or subversion of gender (see especially Raymond 1982). Fuller understandings of trans lives outside medical-psychiatric discourse were not as available as they are today. Intersexuality was hardly even revealed as an arena of political struggle for revindication. The limitations of Zapata's text can be seen in this light and make useful contrast to *Sirena Selena vestida de pena*, whose more recent 2000 publication makes it even more difficult to comprehend how and why Santos-Febres and her critics persist in subscribing to merely performative and hegemonic notions of trans and gender-variant subjects.

To say that *travesti* or transsexual subjectivity (like other subjectivities) partake of or are shaped by larger regional processes or forces in their intersubjective, collective spaces is not the same as saying that *travesti* and national identity are equivalent to each other. The metaphorization of such subjects—their transfiguration in writing and in reading practices—can further mystify a group of people whose own stories have only begun to emerge in the social text. Surely it is now possible to tell individual stories from Mexico, Puerto Rico, or anywhere else in Latin America that are resistant to monolithic "worlding." Surely it is possible to create narratives that are also resistant to stereotypes, and to the exigencies of regional canon formation in which literature is only deemed significant to the extent that it can speak the language of collectivity, universal experience, and national-cultural inheritance. While these are all valid issues in the context of a people who have never "had" a nation—that is, all Puerto Ricans, *travesti* or not—the question of the emptying out of subjectivity and its appropriation for the needs of national metaphor remains. Surely the tendency that Namaste underlines in which "transsexual and transgendered people are reduced to the merely figural: rhetorical tropes and discursive levers invoked to talk about social relations of gender, nation or class" (2000, 51–52), that both the novels and criticism around them display can be challenged and contradicted? The next chapter examines the work of Pedro Lemebel to further this inquiry.

Chapter 6

Scandalous Embodiments, Shameful Citizenships

Loca and *Travesti* Subjectivities in the Work of Pedro Lemebel

Feminine Identifications

One of the most effusive commentators on *loca* and *travesti* lives is the Chilean performance artist and writer Pedro Lemebel. Like Reinaldo Arenas before him, Lemebel in all his work speaks resolutely in the *loca* voice, and extratextually in his public persona he takes up this position. His adoption of the maternal surname "Lemebel" signals this identification, and through the deliberate privileging of the maternal signifier over the paternal, Lemebel makes apparent his allegiance to the feminine, an allegiance that structures his artistic and political project.[1] This chapter considers this project as it is advanced in three central works, two collections of *crónicas* (chronicles), *La esquina es mi corazón* (1996; *The Street Corner Is My Heart*) and *Loco afán: Crónicas de sidario* (1997; *Mad Undertaking: AIDS Chronicles*), and one novel, *Tengo miedo torero* (2002; *My Tender Matador*).

Although Lemebel himself speaks of his *locas* and *travestis* as "espejo y metáfora de la identidad tercermundista" (mirror and metaphor of Third World identity) and recognizes the allegorical potential of some of his depictions in some interviews, admitting that he writes about certain "causas litigadas" (litigious matters) that are often "reducidas solo a simbolismo literario" (Blanco and Gelpí 1997, 95; reduced to mere literary symbolism), his narrativization of the lives of these subjects in its very versatility and depth refuses containment to the merely figural. If the principal enterprise engaged by Mayra Santos-Febres in her novel *Sirena Selena vestida de pena* could be said to be the appropriation of *travesti* bodies and identities for the needs of national allegory, the same cannot be said for the work of Pedro Lemebel. By stating this, I do not mean to suggest that contexts are not crucial to understanding Lemebel's work. The opposite is true, as his *crónicas* and novel are clearly situated at certain historical and political adjuncts and locales that range from the streets of impoverished Santiago to the mansions of the wealthy in Vitacura. This sense of time and space—both local and national—pervades his writing. Lemebel connects his gender-variant subjects very much to the Chilean social landscape, but he does not use them as an overriding or reductive symbol of national identity in crisis.

Mercifully, the majority of scholarship on Lemebel's texts—which is considerable given that as a *cronista* (chronicler) writer he has been published for little over a decade—recognizes this complexity. Varied in their foci, most critics do indeed acknowledge the real-life subjects behind the kitsch acrobatics of Lemebel's prose, whose metaphorizing tendencies are suggestive and never absolute and intentionally trace lines of contention between certain issues. Jean Franco, Fernando Blanco, and Bernadita Llanos, writing in the collection *Reinas de otro cielo (Queens of Another Heaven)*, comment on the deep political commitment that lies behind Lemebel's output (2004, 13, 37, 75). Blanco in particular notes the social function of Lemebel's work, which always implies a set of addressees, and whose discourse is supremely shaped by this sociopolitical purpose (40–41).

A consideration of Lemebel's work, which crosses both genre and gender, is pivotal to an examination of the textual possibilities of inscribing *loca* and *travesti* subjectivities in the contemporary period. Lemebel's texts work both as histories and stories: they excavate and reanimate from the entombment of memory long-buried artefacts of popular culture from the era before Pinochet's aggressive wresting of power from Allende's *Unidad Popular*, right through the period of the regime with its techniques of *olvido* (forgetfulness) and *desaparición* (disappearance), to the so-called *años de transición* (transition years) and return to "democracy." His reclamation and historicization of the most maligned and invisibilized aspects of Chilean culture fits precisely in the period of cultural production of the last twenty-five years on which the present study focuses. Lemebel's work also achieves a degree of self-conscious and politicized representation that seemingly evades many of the other writers and filmmakers studied here. His *crónicas* and novel provide the most nuanced and theoretically sophisticated explorations of *loca* and *travesti* subjectivities and embodiments. Lemebel's oeuvre is a provocative performance in itself that very ironically invokes the terms of scandal and shame to contest the forces of marginalization exacted upon those toward whom the writer expresses unreserved sympathy, groups traditionally misunderstood and ill conceived on both sides of the political spectrum: *locas, travestis,* and transsexuals centrally among them.

Crossing Genres, Crossing Genders, and Speaking Back to Power

Lemebel erupted onto the Chilean cultural scene in 1988 alongside Francisco Casas in their performance group Las Yeguas del Apocalipsis (*The Mares of the Apocalypse*), during a period that, as Victor Robles recounts, was characterized by intense repression as society became more militarized (1998, 37). The 1980s also marked a period of increasing protests against the state. A fledging lesbian and gay movement began to appear as limited social freedoms were obtained, freedoms that were associated with the push toward consumption with the institution of free-market ideology in the country. However, this movement was rather middle class in character and not openly antistate. Las Yeguas del Apocalipsis were without precedent. Their actions challenged the staid and reiterative cultural scene and scandalously provoked debate about the situation of the most stigmatized of those ignored or repressed in Chilean society.[2]

Additionally, Lemebel's insistence on the presence of *locas* and *travestis* as individuals also exposed to the horrors of military persecution and social erasure grew out of a response to the Left. Long involved in the underground left-wing movement against the Pinochet regime, Lemebel experienced a profound disenchantment with these circles and their demonstrated phobia toward and trivialization of sexual minorities. His performances in *Las Yeguas* anticipated a series of indictments and counterdiscourses delivered in his *crónicas* in which Lemebel always speaks from the Left. Additionally, his works very frequently speak *to* the Left, which Lemebel frames as just as susceptible to the phobic machismo that structures the Right and its political violence.

His *crónicas* began life literally as spoken pieces: their dialogic character was heightened by radio's medium of dispersal. Moreover, they demonstrate a compelling attention to detail and linguistic play like the best oral storytelling—aspects that gained more emphasis as they were set down on paper, edited, and published in the various collections available to date—those texts chosen for analysis, as well as *De perlas y cicatrices* (1998; *Of Pearls and Scars*), *Zanjón de la Aguada* (2003), whose title refers to a water delta in Chile, and *Adiós mariquita linda* (2006; *Goodbye Beautiful Butterfly*).

In his *crónicas*, moreover, Lemebel engages in what Dino Plaza Atenas calls a "minority genre" (1999, 123) or what Deleuze and Guattari (1996) categorize as minor literature. Deleuze and Guattari use this term in relation to the works of Franz Kafka. For these theorists, such a literature is not minor in the sense of being inferior. It is minor in the sense that it evolves out of a minoritarian position—speaking back to power. Two facets of their description of minor literature are surely applicable to Lemebel's work: its thoroughly political nature and its collective, enunciative value (Deleuze and Guattari 1996, 17–18). Deleuze and Guattari also note that this type of literature escapes figuration and metaphor, as it constantly deterritorializes, that is, it works across vernaculars and registers of language to occupy several at once—it therefore does not refer to one subject or voice, but many voices (22).

Such characteristics are present in Lemebel's writing. Its multivocality may tempt the critic to see Lemebel's work as invariably postmodern, a qualifier that Palaversich vigorously contests (2002, 101). For Palaversich, Lemebel's *crónicas* are best located in the tradition of the *testimonio*. A chief feature of the *testimonio*, it will be recalled, is that it speaks in the collective "we." Lemebel's work speaks for a very specific set of "wes" at different adjuncts. These are those subjects who are disinherited or dispossessed in the national panorama, those formerly condemned to whispers, mute speech, rumors, and "la oralidad en baja voz" (hushed oral storytelling) as Ángeles Del Pino describes it (1998, 21). The pitch of his *crónicas* raises the volume of these rescued and resurrected voices to memorialize the demoralized and to scandalize the regime and complicit—as well as complacent—Chilean society.

Whether seen as postmodern or testimonial or as constituting a minor literature that has launched Lemebel as a major figure in Chilean letters, his *crónicas* are generically different from the fictional form. Yet neither are they realist or naturalistic—they, too, are literary recreations, suffused, at times inordinately so, with subjectivity. As Lucía Guerra Cunningham argues, they constitute histories with a lowercase "h," "epopeyas humildes" (humble epics), that is, tales that inscribe the no less ingenious and heroic struggles of those never previously lionized in official discourse, whose exploits are missing from the history books (2000, 110–11).

In interview, Lemebel himself defines his use of the *crónica* in the following terms:

> Digo crónica . . . por la urgencia de nombrar de alguna forma lo que uno hace. También digo y escribo crónica por travestir de elucubración cierto afán escritural embarrado de contingencia. Te digo crónica como podría decirte apuntes al margen, croquis, anotación de sucesos, registro de un chisme, una noticia, un recuerdo al que se le saca punta enamoradamente para no olvidar. (Blanco and Gelpí 1997, 93)
>
> [I say *crónica* [chronicle] . . . because of the urgency in naming in some way what I do. I also say and write *crónica* to cross-dress via a style of expression a certain writing exploit smeared in contingency. I say *crónica*

in the way I could say marginalia, scribbles, field notes, record of a piece of gossip, news, a memory one sharpens lovingly in order not to forget.]

Lemebel carries through this approach to the novel studied here. Added to this, he utilizes the more extended form that the novel offers to focus more minutely on the emergence of the political subjectivity of one particular gender-variant personage known only in *Tengo miedo torero* as La Loca del Frente. This text constitutes Lemebel's first foray into the novel form. Although there are logical limits between what he achieves in his *crónicas* and what he achieves in his novel, the commitment to the rescue of forgotten histories remains a major motivation in the novel's elaboration. In both the *crónicas* and novel, Lemebel comments, in part, on attestably real-life events largely forgotten by the public. This is not to say, however, that simply by virtue of their genre his use of the *crónica* orients the writer's work more to the representational function than the other texts that we have considered in the previous chapters; Lemebel is too unconventional to embark on such a realist enterprise. Lemebel uses the *crónica* in somewhat unorthodox (fictive and poetic) ways and the reader at times gets the sense that they are *mini-relatos*, or sketches, for what Lemebel eventually turns into the more ambitious project of the *novela-testimonial*. Throughout, then, Lemebel remains faithful to his project: redressing history, talking back to power, and politicizing subjectivity.

The tracing of personal-political conscience from a sexual minority perspective is most apparent in the three texts examined here. Far from merely appropriating *locas* and *travestis* as rhetorical vectors that point to other issues, Lemebel poetically humanizes them and places them at the center of both the interpersonal struggles of the everyday as well as the larger panorama. In the three texts discussed in this chapter, the slippery terrain of belonging and becoming is made manifest via interrogations of socioeconomic inclusion and exclusion, the state and the citizen, techniques of surveillance and the body, and subjection and freedom from subjection via the body.

These issues, we have seen, are nodal points for understanding both theoretically and concretely the emergence of subjectivity. For Lemebel, they become the means of insistently inserting his marginalized sexual citizens into contemporary and historical view and contesting productions of both Left and Right persuasions of *locas* and *travestis* as politically inconsequential. Lemebel upends these preconceptions, mocks the rapprochements and pretensions of the market language of pluralism and freedom, and makes evident how his subjects struggle from outside the current conditions of admission into the Chilean economic "miracle." With an eye very different from that which is merely sartorial and submissively co-opted—vastly removed from the role occupied by syndicated homosexuality in U.S. popular culture—Lemebel the *cronista* and his multivoiced and shifting narrators in *La esquina es mi corazón*, *Loco afán: Crónicas de sidario*, and *Tengo miedo torero* challenge complacent views of the connections between gender, sexuality, poverty, and class by playfully histrionic and historical turns.

In the following, I consider these three texts in terms of the principal obsessions that animate them and summon the interlocutor to dialogue: the fields of citizenship, marginalization, resistance, transformation, subcultural knowledge, and subversion of the masculine order. The inversion of looking relations that places the *loca* as viewer of the social order—Lemebel's furtive "ojo coliza" (Lemebel 1995, 56)—visibilizes difference and difference between bodies and charges this space with significance. Unlike in the work of Arenas, the visual inspection of different bodies does not engender distance or abjection: the reader becomes thoroughly involved with the subjects and environments so envisioned. Lemebel in fact continues and completes the project to which Arenas initially pledges himself but that he ultimately fails to achieve: the political restoration of marginalized sex and gender minorities and the viability of their subjectivities.

OF *ROTOS*, *POBLADORES*, AND *COLAS*: CONTESTING CITIZENSHIP

Composed of twenty *crónicas* that overlap thematically and complement each other, *La esquina es mi corazón*, as Karina Wigozki illustrates, takes place in the euphemistically dubbed "transition to democracy," which supposedly ended the dictatorship (Wigozky n.d., 9). As Wigozky states, it investigates the marks this dictatorship has left behind: the persistence of the fear of surveillance and repression and the effects on Chile's most marginal sectors of the neoliberal economic model and its processes of globalization (9). The title of the collection is also significant: it locates the reader very much in the *vía pública* (public eye) of the streets of "peripheral" Santiago, with its traffic of persons who inhabit the (in)famous *poblaciones*, that is, the poorest suburbs of the urban city sprawl. And yet as it refers to a street corner, it also evokes a particular vantage point—that of the solitary *travesti* prostitute plying her trade, the poor beggar, the indigenous Mapuche selling *choclo*, and the sex-crazed older family man lusting after younger men, among others.

The title *crónica* deals with the young men of the *pobla*—a Chilean abbreviation for *población*—the theft, drugs, and violence in which they become enmeshed, and their parallel confrontations with the police. We perceive the many forms of trespass and the sense of hopelessness and lack of a belief in any real future in a country touted for its economic "miracle."

The street corner may constitute the heart of this narrator's passions, but the collection's allegiance is toward all those linked by their nonideal status, their failure to be "ciudadano[s] de cinco estrellas" (Lemebel 1995, 81; five-star citizens), many of whom are in attendance at a football match described in "Cómo no te voy a querer." Among them are people of the lower class who are out of work, alcoholic, and have six children to feed. Lemebel finds a loyalty with these subjects that transcends their outwardly aggressive masculinity, as they share class origins with *locas* and also experience abuse at the hands of the police. Graffiti—that most rebellious act of repressed youth—is described as black rouge smearing the contours of the city's skin. Described in terms both *loca* and feminine, the apparently mismatching forms of expression become the cause for linking radicalisms. That is, the *loca*'s expression is just as valid, expressive, and political as graffiti. Together these groups contend equally with the "ojo punitivo" (punitive eye) of the authorities and their surveillance cameras (56); as the poor, as prostitutes, as homeless, as drug users, and as "thieves," they all experience the weight of criminalization.

These sectors combine to form a social body under siege in *La esquina es mi corazón*, whose belonging in the junta's vision of orderly and prosperous Chilean society is constantly eroded by techniques of state repression and the onslaught of its economic programs that favor the elite rich. They are a citizenry in the process of disappearance, one that continues that which was literally and perniciously enforced in the years following the coup. However, by their very presence they expose the limits of terms of admission to full citizenship and the ways in which it is ideologically manipulated to suppress protest and dissent. Lemebel incisively mines the concept offering a radical view of the term.

The notion of citizenship is ubiquitous in much political and social theory, and yet, as Surya Monro points out, "studies of citizenship have traditionally paid little attention to women, trans and intersex people, and non-heterosexuals. The 'citizen' is generally assumed to be a white, male, heterosexual, able-bodied person" (2005, 147). This acknowledgment also structures Lemebel's interrogation, as the citizen in the era that he describes in his *crónicas* is a concept with contingently racial, class, and gender dimensions and moral corollaries that highly regulate sexual normativity in the public gaze. If citizenship even in so-called democracies is, as Monro argues, "a slippery concept, involving the inclusion of some groups and the exclusion of others, often along ethnic and national lines . . . historically and culturally situated" (148), then under dictatorship and a system that pushes the idea of consensus but inherits the punitive methods, policies, and structures of the previous period, as is the case in 1980s and 1990s Chile, such fractures are all the more points of concern for a socially aware writer like Lemebel, who never loses sight of the ways in which citizenship is layered culturally via institutions and state actors.

It is this relation between the state and the so-called ungovernable floating groups of Chilean *rotos*—a word used disparagingly in the country for what Marxists define as *lumpenproletariat*—that most obsesses Lemebel. *Roto* means of low standing, plebeian. For Herbert Marcuse, the lumpen are understood as that "substratum of the outcasts and outsiders, the exploited and persecuted of the other races and other colors, the unemployed and unemployable" (1964, 256–57). Lemebel highlights their status as marginalized citizens who, while they are not his ironically named "five-star citizens," do exist and struggle. Chilean society is deeply cleft by class differences. While the "pitucos" (snobs) glorify in their houses in Vitacura and Las Condes, toasting champagne to the "successes" of the free market and waxing lyrical on the order that Pinocho (the pet name for Pinochet) "restored" to a country that was "riddled" by the communist "cancer," the indigenous poor, urban *huachos*—Chilean slang for "orphan"—running the gamut from street kids to ex-cons, and *travestis* and transsexuals who perform in a poor drag circus troupe, contend with the institutions of that state and the sociocultural forces of marginalization that maintain the asymmetries of "center" and "periphery."

Lemebel intricately focuses on the agents of the asymmetries of power in the era of market ideology in which all are said to be able to participate equally. He challenges the resituating of Chile in the Aylwin transition years and its notions of what Tomás Moulian labels "El Chile Modelo" ("Model Chile") and "el Pinochet Necesario" ("The Necessary Pinochet"; 1997, 12). He puts in check the vague and soporific notion of participation and pluralism mythically eulogized through the period. This is the Chile of the blandishments of shining metallic shopping malls, glossy advertising, and the soft-core eroticism of video clips in which even revolutionary libidinal potential is repackaged and sold as one more product in the market (from the *crónica* "Barbarella Clip"). Citizenship, now another word for clientelism or consumerism, offers no guarantees for the systemically persecuted, the homeless, the ill, the denigrated, and the abused. For these marginalized populations, the repression is anything but over, and full citizenship is routinely denied.

In *La esquina es mi corazón*, Lemebel gets under the skin of his *loca* and *travesti* characters in particular: he inhabits them. And he inhabits them to a far greater degree than any other of his "non-five-star citizens." This is accentuated in the next collection of *crónicas*, *Loco afán: Crónicas de sidario*, which deals most specifically with *locas*, *travestis*, and AIDS and whose exploration of sexual citizenship is also more pronounced. By strategically situating *locas* and *travestis* among other *rotos* in the ruined landscape of neoliberalist Chile, Lemebel challenges the notion prominent on the Left that one's experience of marginalization as a member of a sex or gender minority is not a valid focus of radical attention. He proposes *locas* and *travestis* as worthy of consideration as political subjects, who can be understood as individuals implicated in the terms of social and economic exclusion in a similar way to which Marxists have already pinpointed in terms of class. The class dimensions to the subjectivities and lived experiences of Lemebel's *locas* and *travestis* is a point to which we shall return later.

"*Lucho luego existo*": Creatively Resisting Marginalization

As much as the experience of marginalization—one that unites a range of seemingly fragmented subjects—profoundly orients his depictions, in *La esquina es mi corazón* and *Loco afán: Crónicas de sidario* Lemebel does not approach marginalization as if it were a fixed property. The dangers of assigning people the moniker "marginal" or speaking of "marginality" are in the tendency to locate the problem in the people themselves, as if they were a "social disease." This accrues by the use of the adjective and the abstract noun based on the adjective—it suggests a quality, not an outcome of a process or set of forces. It also erases the process and forces whereby marginality is reproduced. Poor people, the indigenous, *travestis*, and the homeless among them thus become the standard bearers of what has been done to them, and the focus shifts away from the agents and forces of marginalization. Added to this, it does nothing to make visible the quotidian efforts of these groups to sustain their own families, communities, and livelihoods and continually renegotiate and engage with the so-called center—they are implicated in it and, although socially ostracized, also contribute to it and permeate the imaginary boundaries of "margin" and "center."[3]

La esquina es mi corazón and *Loco afán: Crónicas de sidario* make plain these quotidian efforts, that is, the intra- and intergroup networks of support and survival in the face of social and economic exile. This view of alternative citizenships concurs strongly with the models advanced by Latino/a scholars in the United States who tackle the prospect and possibilities of resistant forms of cultural citizenship in the face of dominant U.S. Anglo culture (Flores and Benmayor 1997; Rosaldo 1997). Such a form of citizenship, in the words of Paul Allatson, "refers to the ways in which Latino/a sociocultural practices establish distinct venues of belonging that, in turn, challenge dominant political discourses about citizenship that have historically excluded Latino/as from the national realm" (2007, 69). The term "Latino(a)" could easily be replaced by "roto" in the context of Lemebel's work. Earlier I asserted that citizenship, as a sociopolitical reality, is ordered by the institutions of the state. For Lemebel, ironically, the practices of these institutions become the sites and occasions of compelling *roto/a* cultural resistance. In "Censo y conquista" ("Census and Conquest") included in *La esquina es mi corazón*, Lemebel provides a view of the work of institutions and their neocolonial attitude to *mapuche* descendants. But he also reveals their resistance to the same; he shows the way the poor dodge government bureaucracy to survive—elements invisible in the statistics—and how they collaborate to protect each other from officials, declining to declare their full income or the birth of a new family member. Likewise, in "El resplandor emplumado del circo travesti" ("The Feathered Brightness of the *Travesti* Circus") from the same collection, a group of *travestis* and transsexuals perform in the circus, and this venue provides a way of turning around the apparent social disadvantage of their "transness." They resist the center, which ultimately tries to appropriate their energies but fails.

Although *locas* and *travestis* may risk expulsion from their families and communities in some parts of Latin America, this belies situations in which families and communities maintain loyalties toward their "errant" sons and daughters due to force of circumstance, an uneasy acceptance and, occasionally, a parental love that undoes societal stigma. The portrait of La Chumilou, a *loca* who falls under the spell of the plague, that is, AIDS, called variously "la sombra" (1997, 17; the shadow), "el Orfeo Negro" (19; Black Orpheus), and "el misterio" (33; the mystery) in *Loco afán: Crónicas de sidario*, is a case in point. La Chumilou, favorite working-girl *travesti* of married men, contracts AIDS, which leads her into a downward spiral and a loss of both social and literal capital. Her previous existence was one of exuberant luxury, position, and buying power, characterized by so much money, so much makeup, so many depilatory creams, so many gringos, dresses, shoes, food bought for the family, children's teeth filled. Lemebel's portrait of La Chumilou places her at the heart of popular class life. She is not a social pariah without connections to her setting; rather, she still lives with her mother, who cleans her "work clothes" (19). She is very aware of Chumilou's profession and lifestyle and yet does not throw her out. Instead she actually helps her and constantly worries, "diciéndole que tuviera cuidado, que no se metiera con cualquiera, que no olvidara el condón, que ella misma se los compraba en la farmacia de la esquina" (19; "telling her to take care, not to go with just anyone, not to forget her condoms, which she herself bought for her at the corner pharmacy"). This is a portrayal of considerable social integration in spite of adversity and discrimination.

Locas and *travestis* form alliances and forge solidarity among themselves. *Tengo miedo torero* reveals the tight-knit relations between its protagonist, La Loca del Frente, and her friends and cohorts, La Rana and

La Lupe. In spite of the assertion early in the novel by La Loca that "las locas eran tan ladronas, tan pérfidas, tan envidiosas" (Lemebel 2002, 25; the *locas* were such lying, envious thieves), she and her friends support and look out for one another; for La Loca, they are the family who take the place of the parents and siblings she never had or who abandoned her. Years previously, we learn that La Rana had taken La Loca in from the street, cleaned her up, and put her to work sewing, but when La Loca ultimately took her *clientela*, La Rana threw her out. In spite of this, their friendship endures. La Rana is a mother figure to La Loca.

Similarly, in *Loco afán: Crónicas de sidario*, the *colas* devotedly care for their sisters when they are dying of AIDS (from the *crónica* "El Último Beso de Loba Lamar"; "The Last Kiss of Loba Lamar"); they attend funerals and transform them from the customarily sad affairs into something glorious, camp, and scintillating—an excuse for a fashion show (from the *crónica* "Esas largas pestañas del sida local"; "The Long Eyelashes of Local AIDS"); they invent their own myths of origins, religiosity, and divine *travesti* and transsexual redemption (from the *crónica* "La transfiguración de Miguel Ángel"; "The Transfiguration of Michelangelo"); they enter in the public consciousness in ways that are both shocking and deeply human (from the *crónicas* "El rojo amanecer de Willy Oddo,"; "The Red Dawn of Willy Oddo", and "Berenice"); they lessen the impact of stigma and ostracism for having HIV by playfully and poetically rebaptizing themselves with new names (from the *crónica* "Los Mil Nombres de María Camaleón"; "The Thousand Names of Maria Chameleon"), a technique of self-conscious display through local argot and the stylish resemanticization described by Lemebel's critics as "neo-barroso," a term that comes from the Argentinian Néstor Perlongher's work, whose sensibilities run parallel to Lemebel's own.[4] As this *crónica* details,

> existe una gran alegoría barroca que empluma, enfiesta, traviste, disfraza, teatraliza o castiga la identidad a través del sobrenombre. Toda una narrativa popular del loquerío que elige seudónimos en el firmamento estelar del cine. Las amadas heroínas, las idolatradas divas, las púberes doncellas, pero también las malvadas madrastras y las lagartas hechiceras. Nombres adjetivos y sustantivos que se rebautizan continuamente de acuerdo al estado de ánimo, la apariencia, la simpatía, la bronca o el aburrimiento del clan sodomita siempre dispuesto a reprogramar la fiesta, a especular con la semiótica del nombre hasta el cansancio. (1997, 57–58)
>
> [a grand baroque allegory exists that feathers, fetes, cross-dresses, disguises, dramatizes, or punishes identity via the nickname. An entire popular *loca* narrative that chooses pseudonyms from the starry firmament of cinema. The beloved heroines, idolized divas, budding maidens, but also wicked stepmothers and snaky sorceresses. Noun and adjective names that rebaptize continually according to the state of mind, appearance, attitude, ire, or boredom of the sodomite clan, which is always willing to rejig the

festive proceedings, to speculate unto exhaustion on the semiotics of the name.]

These are all techniques of survival that are creative, furtive, and political. This is only made possible when one finally is able to "saberse diferente" (know oneself as different) and by means of the crucial taking up of the terms of that very difference—with all its cultural baggage—in a response to marginalization.

As a dissident writer and gender-variant person himself, Lemebel fractures and remakes the notion of the citizen via the scandalous reworked concept of the "ciudad-ano,"[5] a concept that transits Butler's space of abject beings and remains outside the terms of normalization and the official subject-citizen. This is also a highly eroticized citizenship; the emphasis on "ano" (anus) is surely crucial here, as it plays with what has been denigrated as passive, feminized, and inferior in Chilean culture and overtly sexualizes it. Although Butler characterizes this zone of exclusion from the domain of the subject as "unlivable," Lemebel's portraits demonstrate quite otherwise.[6]

The public presence of *locas* and *travestis*, as effeminate and feminine-identifying individuals who transgress both the bipolar gender system and male (heterosexual) space, as *aves sin nido* (birds without a nest) unable to be pinned down,[7] is surely key in the elaboration of alternative understandings of citizenship. Recently, research has been done on the issue of where the notion of citizenship and sexualities intersect, notes Surya Monro (2005, 153). There are several works that have established this field of inquiry. In *Sexual Citizenship: The Material Construction of Sexualities* (1993), David Evans writes of the interplay between the state and the market and the impact on sexuality, especially the kind viewed historically as immoral. While capitalism allows a certain degree of nonnormative sexual expression, argues Evans, this becomes ghettoized away from the mainstream, the kind of ghetto that middle-class gays form (36–37). In *Telling Sexual Stories: Power, Change and Social Worlds* (1995), Ken Plummer, meanwhile, talks of "intimate citizenship," which refers to peoples' choices about what they do with their bodies, emotions, gender identities, and desires (151). In *The Sexual Citizen: Queer Politics and Beyond* (2000), David Bell and Jon Binnie urge the queering of citizenship, which requires bringing the erotic and peoples' experiences of embodiment into discussions of citizenship (20–25). They advocate the provision of space for dissident citizenship, that is, in order to reshape the very terrain of citizenship by remaining outside of it (21). This further requires the recognition of myriad dissident sexualities, the kind described by Lemebel when he speaks of a "zoológico gay" (1997, 57; "gay zoo"). How this dissident citizenship—a sexual citizenship—emerges in all its political radicalism will be explored subsequently. However, first it is important to consider how the *loca* narrative gaze on neoliberalist Chile allows Lemebel to reposition questions of difference, otherness, the place of *locas* and *travestis* historically, and their expulsion from the national story itself in order to demonstrate the impossibility of arrogating Lemebel's marginalized sexual subjects to the terms of the national subject.

THE *OJO COLIZA* THAT SPIES FROM BEHIND: THE *LOCA* GAZE ON NEOLIBERAL CHILE

In *La esquina es mi corazón* the third-person perspective leads us through various parts of the city—a Santiago not shown on the usual tourist maps—some communally shared and others more intimate. It starts in a suitably lascivious and transgressive way, voyeuristically trespassing on the realities of beat sex, all registered by the eyes of a not-disinterested *cola*. Public space is masculine and heterosexually dominated; the darkened space of a park at night offers opportunities to slip by the administrative punitive gaze of the *milicos* and *carabineros*—the army and the police respectively—and their methods of social control. This is the kind of public sex that scandalizes straight passersby in their matrimonial bliss, the kind of sex parents warn their sons about; corporeal encounters under constant threat of police brutality—and all the more intense for that reason.

The reader is then led by the perverse *flâneur* of a narrator into a beach club frequented by the high-class "beautiful people" of the city, following a well-known prostitute, Babilonia, who crosses the gridlines of the classed city to solicit among the "perraje," alongside other familiar sexual fauna, *unas locas* (Lemebel 1995, 38, 40). The narrator-voyeur fixes our gaze on one constant fact: there is always a *loca* somewhere in the changing landscape, even in the most heterosexual of environments; this *loca* is both the viewed and the viewer. We are taken to an all-male sauna where a *loca* returns to her old haunts twenty years after the coup, the day the *milicos* (soldiers) broke into *Los Baños Placer*. In her old age, she defies the stereotype of the body beautiful and flaunts publicly her phallic obsessions.

The narrative gaze also constantly homosexualizes this landscape: Bruce Lee movies dubbed into Spanish form the homoerotic background for the meeting of two ethnically different men in a sticky embrace; football, the national religion, is homoeroticized. When a *loca* haunts the stadium suddenly everyone turns a little homosexual.

The primordial *loca*—so untamable and ubiquitous—is eminently figured in the landscape of *otros* brought so clearly into view within the *loca*'s own gaze. She is part of the *fauna popular* (street life) that persists in spite of the current climate, even as it is in danger of crashing out of existence, because of the social violence of the repressive state, the AIDS epidemic, or the dispossession of neoliberalism, a fact that "Coleópteros en el parabrisas" amply illustrates. In this *crónica*, in the midst of all the transnational products and signs that mark the globalizing urban landscape, we have set in relief the kitsch confluence of old buses with their popular ballads blaring out of wonky loudspeakers, a traveling marketplace of suburbanites brimmed to the hilt, and a driver-disc jockey who hugs the curves dangerously. A *loca* is in the melee:

> Entonces se toma del pasamanos a la altura del marrueco y cada vez que el chico afirma el bulto la loca no respira. Más bien desfallece cuando se da cuenta de que el péndex no se quita, es decir, se refriega en sus dedos agarrotados. Y así mano y nervio, fierro y carne, loca y péndex, van agarrados de la misma fiebre, sujetos del mismo deseo clandestino que nadie ve. Ni siquiera el paco sentado que se hace el civil y no se da cuenta de la paja que le corren al estudiante en sus propias narices. (142–43)
>
> [So she slides her hand along the railing down to where his fly is and every time that the guy pushes out his package, *la loca* stops breathing. She practically faints when she realizes the guy doesn't pull away, but rubs himself against her fingers on the railing. And so hand and nerves, iron and flesh, *loca* and trade, both prey to the same fever, both subject to the same clandestine desire that no one sees. Not even the cop dressed as a civvy who doesn't twig at the smell of cum wafting under his very nose.]

Passengers, driver, goods, and metal become intertwined in a violent stew of modernity when the bus flies out of control, providing a snapshot of the collision of cultural norms, where the most seemingly unlikely blends together, if violently, in an epistemological upending.

The "ojo coliza" brazenly gazes from behind, winking seductively in a turn that literalizes Lemebel's emphasis on the "ano" in "ciudad-ano" (55). The attributed passivity of the *loca*'s sphincter-eye—made ironically active by the perspective of the *loca* viewer that embellishes the landscape—has prompted Wigozki to describe the transformative potential of the *travesti*'s visual demarcation of space. This creates a "travestied space": the ownership of the gaze takes possession of territory and redefines it, in spite of the perils of the authorities who hound and delimit one's movement in the city. As Wigozki states, "con su presencia y comportamiento en la ciudad, el travesti se constituye como una figura desestabilizadora que confronta el paradigma de la ciudad 'ordenada'" (Wigozki n.d., 2; with her presence and behavior in the city, the *travesti* becomes a destabilizing figure that confronts the paradigm of the ordered city). With her persistent insertion in space, the *travesti* asserts her right to be, following Gónzalez Pérez's invocation of Erving Goffman's "revindication of the 'I'" in his study *Travestidos al desnudo* (2003; "*Travestis*" *Stripped Bare*).

Space is contested among a variety of actors, including some formal representatives of the state and other informal representatives of "morality." The formal representatives of the state—the police and the army among them—exploit existing frameworks that criminalize the lives of the poor, *locas* and *travestis* among them, and curtail their movements. The "ojo vigilante" of the state, is, however, profoundly challenged by the answering "ojo coliza," which undermines the strictures of the order, conventional morality, and permissibility. As González-Pérez observes, in the case of *travestis*, their territories are vindicated by different tactics, but they are never fixed (2003, 93). This tallies with Lemebel's visions, which inscribe a kind of nomadism to *locas* and *travestis*, something that will be discussed in length later.

The contested movement of the *loca* or *travesti* through besieged space also configures the emergence of their subjectivity. As mentioned in Chapter 1, one's presence and coursing through physical space informs one's subjectivity, as space becomes the nexus of intersubjective relations and the articulation of difference. As González-Pérez understands this process, following Goffman, "cuando un individuo interactúa pone en juego estrategias que marcan su diferencia ante el 'otro'" (93; when an individual interacts s/he puts into play strategies marking his/her difference from "another"). One's interpellation in space acts in such a way that the conjoinment of space and social articulation are given new meaning, that is, in terms of one's existence and position in the world (93).

Wigozki calls this revindication or differentiation in its *travesti* mode a *travesti* discourse (Wigozki n.d., 1). The eye-I is central in the configuration of the *loca* and *travesti*'s belonging to the landscape—roving, moveable but active, fundamentally challenging cultural equations of sexual "passivity" and femininity with weakness and submission. In the work of Lemebel, the terms of "otherness" are in fact turned around—the *loca* is at the center, and heterosexual normativity and the terms of patrimonial history, tradition, and nation are made strange, even superfluous.

With his *loca*'s denaturalizing gaze, Lemebel exposes the performativity at the heart of cultural and national "givens," piercing through to the core and beyond the pretensions of superficial neoliberalist fantasies of unity and participation. The willful injunction to forget the past and wallow in the irreducible present of collective consumerism has resulted in what Moulian calls the "blanqueo" and homogenization of Chilean culture (1997, 33). This market homogenization works together with the state's political nationalism as seen in the national-holiday celebrations, whose underlying character is viewed by Lemebel as patriarchal and as a reinscription of colonial relations between the state and its various others. In "Chile mar y cueca," included in *La esquina es mi corazón*, these national festivities become a means of false participation, in the style of the "bread and circuses" realized by the Romans in which the people of the *pobla* lose themselves in the alcoholism of the free beer and *pisco*, and an imposed national identity replaces the lost community one. Desire becomes, following Molloy, national desire.[8] Yet the loss of previous identities is not just an effect of media and symbolism but rather the very institutionalized processes that continue to allow the "desaparición del Otro" (Moulian 1997, 38–39; the disappearance of the Other). The *loca*'s lascivious desire is not equated at all to this national desire, but rather, undoes it, complicates it, and destabilizes its heterosexual and masculine center. It is a desire that is particular and transgressive of all that is deemed holy.

In the neoliberalist landscape viewed by the "ojo coliza," there are multitudes of *otros*, as we have seen. And yet *locas* and *travestis* remain insistently among them, as both viewer and viewed—self-aware and aware of others, necessary in the condition of a state of siege. The tendency for the gaze of the *cronista*-voyeur to locate constantly the *loca* in the landscape is also evident in Lemebel's homosexualization of the Chilean national dance, *la cueca*, which undoes the male heterosexual domination of the woman partner by describing how "amariconado" (faggy) the male looks as he moves his "culito" (Lemebel 1995, 96; "little ass"). Heterosexuality is a performance, seeing is believing, and appearances can deceive. These terms are not linked to *travestismo* but rather seeming "gender normativity." The difference between heterosexuality and homosexuality is a matter of degree as well as dependent on one's viewing position. This is a wonderful reversal that draws attention not to the performativity of queer and transgender subjects, but rather, to that of the so-called central and heterosexual national subject. Lemebel is conscious of the fact that *locas* and *travestis* have been and continue to be excluded from the national story and its modes of enunciation, as he ironically subverts this rite of national identity and the foundation of the *criollo* nation.

In this way, the identities of *locas* and *travestis*, although seen by Lemebel as part of a folkloric landscape of Chilean or Latin American cultural "originality," do not embody any kind of project of nation, contrary to the assertions of Sandra Garabano, who states,

> En el cuerpo de la cultura gay y en el cuerpo de la loca se pueden leer ciertos proyectos de nación articulados alrededor de las fricciones entre un presente, marcado por el discurso de la modernización, y un pasado, quizás arcaico, que plantea las relaciones entre metropolis y periferia en términos de una invasión imperialista. (2003, 50)
>
> [In the body of gay culture and the *loca*'s body one can read certain projects of nation articulated around the tensions of the present, marked by the discourse of modernization, and the past, perhaps more archaic, which proposes relations between the metropolis and the periphery in terms of an imperialist invasion.]

Lemebel may position the "míster gay" as a product of imperialistic projects of cultural homogenization and the *loca* or *travesti* as a point of difference as well as a "native" sexuality—elements that are addressed in the next section—but *locas* and *travestis* are never tied to any sort of national project, before or after Pinochet, pre- or postneoliberalist policy in Chile. Lemebel may look back nostalgically to the possibilities for Chilean minorities of Allende's all-too-short period in power (a nostalgia captured in *Loco afán: Crónicas de sidario*), but this is sobered by an implicit and historical recognition that the Left did not make life any easier for sexual minorities in particular.[9] Further, the insistent "ojo coliza" in his *crónicas* elicits a desiring gaze that interrupts, diverts, and overtakes the sublimation of desire into "national desire" and is hence also radical in libidinal-political terms: revoking the pretensions of nation and heteronormativity.

Class, Nomadism, and *Locas*: Transformational Power and Subcultural Knowledge

Ultimately, Lemebel is not interested in employing figures of gender-variant homosexuality, *travestismo*, or transsexuality to embody a national-cultural problem or situation; rather, he looks to these subjects as subjects who exist in the real world and appraises them for their radical political potential, as unique and unrepeatable subversive forms of diversity in an increasingly homogenized cultural landscape. If they represent anything at all, then it is the maligned and marginalized aspects of Chilean culture—not the "national" collective, which for Lemebel is little more than a performance, updated and falsely evoked again in the era of neoliberalism.

The typical class origins of many of his *locas* and *travestis* forms a central element in their power of transgression and hence marks an important part of his representations. In spite of this, the diversity of his subjects is always palpable: one cannot generalize about *locas* or *travestis*, like any other group of individuals, they are not uniform and show differing political allegiances, movement in and out of "marginalities." *Locas* in particular may come from divergent class backgrounds, although *locas* and *travestis* are principally associated with the popular classes or the *rotería* that Lemebel celebrates (a proposition that confirms the work of Annick Prieur).

In spite of this, Lemebel is interested in exceptions and not simplistic paradigms. He describes a type of culturally accommodated "queen" who is a relative of Arenas's *loca regia*—an opportunistic individual who has contacts in high places and is thus protected. Gonzalo Cáceres is depicted in this light in one of the pieces in *Loco afán: Crónicas de sidario* and also in *Tengo miedo torero*. Cáceres was the official stylist for the presidential couple and moved in elite circles both during and after the dictatorship, somehow avoiding scrutiny for his connection to Pinochet in the transition to democracy period. When Lemebel talks of Gonzalo's artistry as a *loca* as a form of betrayal and concealment, he does not trope *loca* styles or embodiments themselves—he consciously highlights the exceptional class allegiances that overwrite any positive appraisal of this figure. Thus the following attributions cannot be extended to *locas* or *travestis* generally: "su elefántica silueta maquillando la cara de la dictadura" (1997, 123; "his elephantine silhouette making up the dictatorship's face"); "espolvoreaba de luz y coloreaba de hiprocresía la cara de la represión" (123; "powdered with light and colored with hypocrisy the face of repression"); "pintando de tornasol los discursos oficiales" (124; "painting sunflowers around the official discourses"). It is Gonzalo's hypocrisy that is exposed here. In exploring the subjectivities of *locas* and *travestis* whose class backgrounds and allegiances Lemebel perceives as progressive and antiestablishment, these images that connect "making up" to deception and corruption are absent. Lemebel privileges a class analysis over an emphasis on shared homosexual desire, as Palaversich notes (2002, 102). He does not show sympathy toward his subjects simply by virtue of their homosexuality nor does he view shared "homosexual desire" as a basis for identity, community, or radical subjectivity, as we shall see.

Those *locas* with delusions of wealth and class—the kinds of delusions that structure much of Chilean society itself—are lambasted by the narrator of *Loco afán: Crónicas de sidario*. These are the "locas jai," who in the first *crónica* of *Loco afán: Crónicas de sidario*, "La noche de los visones (o la última fiesta de la Unidad Popular)," which takes place on New Year's Eve, 1972, mock the poorer *locas* and *travestis* who support la Unidad Popular (1997, 13). These *locas* share the same class prejudices as the heterosexual, upper- and middle-class *pitucos* (snobs) who live across town; and yet, the greatest irony is that, for all their pretensions, they are pursued by police and harassed just the same. This *crónica* fittingly opens the collection, setting the scene for the tumultuous political change that the coup occasioned and that would modify and reshape homo and trans subjectivities in Chile, especially with the application of neoliberal policies, the widening gulfs between social classes, and the severe mismanagement of the HIV/AIDS epidemic in the era of the dictatorship.

Readers may detect the strong tone of nostalgia in this *crónica*, alluded to earlier; however, in my view, it is more apocalyptic and mordant, as it adumbrates the shape of things to come. The coup changes the rules even in the most geographical sense:

> Vino el golpe y la nevazón de balas provocó la estampida de las locas que nunca más volvieron a danzar por los patios floridos de la UNCTAD. Buscaron otros lugares, se reunieron en los paseos recién inaugurados de la

dictadura. Siguieron las fiestas, más privadas, más silenciosas, con menos gente educada por la cripta del toque de queda (15–16).

[The coup came and the shower of bullets provoked the stampede of *locas* who never again danced in the florid patios of UNCTAD (The United Nations Conference for Trade and Development). They looked for other places, in the pathways newly erected by the dictatorship. The parties continued, more private and silently, and with fewer high-class people because of the curfew.]

Surveillance becomes the order of the day with the consequent normalization of those who stand out because of their gender expression.

Ironically, if we compare Chile to Cuba, the fact that one form of militarized order was right wing while the other left wing matters little: in both cases *locas* and *travestis* were among those targeted for their heightened visibility as subjects that led them to being rounded up, shipped off, and abandoned or tortured, in the case of several in the early months of the junta in Chile or sent off to UMAP (Unidades Militares de Ayuda a la Producción) work camps in the case of Cuba.[10] In both countries, *locas* and *travestis* as well as street prostitutes were rounded up. The former were subject to random removal of hair and forced masculinization, the latter, to methods of "reform" and abuse. Those *locas* and *travestis* who survived the horrors contended instead with HIV/AIDS. The "pestilencia" of the coup equated to the later one of AIDS (16). These are the lines of contention that serve to frame the lived experiences of *locas* and *travestis* in ways that are intelligible to the Left and its traditional causes. Traditional Leftist groups have failed to extend the solidarity they customarily express, for instance, to political prisoners or to the indigenous and (heterosexual) working class to sexual minorities. This, then, centers Lemebel's passionate reconsideration of the subjectivities and lived experiences of *locas* and *travestis*.

Furthering his examination of categories of social relations and the construction of subjectivities, in "Tarántulas en el pelo," also featured in *Loco afán: Crónicas de sidario*, Lemebel focuses on hairdressing salons as a site of transformation and the molding of fantasies of class, glamour, and superiority. Crucially those responsible for the makeover are *locas*, who, with their vedette images of femininity, are permitted this sole cultural space. The hairdresser and his art form point to a uniquely *loca* or *coliza* space: "Detrás de la imagen de mujer famosa, casi siempre existe un modisto, maquillador o peluquero que le arma la facha y el garbo para enfrentar las cámaras. Una complicidad que invierte el travestismo, al travestir a la mujer con la exuberancia coliza negada socialmente" (104; Behind the image of a famous woman, there's almost always a fashion designer, cosmetician or hairstylist who will make her over for the cameras. A form of complicity that turns *travestismo* upside down, by cross-dressing women with an exuberance socially denied to *locas*). Where publicly such skills of self-transformation meet with ire and rejection, they are manipulated and accommodated to the needs of those with money and a desire to flaunt it—a dark-skinned woman becomes the image of Lady Di, thanks to this "alquimia que transmuta el barro latino en oro nórdico" (107; alchemy that transforms Latin clay into Nordic gold). In this way, *locas* or *travestis* themselves are not presented as symbols of some flight from class or race, but rather, the system of inequitable relations and social privileges that accumulate via the signifiers of wealth and ransack the poor artisanry of their visual talent and hence become targets of Lemebel's critique:

> Como si en este aclarado se evaporaran por arte de magia las carencias económicas, los dolores de la raza y clase que el indiaje blanqueado amortigua en el laboratorio de encubrimiento social de la peluquería, donde el coliza va coloreando su sueño cinematográfico en las ojeras grises de la utopía tercermundista. (107–8)
>
> [As if in this bleaching economic scarcity, the pains of race and class softened and masked by whitened Indianness, would magically vanish in the hairdresser's social laboratory, where the *loca* dyes with her cinematographic dream the dark grey circles under the utopian eyes of the Third World.]

The new era of market dreaming offers the promise that one merely requires the look of wealth to become a wealthy person. We recall that the notion of transformation and transcendence of race and class is also present in *Sirena Selena*. And yet here, the pressures of the globalizing utopian setting are foregrounded, and this tendency to adopt the poses of an idealized other in an attempt to become that other are not attached to *travesti* or *loca* identities themselves. As hairdressers and stylists, they merely respond to the need that the market creates—they are implicated, like their own clients who insist on another bleach job or hairset, in this recreation, but they are not its symbol. They work in the increasingly rare privately owned downtown salons because no other work is available to them; neither is the opportunity to receive higher education, Lemebel notes (110). Their own ambitions are comparatively humble: to make enough money to buy some "pilchas" (threads) to dress up and go to the discos, have some fleeting pleasure with the young boys available (106). That *travestismo* is described as inverted may have two explanations: the *travestismo* of a poor and wearied woman into diva, where usually it serves to transform from male to female, but also, the relocation of the skills of *travesti* transformation to serve different, indeed opposite, ends. Lemebel thus avoids the troping moments found in Santos-Febres's novel.

In "La música y las luces nunca se apagaron," we revisit the scene of a crime: the firebombing in 1996 of the gay disco, Divine. Lemebel uses this event to focus on the detached transnationalist consumerist dreamworld that already structures commercial gay culture. The patrons are so distant from reality that they do not realize the club is under attack. This disco culture is not the domain of *travestis*, but rather, those who emulate North American models of homosexuality, increasingly sellable in the ghetto scene of the upwardly mobile gay of Santiago. This class critique of different homosexualities is also present in "Las locas del verano leopardo" from *La esquina es mi corazón*, which deals with the emergence of a gay culture in Chile, and the mobility and tourism of several older homosexual men to towns who take their desires across class lines. These features intensify in the collection *Loco afán: Crónicas de sidario*.

Once again, we have difference dispersed across several domains—the difference of class origins of *locas* and *travestis* from normative gays as well as the difference in class allegiances between these very *locas* and *travestis*, which provides a historical picture of the evolution of sexually and gender-diverse subjectivities. As Guerra Cunningham surmises, Lemebel thus rejects "las postulaciones intelectuales que abstraían la condición *gay* al plano puramente filosófico de la identidad, [y en lugar de ésto] elige historiar esa condición haciendo eco de la praxis política de Foucault" (2000, 110; intellectual theorizations that abstract the gay condition to the purely philosophical plane of identity, [and instead of this] chooses to historicize this condition echoing the political praxis of Foucault).

La Chumilou, mentioned earlier, dies the same day that democracy "arrives." The passage of her cortege blends unexpectedly with the happiness and celebration at the successful "abnegation" of Pinochet in the first general elections—two ends of an era. By this stage, *travesti* life as it has been is no longer. At her funeral, topless boys with rainbow flags dance in a frenzy. "Is this the future emancipation the *colas* dreamed of?" the reader is prompted to ask, or in the words of the text,

> antes que el barco del milenio atraque en el dos mil, antes, incluso, de la legalidad del homosexualismo chileno, antes de la militancia gay que en los noventa reunió a los homosexuales, antes que esa moda masculina se impusiera como uniforme del ejército de salvación, antes que el neoliberalismo en democracia diera permiso para aparearse. (Lemebel 1997, 21–22)
> [before the millennium ship moored in the year 2000, before even the status of legality was granted to Chilean homosexuality, before the gay militancy of the 1990s brought homosexuals together, before masculine fashion was imposed like a Salvation Army uniform, before neoliberal democracy granted permission for civil unions.]

There is evidence that in Chile the earliest rumbles of a gay movement were spearheaded, as in Stonewall in the United States, by street queens and transvestites.[11] Now such facts are largely forgotten in both places and trans people have been successively marginalized in homoerotic communities. This was 1973: before the era of neoliberalism and AIDS, before the coup, before the gay uniform of masculinity, before the metamorphosis of homosexualities by the end of the century, and before the demise of the *loca* consumed by AIDS and decimated by what Lemebel positions as an imported gay model. As Lemebel sees *loquerío* and *travestismo* as indigenous forms of homosexuality, AIDS hence becomes a recolonization, contracted in the North, knocking off the natives, the *locas*, with bodily fluids. This facilitates the arrival of the "Modelos de Olimpio del Primer Mundo" (Olympian Models from the First World) with their "bíceps y clases educativas de fisicoculturismo" (biceps and weight-lifting classes) that is "el míster gay" (23):

> Una nueva conquista de la imagen rubia que fue prendiendo el arribismo malinche de las locas más viajadas, las regias que copiaron el modelito de Nueva York y lo transportaron a este fin de mundo. Y junto al molde de Superman, precisamente por la aséptica envoltura de esa piel blanca, tan higiénica, tan perfumada por el embrujo capitalista. (23)
>
> [A new conquest of the blond image that gradually ignited the love of all things foreign and the social climbing of the most well-traveled *locas*, the elegant ones who copied the New York fashion model and brought him to this end of the world. And together with the Superman mold, sought precisely for its antiseptic white skin wrapping, so hygienic and perfumed by the capitalist spell.]

Lemebel sees no power of resistance in this globalizing gay model and laments the disappearance of many of his fellow queens and *travestis*, in whom one finds a true potential for transgression: "Todavía es subversivo el cristal obsceno de sus carcajadas, desordenando el supuesto de los géneros" (22; The obscene crystal of their laughter is still subversive, disordering the supposed norm of genders).

In "Nalgas Lycra, Sodoma Disco," Lemebel sarcastically critiques this new gay model and its seemingly neoliberalist-friendly commercial appeal. For Lemebel, this kind of gay clone image that pretends to an establishment masculinity is depoliticized and accommodated to the capitalist climate. The homo-dance ghetto disco unites these gays better than any political militancy—their only cause is "imponiendo estilos de vida y una filosofía de camuflaje viril que va uniformando, a través de la moda, la diversidad de las homosexualidades locales" (53; imposing a philosophy of virile camouflage that dresses in uniform, via fashion, the diversity of local homosexualities). The John Travolta macho image becomes institutionalized in the 1980s in Chile. Lemebel characterizes this new club environment as a Mapuche Olympus—they could be queens, except for the cut of their clothes; they could be stars, except their Levis are knock-offs;

they could be young, except for the horrendous bags under their eyes. They seem almost straight, except for the smell of freshly pressed jeans and cologne—Obsession for Men by Calvin Klein—and the phrases they utter that always begin with "Ay." This is a tame, defanged homosexuality that answers to middle-class imperatives and the myth of a homosexual ethnic-style identity, a homosexuality that gingerly conglomerates in the ghetto, secluded from the tribulations of the sexphobia and homophobia of the wider culture. It represents acceptance purchased by credit card, quite literally in the form of "la tarjeta Rainbow," transposed from North America. It constitutes a contained and co-opted homosexuality, content to construct its own image in the image of the market.[12] Such a community is little more than a "gueyto": a gay-market ghetto.

And yet it goes further than this. In the present day, *locas* and *travestis* have increasingly become sidelined in many upwardly mobile gay districts and the association of homosexuality with *lo femenino* vigorously disavowed. Such a development is not confined solely to Chile or Latin America but has taken place in Australian, European, and North American contexts as well, in an increasingly globalized climate. Before the gay liberation movement, subjects now commonly called "transgender" and "homosexual" were not always theoretically separated. In major U.S. cities such as New York, where the Stonewall rebellion occurred, and San Francisco, where the earlier Compton's Cafeteria riots took place, the working class bar dykes, nellies, butches, and street queens who fought on the front lines understood each other as "camp" or homosexual, in spite of their wide range of gender behaviors. They did not necessarily see themselves as part of that same-sex-desiring identity ascribed to, however, by the middle class, as the work of George Chauncey shows (1994). As Steve Valocchi explains in "The Class-Inflected Nature of Gay Identity" (1999), previously "men who had an erotic interest in other men encompassed many different gender styles, sexual habits, and class positions" (1999, 211). As he further indicates, "it was in middle class communities . . . that the core identity of sexual object choice emerged as the defining feature of the homosexual person. Growing up beside the working class gay communities of fairies, trade, and husbands were middle class homosexuals who used these groups as 'negative examples' of their own identities" (211). The socioeconomic changes that the post–World War II years brought and the example of the black civil rights movement promoted the consolidation of middle-class homosexual populations who redefined the homosexual in the terms of an ethnic-like minority. Although street queens and bulldaggers brought the oppression of sexual minorities to national attention, these middle-class groups possessed the economic resources to build the movement in their own image—and to exclude those deemed bad for its image.

The historical rejection of anything gender variant in homosexualities continues to this day. As Wayne Martino states in an article in the book *Gendered Outcasts and Sexual Outlaws*, "Although it could be argued that there is a subversive potential in the appropriation of straight-acting masculinities for gay men who defy the mainstream culture's representation and positioning of gay men as 'feminized faggot,' the 'masculinity confirming' . . . discourses that are mobilized by these men are circumscribed within the regulatory apparatus of heterosexuality that is invested in essentializing, naturalizing, and eroticizing a form of masculine power—a power that is produced through the force of constituting an abjected feminized Other" (2006, 38). Similar developments have occurred in the Chilean context, and the rise of neoliberalism might be seen as facilitating this erasure of *locas* and *travestis* as transgressively gendered (homo)sexualities by the gay community. The disavowal of what is seen as "abnormal" and "perverse" amounts to a sort of "cleansing" of this feminine abject other, and her "low class" associations (55). As Lemebel's allegiance is primordially positioned toward the feminine, the so-called perverse and abnormal form loci for the elaboration of a radical, politicized subjectivity, which he passionately seeks to rescue and restore in *Loco afán: Crónicas de sidario*, in all its color and proletarian potential. Accommodated gay sexualities simply reinscribe their allegiance to the classist, heterosexist, and paternalistic order. Working class *loca* and *travesti* subjectivities challenge that order: its precious concepts of *hombría*, in both Left and Right persuasions.

In "Manifiesto: hablo por mi diferencia," ("Manifesto: I Speak From My Difference") placed midway through the *Loco afán*, Lemebel directly occupies this "abnormal" and "perverse" difference, speaking in the first person. He resituates *hombría*—what it is to be truly valiant—in terms of *loca* and *travesti* lived experience. He says "no me hable del proletariado / Porque ser pobre y maricón es peor" (83; Don't speak to me about the proletariat / Because being poor and a faggot is worse). This text was read as an intervention in a political action undertaken by the Left in 1986:

> ¿No habrá un maricón en alguna esquina desequilibrando el futuro de su hombre nuevo?[13]
> [Won't there be a faggot in some corner upsetting the future of the New Man?]
> . . .
> No sabe que la hombría
> Nunca la aprendí en los cuarteles
> Mi hombría me la enseñó la noche
> Detrás de un poste. (1997, 85–87)
> [You don't know manliness

I never learnt it in the barracks
I learnt manliness at night
behind a post.]

In a similar way to many of the *locas* and *travestis* in *La esquina es mi corazón* and *Loco afán: Crónicas de sidario*, the protagonist of *Tengo miedo torero* is notable for her class background. La Loca is a dressmaker who lives alone and gains the attention of the neighborhood by singing boleros. She sews clothes for the rich. An aging *mariposuelo* (gay butterfly) who needs a boyfriend according to the local gossips, she is oblivious to the current political upheavals and their import. Everything about her is *loca*: "pájara," "emplumado," (bird-like, feathered) scandalously different (Lemebel 2002, 12, 16). La Loca, the text relates, is "De origen humilde—no sabía de esas cosas universitarias" (33; From a humble background—she didn't know about university things). Like the *locas* and *travestis* depicted in *La esquina es mi corazón* and *Loco afán: Crónicas de sidario*, she possesses a class-specific, subcultural knowledge, having learned from "las lecciones sucias de la calle" (34; the dirty lessons of the street).

Poet and anthropologist Néstor Perlongher, mentioned earlier, also sees in *locas* and *travestis* a kind of identity distinct from the homogenized gay identity, one that is increasingly minoritized and threatened but that offers a kind of radical critique of the order not possible under the gay model. He speaks of the "feminidad radical del travesti" (1997, 47; radical femininity of the *travesti*). He is highly critical of what he perceives as a normalizing project within the homosexual community, which mirrors the overall normalizing project of heteronormative culture, whereby straight-acting gay masculinities buy acceptance in mainstream circles (33). Moreover, Perlongher urges us to resist subsuming the variant singularities of identities like *loca, el chongo*,[14] *el travesti*, and so on into a "generalidad personológica: 'el homosexual'" (a general typology: "the homosexual"):

> Esta normalización de la homosexualidad erige, además, una personología y una moda, la del modelo gay. Siendo más concretos, una posibilidad personológica—el gay—pasa a tomarse como modelo de conducta. Este operativo de normalización arroja a los bordes a los nuevos marginados, los excluidos de la fiesta: travestis, locas, chongos, gronchos—que en general son pobres—sobrellevan los prototipos de sexualidad más populares. (33)
> [This normalization of homosexuality constructs, as well, a whole typology of persons and a fashion, that of the gay model. To be more concrete, this set of subject possibilities—the gay type—ends up being taken up as a model of conduct. This operation of normalization consigns the newly marginalized to the edges, those not invited to the party: *travestis, locas,*

chongos, gronchos—who in general are poor—overtaking the sexuality prototypes most associated with the popular classes.]

Lemebel, as we have seen, does not pledge himself to the idea of a homosexual ethnic-style identity, as this he sees as primarily a middle-class formation that erases local specificities. His *crónicas* make visible a whole range of homosexual possibilities, from the "tíos carrozas" of the older generation to the taxi boys and "cafiches" of the younger generation, whose interaction is not based on some idea of shared gay identity.[15] Then we have the *loca* and *travesti* who simultaneously are homoerotic and crossgendered and in a constant state of elaboration, following Lemebel's own baroque linguistic dispersals: *cola, coliza, coliflor, colipata, maraco, marifrunci, mariflauta,* and *maripos*ón (Lemebel 1997). These are all puns that work via orthographic and phonological extensions of *cola* and *maricón*, both of which signify queen or faggot, and also the word for butterfly in Spanish, which is *mariposa*.

Perlongher, in a manner that fits very well with Lemebel's vision, argues for a model that guarantees a proliferation of identities, sexualities, and possibilities of becoming that are not restrained by a dominant normalizing identity model. Taking inspiration from Deleuze when he speaks of "becoming woman," Perlongher argues the need to "soltar todas las sexualidades, abrir todos los devenires" (Perlongher 1997, 33; unleash all sexualities, open up all becomings). Foremost here is the *loca* who is nomadic and unfixed in her identity, who proposes for Perlongher, as her name may suggest, "la sexualidad loca, la sexualidad que es una fuga de la normalidad, que la desafía y la subvierte . . . corroe a la normalidad en todos sus wings" (33; *Loca* sexuality, a sexuality that is a flight from normality, which challenges and subverts it . . . undermining it in all its wings). Lemebel's *locas* and *travestis*, via their camp humor and an ever-changing and performative poetics of being and acting in their worlds, possess a true transformative power. The *loca* "mode" is both a politics and a poetics that is transcendental and not fixed to a particular identity, lifestyle, or fashion. Neither is it rational, schematic, or politically correct for that matter. The flipside of the negative valence of *loca* as mad is one that proposes this identity as a modus operandi that cannot be second-guessed and that constantly refuses normalization.[16]

Subversive Subjectivities: *Travesti* Bodies, Prostitute Bodies

Elijo la palabra travesti porque es importante resignificar el término con el cual nos refieren a nosotras . . . Tenemos diferencias físicas y culturales con las mujeres. Acepto que hemos sido criadas con toda una carga patriarcal . . . [pero] somos, como las mujeres, traidoras del patriarcado, y eso es algo que muchas tenemos que pagar con nuestras vidas . . . El género que queremos construir no es el femenino, pero no podemos negar que algunas de las características que asumimos se encuentran en las mujeres. Pero aquí tenemos dos opciones: somos las mujeres que consumen el sistema, lindas, dulces, etc. O nos identificamos con quienes luchan por el aborto, por la libre elección sexual y con las bolivianas que luchan por sus tierras, entre otras . . . Es aquí en donde nosotras somos lo que queremos ser en solidaridad contra un enemigo común . . . que se manifiesta en la opresión social—desprecio y falta de trabajo—y en la violencia institucional. Somos mujeres y somos un escándalo, esta es una respuesta a la condena.

[I choose the word travesti because it's important to resignify the term used to refer to us . . . We possess physical and cultural differences from women. I accept that we are brought up under patriarchal power . . . but, like women, we are traitors of patriarchy, and this is something that many of us have to pay for with our lives . . . The gender that we wish to construct isn't a feminine one, but we can't deny that some of the characteristics that we take on are found among women. Here we have two options: either we are women who consume, pretty, sweet, etc. Or we identify with those that fight for abortion, for free sexual choice and with Bolivian women who fight for their land, among other militant women . . . This is where we become what we want to be in solidarity against a common enemy that is visible in forms of social oppression—derision and lack of employment—and institutional violence. We are women and we're a scandal, this is our response to social condemnation.]

—Lohana Berkins, quoted in Flavio Rapisardi, "Regulaciones políticas. Identidad, diferencia y desigualdad. Una crítica al debate contemporáneo"

In *Loco afán: Crónicas de sidario*, we are exposed to the body in flames, a place of intensities, but also the body with wounds: bearing the marks of the epidemic in a manner similar to the gender-variant bodies that turn up to the *salón de belleza* (beauty salon) in Mario Bellatin's eponymous novel. However, this particular body is displayed by Lemebel as a protest body, a shamed and scandalous site of transgression. These bodies in *Loco afán: Crónicas de sidario* are also the site of the emplotment of difference, that is, from both hetero- and homonormativity. Such elements are key to Lemebel's envisioning of *loca* and *travesti* subjectivities. In both *Loco afán: Crónicas de sidario* and *Tengo miedo torero*, Lemebel pays close attention to the many dimensions of subjectivity—psychic, intersocial, class, race, and sexuality, to name a few. As in *Salón de belleza* and *El Rey de La Habana*, in these *crónicas* the body becomes a site through which subjectivity is constructed and difference is articulated.

In "La Muerte de Madonna," we learn of the Mapuche version of Madonna—a *travesti* street sex worker, the first to get HIV/AIDS among the *travestis* in San Camilo. She used to have another name, but when she saw the Blond Ambition girl on television, she went crazy imitating her, copied all her moves, and bleached her hair to insanity until it started to fall out in clumps. She mouthed words that she did not understand from Madonna's songs in English—she knew them by heart. You could close your eyes and you would think it was Madonna—the Mapuche copy.

In this *crónica*, Lemebel depicts a performance art and video installation event "Gone with the Epidemic" (punning on *Gone with the Wind*) that took place in the 1980s. This was a *loca-travesti* broadway send up by Las Yeguas del Apocalipsis performed to expose the lack of response to AIDS. Among the *travestis* who attended the event, lascivious and pumped up on silicone, La Madonna was the most photographed that night, the center of attention. Seeing her moment, she grabbed a female video artist and began posing naked for the camera—like her idol—using the special *travesti* tuck to hide her candy called "el candado chino," (the Chinese padlock) all Venus, all virgin. However, under the heat of the lights and cameras her offending member pops out. Years later, after the end of the dictatorship, the video is screened uncensored to an unsuspecting public of boy scouts. A barrage of criticism prompts the gallery director to shut down the screening, which raises the question: is there still censorship in the new era of "democracy"? How much have things changed?

Thus in a very direct way, *travesti* embodiments are used as an object of scandal by Lemebel that subverts the "pulcra moral" (stiff morality) of the social order and is hence threatening on several levels (1997, 15). He recalls the way that displaying the body was used to denounce the excesses of the regime in actions such as those undertaken by Las Yeguas del Apocalipsis. Lemebel in fact extends this place of the body for the politicization of subjectivity in his writings. This body is dramatized by the agony of the epidemic but also by the folkloric moments of popular romance and the bolero. Here we can see some continuities between Lemebel's work, that of Mayra Santos-Febres and her predecessor, Manuel Ramos Otero. As closeted and conforming to the Apollo gay North American ideal that they may be, the diva that all homosexuals hold inside is given full rein in *travesti* lives, loves, in short, in their habitus, their way of being and situating themselves in the world. Such features of identification can be observed in the *crónicas* "El Último Beso de Loba Lamar," "Carta a Liz Taylor" ("Letter to Liz Taylor"), "Los Mil Nombres de María Camaleón," all redolent of acerbic irony. And they are also of centrality in *Tengo miedo torero*, which is littered with verses from boleros, the title of the novel itself is taken from one.

The *crónica* that closes *La esquina es mi corazón*, "Las amapolas también tienen espinas" ("Poppies Also Have Thorns"), is also a good example of this use of melodrama, scandal, and romance. The drama and danger of *loca* life are staged by reference to what is usually relegated by tabloid press to a crime passionel. With camp and mordant romanticism, Lemebel inscribes violence tied up with desire—the spider and fly dance between the *loca* and the macho—and the hate crimes mercilessly undertaken that are normally reported via homophobic epithets in the media, which treats such deaths as "deserved." The terms of scandal and shame, so often invoked by tabloid journalism in reference to *travestis*, are deployed in a histrionic reversal that draws attention to the construction of *locas* and *travestis* in such media forms. Lemebel thus revivifies the popular and the obscene in order to understand how his lumpen *locas* and *travestis* are discursively described—and ironizes them. The tactics of irony, black humor, and the reversal of terms are central components in the deployment of gender-variant subjectivities and embodiments.

The body on display in *Loco afán: Crónicas de sidario*—the public body of the *travesti*, a place of the inscription of myriad forms of cultural contest and dispute in the work of many of the other writers and directors examined in this book—forms the site of the emergence of resistant identities. *Locas* and *travestis* hold this promise as they stand outside the co-option of both mainstream culture and the *gueyto*. Lemebel proposes the insertion of the "unpredictable" embodiments of *locas* and *travestis* in all their visibility into the domain of citizenship, but—crucially—without eliminating the terms of "shame." We recall that AIDS—a typical source of cultural stigma—is resignified by *locas* and *travestis* in highly ironic ways as a fashion accessory: "Te queda regio el sarcoma linda!" (69; The Kaposi's sarcoma looks great on you darling!) This is a reversal that draws attention to itself. The very terms of shame might be used to challenge the notion of the citizen itself, following the insights of Kulick and Klein (2003) in their study on the use of shame by Brazilian *travestis*. To cite again how this functions, "in both scandals and their more recognizably activist modalities of political action, *travestis* transgress public decorum and civil society not by rejecting shame (and championing something like '*Travesti* Pride'), but by inhabiting shame as a place from which to interpellate others and thereby incriminate those others. In doing this, we want to argue that *travestis* are deploying what Eve Kosofsky Sedgwick has called a 'shame-conscious' and 'shame-creative' vernacular; one that inflects the 'social metamorphic' possibilities of shame" (2003, 284). All of these highly embodied strategies, to invoke Elizabeth Grosz, point to the ability of (marginalized) bodies to "seep beyond the domains of control" with unforeseen creativity (1994, xi). While Arenas originally holds out the promise of such *loca* potential but ultimately recapitulates and reinforces the terms of stigma, Lemebel insistently reappraises the subcultural norms and tactics of survival of his subjects and emphasizes their power of subversion.

The place of prostitution in the articulation of *travesti* subjectivity in Lemebel's work is central to his visualization of their lives and their subversiveness. As we saw in reference to several of the other works analyzed in this book, the site for the *escenificación* of *travesti* identity is commonly the street. This is the only cultural space fully available to them as subjects, apart from working as hairdressers or dressmakers. In "Su ronca risa loca (El dulce engaño del travestismo prostibular)," Lemebel sharpens his view of this world. His *travesti* exercises "el laburo filudo del alma ramera" (1997, 77; the sharp-edged labor of the whore's soul). She occupies the street corner, rain, hail, or shine, shivering and smoking a cheap cigarette to keep herself warm. Lemebel refers to "la noche milonga del travesti" (77; the *milonga* night of the *travesti*).[17] Her look is a complicit wink—just like that of the "ojo coliza" described earlier— a glimpse that convinces but then shocks the public. Something in her femininity exceeds the mold: the deep-plunging necklines, the last sexual trick ("engaño"), "la cirugía artesanal" (provincial make-do surgery) of the tucked away penis (77, 78). This is by no means an "average" woman; most men who cruise for *travesti* prostitutes know this, even if they pretend not to; her gruff *loca* laugh is a giveaway. At 5 foot 10 inches tall she overtakes femininity and overacts it. And yet Lemebel is at pains to show this in the context of her trade. Many of his *travestis* dress down outside the context of sex work. The overacting of femininity is not attributed to her as an inherent characteristic, rather, it is a necessary and self-conscious one.

Lemebel describes this *travesti* prostitute as "trashumante"—like a migratory bird (78). He emphasizes the threat of the masculinist state and its agents of control, the police: "Nunca se sabe si una bala perdida o un estampido policial le va a cortar el resuello de cigüeña moribunda" (78; One never knows if a stray bullet or a police stampede will cut the slender neck of a dying swan). He also reminds the reader of the social ostracism sex workers suffer, the neighborhood teenagers who roam in cars throwing bottles and harassing prostitutes: "expuesta a la moral del día, que se asoma tajeando su dulce engaño laboral" (79; exposed to the morality of the day, she goes out plying her sweet labor of trickery). The quotidian worlds of *travesti* sex workers—peripatetic, nomadic—mark the most liminal and perilous space that paradoxically is also the space of utmost possibility, that is, for forging radical subjectivities. Lemebel, like the Argentinian *travesti* activist Berkins, offers his *locas* and *travestis* as "traidoras del patriarcado" (traitors to patriarchy) becoming-women whose scandalous identities are indeed a response to deep sociocultural "desprecio" (disdain), the routine exclusions and condemnation of both mainstream and gay worlds alike.

With the novel *Tengo miedo torero*, the scandalous and shamed body of the *loca* that forms the site of the emergence of resistant identities is manifest in the main character and her slow but overt politicization. La Loca, who to be sure enjoys being sexually passive, must overcome her political passivity to earn the title "La Loca del Frente." The swirling of her consciousness is rendered in language that resembles French feminist *écriture feminine*: evocative of the "other sex," inscribing a certain sexual difference that is also profoundly embodied. Lemebel himself calls this a "lengua marucha," the internal language of all amorous and enamored homosexual subjectivities (2002, 11). This language has also been labeled by Lemebel elsewhere in an online interview with Solange Gónzalez as a "locabulario" (González 2004).

Through the protagonist, La Loca, history is personalized and imbued with subjectivity—*lo vivido*. In this way, the novel clearly remains true to the impulse that propels the two previous collections that we have analyzed. It is based on a real-life event: the assassination attempt on Pinochet in September 1986 carried out by members of the Frente Patriótico Manuel Rodríguez, a Leftist underground guerrilla movement. The text in no way resembles a dry historical document, however, and every word is suffused with subjectivity. Although told via a third-person narrator, it obtains a seductive multivocality, as this narrator focalizes continually through the minds of the characters and recounts two parallel stories: that of the emerging romance between La Loca and a *militante*, Carlos, and the presidential couple, Lucy and Augusto Pinochet.

Immediately the reader will note the ancestor to this configuration—the romance between Molina and Valentín as presented in Puig's *El beso de la mujer araña*. Like the romance between the *loca* and the radical Leftist revolutionary in that novel, the relationship between La Loca and Carlos in *Tengo miedo torero* follows the politicization of a previously passive and apolitical gender-variant character by a committed and passionate guerrilla.

La Loca—*encandilada* (enchanted) as in the classic bolero by her new object of desire—sees her friends La Rana and La Lupe less and less, and a real warmth arises between La Loca and Carlos. As if by osmosis, La Loca begins to imbibe the radical atmosphere that fills the attic. In spite of what the text refers to as the commonplace distrust of *locas*, based on the idea that they cannot keep secrets or be trusted because of their touted "inauthenticity," histrionics, and drama (Lemebel 2002, 198), Carlos entrusts La Loca with a vital mission that is crucial to her voyage out of political ignorance and inaction: the transport of a package. Eventually La Loca confronts Carlos about his comings and goings—and Carlos reveals that he is, indeed, working *en la clandestinidad*. "Carlos" is a pseudonym, something that La Loca grasps by reference to her taking on "nombres de fantasía" (fantasy names) when doing drag shows (133).

Under the influence of Carlos, her consciousness is politicized. A telling scene in which La Loca goes to hand over a tablecloth she had embroidered for a certain general's wife displays the clarified thoughts of a person who has suddenly realized the extent of the ugliness, pain, and death inflicted by those in power. She imagines the general, his wife, and their honored guests feasting on it and drinking to the spilt blood of Marxist students that they killed. La Loca absconds with the cloth she embroidered, no longer content to sew little angels and birds on the edges of the official discourses of power or to beautify and cover up their lies, unlike the chief maidservant of the presidential couple, Gonzalo.

In *Tengo miedo torero*, the subversive embodied subjectivity of the paradigmatically named protagonist is clearly proffered as the grounds for the evolution of a political consciousness, which furthers Lemebel's writerly project of politicizing subjectivity. This consciousness is awoken by love, instinctive feeling, and interconnectedness—not political lectures on the part of Carlos. These may be termed an *ars loca*—sentiment and intuition become virtues in the novel; consciousness emerges as La Loca is awoken to herself and the setting around her under their force.

Moreover, the complexity of her identity is valorized as crucial to this kind of transformation, since, as Paola Díaz claims in "Homosexualidades: ¿Entre feminidades y masculinidades?," La Loca as a figure "perturba el orden de los lineamientos genéricos, dado que contiene en un solo espacio—su cuerpo—contenidos masculinos y femeninos, resultando un bricolage de estilos inacabados, incompletos, donde el orden de las cosas no es el establecido, pero tampoco el opuesto, que no cierran su proyecto genérico" (qtd in Candía Cáceres n.d.; disturbs the order of gender norms, given that within a sole space—her body—she possesses both male and female aspects, resulting in a bricolage of unfinished styles, where the order of things is not the established one, and does not foreclose her gender trajectory.)

Inhabiting this body we have a subject who asserts and articulates herself in multiple, unpredictable, and sensual ways, ways that *Tengo miedo torero* and the two collections of *crónicas* trace: the spark of the old argot, the humor, "la única distancia politizable" (the only politicizable element), a remnant of "folclor mariposón" (fag folklore; Lemebel 1997,

53). Lemebel's highly political and politicized *loca*, then, challenges traditionalist Leftist frameworks that trivialize the experiences of these subjects as *rotos* and lumpen and that understand them as incapable of a political consciousness. For Lemebel, this is patently not the case: they are in fact the prime site for its emergence.

Inverting the Masculine Order

If the "feminidad radical del travesti" (Perlongher 1997, 47) or the *cola*'s complex embodied differences of class and sexuality represent for Lemebel a heightened political point of critique of dictatorial and postdictatorial Chile in all its homogeneity, so, too, do these subjects who bystep the masculine order resist and contradict its mechanisms of reproduction. Their very presence interdicts this order and its suffocating methods, and hence Lemebel is able, by virtue of example, to illustrate further the viability of both *loca* and *travesti* resistance to this order and nonalignment with its principles.

In Lemebel's work, the state is always identified with this masculinity. It is not simply any masculinity, but, rather, the kind of hegemonic masculinity, to use Raewyn Connell's term (1995), reinforced by power and domination: a cold and calculating masculinity that refuses emotions, demands obedience, terrorizes, denigrates the feminine, and vigilantly monitors all borders—in a literal sense, embodied by the *pacos* and *milicos*, and figuratively, in the rejection of homosexuals. This masculinity represents the Law of the Father. *Locas* and *travestis* are very much at cross-purposes in this setting.

Once again, Lemebel extends the lines of connection to include all those who are up against the state and bear the brunt of this masculinity. In the *crónica* "Lagartos en el cuartel," included in *La esquina es mi corazón*, the space of the army barracks is where the masculine domination of the state is most keenly felt, a species of domination that requires "el quebrantamiento del femenino" (81; the breaking down of the feminine). Here, predictably, part of the training is to avert homosexuality. Lemebel makes links between Jews, blacks, women, the disappeared, and homosexuals, as all share the plight of being "pisoteados" (trodden on) by the black boots of the military (82). Lemebel hence forges a horizon of solidarity with those "up against it"—and who are read and located as "feminized" by the coercive forces of the state.

In *Tengo miedo torero*, the state embodies phallocentricism par excellence, which, with its rigid demands for unity, strength, patriotism, stability, and homogeneity, is imperiled by anything ambiguous, "the incongruous, jarring, asymmetrical, arbitrary and unfinished" (Mansfield 2000, 70). *Locas* and *travestis* represent this, as we have seen, with their dynamically changing identities. While Irigaray writes in *This Sex Which Is Not One* of woman as that being that "goes off in all directions . . . in which 'he' is unable to discern the coherence of any meaning" (1991, 353); for Lemebel, it is the *loca* who constitutes this strategy of movement outside the strict domains of control. This might be termed the politics of the everyday. It is surely a modus operandi used by La Loca who, even in the midst of the danger and repression prior to the assassination attempt carried out by the Frente, goes out seeking a bit of fluff—her sexcapades detailed by the narrator become mixed up with a street protest. La Loca, to further the connection to Irigaray's notion of the possibilities of "woman" as opposed to "man," is not quite woman, and yet she feels most at home socially with them—and is recognized as "not man." In the midst of the protests and after her cruising of a random guy on the street, the text notes, "Era extraño, pero allí entre las mujeres no sentía vergüenza de levantarse el grito mariflauta" (Lemebel 2002, 164; It was strange, but there amid the women she wasn't ashamed to raise her high-pitched faggy voice). She joins the loud pots and pans protest, the symbolic *cacerolazos*. She observes the homophobic police and the violence they exact with impunity.

In an online article, Iván Alexis Candia Cáceres sustains that *Tengo miedo torero* functions to parody hegemonic masculinity and its institutions of formation that are so central to Chilean society (n.d.). This masculine order starts within the most basic ideological unit of Chilean society: the family. On page 16 of the novel, the narrative segues from third to first person as La Loca retells her childhood to Carlos. Her father used to belt her to make her a man, so she would not turn out twisted and bring shame on her family. By then her mother was already dead. In high school, teachers would say that La Loca should be sent to a psychologist—only a doctor could deepen that voice, correct that mincing. Her father adds, ominously, that only military service would make a man out of her, a comment that connects the gender coercion of family and school life to the state's.

This serves to underscore the novel's principal point: that the paterfamilias is a miniature image of the dictator-fatherland. Through the parallel articulation of the voices of the dictator and his wife, Lucy, *Tengo miedo torero* makes apparent the paranoia of Pinochet and his obsessive hatred of anything "feminine," passionate, and nonlinear. Pinochet sees students as wannabe guerrillas—*maricones* and lazybones, reading poetry about love and machine guns. Pinochet hates poetry; he has never read Neruda and would have sent him off to the military to "make a man" out of him. He is also portrayed as being aggressively homophobic; at one point he demands the removal of someone he suspects to be a *maricón* cadet soldier from his property, asserting, "Maricones traen mala suerte . . . igual que comunistas" (Lemebel 2002, 157–58; Faggots bring bad luck . . . just like communists"). In this sense, then, both Carlos and

La Loca are implicated as threats to the order, an order that is demonstrably masculine.

The "disvirtualización de la masculinidad hegemónica" (the undermining of hegemonic masculinity) is first seen in one of several transitions from the principal plane of the narrative that relates the lives of Carlos and La Loca to that of the presidential couple (Candia Cáceres n.d.). Pinochet is shown as paranoid and insecure. Far from the public image of stolid masculinity, the voice of the dictator is truculent and whiny; he is forever pestered by his wife who seemingly dominates him. As Lemebel ventriloquizes the voice of this apparently unassailable man, his masculinity itself is deconstructed. He is a lonely figure, almost congenitally so. The telling of Carlos's birthday in one part of the novel is paralleled to Pinochet's terrified memories of his tenth: when his father insisted he invite his high-society classmates, who were in fact his enemies. The little Pinochet puts insects in his birthday cake to exact revenge on his "friends." When they do not show, he has to eat it himself. During the retold ambush performed on the presidential car that fateful day in September 1986, Pinochet is revealed as a shivering mess. The cold and hard marble statue of masculinity and military might is shown as lacking in any kind of courage.[18]

The stripping down of Pinochet's aura of indestructibility forms a central plank of the critical enterprise of the novel. This is because Pinochet as father of this nation formed on violence—the violence of the dictatorship and the violence of hegemonic masculinity—is at the same time the state. Bernadita Llanos addresses these relations as manifest in Lemebel's work in her article "Masculinidad, estado y violencia en la ciudad neoliberal" (2004), in which she argues that gender relations and gendered subjectivities—forced into a binary frame—are tied up with this more general political and social violence exercised by the state on its own people, from the time of the 1973 coup to the years of "consensus." Not coincidentally, the relations of violence shape and influence the rigors of the frameworks for reproducing identities and relations of inequality at virtually every level. And yet just as gender relations are the arena for struggle and transformation, so, too, can other arenas be uncovered and claimed for restitution in order to overcome the effects of state ideology and systematic abuse, violence, and terror. As Bernadita Llanos holds,

> La dictadura en tanto proyecto político, social y económico potencia las identidades que la racionalidad moderna instala como deseables en el imaginario chileno urbano, obligando a la masculinidad hegemónica a variar sus estrategias de afirmación y diferenciación a través del uso de la violencia. El narrador . . . devela lo silenciado y oculto por la doble moral que mantiene la hegemonía masculina. Sus pactos, traiciones y abusos aparecen tematizados . . . La denuncia de los abusos y el atropello sobre sujetos sociales diferentes y desprotegidos caracteriza esta escritura. (2004, 79)

[As a economic, social, and political project the dictatorship makes possible identities that modern rationality posits as desirable in the Chilean urban imaginary, making hegemonic masculinity vary its strategies of affirmation and differentiation via the use of violence. The narrator . . . unveils what is silenced and hidden by the double standard preserved by hegemonic masculinity. Its pacts, betrayals, and abuses are thematized . . . The denunciation of the abuses and the roughshod treatment of different and vulnerable subjects characterizes this writing.]

As in any social arrangement, the danger exists in internalizing and reproducing this violence, even, and perhaps especially, among marginalized groups. Lemebel offers his protagonist La Loca as an instance of one subject capable not only of transforming herself but also of transforming those around her. When La Loca muses on men and their brutal eroticism, she realizes that Carlos is different, even if he—like other men—has been socialized in the patriarchal order to fulfill that kind of masculinity. At the beginning, he does not wish to involve her in the meetings in the attic, arguing "son cosas de hombres" (Lemebel 2002, 13; they're men's things). But by dint of their proximity, and beguiled by the wiles of this dreamy being with the voice of a *mariflauta*, they share intimate parts of their personal histories. The transformation in Carlos is that he learns to take his *colipata* seriously.

Candia Cáceres asserts that Carlos is feminized by his involvement with La Loca (n.d.). Such a claim, however, does not bear close textual scrutiny. Carlos does not lose his manhood in any way—from the beginning, in fact, he is a fascinating mixture of masculinity and tenderness. The title of the English version of the novel is "My tender matador." Given that a large part of the text's "lengua marucha" forms a love song to the young revolutionary, where the *loca* takes the female bolero role, it is not difficult to frame Carlos as that tender matador himself—one who is brave and sweet, who takes risks and yet is loyal to those he loves. His masculinity, after all, is not the kind of masculinity of those indoctrinated in the military. Given his political tendencies, it is a different kind of masculinity, and one not under critique in the novel. And as in *El beso de la mujer araña*, the transformation of sexual and gender possibilities that occurs between them is twofold: La Loca learns to be strong and active in her femininity, and Carlos's sensitive masculinity is nourished by his involvement with La Loca. The implicit argument, then, is that a Leftist alliance with oppressed sexual minorities and a recognition of their radical potential points the way to true social transformation where other projects have failed. Carlos is a representative of that Left. La Loca del Frente is that potential. And as we have seen, *roto*-identified *locas* and *travestis* hold this promise in all their subversiveness—never middle-class mainstream gays, whose commercial and Aryan-style masculinity refashions itself along imperialistic lines and in uniform ways that merely reflect the state's call to linearity, order, and establishment masculinity for Lemebel.

Deep Focus: Extending Subjectivity's Field of Vision

Taken together, *La esquina es mi corazón*, *Loco afán: Crónicas de sidario*, and *Tengo miedo torero* advance a vision of *loca* and *travesti* subjectivities that casts them in a new political light, the dimensions of which this chapter has explored in some detail: their inseparability from neoliberalist Chile's landscape of *otros*, who test the terms of their "marginalization" by living outside the zone of the "five-star citizen" in often creative and challenging ways; as people who exist in spite of the forces of socioeconomic exclusion; as persons who usurp the punitive methods of the state in their public visibility as gender-variant prostitutes; as individuals who look back and insert themselves into the panorama and obtain agency; as subversive beings with real transformational power and subcultural wisdom; as *colas* and *maripozuelos* who, though they represent for Lemebel generally the creativity of popular sectors in many parts of Latin America in resisting imperialism and economic exclusion, are not reducible to mere symbol.

By highlighting the issues of cultural and economic imperialism in framing the subjectivities of working-class *locas* and *travestis* and distinguishing them from the upwardly mobile, gender-normative gay, Lemebel seeks to address the complex factors that can account historically for the processes of identity formation and erasure. Thus the *loca* and *travesti* lived experiences as given in his *crónicas* and his novel cannot ultimately stand in to represent the national situation, as in previous works studied in this book; Lemebel refuses such facile equations that undermine the specificity of the realities he endeavors to address and radicalize.

Additionally, although Lemebel draws lines of contention around issues of pestilence, the violence of the state, and colonialism; these are suggestive and used to contour the political setting, in line with Lemebel's own commitment to the Left. They help place the lived experiences depicted in his work in ways that consciously resonate with questions of utmost import to that Left, to give them a new spin, and to tweak the consciousness of those who often dismiss the concerns of sex and gender minorities as being of minor consequence in comparison to the "main issues" at hand. Lemebel challenges this with his writing and mounts a response in direct dialogue with the Left that posits that *loca* and *travesti* lives are, in fact, central. The experience of AIDS so minutely exposed by Lemebel, does not conveniently adhere to the experience of the national body. He may draw connections that underline the shared gravity of experiences of trauma, abuse, and social disappearance among seemingly distinct groups, however, in radicalizing *loca* and *travesti* subjectivity, Lemebel engages with this political discourse of protest in order to be heard and to make visible the particularity of the subjects he portrays. Clearly the social disappearance of *locas* and *travestis* by economic exile, by AIDS, and by military violence may be like the disappearance of indigenous in colonial times—but the comparison is temporary, strategic, and never occluding of specificity in experience, which Lemebel is so careful to portray. By tracing these dimensions of the wider sphere, Lemebel seeks to demonstrate that *loca* and *travesti* realities of socioeconomic exclusion are not "merely cultural" but rather intersections with the struggles of many others under the neoliberalist global setting, whose pledge to market freedoms does not translate to the touted sociopolitical pluralism and justice in the "return to democracy" era.

Neither is Lemebel interested, ultimately, in presenting the *loca* and *travesti* body as one version of the project of nation—original, authentic, Chilean, now discarded—and the gay body as the latest, globalizing project of nation currently in vigor, as Garabano implies. His texts serve a volley of disjunctures to complicate such a totalizing view. *Locas* and *travestis* have never "had" a nation as such and their rejection by the Left both before, during, and after the dictatorship makes this painfully obvious. Lemebel's poetic diatribe "Manifiesto" in the middle of *Loco afán: Crónicas de sidario* serves as recognition of the ongoing tension between how the Left would view people like him as *maricas* and whether they might include them in their revolution.

Lemebel's revolution, of course, places poor women and men, prostitutes, *locas*, *travestis*, and transsexuals at the vanguard. His texts employ an arsenal of linguistic *cargas* to brush off the tarnished image of his maligned subjects and recuperate them as the most exemplary nomadic radicals whose revolution is the revolution of everyday. He thus redirects and surpasses the previous politicization of *locas* attempted by the work of Arenas.

This politics of cultural and systemic transgression is reminiscent of the efforts of much queer and transgender activism of the eighties and nineties in articulating an at once revisionist and restorative view of so-called minor players in the gay, lesbian, bisexual, and transgender struggle— to forge alliances among groups still complexly oppressed in ways that demand a sophisticated understanding of how one becomes subjected and how one emerges as a political subject in the contemporary scene. Leslie Feinberg in *Transgender Warriors* engaged in this tactic, as have others.[19] In many ways as a tactic it forms the basis of a queer and transgender politics, which reappraises what is troped as "unnatural," "beyond the norm," monstrous, abject, or marginal and recasts it as the center of subversive potential, bringing in from the cold the outlawed and the excluded and celebrating what is valorized as its ability to threaten the established order and its cleaving divisions: sex and gender, as well as class and race.

In *Tengo miedo torero*, this order is exerted via the hegemonic masculinity of the state. The novel minutely ridicules and undermines its foresworn rigidity, its paranoid obsession with the linear, the unambiguous, and its drive to vilify what is perceived as threatening to these terms in a move that equates *maricones* to *comunistas*. Lemebel proposes that *locas* and *travestis* do indeed present such a threat, and yet chiefly to the extent that their class origins, affiliations, and a consciousness informed by their lived experiences are able to marshal this form of transgression, macro- and micropolitically. Lemebel offers La Loca del Frente and her evolution in the novel as an instance of a political subjectivity whose consciousness can, indeed, undergo politicization—and affect others. The scandalous embodiments and shameful alternative citizenships that are positively valorized in the collections of *crónicas* form the basis for this politicization and cue convincingly with recent reconsiderations of notions of belonging, community, dissident sexualities and escaping dominant forms of normalization, the co-option of capitalism, and the containment of bodies, desires, and identities to the strictures of social control. In this way, *loca* and *travesti* radicalisms place these subjects at the forefront of social change, that is, the transformation of personhood and cultural coexistence, resisting patriarchy, and resisting hegemony.

This compelling revalorization that Lemebel provides may appear to some readers as programmatic to the degree that it answers to the exigencies of questions of identities and their viability implicitly raised on the Left. Why is it even necessary to politicize *locas* and *travestis* in this way in giving account of their existence in contemporary culture? Is this poetics of transgression simply another attribution, considerably less vituperative, to be sure, than the attributions of colonial backwardness or hegemonic reinscription of norms that we saw, for instance, in the previous chapter? These are questions that are not raised by Lemebel's texts themselves, in their passion for the restitution of his subjects, and yet, they are worthy of some reflection. While Lemebel, in exploring and then politicizing *loca* and *travesti* subjectivity, sidesteps pledging his representations to mere national-cultural metaphors, he nonetheless implicitly tees his visions with those queer and transgender notions that themselves generate ranked degrees of transgressiveness as their main conceptual tools. And yet critics like Namaste (2000; 2005), Rubin (2003), and Prosser (1998) would question the practical value of such appraisals, which appear to impose another set of hierarchies around identities. Is it necessary to even frame *locas* and *travestis* this way to gain insight into their subjectivities? Namaste argues in *Sex Change, Social Change* that we risk setting "a dangerous precedent if we maintain that people's identities are acceptable only if and when they can prove that they are politically useful" (2005, 8). For Namaste, we should simply accept that gender-variant, transgender, and transsexual people exist and move past the demand to explain, rationalize, or dismiss their identities.[20] If Lemebel posits that some cross-dressing *locas* can be politically retrograde, while others are not, surely gender-normative gays can, by the laws of variability, be progressive—neither of these facts having anything to do with their "identities."

Whether or not the reader will perceive Lemebel's move as a swing in the other direction of the seesaw debate about transgender subjects as conservative or subversive, what is patently clear is that Lemebel's speaking back to power using the voices of *locas* and *travestis* achieves a depth of vision of subjectivity and context that makes his representations the most challenging and engaged representations emerging in Latin America.

Epilogue

You see me as a symbol, not a human being.

—Ani DiFranco, "Crime for Crime"

El poder de representar se refiere al poder de nombrar la realidad, de clasificarla, de adjetivarla y hacer valer esa representación en la mente (y en el corazón) de los individuos, construyendo de esta manera una estructura de posibilidades de acción, así como un sistema de diferenciación y distinción social.

[The power of representation refers to the power to name reality, to classify it, to describe it, and to make that representation matter in the minds (and in the hearts) of individuals, constructing in this way a structure of possibilities for action, as well as a system of social differentiation and distinction.]

—Guillermo Núñez Noriega, *Sexo entre varones. Poder y resistencia en el campo sexual* (*Sex Between Men: Power and Resistance in the Sexual Field*)

Brevemente dicho, las travestis sufrimos de dos tipos de opresión. Por un lado, la opresión social basada en el imaginario colectivo de lo que es una travesti: misterio, ocultamiento, perversión, contagio, etc. . . . Por el otro lado, sufrimos la violencia institucional.

[Briefly said, we travestis suffer from two kinds of oppression. On the one hand, the social oppression based on the collective imagination about what a travesti is: mystery, concealment, perversion, contagion, etc. . . . On the other hand, we suffer institutional violence.]

—Lohana Berkins, "Un itinerario político del travestismo" ("A Political Itinerary of *Travestismo*")

This inquiry into the representation of gender variant homosexualities and trans manifestations in contemporary Latin American narratives responds to the circulation of an increasing number of texts featuring figures identifiable for their differently gendered embodiments, a selection of which has been examined here. A compelling connection can be made between the advent of the articulation of *locas, travestis*, and transsexuals as political subjects in Latin America and this increase in textual representation in the last two decades. As trans and marginalized homosexual subjectivities have gained visibility and social currency, so have representational modes of all kinds begun to respond to their presence.

This increase in representation is not without its own problems, which might be related to the very problems of the emergence of subjectivity from the obfuscations of dominant discourse. *Locas, travestis*, and transsexuals in the real world have emerged as subjects in circumstances of intense contestation. As outlined at length in this study, where they are depicted in texts in the contemporary period, their very bodies have often functioned as spaces of contestation.

There is, however, a vast difference between recognizing the problematic nature of subjectivity, the fraught terrain of its emergence, as well as the challenges of its textual inscription, and positing that subjectivity as a problem unto itself, which is then employed as a site from which to broach a range of cultural dilemmas, at times quite abstractly removed from the lives of the subjects so depicted. While the figuring of gender-variant and trans bodies as agonistic sites is noticeable in a range of texts and realized in certain ways in the contemporary period, few scholars endeavor, as we have seen, to deconstruct the rhetorical movements that make possible the employment of the bodily signs, positionalities, and styles of *locas, travestis*, and transsexuals to polemical ends. Nor, for that matter, have they sought to examine the implications of this allegorization for such subjects.

The effect of this use of trans bodies for rhetorical ends in the works of Arenas, Novaro, and Rojas, examined in Chapters 2 and 3, confirms Viviane Namaste's thesis of the textual erasure of subjectivity, which orients the conception of metaphor and its effects advanced by this study. A major consequence of troping, according to Donna Haraway, is inherent in the Greek meaning of the phrase *tropos*, from which it derives: to turn (1992, 296). Troping effects a detour of other elements in the subject that may not fit the rhetorical needs of metaphor. Metaphor does not join two items that possess any inherent, a priori similarity; rather this similarity is produced by their placement together and the transfer of certain discursively constructed features to the principal term under discussion. A culturally determined field of meaning is drawn upon to construct this allegorical relationship. In Namaste's terms, through the rhetorical operations of metaphor, trans figures—including *locas, travestis, transformistas,* and *transexuales*—may be "textually inscribed as *purely figural*—that is, *literally impossible*" (2000, 93, emphasis in original).

In the work of Arenas, Novaro, and Rojas, the troping of *locas, travestis*, and *transformistas* forecloses any complex view of subjectivity. The same can be argued for Zapata's *La hermana secreta de Angélica María* and Santos-Febres's *Sirena Selena vestida de pena*, analyzed in Chapter 5. If any texture is provided for the vision of what might be a subject position, it is mainly found in the world of the stage, the cabaret, or the song. In particular, a tropicalized link to bolero emerges in many of these texts, which might be seen as part of a Latin American tradition of imagining androgyny and gender mixture aesthetically, especially in modernity (Zavala 2000). This is also present in the work of Lemebel. Unlike in Lemebel's work, however, the use of such points of reference by Zapata, Novaro and Santos-Febres does not move the reader or viewer beyond the metaphorical and performative function of each text's *loca, transformista*, or *travesti*, and as such, the place of the popular lyricism of stage and song serves to broach the scripting of desire and identity and their connections to national stories or cultural fables. Thus contained in the figurative, the possibility of transcending the typical representational modes of picturing these subjects is at best deferred for the sake of the glories and agonies of allegory.

What might be the extratextual implications of such representations, especially those that reinscribe the terms of corruption, falsity, deception, criminality, and transgression? I write this epilogue having just filed an affidavit for the case of a trans person of Latin American origin, X, seeking asylum in the United States. I am hoping my words have their desired effect on the arbiter of justice in this case. I am hoping that my own form of representation is powerful enough to overcome what does not get represented in dominant knowledges, and I do not just mean the statistics and facts missing from official reports. Confidentiality decrees I cannot name any particulars, and yet her story is not atypical. X faces violence and the very real risk of death if forcibly returned—three of her friends have already been murdered the year in which I write, 2008, of the thirty-five people counted as dead this year from the capital's lesbian, gay, bisexual, and transgendered (LGBT) community, the most visible of whom are *travestis* and transsexuals. Most of her peers do not look forward to a long life; if death does not come from homicide, it might be undertreated AIDS, an overdose, an accidental infection as a result of a risky silicone injection to more fully embody one's femininity and sexuality; it might be suicide. Every week there are reports of such grisly ends all over the continent, although most stories sensationalize such accounts and neither bother to investigate what led to the circumstances nor delve deeply into the conditions of existence in which the victims had lived. X, for her part, was harassed every day by local police, who would approach her, sometimes on the assumption she was involved in criminal dealings and other times under the assumption that she was engaging in prostitution in off-limit areas and offending public morality.

For most sex and gender diverse people, especially male-to-female *travestis* and transsexuals, life in many Latin American jurisdictions is a life of everyday persecution at the hands of police, by those who see them as society's ills, and by moral majority representatives, among many others. In the media, violence against *travestis* gets turned around so that *travestis* themselves become the harbingers of that violence: a threat to decency and order, to the good citizen and their right to security. Everyday *travesti* existence, as Josefina Fernández, the Argentinian sociologist acknowledges, is mediated by a symbolic violence. Fernández (2004) deftly works the insights of Bourdieu into her analysis, but one does not require knowledge of the nuances of reflexive sociology to grasp the point. Epistemic violence, the violence committed by the paradigms of discourse about *travestis*—in the media, in the law, and in many domains and institutions of culture—curtails their lives and living space in very minute ways that appear invisible to a society that does not even recognize their validity as subjects. Dominant representations of *travestis* both limit and create the phantasms of their own discourses. Exiled from mainstream culture and its institutions and, in the case of X, compelled to cross borders in an effort to move outside the discursive and social spaces in which this violence becomes bodily, (s)exiled, to use a term used among the *boricano* queer and trans community in the United States, what space outside these representations exists?

Looking for this textual space—and the possibility of freer representations—I would cite here those texts analyzed in which subjectivity and situatedness are points of major elaboration and that bypass or undo the metaphorical use of gender crossing as symbolic of national issue. Karim Aïnouz's *Madame Satã* examined in Chapter 3, the novels *El Rey de La Habana* and *Salón de belleza* by Pedro Juan Gutiérrez and Mario Bellatin, respectively, discussed in Chapter 4, and, of course—and perhaps most profoundly—the work of Pedro Lemebel, analyzed in Chapter 6, all engage with subjectivity.

Instead of restrictively confining their *locas*, *travestis*, and transsexuals to a sole plane for the sake of negotiating or embodying some anxious point of tension, dispute, contradiction, or duality, these texts reveal the lives of these subjects they portray as livable and possible, enmeshed in an array of intersubjective complexities. *Locas* and *travestis* in particular are revealed as subjects who contend with marginalization in the bipolar gender order and the realities of economic inequality in Latin America; these form narrativized experiences not simply equated to some national order or collectivity. In texts such as *Salón de belleza*, Lemebel's *La esquina es mi corazón, Loco afán. Crónicas de sidario*, and *Tengo miedo torero*, the forces of homophobia and travestophobia, as well as classism, are pervasive. In these works, the popular class affiliations of *locas* and *travestis* are made explicit, as well as their tenuous and troubled presence within the dominant gay culture. In the work of Bellatin and Lemebel, *travestismo* is explored on its own terms but also in connection with the wider setting. *Travestis* are visualized as juridically circumscribed identities that are stigmatized in culture but also as unique and unrepeatable forms of creative and erotic potential in danger of extinction due to state repression, neoliberalism, stigma-enabling epidemics like AIDS, and, in the case of Lemebel, the globalizing gay model. On the matter of HIV/AIDS, it is stunning to see the number of recent texts that deal with the epidemic in pursuing narrative depictions of *travestis* and *travesti* lives. The unique challenges faced in this arena by a population invisible not only in terms of their experiences of violence but also in relation to the official statistics and institutional responses to the disease help to explicate the sensitivity to the topic in these works. The virus continues to impact *travestis* and transsexuals in dramatic ways in Latin America, as revealed by the work of critical social researchers and community activists (Surratt et al. 1996; Varella et al. 1996; Berkins and Fernández 2005). In engaging *loca* and trans realities in all their qualitative nuances, the epidemic is something few of these authors fail to register in human terms.

In all the texts that make visible these subjectivities of difference, the street sex trade is key to the social spaces and publicly presented selves that emerge. *Vedettismo* is highlighted as a key manifestation of the public *travesti* body in the setting of sex work in the prose of Bellatin and Lemebel, and also in that of Gutiérrez. Gutiérrez's and Lemebel's depictions, in particular, insistently eroticize *travestismo*. Lemebel and Bellatin link this to the phenomenon of Latin American homosexualities. Street sex work is depicted in all these works as a site of both possibility and risk. These genre diverse texts also render the forces of religiosity and moral censoriousness, which reinforce a general sexphobia in their fictional or semifictional worlds. Lastly, they all insert their characters into interpersonal contexts in which relationships of community, spirituality, race, ethnicity, conflict, inclusion, and exclusion are foregrounded.

Representations, as knowledge constructions, are intimately related to power. As a critical reader of the representations tracked and scrutinized in the course of this book, I hold up the facts of everyday existence, careful not to relativize the power of representations to the point that I might dislodge them from any account of lived, quotidian lives and the impact of knowledge constructions that repeat and do violence. Of course, any of us from minoritarian experience—sexual, gendered, raced, or classed—looks to representations that might afford some breathing space, through which and by which we might (continue to) exist. How do others see us? How do we see each other? Ourselves? Representations speak many languages and are multiple; I am only ever seeing with a partial gaze, informed by my own set (and therefore lack) of awarenesses. And yet through representations we communicate, share codes, and transmit schemes of perception. This often can, and does, happen differentially. And yet the dominant images of *lo loca y lo trans* have been so influential and congealed to form a way of thinking—an episteme—whose power cannot be underestimated. Deception, charade, crisis, risk, threat, and even political corruption count among the chief perceptual categories that are generated by this episteme. But as I have shown here, such categories themselves are under revision. This book has sought to propitiate that shift in the critical arena.

NOTES

INTRODUCTION

1. Examples include Ana Clavel's *Cuerpo náufrago* (Alfaguara, 2005; *Shipwrecked Body*) and Antonio Benítez Rojo's *Mujer en traje de batalla* (Alfaguara, 2001; *Woman in Battle Armor*). These works do not represent a longstanding trend and are not examined here. Although the true story of the seventeenth-century Monja Alferez, a *Novohispano* nun who lived in male mode, has been subject to diverse treatment in cinema and on stage well into the twentieth century, s/he was but one figure. Cultural visions of effeminacy and male-to-female *travestismo* have a historical pedigree that populates the imaginary in numbers exceeding female-to-male gender crossing. This book is limited to an analysis of visions of male-to-female crossing because of this and also for the simple reason that male-to-female figures upset reigning paradigms in ways that are distinct from female transvestism or female-to-male gender changes.
2. Puig wrote from a time of totalitarian rule in his country of origin, Argentina, which had a system strongly characterized by its paternalism and masculinist visions of the nation. Donoso's 1966 novel precedes the Pinochet regime, but represents a sustained critique of those aspects of Chilean political culture that even then sought to turn back the clock and reinstall traditional Latin American *caudillismo*.
3. I have placed the terms "Latin American" and "Latin America" (initially) in scare quotes recognizing the inadequacy of understanding the region, its diverse cultures and peoples, in any fixed and totalistic way. Although not the first to interrogate the idea of Latin America, Walter Mignolo's (2005) point that such a label is more aptly understood as the product of colonial history, an invention that has given rise to an imaginary entity, guides my use of the term. Yet, like identity itself, stating that "Latin America" has a genealogy and is constructed does not do away with its applicability, however fraught the term can be, and shifting in meaning. Although the putative "Latin"—a French coinage that unites disparate zones on the basis of the colonial Latinate linguistic heritage found there—makes sense to those who speak Spanish or Portuguese (as well as French) and understand themselves as part of a European *and* "American" heritage, the word is obviously inadequate for a large number of non-Spanish, non-Portuguese, and non-French speakers and those who identify ethnoculturally as indigenous, for instance. That said, this book deals precisely with productions from an avowed *mestizo* tradition, one that could be described pertinently as "Latin American," remembering the persistence of national and regional logics that structure much of the rhetorical work in the visualizations of sex and gender variance under study here.
4. These developments arose in work now recognized as fundamental to the birth of European sexology. Karl Heinrich Ulrichs characterized what he called "male-male love" using the Latin phrase *muliebris virili corpore inclusa*: a female psyche confined in a male body (1869, xx). What he termed "Uranians" could outwardly be men or women who desired members of their same sex but possessed souls of

the opposite. ("Uranian" as a term was invented before "homosexual," which was coined in 1869 by Karl-Maria Kertbeny.) The later work of independent researchers such as Magnus Hirschfeld, who coined the word "transvestite" in 1910, vied with those claims of sexologists such as Richard von Krafft-Ebing, who stated that any behavior that differed from procreative sex in the context of heterosexual matrimony was deviant and inferior (Stryker 2006a, 21). These and other theories that described same sex behavior and cross dressing understood them as linked phenomena and dispositions. In 1910, Hirschfeld, for instance, plotted both same sex desiring people and transvestites in the terrain of sexual intermediacy, between two poles: "pure man" and "pure woman" (Hirschfeld 2006, 35). He also understood both homosexuals and transvestites as constituting a "third sex," although this term did not become popular in his time. In Krafft-Ebing's *Psychopathia Sexualis* (first published in 1877), homosexuality is described as either a congenital or acquired psychosexual disorder. He considered homosexuality to be a form of gender variance, that is, that men who desired other men were more like women, and women who desired other women were more like men (Krafft-Ebing 2006, 22). The differences were one of scale, but all types were cross-gendered in some fashion. All these phenomena, regardless of their differences, were subsumed under the category "contrary sexual feeling." Havelock Ellis's treatise *Sexual Inversion* became influential. Ellis understood those involved in sexual practices with members of their same biological sex as "inverts," displaying—openly, in the case of cross-dressers of the time—reversed sexual dispositions in a contrary outer body (Ellis, 1897).

5. The work of David Valentine is very pertinent in this regard. As Valentine shows in *Imagining Transgender: An Ethnography of a Category* (2007), in African American and Latino/a communities of the sexually diverse in New York, there is a long tradition of combining these two categories in describing oneself; one may be simultaneously gay and transgender. Transgender itself is a somewhat recent concept not always used by non-Anglo residents of Manhattan's Lower East Side. Forms of trans subjectivity in Latin America, most notably *loca* homosexuality and *travestismo*, manifestly resonate with the kinds of multiple identifications Valentine's subjects displayed.

6. The conceptual distinctions between "homosexual" and "transvestite" evolved slowly in the twentieth century in Europe and North America. By the mid-twentieth century, "homosexual" and "transvestite" were no longer seen as synonymous in scientific circles, although in popular ones this association was to persist. A further category of persons was in emergence as well: "the transsexual," first referred to in a paper by David O. Cauldwell in 1949 (see Cauldwell 2006). Many of those subjects whose behaviors, expressions, and desires had formerly qualified them as "inverts" were now isolated and rearticulated in social-scientific and medical discourse via these modern terms. Subjects identified this way also engaged in the production of knowledge that made these distinctions apparent. "Homosexual" was increasingly used to designate same-sex object choice in erotic and affectional relations, without reference to gender atypicality. "Transvestite" referred to individuals who experienced the need to wear the garments associated with those of the opposite sex, either periodically or full time, and "transsexual" to those who presented an ardent longing to change their sex in all respects and live socially in the gender role not designated at birth. In the wake of gay liberation movements in many parts of the globe, homosexuality began to be both decriminalized and depathologized from the 1970s onward. Transvestism and transsexuality have remained on many medical diagnostic-criteria lists as psychosexual disorders, however, and from the period of their emergence and to a large extent to the present day, they are viewed in their capacity as deviant phenomena in many parts of the world.

7. Again, the work of David Valentine (2007) usefully historicizes the hardening—in contradistinction—of the analytic categories "sexuality" and "gender" that the separation of "homosexuality" from "transgender" indicates. Drawing on the work of Chauncey (1994), Valentine demonstrates that before Stonewall, conceptual schemes or mapping of male sex practices and identities that existed included the queer, the fairy, and the masculine trade, among others. The fairy had a womanlike appearance; the queer, homosexual interest without a womanlike appearance. Homosexualities existed along a continuum, inflected by class and race differences. The very notion of gender and sexuality as unrelated in both gay and transgender accounts is, Valentine argues, an implicitly raced and classed understanding of selfhood, one that is white, but not, for that reason, always right (my phrasing). More than right or wrong, the historical separation of "gender" and "sexuality" is merely a variant that became hegemonic. This is important to bear in mind in navigating cultural differences informed by language, ethnicity, and political economy.
8. All translations from the original Spanish or Portuguese of this and other texts are mine.

CHAPTER 1

1. Rosamond S. King, referenced in the introduction, is a notable exception to this rule. The recentness of her sole article (2008) suggests perhaps some critics may be open to asking the kinds of questions that orient this book. Although her work has not yet developed beyond this article, it is an encouraging sign that this study's concerns are not alone.
2. Sifuentes-Jáuregui relates that when he mentioned the project that became the book *Transvestism, Masculinity, and Latin American Literature: Genders Share Flesh* to colleagues, they would ask if there is much cross-dressing in Latin America, which he assumed was a rebuff about its "marginality" and lack of importance, instead of affirming that, yes, there is much cross-dressing and gender crossing going on and looking into the lives and experiences of trans subjects in Latin America. This provides a rich opportunity to the scholar that Sifuentes-Jáuregui misses (2001, 9).
3. The connection of individual situations and libidinal investments to the national sphere is posited as an inherent property of Third World texts by American Marxist critic Fredric Jameson. In his article "Third World Literature in the Age of Multinational Capitalism," Jameson insists that novels from the Third World are always about a national situation or collective story. Jameson includes Latin America in the category "Third World." For this critic, any individual history told is inevitably metaphorical of—and less important than—the perceived larger scheme of things. Moreover, libidinal investments are always read and readable in primarily political and social terms. Jameson's thesis was challenged from the beginning in a reply made by Aijaz Ahmad (1987). Postcolonial scholar Arif Dirlik (1994) has also questioned his argument, as has Hispanist John Beverley (2004), among a multitude of others. My own position likewise strongly rejects as reductive Jameson-inspired formulations that understand non-European fictional texts as always concerned with the narration of nation.
4. Many current legal statutes and police codes across the continent derive from this era. These statutes and codes proscribe "ofensas al pudor público," provoking "escándalos" or transgression of "las buenas costumbres" and are regularly used to arrest *travestis* and transsexuals everywhere from Argentina and Chile to Ecuador, Perú, Honduras, and Costa Rica, among other nations. See Reding (2003).

5. In *Sexual Anarchy: Gender and Culture at the Fin de Siecle* (1990), Elaine Showalter talks of the end of centuries as intense moments of excitement and dread before the prospect of radical change in the midst of opulence. Gender and sexuality become its fields of visualization, that is, of the possibilities of radical change and the embodiment of monstrous cataclysmic fantasies. Showalter's work draws striking cultural parallels between the end of the nineteenth century and the end of the twentieth century, positing a resurgence or reiteration of the hysteria of "end times" at the recent change of centuries and beginning of the new millennium.

6. Sarmiento was president of Argentina from 1868 to 1874. His work, *Facundo o Civilización y barbarie* (1845; *Facundo or Civilization and Barbarism*), was based on a conceptual opposition between urban and rural centers and the supposition that these two formed the sites of the nation's civilized and barbaric life, respectively. In *Conflicto y armonías de las razas en América* (1884; *Conflict and Harmony Among Races in Latin America*), Sarmiento expounded more specifically his views on the problematics of race. These views, while more implicit, also structure his thesis in *Facundo o Civilización y barbarie*.

7. The work of Octavio Paz in *Laberinto de la soledad* (1950; *Labyrinth of Solitude*) investigates the links between notions of male "active" sexuality and female passivity on the one hand with the discourse of coloniality in Mexican history on the other. Other writers have also explored this nexus. Gloria Anzaldúa in *Borderlands/La Frontera: The New Mestiza* (1987) looks at the figure of La Malinche as "la chingada" (the penetrated one)—a symbol of the colonized land and the colonized woman. José Rabasa in *Inventing America: Spanish Historiography and the Formation of Eurocentrism* (1993) and Matthew Gutmann in *The Meanings of Macho: Being a Man in Mexico City* (1996) have also written on this dynamic in their works.

8. *The Famous 41: Sexuality and Social Control in Mexico, 1901*, edited by Robert McKee Irwin, Edward J. McCaughan, and Michelle Rocío Nasser (2003), offers a detailed examination of this case and its relevance to ideas of homosexuality as effeminacy in Mexican popular culture.

9. Referring to the present day setting, one of the respondents in the study conducted by Josefina Fernández states that in Latin America there prevails the myth of the violent, marginal, and criminal *travesti* (2004, 118). In television and newspaper media they are comic performing caricatures (at best) but most often depicted as abnormal, unnatural, grotesque, sexually aggressive, as well as murderous, thieving, corrupting, pathological, and mentally ill. *Travestis*, if they merit mentions at all, most frequently appear as the fodder of scandal sheets. Guatemala's paper *Extra* for instance, fills its *policiaca* pages with references to drug addicted cross-dressing "homosexuals," principally equating *travestis* with HIV/AIDS and prostitution through its *nota roja* style reporting of crimes and misdemeanors, assaults and arrests. The murders of *travestis* are more often than not depicted as an outcome of their lifestyle or nature (Reding 2003, 51). In television discourse, *travestis* are constructed stereotypically as a group that possesses no discernible variation or individuality. They are visualized as an exaggeration, represented as artificial, and therefore less real. Dominant imagery and debate depicts them as fraudulent tricksters fooling people with their appearances, and as nothing more than freaks or monstrous betrayals of nature.

10. In Chilean media discourse around the 2005 political contest between Michelle Bachelet and her chief National Renewal (RN) opponent, Sebastián Piñera,

Bachelet used the figure "political transvestism" in describing what she saw as Piñera's attempt to appropriate aspects of another party, the Christian Democrats' (DC) platform to gain votes. This made headlines all over Chile, but no single group interrogated the deployment of *travestismo* in the name of corruption, theft, and deceit. The phrase sounds odd in English. Certainly the idea of one party taking aspects of another's policy and calling them their own is notionally present in English—former British Prime Minister Tony Blair's New Labour and the media reporting on this is a case in point. Blair's touted renovation of the political landscape to supersede "Old" Labour was challenged by critics who observed that the only new feature of Blair's platform was the ironic absorption of Tory-style policy into an ostensibly Center Left party. However, nowhere in the media discourse about New Labour do we find references to political cross-dressing or transvestism; the metaphor and its extensions—deception, appropriation, stealing, concealment, dressing up as something one isn't—belong very much to Latin American mass cultural understandings of both *travestismo* and *travestis*. Neither is it the first occasion that we find its use in mass-media and political discourse. It offers yet another indication of the tendency to connect gender variance or sexual "marginals" to the some national-cultural issue. The conjunction of talking about *travestis* this way and aligning them with political manoeuvres or elite and state-level deception is not just a turn of phrase; it is a figure of thought. The phrase "travestismo político" was also used in Nicaragua in 2001 in reference to the political run-off between the conservative Alemán government and the unusual alliance forged between the liberals and Sandinistas in that year (Equipo Nitlápan-Envío 2001). It is a very common phrase associated with deception, acting and blending of party tactics in many political arenas of the continent.

Another variation of this rhetorical device found in public discourse is "transformismo político." Even Tomás Moulian (1997), whose analysis of Chile under the dictatorship is referenced in this book's final chapter, compares the impact of the Pinochet junta on Chilean society to "cirugía transexual."

11. Readers of Sarduy in English frequently refer to his theorizations of transvestism and the transvestite. Here I keep the original Spanish in which he wrote. It is not entirely clear to what kind of *travesti* Sarduy is referring, but given the influence of Lacan on his ideas, these are influenced by psychiatric notions of the "transvestite"—not just an identity, but rather a paraphilia: the "erotic drive to cross-dress" (Hirschfeld 2006). However, the slippage and ambiguity provided by the untranslated *travesti*, especially when read by the Latin American scholars profiled here, collapses any meaningful distinctions, and as such, the *travesti* is imagined purely in terms of a manoeuvre, not a gendered identity in itself. Psychiatric definitions clearly predominate.

12. In *La simulación*, Sarduy claims that, "El travestí no imita a la mujer. Para él, *a la límite*, no hay mujer, sabe—y quizás, paradójicamente es el único en saberlo—, que ella es una apariencia, que su reino y la fuerza de su fetiche encubren un defecto." (1982, 13, emphasis in original; "The *travesti* doesn't imitate women. For him, *in the end*, there is no woman, he knows—and perhaps paradoxically he is the only one to know—that she is all appearance and the strength of his fetish covers over a defect").

13. As Sarduy describes the *travesti* in *La simulación*:

> La erección cosmética del travestí, la agresión esplendente de sus párpados temblorosos y metalizados como alas de insectos voraces, su voz desplazada,

como si perteneciera a otro personaje, siempre en *off*, la boca dibujada sobre su boca, su propio sexo, más presente cuanto más castrado, sólo sirven a la reproducción obstinada de ese ícono, aunque falaz omnipresente: la madre que la tiene parada y el travestí dobla, aunque solo sea para simbolizar que la erección es una apariencia. (1982, 13)

[The cosmetic erection of the *travesti*, the radiant aggression of his trembling and metallic eyelashes like the wings of voracious insects, his displaced voice, as if it belonged to someone else, always dubbed, the mouth drawn on the mouth, his own sex, more present the more castrated he is, only assist the obstinate reproduction of that icon, even as it is omnipresent: the mother with a hard-on that the *travesti* mimes, even if only to symbolize that the erection is an appearance.]

14. The influence of the thinking of Homi Bhabha, the postcolonialist theorist, is evident in Garber's formulation. Bhabha himself calls the third space a mode of enunciation, which he links to that which is hybrid, moves outside binaries of either-or, master-slave, colonizer-colonized and so on. In "The Third Space: Interview with Homi Bhabha" featured in *Identity, Community, Culture and Difference* (1990), Bhabha states, "For me the importance of hybridity is not to be able to trace two original moments from which the third emerges, rather hybridity to me is the 'third space' which enables other positions to emerge. This third space displaces the histories that constitute it, and sets up new structures of authority, new political initiatives, which are inadequately understood through received wisdom" (211). Although Bhabha's formulation does not refer in any measure to queer or trans identities, Garber reconstitutes transvestism and transgender as the symbol par excellence of this third space. One could argue, in fact, that Bhabha's formulation, in its absence of accounting for the terrain of queer cultural spaces, relies already on primarily heteronormative logics. That is to say, within his framework of analysis, straightness and normatively gendered identities are unquestionably universal. Moreover, in understanding hybridity, the assumption is of two differing "parent" cultures, whose offspring displays mixture. The very scheme of parentage and reproduction is based on heteronormative logics. Garber's usage of the "third" might be seen as an allegorization both of transgender and Bhabha's theories of cultural hybridity (see also Bhabha 1994). It is arguably an allegorization that collapses gender and ethnicity together, occluding the proposition that they are not immediately commensurate. This represents a clear metaphorical leap, wherein a gendered subject stands in to represent the horizon of cultural hybridity as outlined by Bhabha's analysis. Bhabha's theories of hybridity and the "third," do not, it should be noted, consider class or gender either.
15. Butler's use of drag to illustrate the mechanisms of gender performativity has led to a (con)fusion between the idea of gender as a forced reiteration of acts and styles in accordance with the cultural demand for sex-gender coherence and the idea that gender can be willed and performed in the sense of a stage performance. Butler attempted to revise this notion of the voluntaristic possibilities of gender performance by elaborating in *Bodies That Matter* (1993) her notion of citationality, which severely limits the subject's will in constructing their own gender. Such terms are nonsensical to Butler; she insists that the subject cannot even be thought of as prior to the production of gender, but rather emerges through its production, so it is illogical to think about gender performativity as something one can consciously decide—today I will perform male; tomorrow, female; and so on.
16. Although Butler's theorizations of transgender represent a hegemonic strand of Anglophone North American queer theory, I do not mean to suggest that they are the only interpretations that have been advanced in Anglophone North

American scholarship. Indeed, Karen McCarthy-Brown (2001), a U.S. queer ethnographer, provides some challenges to Butlerian readings of the balls featured in *Paris Is Burning*. McCarthy-Brown has studied these balls in some detail. Chapter 5 reengages the Bulterian reading of the film and contrasts it to McCarthy-Brown's work in more detail, thus problematizing any generalization that all U.S. and North American Anglophone queer theory responds to "transgender" in the same way.

17. Katrina Rolley, writing in *Feminist Review*, also finds Garber to be sweeping, imprecise, and glib in some of her statements. When Garber enumerates the presence of transvestites in such widely different cultural contexts and traditions such as Kabuki theater, Shakespearian drama, Greek tragedy, Chinese opera, and Japanese Noh theater, she states that all show an interrelation between transvestism and theatrical performance that is intertwined culturally, historically, and psychologically but never expounds on these cultural, historical, or psychological settings or forces in any convincing manner. Rolley further observes, in sum, "to utilize a wide variety of texts, while also respecting their inherent differences, and simultaneously to sustain an argument throughout a book of this length is a difficult undertaking, and one to which Garber appears unequal" (1993, 102).

18. A glance over the titles and abstracts of any number of articles, conference papers, and monographs that choose transgender as their object of inquiry immediately reveals this; queer's obsession with "queer gender" or transgressive gender—that the subversion of identity is part and parcel of transgender—commonly frames this work. In fact, gender performativity is most often mentioned in reference to transvestism, transsexuality, and drag. This, in spite of the fact that, in Namaste's words, "these works have shown very little concern for the individuals who live, work, and identify themselves as drag queens, transsexuals, or transgenderists. Although the violation of compulsory sex/gender relations is one of the topics most frequently addressed within queer theory, this body of knowledge rarely considers the implications of an enforced sex/gender system for the people who have defied it, who live outside it, or who have been killed because of it" (2000, 9).

19. It should be noted that these North American scholars who have studied Latin(o/a) American sexualities have been criticized as offering formulaic and exoticizing perspectives. In the insistence on the active-passive model, and in advancing the perception that the masculine penetrative partner may completely escape the attribution of homosexuality, their conclusions have been shown as generalizing and as evidence of the projections of a fantasized "difference of the other." The models of "antiquated" and "modern" varieties of homosexuality may constitute an outsider imposition, as many Latin Americans acknowledge that both potentialities of "organizing" homosexual attractions coexist. Pedro Bustos-Aguilar (1995) is a notable opponent of the approaches of scholars like Lancaster, Carrier, and Lumsden. Other critics have complicated the idea of a rigid active-passive distinction by reference to research that shows that actual sex roles may, and often do, change in relationships whose participants appear gender differentiated. That is to say, the fact that one is macho in public does not necessarily nor always signify preference for the active role. Actual sexual behavior can differ from perceived or attributed preferences (Carrillo 2002; Palaversich 1999).

20. Dyer develops this distinction between "social types" and "stereotypes" in *The Matter of Images. Essays on Representation* (1993). Social types are those who "belong" to society. They are the kinds of people that one expects, and is led to expect, to find in one's society (14–15). Usually more fluid and flexible, they can have many roles in relation to the plot. Stereotypes, on the other hand, exist

outside the society: they constitute the other, the peripheral, or the outcast (14). Usually they carry an implicit narrative pattern (15). Stereotypes emerge from where a line is drawn between what is deemed different, in order to contain it, and "map the boundaries of what is acceptable and legitimate behaviour" (16).

Chapter 2

1. Due to state sanctions against the formation of independent political-interest groups, Cuba has not witnessed the emergence of an openly politicized *travesti* subjectivity openly politicized travesti subjectivity. Most recently, however, the rights and humanity of gays, *travestis*, and transsexuals have been placed on the national agenda by none less than Castro's niece, Mariela Castro Espín. Castro Espín is director of the Cuban Centro Nacional de Educación Sexual (CENESEX), which has been instrumental in putting together a proposal to the Cuban parliament to make sex-change treatments and surgeries legal and publicly funded and to allow transsexuals to change their name and sex details on official documents. CENESEX works for all those who have been marginalized because of their sexual difference, including bisexuals, homosexuals, and lesbians. In a 2006 article featured in *La Jornada*, Castro Espín clearly acknowledges past Cuban "mistakes" in the mistreatment of the sexually diverse (Arreola 2006).
2. The image of Che's New Man implied elements of gender normativity and heterosexism that precluded the most visible homosexuals, whose "extravagance" in dress and fashion were viewed as signs of bourgeois decadence, from national life (Leiner 1994, 32–33). The New Man displayed a serious attitude toward work, not "frivolity."
3. The UMAP camps were an "educational form of aversion therapy," the objective of which was to instill the revolutionary ideals of hard work and masculinity in anyone who displayed such tendencies (Leiner 1994, 34). Several sources (interviewees in Orlando Jiménez Leal's 1984 documentary *Conducta Impropia*, for example) mention the ironic parallel to Nazi camps by noting that the gates of the UMAP camps also had their own plaque that read "Work will make you men," which evokes the "Work will make you free" slogan looked at by prisoners of the concentration camps in 1940s Nazi-occupied Europe.
4. Molloy uses the figure of posing referring to fin-de-siècle Europe and the personage of the fop. However, this idea of imposture and *loca* and *travesti* visibility has continued in mass cultural contexts in many parts of Latin America. See Lewis (2008) for an explanation of historical discourses on *travestismo* in Latin America.
5. Or, as Eduardo Nabal says,

> El homosexual era identificado por su forma fallida de representar el género masculino: su indumentaria, sus gestos al andar o hablar, su peinado e incluso su actividad (los escritores y artistas eran vistos como mucho más sospechosos que los miembros de otras profesiones). La homosexualidad es vista así desde el régimen y desde la cultura que promueve como una traición íntima al corazón de la revolución ya que la imagen arquetípica del revolucionario, la imaginaría sociosexual en la que se sustenta, es la del varón heterosexual, guerrero, pater familias, transmisor de valores y actitudes. Varón cuyo cuerpo ha sido modelado por el trabajo, la militancia, el combate y el esfuerzo revolucionarios. El género fallido que representa la homosexualidad es así un desafío

a la regulación de los cuerpos y las mentes masculinas necesaria para la supervivencia del régimen y su legitimación sociocultural. (n.d.)

[The homosexual was identified by his failed way of representing the masculine gender: his clothing, his gestures while walking or talking, his hairstyle, and even his exploits (writers and artists were seen as much more suspicious than members of other professions). Homosexuality was seen from the viewpoint of the regime and the culture it promoted as an intimate betrayal of the heart of the revolution, since the archetypical image of the revolutionary, the sociosexual imaginary that supports it, is that of the heterosexual male, the warrior, the pater familias, transmitter of values and attitudes. A male whose body has been molded by work, militancy, revolutionary combat, and effort. The failed gender represented by homosexuality is hence a challenge to the regulation of the masculine bodies and minds needed for the survival of the regime and its sociocultural legitimation.]

6. In the public (hetero) imagination, the *loca*'s effeminacy can only equal the assumption of the passive role in sexual penetration by other men. As several observers note, however, this sexual script (*activo-pasivo*) is occasionally reversed and interchanged in private. It is more a symbolic paradigm related to conceptions about gender and may have inconsistent applicability in everyday sexual practice (Palaversich 1999; Prieur 1998). While identifying with the *loca*-macho ideal, Arenas himself subverts this script of positionality as he recounts in his autobiography. This tees with the strategy of disturbing the macho's claims to superiority: the "bottom" topping the "top."

7. As Epps states in his article "Proper Conduct," "Arenas . . . struggles to script his singularity, his individuality, through and against and within what is already scripted; perhaps it might be better to say that he struggles, through a sort of ironic inflation, to break the script altogether . . . the struggle is not only with heterosexuals but also with homosexuals, for they too script and are scripted" (1995b, 246).

8. Volumes of scholarly and nonscholarly literature have been written on the phenomena of camp, camp style, and camp culture. Camp is, however, rather difficult to define. Originally employed as an adjective to describe men identified as "ostentatiously and extravagantly effeminate," its meanings and use have extended over time to also include any phenomenon viewed as exaggerated or theatrical. One of the first to place "camp" logics in academic purview was the U.S. American theorist Susan Sontag. In "Notes on 'Camp'" (1964), Sontag connects camp to the subversion and mimicking of categories of conventional "good taste" and artifice. Sontag viewed camp as an irreverent aesthetic and sensibility, but inherently apolitical. Since the release of her essay, much debate has emerged in terms of the general applicability of the term and its status as conservative or progressive. Camp has also been linked to the popular culture and popular icons and has traveled outside of homosexual cultures and into "the mainstream."

9. Referring to this description, Carmelo Esterrich makes the following comment:

El maricón areniano es aéreo porque jamás echa raíces, es errante, sin rumbo seguro o planeado. Si bien hay un deseo de retorno, su desplazamiento está consciente de que ese espacio que se busca no existe como tal: la meta es sólo una excusa para continuar moviéndose sin parar en el desarraigo, sin propiedad, siempre desvalijado y desválido. Es decir, la condición exílica. (1997, 182)

[Arenas's queen is ethereal because he never sets down roots; he is errant, with no fixed or planned route. Even if the desire to return exists, in his displacement he is conscious of the fact that space he looks for does not exist as such: the goal is only an excuse to keep moving without stopping in his rootlessness, without belongings, always without luggage and undone. In other words, the exilic condition.]

10. This chapter, among other things, implicates the dictator, Fifo, in effeminacy, a kind of repressed *mariconería* responsible for his eventual personality split: an exaggerated violent masculinity struggling with its homosexuality in denial. This is typical Arenas satire: hitting the macho where it hurts. However, it also extends the link between the duality of power and the duality in gender identifications that form the centerpiece of Arenas's complex appraisal of the regime.
11. As the setting intensifies, so the *Reprimero* becomes the *Reprimerísimo*.

CHAPTER 3

1. *Fichera* refers to a female cabaret dancer-prostitute who gets a paid with a *ficha*, or token, for every drink her client buys. These films featured such characters.
2. A very similar film, controversial for its time, was also made in Peronist Argentina: *Mi novia, el travesti* (*My Girlfriend the "Travesti"*).
3. Together with NAFTA, a policy whose fragmenting impact on labor laws, tariffs, and trade was without precedent, Salinas de Gortari instituted a wave of privatizations of public companies that redrew the map of industrial relations. Salinas de Gortari encouraged massive runaway spending and investments on credit. His administration and its economic policies are widely held responsible for the 1994 Peso Crisis.
4. The biography of Maria Novaro featured in the Internet Movie Database mentions that "Danzon was an instant hit in Mexico and was well received overseas," something especially difficult to achieve as a foreign language film in the international circuit and also given its arthouse/women's film associations locally in Mexico (Berthiaume, n.d.).
5. Known in Cuba as the *Período especial en tiempo de paz*, this refers to the period that began in 1991 with the collapse of the Soviet Bloc when Cuba lost its chief trading partner and descended into economic disarray. The loss of crude-oil supplies from the Soviet Union and its satellite states significantly impacted on Cuban industrial and agricultural activity. The most severe years of the Special Period were felt in the mid-1990s. Recently the situation has been somewhat alleviated by the support of Venezuela under Hugo Chávez and the bartering exchange of Venezuelan oil for Cuban medical experience. Most commentators sustain that the Special Period ended in 2004. In the Special Period, the crisis was worsened by the continuation of the trade embargo imposed by the United States in 1962, an embargo still in place today and representing one of the longest in modern world economic history. Tourism has displaced sugar production in Cuba as the chief avenue of foreign revenue coming into the country.
6. One of these sequences includes a bondage fantasy led by Fresa and Vainilla, whose use of feathers to tickle a clearly terrified Hernán, who is naked and tied to a tree, is particularly memorable. The feathers simultaneously point to their *transformista* artistry and their association with popular Afro-Cuban divination

rituals, as this scene is juxtaposed with images of Pachi cutting open a chicken and the sound of drums and other santeria elements. It reinforces the heterosexual panic of seduction, reinforced by fear, into queerness. Queer *rarezas* are clearly the subconscious limits of perversity as imagined by the straight character, Hernán, whose viewpoint centers the film
7. Castro comes from a wealthy farming family and is the son of a Galician immigrant; hence, he is more white and elite than mulatto or black.
8. Before Castro's "temporary" withdrawal from power (now permanent) due to illness in August 2006, ongoing reports had speculated on his health and imminent death. The U.S. Central Intelligence Agency (CIA) monitored hundreds of hours of video footage to determine if Castro had Parkinson's, something that Castro himself has mocked in public speeches ("Castro has Parkinson's says CIA" 2005).
9. The film is awash with Biblical references—literally. In one moment, a "flood" occurs upstairs, an image that points to the end of one world and the beginning of another. The seven days points to the (re)making of a world, as in Genesis. The main and most treasured *cuadro* is a rendering of Adam and Eve in the garden, which reverberates with the film's notions of a loss of innocence, a gaining of sexual knowledge, and the banishment from "paradise"—the Cuban revolutionary utopia.

CHAPTER 4

1. Lee Edelman's *Homographesis* (1994) and Annamarie Jagose's *Inconsequence* (2002) both examine queer bodies as intensely inscribed with contested meanings. Trans bodies are the latest in a long line of "bodies of difference" to form sites of contemporary obsession over cultural meanings.
2. Koo argues that Gutiérrez endeavors to show, through the male-female relations of the novel as well as the material facts of existence for Cuba's poor, just how far the island has strayed from its initial ideals. Suffice it to say that although gender-bipolar ideology as an overarching horizon persists, the micropolitics of relations between poor men and women exhibit differences from their historically based schema. The longer standing naturalizing notions of what makes a man or a woman therefore mark *travestis* like Sandra as distinct, but the day-to-day negotiation of gender among people may simultaneously allow her appearance and limited acceptance in the community. The novel does not advance this point, but it is a theoretical consideration that may apply to the environment to which Gutiérrez's novel refers.
3. As Murray observes, in Latin Mediterranean societies, people "take for granted . . . that some men won't attain masculinity" (1995, 13). Although this is undesirable in a son, it is sometimes tacitly acknowledged as an unfortunate inevitability for some males.
4. *Aguardiente*, which means literally "burning water," is a strong alcoholic spirit. There are several varieties in Latin America. There is no cognate word in English.
5. In talking of the composition of his first work, *Trilogía sucia de La Habana* with Stephen Clark, Gutiérrez claims, "Todos son personajes reales, yo lo único que hago es cambiarles los nombres a la gente, y en *El Rey de La Habana* lo mismo" (Clark 2001; "All of my characters are real, the only thing I do is change peoples' names, and in *El Rey de La Habana* I did the same thing").
6. Aparicio and Chávez-Silverman deliberately deploy their term in the plural, arguing that in the contemporary period multiple troping possibilities and effects are in evidence, which differ primarily in terms of location, use, and intent. On the one hand, the imperial gaze reductively characterizes a diverse collection of people

via stereotype and the use of debasing rhetorical language. On the other hand, however, these discursive formations have also been deployed by colonial subjects themselves to contest hegemonic representations and, by so doing, express and reaffirm difference. Further, this is not just limited to cultural production; Latino/a ways of being in the world interact with preexistent and reproduced schemes of the exotic and the sexual, schemes that so often underwrite the dominant motifs of tropicality.

7. Bellatin himself formulated his position on the question of nationality, writing, and national literatures in an interview by Francisco Melgar:

> Me parece interesante porque remarca el hecho de que la escritura no tiene una nacionalidad definida. Si me preguntas por la nacionalidad a un nivel personal, te podría decir muchas cosas, pero esas cosas no tienen ninguna importancia para mi trabajo, porque lo que yo intento es que los libros hablen por sí mismos, que los textos se vuelvan autónomos, que se vuelvan textos sin autor. Entonces esta posibilidad de tener dos nacionalidades, porque es cierto que tengo dos, pero al mismo tiempo ninguna, permite que la escritura aparezca como de la nada, como no sustentada en una nacionalidad que ha sido, en mi opinión, un lastre para nuestras tradiciones literarias . . . Creo que [la categoría de literaturas nacionales] es un invento académico para poder clasificar una serie de escrituras, y que a la larga ha hecho más daño que cualquier otra cosa. Para mí, esta segmentación a la que llevan las literaturas nacionales puede acabar impidiendo que un escritor diga lo que tiene que decir, solo por respetar una suerte de patrón o idea preconcebida con respecto a la literatura. En especial si esta persona recién comienza a escribir y todavía no se compromete con una palabra determinada. (Melgar 2007)
>
> [I think it's interesting because it underlines the fact that literature doesn't have any defined nationality. If you ask about my nationality on a personal level, I could say many things, but these things aren't at all important to my work, because what I try to do is let the books speak for themselves, so that the texts are autonomous, so they're texts without an author. So the possibility of having two nationalities, because it's true I have two, but at the same time none, allows the writing to appear from nowhere, without a basis in any nationality, which has been, in my opinion, a real dead weight for our literary traditions . . . I believe that [the category of national literatures] is an academic invention that only ends up preventing the writer from saying what they want to say, all for the sake of respecting a kind of model or preconceived idea in connection to literature. Particularly if this person has only recently begun to write and still hasn't committed themselves to a certain line.]

8. The quality of distant observation—that of a stranger in a landscape—pervades his work. One detail that assisted in "placing" the author, whom I met while in Mexico City in 2006, was in his transcultural religious identification. On hearing me remark on my own veganism and a friend's interest in India and homeopathy, Bellatin identified himself as an adherent of Sufism, a mystical branch of Islam. My intent to place Bellatin led to still more ambiguity and an implicit resistance on the part of the author to be pinned to a Mexican or Latin American cultural landscape. Of interest, too, is that Bellatin works at a writing center that is also a refuge for artists who have sought asylum because of political persecution in their countries of origin. Bellatin, then, lives to some degree alongside the conditions of nationlessness inhabited by his colleagues at the writing school, Casa Refugio

Citlaltépetl. In his novels, moreover, his plotting of place articulates a series of elsewheres that are somewhere but also nowhere, reflecting their antirealist drive. It is in the act of reading that the location or potential location is constructed. Implicit in my interpretation is that part of Bellatin's act of writing is intent on disrupting the possibility of reading "nationally."
9. The work of Jorge Luis Borges resolutely refuses the tradition of literature as representative of national reality. Borges's work does not bear any realist relation to the social or political world. He is fundamentally uninterested in that function of literature. Bellatin hence might be seen to belong more to the tradition of writing like that of Borges, which is intrigued by the possibilities of creating worlds in fiction that are not mimetic of some immediately traceable reality. This tradition of writing is concerned with metatexuality and self-referentiality, philosophy, erudition, linguistic play, image, the fantastical, identity, and psychological landscapes.
10. This provides an excellent example of the way "*travesti*" accrues different meanings in different contexts. Like "transgender," it may contain a number of subcategories, for instance, transvestite, transgenderist, and even transsexual in some cases. Where the word is being evoked for political concerns, it is invariably linked to a lived day-to-day sense of gender—living full time in the gender one has identified as and embodied through hormonal and sometimes surgical means. But there is still considerable blurring between the categories in the cultural imaginary.
11. "In Greek drama, violent or unsavory acts tended to happen off-stage, or 'off-scene', which is where the modern word 'obscene' comes from (more precisely, 'ob' is Latin for 'against' whilst 'skini' is Greek for 'scene', or 'stage.' 'Obskini' has become 'obscene' in the intervening centuries). Technically it refers to any dramatic element which we do not see with our own eyes, and which we are merely informed about" ("Obscene" n.d.).
12. Some examples include the written and visual diaries of Hervé Guibert, Tom Joslin, David Wojnarowicz, Eric Michaels, Gil Cuadros, Alberto Sandoval Sánchez, Derek Jarman, and Paul Monette.
13. *Axolotls* are amphibians that do not ever develop to the stage where they can leave the water. They are thus considered to be perpetually in a hybrid state between developmental phases.
14. In countries such as Peru, the rate of infection has been roughly over half the rate of that in the United States, as recently as 2001 (Reding 2003, 41). In Honduras, it stands at two-and-a-half times the U.S. rate. A tiny minority of people in both countries have access to medical funding arrangements that allow availability of antiretroviral drugs (54–55). In Peru, as many as nine out of ten people with AIDS are left to fend for themselves (41). Similar scenarios exist in El Salvador, Guatemala, Nicaragua, and Honduras (47, 50, 53, 54). Countries like Uruguay and Costa Rica are notable exceptions (42, 46). Where the church and right wing and paramilitary moral majority groups have a strong hold and economies are most regulated by restructuring programs, as in Honduras and Peru, the situation is particularly dire (41, 55).

CHAPTER 5

1. Mexico, neutral in the fight against the Central Powers in World War I, aligned with the Allied Forces against the Axis Powers in World War II.
2. The term "afterlife of colonialism" is derived from the work *Queer Globalizations: Citizenship and the Afterlife of Colonialism* (2002), edited by Arnaldo Cruz-Malavé and Martin F. Manalansan. It relates to the residues, or the persistence of the influence of colonial forms of hegemony, and their rearticulation in diverse

sites of identity and struggle over signification in the contemporary era of global capital.
3. Zapata's novel predates the publication of Judith Butler's *Gender Trouble* in which she expounds on her theory of performativity; and yet, it should be observed that ideas about the social construction and daily enactment of gender were already in circulation before Butler, most notably in the work of ethnomethodologists such as Garfinkel (1967) and Suzanne Kessler and Wendy McKenna (1985).
4. The 1950s and 1960s were a time in Mexico where "youth" as an important cultural category made itself known—in all its conflicts and troubles—as in the United States, with James Dean being the iconic representation. It was also the era of the inauguration of television and mass consumer culture and a consolidation of gender-role norms. The novel makes references to this temporal frame in various parts. The mid-to-late-1960s saw a wave of countercultural youth activity in the country, which Angélica María largely bypassed. As detailed in the official Web site of the star, *Angélica María. Sitio oficial*, in her twenties, with the arrival of the 1960s, she initiated a new trajectory in the public imagination as a singer, which would reach a peak when she recorded with that other icon of Mexican (and queer) culture, Juan Gabriel. The two popularized on a mass scale the genre of the *balada ranchera*. Angélica María continued to star in hit films at a time when Mexican cinema was in decline stylistically, the golden age of the film industry having come to an end (Biografía).
5. The sight of blood and female reproductive organs unite to create this abjection in horror films, especially as it pertains to the experience of beginning female puberty. *Carrie* is an example of this in Hollywood cinema.
6. Deneuve plays a sexually repressed young woman, Carol, whose disgust for sexual and bodily life and male attention is highly at odds with the tone of the "swinging sixties" and the heady liberation the film portrays. Like Alba, Carol murders men who threaten her sense of sexual and bodily limits. So, too, like Alba, she is seemingly incapable of distinguishing between reality and fantasy. The Roman Polanski film, made in 1965, provides yet one more intertext to the whirling cinematic references the novel engages and is also placed at a similar juncture of time, with the concomitant changes in sexual mores.
7. The narrative voice variously refers to Alba María in all her suffering as Sancha María, Prana María, and Asma María (Zapata 1989, 42).
8. Alba-Alexina ends up in a *manicomio* herself by the novel's end, still living between fantasy and reality and thus recalling the character Blanche DuBois from *A Streetcar Named Desire*. She is committed after stalking the real Angélica, whom she wishes to replace, as an extension of the desire to be the original and not a mere copy of an identity. She imagines the other patients as adoring fans, and Dr. Marenti, the hospital's head, as a director in a new film she will star in.
9. In Lacan's formulation, three planes to the psychic structure exist: the Real, the Imaginary, and the Symbolic. The Real is a difficult concept. The Imaginary, or nonlinguistic aspect, formulates human primitive self-knowledge. The Symbolic is the linguistic realm, a shared set of collective rules and terms. The Real cannot be spoken but is always present and continually mediated by both the Imaginary and the Symbolic. All subjects from the time of childhood develop a sense of self through identification. The Imaginary is the space of this identification that begins at the mirror stage, when the young infant is able to perceive a reflection of itself in the mirror and recognizes that other as self and therefore distinct from the maternal body. The subject achieves proper selfhood through language, when it enters the Symbolic order, and is able to express desires and relations. The Real cannot be spoken of—and is only mediated in those terms of self-other relation

both in the Imaginary and the Symbolic. Millot seems to understand sexual difference as prior, as a base characteristic that automatically comes in twos—male or female—as the Real itself.
10. The book's back cover summarizes Millot's argument in the following way:

> Transsexuality answers to the dream of pushing back, or even eliminating altogether, the limits marking the frontiers of reality. The male transsexual, who claims to have a woman's soul imprisoned in a man's body, and who often demands correction of this "error" through surgery, is perhaps the only believer in a monolithic sexual identity free of doubts and questions. The female transsexual reverses this equation, seeking to identify with the prerogatives—and even organs—of male power. Sexual difference and its discontents owes much to the cultural interplay of fantasy and reality, dominance and transgression, and the questions that put each of us in touch with what makes us strangers to ourselves. (Millot 1991)

Millot is heavily criticized as reductive, distorting, and transphobic by several trans theorists and commentators, including Patrick Califia and Jay Prosser.

11. Again, the work of Gutmann (1996) points to substantial changes in the conventional ways of understanding the place of women and men in the last few decades. Mexico passed through waves not only of "sexual revolution" and counterculture from the late 1960s on, but also feminism and gay rights, particularly in the 1970s (Lumsden 1991; Mogrovejo 2000).
12. I have yet to find another novel or play from Latin America that depicts intersexuality in any form. The recent Lucía Puenzo film from Argentina, *XXY* (2007), is one of the few cinematic exceptions to this rule. This virtual absence is in contrast to works in English, including Jeffrey Eugenides's *Middlesex* (2002) and others.
13. In this interview, Santos-Febres tells Morgado the following, in response to the question as to whether her story is based on real events or real transsexuals and *travestis*:

> Yo no creo en marginalidades fijas, quizás porque pertenezco a varias. Soy mujer, negra, caribeña y quién sabe qué otras cosas más que me colocan en un margen. Pero he observado que este margen siempre es móvil. A veces estoy en el centro (por cuestiones de educación, de clase quizás) y a veces soy la abyecta (por razones de piel, por pertenecer a un país colonizado por EE.UU.). Precisamente por esa movilidad me doy permiso para transitar por varios mundos, por varios márgenes, a veces hasta por el centro. (Morgado 2000)
>
> [I don't believe in fixed marginalities, perhaps because I belong to several. I'm a woman, black, Caribbean, and who knows what else that would place me in the margin. But I have observed that this margin is always mobile. Sometimes I'm in the center (in regards to education or perhaps class) and sometimes I'm the abject one (because of my skin, because of belonging to a country colonized by the United States). Precisely because of this mobility I grant myself the permission to move between different worlds, different margins, sometimes toward the center.]

14. Women are understood by Pedreira as weak, soft, vain, fickle, and overemotional. Women's role, moreover, is to produce and function from the home, not to participate in public life (120). Pedreira is dismissive, too, of men that do not display masculine strength of will (119) and posits that the essential problem is with those "hombres inservibles," that is, males susceptible to the fragilities normally found

in women and also influenced by these women as teachers. The task before Puerto Rico is the education of men that would lead to "un nuevo tipo de puertorriqueño que sepa hacer y medir la realidad con nuevos bríos, sin azucaramientos ni confusiones" (122; "a new kind of Puerto Rican who knows what to do and how to measure reality with a new energy, without sugar coating or confusions"). His triumphant discourse is hence deeply masculine and generates binaries of active-passive, dominating-submissive, and so on.

15. Rodó's *Ariel* (1990) is a secular sermon directed to the youth of Latin America calling on them to reject U.S. materialist values and embrace the Greco-Roman classic tradition of philosophy and "refined" culture. Ariel, a character drawn from Shakespeare's *The Tempest*, represents the hopeful future of Latin America, and Caliban, the realities of the (Anglo) North. Rodó assumes the wise voice of Prospero in *Ariel*. Pedreira adopts a similar pose—that of teacher and navigator of the nation's course.

16. In the current setting, most Puerto Ricans have disengaged from the argument of independence. Tellingly, a considerable number consider statehood a viable option. At the same time, Puerto Rican society is not simply split between one pole or the other—absorption into the United States on the one hand or autonomy on the other. The famous 1998 Plebiscite, in which 46.5 percent voted for statehood, 2.5 percent for independence, 0.4 percent for the continued commonwealth status, 50.3 for "none of the above," and 0.3 percent did not enter a vote, provides a vivid illustration of the transcendence of binary thinking around the issue. The considerable vote for "none of the above," in which half of the island lodged what might be considered a rejection of the categories offered themselves, suggests that many Puerto Ricans have other issues on the minds apart from those publicly promoted in the name of the collectivity.

17. Duany notes that two subalterns in the Puerto Rican context are those unwanted others excluded from the national imaginary, the Cuban émigré and the Dominican. Often they are conflated to the black Puerto Rican, also eschewed, denationalized, and undocumented, and seen as dangerous, marginal, and clandestine (2002, 21).

18. If we turn to the sociological record of such persons in contemporary San Juan, we find a profile that supports this picture of social and institutional exclusion, police violence, and underground support networks and friendships forged in the face of both. Sheilla Rodríguez Madera's and José Toro Alfonso's work is useful is useful in illuminating the current context for *travestis* and transsexuals in San Juan that the novel makes reference to. In their article "La comunidad de la cual no hablamos" (The community we don't talk about), they furnish us with a similar picture of vulnerability and stigma, providing some key reasons behind this:

> Los factores que vulnerabilizan a los/as transgéneros, trabajen o no en la industria del sexo, están directamente relacionados a la marginación, al prejuicio social, y a la falta de apoyo. Como comunidades marginadas son víctimas de: (a) rechazo por parte de la comunidad en general y por la comunidad *gay* en particular, (b) rechazo de su familia, (c) ausencia de servicios de salud, (d) pobreza, (e) escasez de escenarios laborales que les acepten, (f) adicción, (g) prejuicios, (h) racismo, (i) un sistema judicial que ha sido implacable, (j) maltrato físico y emocional, entre tantos otros. (2003, 12)
>
> [The factors that make transgender people vulnerable, whether or not they work in the sex industry, are directly related to marginalization, social prejudice and lack of support. As marginalized communities they are victims of (a) rejection by the community in general and by the gay community in particular, (b) rejection by their family, (c) absence of health services, (d) poverty,

(e) scarcity of work settings that accept them, (f) addiction, (g) prejudices, (h) racism, (i) an implacable legal system, (j) physical and emotional mistreatment, among other things.]

These aspects shadow the lives of the *dragas* and transsexuals in *Sirena Selena vestida de pena*, even when they are not made explicit. One dimension in Rodríguez-Madera's and Toro-Alfonso's study that strikes a chord in particular is in the observation that in San Juan "las personas informaron que sus redes de apoyo social esencialmente estaban compuestas por sus amistades y por la figura materna" (20; our informants related that their social support networks are made up by friendships and by the maternal figure).

19. This highly parodic sequence is given in English in the first-person voice of a Canadian gay man. It lampoons gay tourism—"our kind of tourism"—as another kind of imperialism. This section implicitly critiques the posturing to cultural superiority around questions of the acceptance of homosexuality in Anglo-America and Europe—the idea that they are more "evolved" to accept gayness than Caribbeans—its underlying valorization of the First World–Third World paradigm, the clichéd ideas about closetedness and gayness and "latin lovers." Moreover it serves to show up the prejudices and hypocrisy of white, middle-class gay men who claim their identities as "normal" and "universal" (not being drag queens, or AIDS activists with chips on their shoulders, or street boys, unlike many of the characters portrayed in the novel) and the potential for (sexual) exploitation by gay North Americans of young men on the island.

20. Xtravaganza's death is judged by Butler as a misreading of the "advantages" of assuming a female identity in the context of the realities of women of color in the United States. And yet there is little evidence that Xtravaganza was murdered for being a Latina. Butler invokes Xtravaganza's gender—her transsexuality—to understand the divergences between idealized gender norms and the implications of their enactment in everyday life. For Butler, Xtravaganza may see her occupying the position of woman as a way of transcending current circumstances, but she does not take into account the very real perils that women of color face, including, for instance, physical and sexual violence. Namaste views Butler's use of the life and death of Xtravaganza and her transsexuality as a misreading itself, a way of allegorizing transsexuality to stand in for other issues. As Namaste states,

> Butler elides both Extravaganza's transsexual status and her work as a prostitute. Here is the point: Venus was killed because she was a transsexual prostitute. An acknowledgement of violence against transsexual prostitutes is explicit in *Paris Is Burning*, although Butler chooses to ignore it. After the death of Extravaganza, her best friend, Angie, insightfully comments, "But that's part of life. That's part of being a transsexual in New York City and surviving." Since Butler has reduced Extravaganza's transsexuality to allegory, she cannot conceptualize the specificity of violence with which transsexuals, especially transsexual prostitutes, are faced. This, to my mind, is the most tragic misreading of all. More than simply denying Extravaganza's transsexuality, Butler uses it in order to speak about race and class. (2000, 13)

21. In a chapter entitled "Is Paris Burning?" in her book *Black Looks: Race and Representation*, bell hooks sees the ball performances as reproductive of not simply gender but also white imperial power. She holds that the drag performers enact "a racialized fictional construction of the feminine that . . . makes the representation of whiteness as crucial to the experience of female impersonation as gender" (1992, 3). This kind of mimesis elicits a "longing to be in the position of the ruling-class woman" as well as "the desire to act in partnership with the ruling-class

white male." (5). Hence, for hooks, the ball stars support the very "brutal imperial ruling-class capitalist patriarchal whiteness" that oppresses them. Such assertions also attain resonance in Mayra Santos-Febres's figuring of *travestismo*. And yet both Butler and hooks do not perceive the potential for disidentificatory strategies at the heart of mimetic practices such as those of the balls, the kind of minority strategies of mockery and resistance suggested by José Muñoz in his already cited book, *Disidentifications*.
22. Zavala devotes a chapter of her book *Bolero. Historia de un amor* to the transgendering possibilities of the bolero, entitled "Mutación, metamorfosis, androginia" (2000, 119–25), underlining the obvious connections made by Santos-Febres between bolero and *travestismo*.
23. This is a very common phrase in Mexico.
24. Alberto Sandoval-Sánchez, editor of the *Centro* Special Issue, states in his introduction that "each critic locates transvestism in a given context (gender, sexual, social, racial, colonial, transcultural, allegorical, or metaphorical)" (2003, 7). This may be true, but also true is that none of them locates *travestismo* in the context of *travestismo* itself, as lived and experienced in the site to which the text refers.

Chapter 6

1. Lemebel makes this allegiance with the feminine through the choice of the maternal name explicit in an interview with Fernando Blanco and Juan Gelpí:

    Tú sabes que en Chile todos los apellidos son paternos, hasta la madre lleva esa macha descendencia. Por lo mismo desempolvé mi segundo apellido: Lemebel . . . El Lemebel es un gesto de alianza con lo femenino, inscribir un apellido materno, reconocer a mi madre huacha desde la ilegalidad homosexual y travestí. (1997, 93–94)

    [You know that in Chile all surnames are paternal, even my mother kept on that male line of inheritance. So for that reason I decided to dust off my second surname, Lemebel . . . Lemebel is a gesture of alliance with the feminine, inscribing a maternal surname, recognizing my poor mother from the point of view of homosexual and *travesti* illegality.]

2. As Robles notes,

    Las Yeguas staged a series of performances that aggressively "homosexualized" the political and cultural discourses of the time. One of their most memorable performances was their staging of the cueca sola in the foyer of the building that housed the Chilean Human Rights Commission. Years earlier, the mothers of the disappeared had appropriated the cueca—Chile's national dance in which a couple flirtatiously dance around one another—to symbolize the disappearance of their male partners by performing the dance alone. On the foyer floor, Las Yeguas placed a large cloth map of Latin America and covered it with broken glass. As these two gay men "danced alone" wearing only long white skirts, their feet bled and made imprints on the map. Through performances like these, the group inserted the issue of homosexual oppression into the larger discourses of the opposition to the Pinochet regime and situated the political demands of homosexuals squarely within the horizons of the left (1998, 37).

3. In *The Myth of Marginality: Urban Poverty and Politics in Rio de Janeiro*, anthropologist Janice E. Perlman makes the following argument for favela dwellers with whom she lived and who she observed over several decades in Río de Janeiro, Brazil:

    The evidence strongly indicates that the *favelados* are not marginal, but in fact are integrated into the society, albeit in a manner detrimental to their own interests. They are not separate from, or on the margins of the system, but are tightly bound into it in a severely asymmetrical form. They contribute their hard work, their high hopes, and their loyalties, but do not benefit from the goods and services of the system. It is my contention that the *favela* residents are not economically and politically marginal, but are excluded and repressed; that they are not socially and culturally marginal, but stigmatized and excluded from a closed class system. (1976, 195)

    Perlman further speaks of the "ideology of marginality," which is manipulated to treat those marginalized as a social problem in need of elimination. Favela dwellers were seen as the source of all forms of deviance, perversity, and criminality, the point of abjection that culturally was used to purify other segments of society (259). She found that claims of marginality were "empirically false, analytically misleading, and insidious in their policy implications" as favela dwellers were used as political scapegoats in the period to which the study refers, principally the 1960s and 1970s. Such an ideology of marginality pertains elsewhere, especially under highly competitive economic regimes that posit the "survival of the fittest," such as the neoliberalism evidenced in Chile in the last twenty-five years. Discourses of marginality hence may mask the real situation and serve to "blame the victim," constituting a sort of symbolic violence, to invoke Bourdieu, which may be internalized. Lemebel unmasks the workings of this discourse in his *crónicas* by showing the fraught realities of their shifting levels of integration of his marginalized subjects with the "center."
4. The term "neo-barroso" is based on "neo-barroco"; Perlongher used it to cite a peculiarly *rioplatense* renovation of the baroque. The baroque, it will be remembered, often combines opposites and fuses seemingly disparate elements in a self-conscious style of excess and ornamentation, making use of both the high and low, the sacred and the profane. Several homosexual writers in different parts of Latin America are associated with a neobaroque sensibility—José Lezama Lima, Severo Sarduy, and Reinaldo Arenas. The "barroso" element that Perlongher points to underlies the confusion or "muddiness" of the marrying of these elements. In the context of Lemebel's writing, we might emphasize the apparent black humor, the kitsch artifice, the celebration of the demotic and the melodramatic, as well as the self-conscious high rhetorical mode both of his writing style and argot of the subjects he depicts. Perhaps "neo-barroso" is preferable for its willing embrace of the ambiguous and its movement away from merely reinscribing the grotesque, to which the work Arenas, as we have seen, is susceptible.
5. The term "ciudad-ano" is deployed in a *crónica* entitled "Homoeróticas urbanas (o apuntes prófugos de un pétalo coliflor)," which is not featured in the Lom Ediciones version of *Loco afán: Crónicas de sidario* but that does appear in the one released by Editorial Anagrama, Barcelona, in 1996. I refer to the LOM Ediciones version published in 1997, as it is the one that was available to me, but the *crónica* not contained in this edition has been published online by *Letra S*.
6. Butler uses this idea of "unlivable zones" that signal the abjected space outside the subject in talking about regimes of cultural intelligibility, especially with regard to gender. The regime of cultural intelligibility forms an exclusionary matrix by which subjects are formed and requires the simultaneous production of a domain

of abject beings, those who are not yet "subjects," but who form the constitutive outside to the domain of the subject. As Butler states, "The abject designates here precisely those 'unlivable' and 'uninhabitable' zones of social life which are nevertheless densely populated by those who do not enjoy the status of the subject, but whose living under the sign of the 'unlivable' is required to circumscribe the domain of the subject" (1993, 3).

7. Locas are described this way in the work of Arenas as well—birds in constant flight—that plays on the pejorative association of "pájaro" with the homosexual. Lemebel also invokes birds, as we shall see, in poetically describing his *colas*. The cover of *Loco afán: Crónicas de sidario* itself plays tribute to this—Lemebel and Casas appear dressed in feather plumage—a baroque turn to be sure, and a play on association, a reclaiming of the notion of effeminacy and "plumas." In Spanish, one who is openly gay is said to be "enplumado," or "con plumas," as opposed to the straight-acting and closeted gay.

8. Sylvia Molloy refers here to the distrust and even phobia toward the subject of homosexuality that has historically affected not only Latin American cultures and their sense of national identity but also investigations of cultural phenomena within Hispanism. She states in the introduction to *Hispanisms and Homosexualities*, "Relations between nationalities and sexualities are uneasy at best; between nationalities and homosexualities, they are downright problematic . . . Hispanism is suspicious of queer studies . . . desire has above all meant national desire" (1998, xi).

9. As Victor Robles notes, the Left during the Allende years were far from accepting of homosexuality:

> In spite of the revolutionary spirit of the times, those years were not a period that would have allowed for a politically organized gay movement. There was no place anywhere on the political spectrum where the virulent homophobia of Chilean society was questioned. In fact, that very homophobia underwrote much of political discourse at the time. In the intense political struggles between supporters and opponents of the Popular Unity government, political figures were often depicted as maricones, or "faggots," in speeches and political cartoons. This was particularly common among the left, which was fond of portraying its opponents as effeminate oligarchs of questionable moral character. (1998, 36)

10. This incident is remembered by a *travesti* prostitute from Talca named Pilar, interviewed by Claudia Donoso for the material that accompanies the photo essay that comprises *La manzana de Adán* (the translation is from the parallel text in the same book):

> Al chico Lucho se lo llevaron y no aparece hasta hoy día. Era dueño de una casa en la calle San Pablo. Los milicos se la incendiaron. Para el golpe estábamos con la Leila en Valparaíso y nos llevaron a todas a un barco que había arraigado en el puerto. Nos llevaron allá con los ojos vendados en una camioneta. Seis días estuve allí amontonado, con los otros en un hoyo. Lo primero que hicieron los milicos fue cortarnos el pelo . . . Mataron a varias para el golpe. A la Mariliz, que era bien bonita igual a la Liz Taylor, la mataron . . . Su cuerpo apareció en el Río Mapocho, entero clavado con bayonetas . . . A la Viviana y a la Juanita las llevaron para el cerro San Cristóbal. (1990, 11)
>
> [They took Chico Lucho who hasn't been there since. He was the owner of a brothel in San Pablo Street. The soldiers burnt it down. We were with Leila in Valparaíso when the coup occurred and they took us all to a ship moored in the port. They took us there blindfolded, in a van. For six days I was left there, piled up with the others, in a hole. The first thing the soldiers

did was cut our hair; they pulled it out by the roots . . . They killed several of us during the coup. They killed Mariliz, who was really pretty, just like Liz Taylor. . . . Her body was found in the Mapocho river, full of bayonet holes . . . Viviana and Juanita's bodies turned up on San Cristóbal hill.]

11. As Salvador Sepúlveda Montoya in an online commentary claims,

    La lucha por los derechos de los homosexuales en Chile, tiene su primer hito, en la protesta que un grupo de travestíes trabajadores sexuales del centro de Santiago, realizaron en la Plaza de Armas de la capital en abril de 1973, la que fue condenada por igual por la Izquierda y por la Derecha. En una coyuntura histórica en la que el país vivía una exacerbada polarización política entre ambos bandos, la irrupción de travestís exigiendo que las fuerzas policiales les dejaran trabajar tranquilos, aparece como uno de los pocos, sino el único, punto de consenso entre ambos bandos. (Sepúlveda Montoya 2004)

    The struggle for homosexual rights in Chile has its first watershed moment in the protest of a group of *travesti* sex workers in the heart of Santiago, carried out in the Plaza de Armas in April 1973, and condemned both by Left and Right. In the context of a country split by the polarized politics of both sides, the eruption of *travestis* demanding that the police let them work in peace, constituted one of the few, if not the only, points on which both sides agreed.

12. As Salvador Sepúlveda Montoya further indicates,

    Cuando se habla del Mercado Gay en Chile, se habla de la serie de bienes, lugares de encuentro y servicios dirigidos al público homosexual y que podemos encontrar principalmente en Santiago y otras ciudades del pais, son espacios en los que se puede vivir la homosexualidad sin temor a la discriminación de los heterosexuales, espacios mediados por el consumo y generalmente marcados en un contexto de diversión, así encontramos discotecas, pubs, restaurants, moteles, sexshops, agencias de viaje, tiendas de ropa. (Sepúlveda Montoya 2004)

    [When we speak of a Gay Market in Chile, we're talking about a series of goods, meeting places, and services aimed at the homosexual community and that we mainly find in Santiago and other cities in the country, which are spaces where one can live one's homosexuality without the fear of discrimination by heterosexuals, spaces mediated by consumption and generally defined in a leisure context, including clubs, pubs, restaurants, motels, sex shops, travel agencies, and clothing stores.]

13. Lemebel alludes here to socialist visions—particularly Cuban ones—via this reference to "el hombre nuevo." His stripping down of revolutionary *hombría* and the inherent homophobia of straight Leftists has resonances with Arenas's project of complicating the macho's claims to superiority, as it was played out in the heteropatriarchal Cuba of the 1970s and 1980s. Lemebel wrote his manifesto with full knowledge of the history of Castro's persecution of homosexuals and *travestis* and was aware of the extraordinary experiences of people like Arenas.
14. "Chongo" is another word for the typically hypermasculine partner of the *loca*.
15. The "tío carroza" is the closeted gay uncle type, who though discreet, continues his sexual activities in the town plaza and exhibits the appearance of being a wealthy gentleman of leisure. Taxi boys are young hustlers who always play the active role, while *cafiches* exchange sex of any type for reward.
16. In interviews, Lemebel notes the influence of Deleuze in his thinking about sexual and other minorities. *La loca* possesses, says Lemebel, "A brilliant means of

perceiving and of perceiving herself, of constantly reaffirming her imaginary as a strategy for survival. The *loca* is constantly zig-zagging in her political-becoming, she is always thinking about her to endure, how to pass, with a bit of luck without being obvious, or too obvious. And she is a type of nomadic thinking; she is the not fixed, solid form of macho reasoning. The *loca* is a hypothesis, a question about herself" (Risco 1995, 16).
17. The *milonga* is a southern cone festive dance but especially associated historically with seduction and prostitutes.
18. In the text, Lemebel infantilizes and mocks Pinochet in the following way:

> ¡Salgamos de aquí ahora que nos hacen mierda!, gritaba como verraco el Dictador, asomando meticuloso la nariz por el vidrio hecho astillas. Pero ¿por dónde?, si nos tienen rodeados, tartamudeó el chofer, mientras ponía marcha atrás chocando con el vehículo trasero. ¡Por cualquier parte, sáqueme de aquí que estos güevones me matan! ¡No ve que no se puede mi General. Agáchese mejor y sujétese bien que voy a intentarlo por atrás! Y en una maniobra de acróbata, el blindado Mercedes reculó con desespero estrellando parachoques y latas, pudiendo salir milagrosamente del tiroteo por la pericia del chofer, que viró en noventa grados rechinando la goma de los neumáticos al retomar el camino . . . En el asiento trasero, el Dictador temblaba como una hoja, no podía hablar, no atinaba a pronunciar palabra, estático, sin moverse, sin poder acomodarse en el asiento. Más bien no quería moverse, sentado en la tibia plasta de su mierda que lentamente corría por su pierna, dejando escapar el hedor putrefacto del miedo. (2002, 173–74)
>
> [Let's get out the hell out of here, the Dictator bellowed like a wild boar, meticulously sticking his nose out of the smashed window. But where to if they've got us surrounded? muttered the driver, reversing against a vehicle at the rear. Anywhere, get me out of here or these bastards will kill me. Can't you see that we can't General? Get down and buckle up good and I'll try to get out from behind. And with an acrobatic maneuver, the bullet-proof Mercedes turned back desperately smashing bumper bars and metal, miraculously managing to escape the gunfire owing to the skill of the driver, who turned ninety degrees screeching the rubber tires on taking the road . . . In the back seat, the Dictator shook like a leaf, unable to speak, without uttering a word, ecstatic, immobile, incapable of settling back into his seat. Or rather he didn't want to move, sitting in the warm slime of shit that slowly ran down his leg, letting off the putrid stink of fear.]

19. In *Transgender Warriors* (1996), Feinberg reconstructs a history of workers and feminist struggles to include transgender people at the heart of many instances of revolutionary action throughout history—against empire, landowners, the ruling class, the church, and so on. Feinberg hence seeks to link transgender struggles to other transformative projects.
20. As Namaste asserts, working against the tendency of the transgender politics of people such as Kate Bornstein, Riki Wilchins, and Feinberg, "Accepting transsexuality means accepting that people live and identify as men and women, although they were not born in male or female bodies. And this needs to be kept separate from political work. Some transsexuals situate themselves on the left, and do their political work from this perspective. Others are moderate, or deeply conservative politically. I want to say that if we accept transsexuality in and of itself, we don't need to make it conditional on a particular political agenda [of gender subversiveness or reiteration]" (2005, 9). This statement could equally be applied to the *locas* and *travestis* invoked by Lemebel in his texts.

REFERENCES

A casa assassinada. 1971. Dir. Paulo Cesar Saraceni. Perf. Rubens Araújo, Norma Bengell, Nelson Dantas, and Joseph Guerreiro. Port Chester, NY: Creative Film Services.
A lira do delirio. 1978. Dir. Walter Lima Jr. Perf. Anecy Rocha, Cláudio Marzo, Paulo César Peréio, and Antonio Pedro. Brasilia: Embrafilme.
Ahmad, Aijaz. 1987. Jameson's rhetoric of otherness and the "national allegory." *Social Text* 17: 3-25.
Aïnouz, Karim. 2003. Macabea con raiva. El ojo que piensa. *Revista virtual de cine iberoamericano* 1 (August). http://www.elojoquepiensa.udg.mx/espanol/numero01/cinejournal/08_rabiosa.html (accessed March 20, 2009).
Alcoff, Linda Martín. 2006. *Visible identities: Race, gender, and the self.* New York: Oxford University Press.
Allatson, Paul. 1998. *Historia de Mayta*: A fable of queer cleansing. *Revista de estudios hispánicos* 32: 511-35.
———. 2007. *Key terms in Latino/a cultural and literary studies*, Malden, MA: Blackwell Press.
Altman, Dennis. 2001. *Global sex.* Chicago: University of Chicago Press.
Amor bandido. 1979. Dir. Bruno Barreto. Perf. Paulo Gracindo, Cristina Aché, Paulo Guarnieri, and Ligia Diniz. Rio de Janeiro: Carnaval Unifilm.
Anderson, Benedict. 1991. *Imagined communities: Reflections on the origin and spread of nationalism.* New York: Verso.
Anzaldúa, Gloria. 1987. *Borderlands/la frontera: The new mestiza.* San Francisco: Spinsters/Aunt Lute.
Aparicio, Frances R. 1998. *Listening to salsa: Gender, Latin popular music, and Puerto Rican cultures.* Hanover, New Hampshire: Wesleyan University Press, 1998.
Aparicio, Frances R., and Susana Chávez-Silverman, eds. 1997. *Tropicalizations: Transcultural representations of latinidad.* Hanover, NH: University Press of New England.
Appelbaum, Nancy P., Anne S. Macpherson, and Karin Alejandra Rosemblatt. 2003. *Race and nation in modern Latin America.* Chapel Hill, NC: The University of North Carolina Press.
Arenas, Reinaldo. 1967. *Celestino antes del alba.* Havana: Ediciones Unión.
———. 1980. *El palacio de las blanquísimas mofetas.* Caracas, Venezuela: Monte Avila Editores.
———. 1982, *Otra vez el mar.* Argos Vergara, Barcelona.
———. 1984. *Arturo, la estrella más brillante.* Barcelona: Montesinos.
———. 1991. *El asalto.* Florida: Ediciones Universal.
———. 1991. *El color del verano.* Florida: Ediciones Universal.
———. 1998. *Antes que anochezca.* 2nd ed. Barcelona: Fábula Tusquets.
Arguedas, Alcides. 1909. *Pueblo enfermo.* La Paz: Ediciones Puerta del Sol.

Arreola, Gerardo. 2006. Estudia el parlamento cubano reconocer derechos a transexuales. *La Jornada*, January 9 http://www.jornada.unam.mx/2006/01/09/index .php section=mundo&article=032n1mun(accessed March 14, 2010).
Arroyo, Jossianna, 2003a. Sirena canta boleros: travestismo y sujetos transcaribeños en Sirena Selena vestida de pena. *Centro: Journal of the Center for Puerto Rican Studies* 15 (2): 38–51.
———. 2003b. *Travestismos culturales. Literatura y etnografía en Cuba y Brasil*. Pittsburg: Instituto Internacional de Literatura Iberoamericana.
Barker, Chris. 2000. *Cultural studies: Theory and practice*. London: Sage.
Barradas, Efraín. 2003. Sirena Selena vestida de pena o el Caribe como travestí. *Centro: Journal of the Center for Puerto Rican Studies* 15 (2): 53–65.
Baudrillard, Jean. 1993. *The transparency of evil: Essays on extreme phenomena*. New York: Verso.
Beauvoir, Simone de. 1973. *The second sex*. Trans. E. M. Parshley. New York: Vintage.
Bell, David, and Jon Binnie. 2000. *The sexual citizen: Queer theory and beyond*. Malden, MA: Polity Press.
Bellas de noche. 1975. Dir. Miguel M. Delgado Perf.Elsa Benn, Carlos Bravo y Fernández, Rosa Carmina, and Jorge Casanova. Mexico City: Cinematográfica Calderón S.A.
Bellatin, Mario. 1992. *Efecto invernadero*. Lima: Jaime Campodónico Editor.
———. 1995. *Damas chinas*. Lima: Ediciones El Santo Oficio.
———. 1999. *Salón de belleza*. Barcelona: Tusquets Editores.
———. 2000. *El jardín de la señora Murakami*. Mexico City: Tusquets Editores.
———. 2001. *La escuela del dolor humano de Sechuán*. Mexico City: Tusquets Editores.
———. 2002. *Jacobo el mutante*. Mexico City: Alfaguara.
———. 2003. *Perros héroes*. Mexico City: Alfaguara.
———. 2004. *Flores*. Mexico City: Editorial Anagrama.
———. 2005. *Obra reunida*. Mexico City: Alfaguara.
Benitez Rojo, Antonio. 2001. *Mujer en traje de batalla*. Madrid: Alfaguara.
Berkins, Lohana. 2003. Un itinerario político del travestismo. In *Sexualidades migrantes. Género y transgénero*, ed. Diana Maffía, 127–37. Buenos Aires: Feminaria Editora.
Berkins, Lohana, and Josefina Fernández. 2005. *La gesta del nombre propio: Informe sobre la situación de la comunidad transexual y travesti en la Argentina*. B.A.: Ediciones Madres de Plaza de Mayo.
Berthiaume, Jean-Marie. n.d. Biography for María Novaro. n.d. *IMDb: The Internet Movie Database* http://www.imdb.com/name/nm0636979/bio (accessed September 17, 2005).
Bettcher, Talia Mae. 2007. Evil deceivers and make-believers: On transphobic violence and the politics of illusion. *Hypatia: A Journal of Feminist Philosophy* 22 (3): 43–65.
Beverley, John. 2004. *Adiós: A national allegory (some reflections on Latin American cultural studies)*. In *Contemporary Latin American cultural studies*, ed. Stephen Hart and Richard Young, 48-60. London: Hodder Arnold.
Bhabha, Homi. 1990. Interview with Homi Bhabha: The third space. In *Identity: Community, culture and difference*, ed. Jonathan Rutherford, 207–21. London: Lawrence and Wishart.
———. 1994. *The location of culture*. London: Routledge.
Billings, Dwight, and Thomas Urban. 1982. The socio-medical construction of transsexualism: An interpretation and critique. *Social Problems* 29 (3): 266–82.
Biografía. *Angélica María. Sitio oficial*. 2002. http://www.angelicamaria.com.mx/ lightbox/galeries/biografia/biografia.html (accessed March 12, 2010).Birkenmaier,

Anke. 2002. Travestismo latinoamericano: Sor Juana y Sarduy. *Ciberletras: Revista de crítica literaria y de cultura* 7. http://www.lehman.cuny.edu/ciberletras/v07/birkenmaier.html (accessed July 22, 2007).
Biron, Rebecca E. 2000. *Murder and masculinity: Violent fictions of twentieth-century Latin America*. Nashville, TN: Vanderbilt University Press.
Blanco, Fernando A., ed. 2004. *Reinas de otro cielo. Modernidad y autoritarismo en la obra de Pedro Lemebel*. Santiago: LOM Ediciones.
Blanco, Fernando, and Juan Gelpí. 1997. El desliz que desafía otros recorridos. Entrevista con Pedro Lemebel. *Nómada. Creación, teoría, crítica* 3:93–8.
Bornstein, Kate. 1994. *Gender outlaw: On men, women, and the rest of us*. New York: Routledge.
Bourdieu, Pierre. 1990. *Logic of practice*. Stanford, CA: Stanford University Press.
———. 1991. *Language and symbolic power*. Trans. Gino Raymond and Matthew Adamson. Cambridge: Polity Press.
Bulnes, Francisco. 1899. *El porvenir de las naciones latinoamericanas ante las recientes conquistas de Europe y Norteamérica*. México: El Pensamiento Vivo de América.
Bustos-Aguilar, Pedro. 1995. Mister don't touch the banana: Notes on the popularity of the ethnosexed body south of the border. *Critique of Anthropology* 15 (2): 149–70.
Butler, Judith P. 1990. *Gender trouble: Feminism and the subversion of identity*. New York: Routledge.
———. 1993. *Bodies that matter: On the discursive limits of "sex."* New York: Routledge.
———. 1998. Athletic genders: Hyperbolic instance and/or the overcoming of sexual binarism. *Stanford Humanities Review* 6 (2). http://www.stanford.edu/group/SHR/6-2/html/butler.html (accessed May 14, 2005).
———. 2004. *Undoing gender*. New York: Routledge.
Cabral, Mauro. 2003. Pensar la intersexualidad, hoy. In *Sexualidades migrantes. Género y transgénero*, ed. Diana Maffía, 117–26. Buenos Aires: Feminaria Editora.
Califia, Patrick. 1997. *Sex changes: The politics of transgenderism*. San Francisco: Cleis Press.
Cambio de sexo. 1977. Dir. Vicente Aranda. Perf. Victoria Abril, Rafaela Aparicio, and Montserrat Carulla. Barcelona: Kruger Leisure Enterprises.
Caminha, Adolfo. 1895. *Bom crioulo*. Rio de Janeiro: Domingos de Magalhães.
Camus, Albert. 1942. *L'étranger*. Paris: Gallimard.
Canclini, Néstor García. 1989. *Culturas híbridas. Estrategias para entrar y salir de la modernidad*. Mexico City: Grijalbo.
Candia Cáceres, Iván Alexis. n.d. Tengo miedo torero. Siete tacos de aguja contra el toro rabioso. *Crítica.cl: Revista Digital de Ensayo, Crítica e Historia del Arte*. http://www.critica.cl/html/candia_01.htm (accessed September 27, 2006).
Cantú, Lionel. 1999. Border crossings: Mexican men and the sexuality of migration. Phd diss., University of California, Irvine.
Carrier, Joseph. 1995. *De los otros: Intimacy and homosexuality among Mexican men*. New York: Columbia University Press.
Carrillo, Héctor. 2002. *The night is young: Sexuality in Mexico in the time of AIDS*. Chicago: University of Chicago Press.
Carvalho, José Jorge de. 1996. Images of the black man in Brazilian popular culture. *Serie antropología* 201 Brasilia: Depto. de Antropologia, Univ. de Brasilia http://vsites.unb.br/ics/dan/Serie201empdf.pdf
(accessed February 27, 2010).
Castro "faints" during speech. 2001. *Tribune India*, June 25. http://www.tribuneindia.com/2001/20010625/world.htm#8 (accessed December 11, 2005).

Castro has Parkinson's says CIA. 2005. *BBC News.* November 17. http://news.bbc .co.uk/2/hi/americas/4444454.stm (accessed December 11, 2005).
Cauldwell, David O. 2006. Psychopathia transsexualis. In *The Transgender Studies Reader*, ed. Susan Stryker and Stephen Whittle. 40-44. New York: Routledge.
Cava, Fiorella. 2004. *Identidad, cultura y sociedad. Un grito desde el silencio.* Lima: Cisne.
Cerqueira, Maeve Mascarenhas, and Marta Enéas da Silva. 2007. A cultura cinematográfica brasileira: uma leitura do filme *Madame Satã. Seara. Revista Virtual de Letras e Cultura.* http://www.seara.uneb.br/sumario/professores/martaemaeve .pdf (accessed March 13, 2009).
Chant, Sylvia, and Nikki Craske. 2003. *Gender in Latin America.* New Brunswick, NJ: Rutgers University Press.
Chase, Cheryl. 1999. Rethinking treatment for ambiguous genitalia. *Pediatric Nursing* 25 (4): 451–55.
Chauncey, George. 1994. *Gay New York: Gender, urban culture, and the making of the gay male world, 1890–1940.* New York: Basic Books.
Chávez-Silverman, Susana, and Librada Hernández, eds. 2000. *Reading and writing the ambiente: Queer sexualities in Latino, Latin American, and Spanish culture.* Madison: University of Wisconsin Press.
Clark, Stephen J. 2001. El Rey de Centro Habana. Conversación con Pedro Juan Gutiérrez. *Delaware review of Latin American studies* 2 (1). http://www.udel.edu/ LAS/Vol2-1Clark.html (accessed November 13, 2005).
Clavel, Ana. 2005. *Cuerpo náufrago.* Mexico City: Alfaguara.
Conner, Randy P., David Hatfield Sparks, and Mariya Sparks, eds. 1997. *Cassell's encyclopedia of queer myth, symbol and spirit: Gay, lesbian, bisexual, and transgender Lore.* London: Cassell.
Conner, Randy P., and David Hatfield Sparks. 2004. *Queering creole spiritual traditions. Lesbian, gay, bisexual, and transgender participation in African-inspired traditions in the Americas.* Binghampton, NY: Haworth Press.
Córdova Plaza, Rosío. 2007. The realm outside the law: Transvestite sex work in Xalapa, Veracruz. In *Decoding gender: Law and practice in contemporary Mexico*, ed. Helga Baitenmann, Victoria Chenaut, and Ann Varley, 124–48. New Brunswick, NJ: Rutgers University Press.
Córtez, Beatriz. 1998. Negociando la construcción de la identidad. La producción de tres directoras de cine latinoamericano. *RLA: Romance Languages Annual* 10 (2): 512–18.
Crónica de un desayuno. 2000. Dir. Benjamín Cann. Perf. María Rojo, Angélica Aragón, and Bruno Bichir. Mexico City: Titan Producciones.
Cruz-Malavé, Arnaldo, 1995. Toward an art of transvestism: colonialism and homosexuality in Puerto Rican literature. In *¿Entiendes? queer readings, Hispanic writings*, ed. Emilie L. Bergmann and Paul Julian Smith, 137–68. Durham, NC: Duke University Press.
Danzón. 1992. Dir. Maria Novaro. Perf. Maria Rojo, Carmen Salinas, and Tito Vasconcelos. Mexico City: Macondo Cine Video.
Dávila, Juan. 1994. *El Libertador.* Utopía exhibition. London: Hayward Gallery.
Defoe, Daniel.1908. *A journal of the plague year.* London: Dent.
De Lauretis, Teresa. 1987. *Technologies of gender: Essays on theory, film and fiction.* Bloomington: Indiana University Press.
Delgado-Costa, José, 2003. Fredi Veláscues le mete mano a *Sirena Selena vestida de pena. Centro: Journal of the Center for Puerto Rican Studies* 15 (2): 66–77.

De la Mora, Sergio. 1992–93. Fascinating machismo: Toward an unmasking of heterosexual masculinity in Arturo Ripstein's *El lugar sin límites*. *Journal of Film and Video* 44 (3–4): 83–105.

———. 2006. *Cinemachismo: masculinities and sexuality in Mexican film*. Austin: University of Texas Press.

De Lima, Paolo. 2004. Peces enclaustrados, cuerpos putrefactos y espacios simbólicos marginales en una novela latinoamericana de fin de siglo. *Ciberayllu*, January 2. http://www.andes.missouri.edu/andes/Especiales/PdL_Bellatin.html (accessed February 26, 2010).

Deleuze, Gilles, and Félix Guattari. 1986. *Kafka: Toward a minor literature*. Trans. Dana Polan. Minneapolis: University of Minnesota Press.

Del Pino, Angeles Mateo. 1998. Chile. Una loca geografía o las crónicas de Pedro Lemebel. *Hispamérica: Revista de literatura* 27 (80–81): 17–28.

Del Río, Joel. 2001. Vuelta al mundo en mil y una imágenes. *La jiribilla*, December 31. http://www.lajiribilla.cu/2001/n31_diciembre/843_31.html (accessed December 11, 2005).

El día del compadre. 1983. Dir. Carlos Vassallo. Perf. Jorge Rivero, Andrés García, Susana Dosamantes, and Rebeca Silva. Mexico City: Alianza Cinematografica Mexicana S.A. de C.V.

DiFranco, Ani. 1995. Crime for crime. *Not a pretty girl*. Buffalo, NY: Righteous Babe Records. Compact disc.

Dirlik, Arif. 1994. The postcolonial aura: Third world criticism in the age of global capitalism. *Critical Inquiry* 20 (2): 328–56.

Donoso, Claudia, and Paz Errázuriz. 1990. *La manzana de Adán*. Santiago: Zona Editorial.

Donoso, José. 1979. *El lugar sin límites*. Barcelona: Seix Barral.

Dore, Elizabeth. 1997. The holy family. In *Gender politics in Latin America: Debates in theory and practice*, ed. Elizabeth Dore, 101–17. New York: Monthly Review Press.

Duany, Jorge. 2002. *The Puerto Rican nation on the move: Identities on the island and in the United States*. Chapel Hill: University of North Carolina Press.

Dyer, Richard. 1993. *The matter of images: Essays on representation*. London: Routledge.

Edelman, Lee. 1994. *Homographesis: Essays in gay literary and cultural theory*. New York: Routledge.

Ellis, Havelock. 1897. *Sexual inversion*. London: Wilson.Engel, Magali Gouveia. 2008. Forbidden sexualities: madness and the male gender. *Hist. cienc. saude-Manguinhos* 15:173–90.

Epps, Brad. 1995a. Grotesque identities: Writing, death, and the space of the subject (between Michel de Montaigne and Reinaldo Arenas). *Journal of the Midwest Modern Language Association* 28 (1): 38–55.

———. 1995b. Proper conduct: Reinaldo Arenas, Fidel Castro, and the politics of homosexuality. *Journal of the History of Sexuality* 6 (2): 231–83.

———. 1996. Estados de deseo: Homosexualidad y nacionalidad (Juan Goytisolo y Reinaldo Arenas a vuelapluma). *Revista Iberoamericana* 62 (176–77): 799–820.

Equipo Nitlápan-Envío. 2001. Sets y escenarios de la película electoral. *Revista mensual de análisis de Nicaragua y Centroamérica* 229, April. http://www.envio.org.ni/articulo/1068 (accessed March 13, 2010).

Espinoza Carramiñana, Claudia. 1999. Forjarse mariposa o la construcción de lo travestí. *Última Década* 10. http://www.redalyc.uaemex.mx/redalyc/pdf/195/19501011.pdf (accessed October 5, 2006).

Esterrich, Carmelo. 1997. Locas, pájaros y demás mariconadas. El ciudadano sexual en Reinaldo Arenas. *Confluencia: Revista hispánica de cultura y literatura* 13 (1): 178–93.

Eugenides, Jeffrey. 2002. *Middlesex*. New York: Farrar, Straus and Giroux.
Evans, David T. 1993. *Sexual citizenship: The material construction of sexualities*. London: Routledge.
Fanon, Frantz. 1968. *Black skin, white masks*. New York: Grove Press.
Feinberg, Leslie. 1996. Transgender warriors: Making history from Joan of Arc to RuPaul. Boston: Beacon Press.
Felski, Rita. 1996. Fin de siecle, fin de sexe: Transsexuality, postmodernism, and the death of history. *New Literary History* 27 (3): 337–49.
Fernández, Josefina. 2004. *Cuerpos desobedientes. Travestismo e identidad de género*. Buenos Aires: Edhasa.
Flores, William F., and Rina Benmayor, eds. 1997. *Latino cultural citizenship: Claiming identity, space, and rights*. Boston: Beacon Press.
Flores Bueno, Daniel. Entrevista con Mario Bellatin. *Terramedia*. http://www.terra.com.pe/terramedia/entrevista2.shtml (accessed December 2, 2005).
Foster, David William. 1997. *Sexual textualities: Essays on queer/ing Latin American writing*. Austin: University of Texas Press.
———. 2002. *Mexico City in contemporary Mexican cinema*. Austin: University of Texas Press.
———. 2003. *Queer issues in contemporary Latin American cinema*. Austin: University of Texas Press.
Foucault, Michel. 1978. *The history of sexuality, volume I: An introduction*. Trans. Robert Hurley. New York: Pantheon.
Franco, Jean. 1970. *The modern culture of Latin America: Society and the artist*. Harmondsworth: Penguin.
Fresa y chocolate. 1994. Dir. Tomás Gutiérrez Alea. Perf. Jorge Perugorría, Vladimir Cruz, Mirta Ibarra, and Francisco Gattorno. Havana: Instituto Cubano del Arte e Industrias Cinematográficos (ICAIC).
Freud, Sigmund. 1989. *The ego and the id*. Trans. Joan Riviere. New York: Norton.
Garabano, Sandra. 2003. Lemebel. Políticas de consenso, masculinidad y travestismo. *Chasqui* 32 (1): 47–55.
Garber, Marjorie. 1992. *Vested interests: Cross-dressing and cultural anxiety*. New York: Routledge.
Garfinkel, Harold. 1967. *Studies in ethnomethodology*. Englewood Cliffs, NJ: Prentice Hall.
Gónzalez, Solange. 2004. Cruzo las fronteras del saber de manera casi pirata, clandestina. Entrevista a Pedro Lemebel. *Identidades* 60. http://www.editoraperu.com.pe/identidades/60/entrevista.asp (accessed December 11, 2006).
González Pérez, César O. 2003. *Travestidos al desnudo. Homosexualidad, identidades y luchas territoriales en Colima*. Mexico City: Miguel Angel Porrúa.
Graham, Richard, ed. 1990. *The idea of race in Latin America, 1870–1940*. Austin: University of Texas Press.
Green, James N. 1994. The emergence of the Brazilian gay liberation movement, 1977–1981. *Latin American Perspectives* 21 (1): 38–55.
———. 1999. *Beyond carnival: Male homosexuality in twentieth-century Brazil*. Chicago: University of Chicago Press.
Grosz, Elizabeth. 1994. *Volatile bodies: Toward a corporeal feminism*. St. Leonards, New South Wales: Allen & Unwin.
Güemes, César. 2000. Las ciudades de América Latina son travestís con ropaje de Primer Mundo. *La Jornada*, October 4.
Guerra Cunningham, Lucía. 2000. Ciudad neoliberal y los devenires de la homosexualidad en las crónicas urbanas de Pedro Lemebel. *Signos: literarios y lingüísticos* 2 (1): 99–119.

Gutiérrez, Pedro Juan. 1998. *Trilogía sucia de La Habana*. Barcelona: Editorial Anagrama.
———.2001a. *El rey de la Habana*. 5th ed. Barcelona: Editorial Anagrama.
———. 2001b. Verdad y mentira en la literatura. *Todo sobre Pedro Juan*. http://www.pedrojuangutierrez.com/Ensayos_ensayos_PJ_Verdad%20y%20mentira.htm (accessed December 2, 2005).
Gutmann, Matthew C. 1996. *The meanings of macho: Being a man in Mexico City*. Berkeley: University of California Press.
Guy, Donna J. 1991. *Sex and danger in Buenos Aires: Prostitution, family, and nation in Argentina*. Lincoln: University of Nebraska Press.
Hall, Stuart, ed. 1997. *Representation: Cultural representations and signifying practices*. London: Sage.
Haraway, Donna J. 1992. The promises of monsters: A regenerative politics for inappropriate/d others. In *Cultural studies*, ed. Lawrence Grossberg, Cary Nelson, and Paula A. Treichler, 295–337. New York: Routledge.
Hausman, Bernice. 1995. *Changing sex: Transsexualism, technology, and the idea of gender*. Durham, NC: Duke University Press.
Heller, Ben A. 1996. Landscape, femininity, and Caribbean discourse. *MLN* 111 (2): 391–416.
Herrero-Olaizola, Alejandro. 1999–2000. Homosexuales en escena. Identidad y *performance* en la narrativa de Luis Zapata. *Antípodas* 11–12:249–62.
Hirschfield, Magnus. 2006. Selections from "The transvestites: The erotic drive to cross-dress." In *The Transgender Studies Reader*, ed. Susan Stryker and Stephen Whittle. 28-39. New York: Routledge.
hooks, bell. 1992. *Black looks: Race and representation*. Boston, MA: South End Press.
Huamán, Miguel Ángel. 2000. La narrativa peruana del siglo XX. *Socialismo y participación* 87:147–68.
Irigaray, Luce. 1991. This sex which is not one. In *Feminisms: An anthology of literary theory and criticisms*, ed. Robyn R. Warhol and Diane Price Herndl, 350–56. New Brunswick, NJ: Rutgers University Press.
Irwin, Robert McKee. 2003. *Mexican masculinities*. Minneapolis: University of Minnesota Press.
Irwin, Robert McKee, Edward J. McCaughan, and Michelle Rocío Nasser, eds. 2003. *The famous 41: Sexuality and social control in Mexico, c. 1901*. Basingstoke: Palgrave Macmillan.
Jagose, Annamarie. 2002. *Inconsequence: Lesbian representation and the logic of sexual sequence*. Ithaca, NY: Cornell University Press.
Jameson, Fredric. 1986. Third world literature in the age of multinational capitalism. *Social Text* 15: 65–88.
El jardín del Edén. 1994. Dir. Maria Novaro. Perf. Renée Coleman, Bruno Bichir, Gabriela Roel, and Jerónimo Berruecos. Mexico City: Macondo Cine Video.
Kaebnick, Suzanne. 1997. The loca freedom fighter in *Antes que anochezca* and *El color de verano*. *Chasqui: Revista de literatura latinoamericana* 26 (1): 102–14.
Kaminsky, Amy K. 1993. *Reading the body politic: Feminist criticism and Latin American women writers*. Minneapolis: University of Minnesota Press.
Kessler, Suzanne. 1998. *Lessons from the intersexed*. New Brunswick, NJ: Rutgers University Press.
Kessler, Suzanne. J., and Wendy McKenna. 1985. *Gender: An ethnomethodological approach*. Chicago: University of Chicago Press.
King, Rosamond S. 2008. Re/presenting self other: Trans deliverance in Caribbean texts. *Callaloo* 3 (2): 581–99.

Klein, Charles. 1998. From one "battle" to another: The making of a *travesti* political movement in a Brazilian city. *Sexualities* 1 (3): 329–43.
Koo, Pedro. 2003. Masculinidad en crisis. Representación masculina en cuatro novelas latinoamericanas. Phd diss., Norman: the University of Oklahoma.
Krafft-Ebing, Richard von. 2006. Selections from "Psychopathia sexualis with special reference to contrary sexual instinct: A medico-legal study." In *The Transgender Studies Reader*, ed. Susan Stryker and Stephen Whittle, 21-27. New York: Routledge.
Kristeva, Julia. 1982. *Powers of horror: An essay on abjection*. Trans. Leon S. Roudiez. New York: Columbia University Press.
Kulick, Don. 1998. *Travesti: Sex, gender, and culture among Brazilian transgendered prostitutes*. Chicago: University of Chicago Press.
Kulick, Don and Charles Klein. 2003. Scandalous acts: the politics of shame among Brazilian travesti prostitutes. In *Recognition struggles and social movements: Contested identities, agency, and power*, ed. Barbara Hobson, 215–38. New York: Cambridge University Press.
La Fountain-Stokes, Lawrence M. 2002. Queer Puerto Rican translocalities: Music, origins, and performativity in Teatro Pregones's *El bolero fue mi ruina* (The bolero was my downfall). *Sexuality and the Public Sphere*. http://hemi.nyu.edu/eng/seminar/peru/call/workgroups/sexpublsphllfstokes.shtml (accessed November 2, 2003).
Lakoff, G., and M. Johnson. 1980. *Metaphors we live by*. Chicago: University of Chicago Press.
Lancaster, Roger N. 1992. *Life is hard: Machismo, danger, and the intimacy of power in Nicaragua*. Berkeley: University of California Press.
———. 1998. Transgenderism in Latin America: Some critical introductory remarks on identities and practices. In Transgender in Latin America: Persons, practices and meanings. Special issue, *Sexualities* 1 (3): 263–76.
Leiner, Marvin. 1994. *Sexual politics in Cuba: Machismo, homosexuality, and AIDS*. Boulder: Westview Press.
Lemebel, Pedro. n.d. Homoeróticas urbanas (o apuntes prófugos de un pétalo coliflor). *Letra S: Escritores y poetas en español*. http://www.letras.s5.com/lemebel37.htm (accessed October 25, 2006).
———. 1995. *La esquina es mi corazón*. Buenos Aires: Seix Barral.
———. 1997. *Loco afán. Crónicas de sidario*. 2nd ed. Santiago de Chile: LOM Ediciones.
———. 1998. *De perlas y cicatrices*. Santiago: LOM Ediciones.
———. 2002. *Tengo miedo torero*. Buenos Aires: Seix Barral.
———. 2003. *Zanjón de la Aguada*. 2003. Santiago: Seix Barral.
———. 2006. *Adiós mariquita linda*. 2006. Barcelona: Mondadori.
Lewis, Vek. 2006. Sociological work on transgender in Latin America: Some considerations. *Journal of Iberian and Latin American Studies* 12 (2): 71–90.
———. 2008. Of lady-killers and "men dressed as women": Soap opera, scapegoats and the Mexico City police department. *PORTAL Journal of Multidisciplinary International Studies* 5 (1): 1–20.
Llanos, Bernadita. 2004. Masculinidad, estado y violencia en la ciudad neoliberal. In *Reinas de otro cielo. Modernidad y autoritarismo en la obra de Pedro Lemebel*, ed. Fernando Blanco, 75–113. Santiago de Chile: LOM Ediciones.
Lola. 1989. Dir. Maria Novaro. Perf. Alejandra Cerrillo, Cheli Godínez, Leticia Huijara, and Gerardo Martínez. Mexico City: Conacité Dos.
López, Ana M. 1991. Celluloid tears: Melodrama in the "old" Mexican cinema. *Iris* 13:29–51.

Ludmer, Josefina. 2002. *The gaucho genre: A treatise on the motherland*. Durham, NC: Duke University Press.
El lugar sin límites. 1978. Dir. Arturo Ripstein. Perf. Roberto Cobo, Gonzalo Vega, and Carmen Salinas. Mexico City: Azteca Films.
Lumsden, Ian. 1991. *Homosexuality, society and the state in Mexico*. Toronto: Canadian Gay Archives.
———. 1996. *Machos, maricones, and gays: Cuba and homosexuality*. Philadelphia: Temple University Press.
Madame Satã. 2002. Dir. Karim Aïnouz. Perf. Lázaro Ramos, Flavio Bauraqui, and Fellipe Marques. New York City: Wellspring Media.
La mala educación. 2004. Dir. Pedro Almodóvar. Perf. Gael García Bernal, Fele Martínez, and Daniel Giménez Cacho. Madrid: Warner Sogefilms.
Manrique, Jaime. 1983. *Colombian gold: A novel of power and corruption*. New York: C. N. Potter.
Mansfield, Nicholas. 2000. *Subjectivity: Theories of the self from Freud to Haraway*. St. Leonards, New South Wales: Allen & Unwin.
Marcuse, Herbert. 1964. *One-dimensional man*. Boston: Beacon Press, 1964.
Mariposas en el andamio. 1995. Dir. Margaret Gilpin and Luis Felipe Bernaza. New York City: Kangaroo Films.
Marqués, René. 1966. *Ensayos 1953–1966*. Barcelona: Antillana.
Marrero, M. T. 1997. Historical and literary santería: Unveiling gender and identity in U.S. Cuban literature. In *Tropicalizations: Transcultural representations of latinidad*, ed. Frances Aparicio and Susana Chávez-Silverman, 139–59. Hanover, NH: University of New England Press.
Martino, Wayne. 2006. Straight-acting masculinities: Normalization and hierarchies in gay men's lives. In *Gendered outcasts and sexual outlaws: Sexual oppression and gender herarchies in queer men's lives*, ed. Christopher Kendall and Wayne Martino, 35–60. New York: Harrington Park Press.
McAlister, Linda López. 1993. Review of Danzón. *Women's Studies Database*. February 13, 1993. http://www.mith2.umd.edu/WomensStudies/FilmReviews/danzon-mcalister (accessed December 20, 2006).
McCarthy-Brown, Karen. 2001. Mimesis in the face of fear: Femme queens, butch queens, and gender play in the houses of greater Newark. In *Passing: Identity and interpretation in sexuality, race, and religion*, ed. María Carla Sánchez and Linda Schlossberg, 208–28. New York: New York University Press.
McRuer, Robert. 2002. Critical investments: AIDS, Christopher Reeve, and Queer/Disability Studies. *Journal of Medical Humanities* 23 (3–4): 221–37.
Melgar, Francisco. 2007. La escritura no tiene nacionalidad. Entrevista con Mario Bellatin. *El comercio*. http://www.elcomercioperu.com.pe/EdicionImpresa/Html/2007-01-28/ImEcLuces0659820.html (accessed May 7, 2007).
Melhuus, Marit. 1996. Power, value and ambiguous meanings of gender. In *Machos, mistresses, madonnas: Contesting the power of Latin American gender imagery*, ed. Marit Melhuus and Kristi Anne Stølen, 230–59. New York: Verso.
Mesa Peña, Janet, and Diley Hernández Cruz. 2004. Transformistas, travestis y transexuales. Un grupo de identidad social en la Cuba de hoy. *Temas. Cultura, ideología, sociedad* 36. http://areaqueer.org.ar/2007/02/transformistas-travestis-y-transexuales.html (accessed March 13, 2010).
Mignolo, Walter. 2005. *The idea of Latin America*. London: Blackwell.
Miller, Marilyn Grace. 2004. *Rise and fall of the cosmic race: The cult of mestizaje in Latin America*. Austin: University of Texas Press.
Millot, Catherine. 1991. *Horsexe: Essay on transsexuality*. New York City: Autonomedia.

Mi novia el travesti. 1975. Dir. Enrique Cahen Salaberry. Perf. Alberto Olmedo, Susana Giménez, and Pablo Cumo, Buenos Aires: Gativideo.
Mogrovejo, Norma. 2000. *Un amor que se atrevió a decir su nombre. La lucha de las lesbianas y su relación con los movimientos homosexual y feminista en América Latina*. México, D.F.: Plaza y Valdés.
Molloy, Sylvia. 1998. The politics of posing. *Hispanisms and homosexualities*, eds. Sylvia. Molloy and Robert Irwin, 141–60. Durham, NC: Duke University Press.
Monro, Surya. 2005. *Gender politics: Citizenship, activism, and sexual diversity*. London: Pluto Press.
Moreno, Antônio. 2001. *A personagem homossexual no cinema brasileiro*. Rio de Janeiro: Funarte.
Morgado, Marcia. 2000. Literatura para curar el asma. *Barcelona Review* 17. http://www.barcelonareview.com/17/s_ent_msf.htm (accessed April 4, 2006).
Morgan, G. 1986. *Images of organisation*. London: Sage.
Mosse, George L. 1985. *Nationalism and sexuality: Respectability and abnormal sexuality in modern Europe*. New York: H. Fertig.
Mott, Luiz R. B. 1996. *Epidemic of hate: Violations of the human rights of gay men, lesbians and transvestites in Brazil*. San Francisco: International Gay and Lesbian Human Rights Commission.
Moulian, Tomás. 1997. *Chile. Anatomía de un mito*. Santiago: LOM ediciones.
Muñecas de media noche. 1978. Dir. Rafael Portillo. Perf. Irina Areu, Diana Arriaga, Alfredo Wally Barrón, and Víctor Manuel Castro. Mexico City: Cinematográfica Calderón S.A.
Muñoz, Carlos Basilio. 2004. Identidades translocales y orientación sexual en Caracas. *Colección Monografías* 2. Caracas: Programa Globalización, Cultura y Economía.
Muñoz, José Esteban. 1999. *Disidentifications: Queers of color and the performance of politics*. Minneapolis: University of Minnesota Press.
Muñoz, Mario. 1996. *De amores marginales. 16 cuentos mexicanos*. Xalapa: Universidad Veracruzana.
Murray, Stephen O. 1995. *Latin American male homosexualities*. Albuquerque: University of New Mexico Press.
Nabal, Eduardo. n.d. Géneros impropios. La representación de la homosexualidad como traición de género en *Conducta Impropia* and *Paris Is Burning*. *Página de Hartza*. http://www.hartza.com/impropio.htm (accessed April 25, 2004).
Nagel, Joane. 1998. Masculinity and nationalism: Gender and sexuality in the making of nations. *Ethnic and Racial Studies* 21:242–69.
Namaste, Viviane K. 2000. *Invisible lives: The erasure of transsexual and transgendered people*. Chicago: The University of Chicago Press.
———. 2005. *Sex change, social change: Reflections on identity, institutions, and imperialism*. Toronto: Women's Press.
Navalha na carne. 1969. Dir. Braz Chediak. Perf. Jece Valadão, Glauce Rocha, Emiliano Queiroz, and Carlos Kroeber. Rio de Janeiro: Ipanema Filmes.
Las noches de Constantinopla. 2002. Dir. Orlando Rojas. Perf. Verónica Lynn, Liberto Rabal, and Verónica López. Havana: El Paso Producciones.
Noches de cabaret. 1978. Dir. Rafael Portillo. Perf. Víctor Manuel Castro, Arturo Cobo, Luis de Alba, and Eduardo de la Peña. Mexico City: Cinematográfica Calderón S.A.
No somos. n.d. *Traveschile*. http://www.traveschile.cl/html/no_somos.htm (accessed May 11, 2005).
Nouzeilles, Gabriela. 2003. An imaginary plague in turn-of-the-century Buenos Aires: Hysteria, discipline and languages of the body. In *Disease in the history of modern Latin America: From malaria to AIDS*, ed. Diego Armus, 26–51. Durham, NC: Duke University Press.

Núñez Noriega, Guillermo. 1999. *Sexo entre varones. Poder y resistencia en el campo sexual.* 2nd ed. México: Miguel Ángel Porrúa.
O anjo nasceu. 1969. Dir. Júlio Bressane. Perf. Norma Bengell, Hugo Carvana, Neville de Almeida, and Maria Gladys. Brasilia: Júlio Bressane Produções Cinematográficas.
"Obscene." n.d. Definition from *Everything2.* http://www.everything2.com/index.pl?node=obscene (accessed November 2, 2005).
O casamento. 1975. Dir. Arnaldo Jabor. Perf. Adriana Prieto, Paulo Porto, Camila Amado, and Nelson Dantas. Rio de Janeiro: R.F. Farias.Olalquiaga, Celeste. 1992. *Megalopolis: Contemporary cultural sensibilities.* Minneapolis: University of Minnesota Press.
Ópera do malandro. 1986. Dir. Ruy Guerra. Perf. Edson Celulari, Claudia Ohana, Elba Ramalho, and Fábio Sabag. Los Angeles: Samuel Goldwyn Company.Ortiz, Fernando. 1940. *Contrapunteo cubano del tabaco y el azúcar.* Habana: J. Montero.
Padura, Leonardo. 1997. *Máscaras.* Barcelona: Tusquets.
Palaversich, Diana. 1999. Caught in the act: Social stigma, homosexual panic and violence in Latin American writing. *Chasqui* 28 (2): 60–75.
———. 1999–2000. El femenino monstruoso y la crisis del género en *La hermana secreta de Angélica María. Antípodas* 11–12:233–48.
———. 2002. The wounded body of proletarian homosexuality in Pedro Lemebel's *Loco afán.* Trans. Paul Allatson. *Latin American Perspectives* 29 (2): 263–82.
———. 2003. Apuntes para una lectura de Mario Bellatin. *Chasqui* 32 (1): 25–38.
Papeles secundarios. 1989. Dir. Orlando Rojas. Perf. Paula Ali, Leonor Arocha, Fernando Bermúdez, and Leonor Borrero. Havana: Instituto Cubano del Arte e Industrias Cinematográficos (ICAIC).
Paris is burning. 1991. Dir. Jennie Livingston, Perf. Pepper LaBeija, Octavia St. Laurent, and Venus Xtravaganza. Burbank, CA: Miramax Films.
Parker, Andrew, Mary Russo, Doris Sommer, and Patricia Yaeger, eds. 1992. *Nationalisms and sexualities.* New York: Routledge.
Parker, Richard G. 1999. *Beneath the equator: Cultures of desire, male homosexuality, and emerging gay communities in Brazil.* New York: Routledge.
Paz, Octavio. 1950. *Laberinto de la soledad.* Mexico: Fondo de Cultura Económica.
Pedreira, Antonio S. 1992 [1934]. *Insularismo.* Piedras, PR: Edil.
Perlman, Janice E. 1976. *The myth of marginality: Urban poverty and politics in Rio de Janeiro.* Berkeley: University of California Press.
Perlongher, Néstor Osvaldo. 1997. *Prosa plebeya. Ensayos, 1980–1992.* Buenos Aires: Colihue.
La Perrera. 2006. Dir. Manolo Nieto. Perf. Martín Adjemián, Pablo Alexandre, and María Sofía Dabarca. Montevideo: Control Zeta Films.
Phillips, John. 2006. *Transgender on screen.* London: Palgrave Macmillan.
Plaza Atenas, Dino. 1999. Lemebel o el salto de doble filo. *Revista chilena de literatura* 54:123–35.
Plummer, Ken. 1995. *Telling sexual stories: Power, change, and social worlds.* London: Routledge.
Portela, Ena Lucía. 2003. Con hambre y sin dinero. *Todo sobre Pedro Juan.* http://www.pedrojuangutierrez.com/Ensayos_ensayos_Ena-Portela_1.htm (accessed December 2, 2005).
Povinelli, Elizabeth A., and George Chauncey. 1999. Thinking sexuality transnationally: An introduction. *GLQ: A Journal of Lesbian and Gay Studies* 5 (4): 439–50.
Pratt, Mary Louise. 2002. Tres incendios y dos mujeres extraviadas: el imaginario novelístico frente al nuevo contrato social. In *Espacio urbano, comunicación y violencia en América Latina.* ed Mabel Moraña 91–105. Pittsburgh: University of Pittsburgh.

Pravaz, Natasha. 2000. Imagining Brazil: Seduction, samba. *Canadian Woman Studies.* 20 (2): 48–55.
Preves, Sharon A. 2003. *Intersex and identity: The contested self.* New Brunswick, NJ: Rutgers University Press.
Prieur, Annick. 1998. *Mema's house, Mexico City: On transvestites, queens, and machos.* Chicago: University of Chicago Press.
Prosser, Jay. 1998. *Second skins: The body narratives of transsexuality.* New York: Columbia University Press.
Puig, Manuel. 1976. *El beso de la mujer araña.* Buenos Aires: Seix Barral.
Rabasa, José. 1993. *Inventing America: Spanish historiography and the formation of Eurocentrism.* Norman: University of Oklahoma Press.
Rainha Daba. 1974. Dir. Antonio Carlos da Fontoura. Dir. Milton Gonçalves, Odete Lara, Stepan Nercessian, and Nelson Xavier. Rio de Janeiro: Filmes de Lírio.
Ramos Otero, Manuel. 1987. *Página en blanco y staccato.* Madrid: Playor.
Rapisardi, Flavio. 2003. Regulaciones políticas. Identidad, diferencia y desigualdad. Una crítica al debate contemporáneo. In *Sexualidades migrantes: género y transgénero*, ed. Diana Maffia, 97–116. Buenos Aires: Feminaria Editora.
Rashkin, Elissa J. 2001. *Women filmmakers in Mexico: The country of which we dream.* Austin: University of Texas Press.
Raymond, Janice G. 1980. *The transsexual empire.* London: Women's Press.
Reding, Andrew. 2003. Sexual orientation and human rights in the Americas. *World Policy Reports.* http://www.worldpolicy.org/projects/globalrights/sexorient/2003-LGBT-Americas.pdf (accessed March 17, 2010).
Reisz, Susana. 2001. Indigencia y creatividad en las letras peruanas. Nueva crisis, nuevos actores-autores. *Hueso húmero* 39 (1):106–23.
Repulsion. 1965. Dir. Roman Polanski. Perf. Catherine Deneuve, Ian Hendry, John Fraser, and Yvonne Furneaux. London: Compton Films.
Richard, Nelly. 1993. *Masculino/femenino. Prácticas de la diferencia y cultura democrática.* Santiago: Francisco Zegers.
———. 1998. *Residuos y metáforas (Ensayos de crítica cultural sobre el Chile de la transición).* Chile: Editorial Cuarto Propio.
Ríos Avila, Rubén. 1998. Caribbean dislocations: Arenas and Ramos Otero in New York. In *Hispanisms and homosexualities*, ed. Sylvia Molloy and Robert Irwin McKee, 101–23. Durham, NC: Duke University Press.
Risco, Ana María. 1995. Escrito sobre ruinas. Interview with Pedro Lemebel. *La nación*, June 18.
Robles, Victor Hugo. 1998. History in the making: The homosexual liberation movement in Chile. *NACLA Report on the Americas* 31 (4): 36–44.
Rodó, José Enrique. 1988. *Ariel.* Trans. Margaret Sayers. Austin: University of Texas Press.
Rodríguez-Madera, Sheilla, and José Toro-Alfonso. 2003. La comunidad de la cual no hablamos. Vulnerabilidad social, conductas de riesgo y VIH/SIDA en la comunidad de transgéneros en Puerto Rico. *Revista de psicología de la salud* 15 (1–2): 111–35.
Rojas, Yumber Vera. 2008. La cumbia villera se parece al funk carioca. *Página 12*, June 19. http://www.pagina12.com.ar/diario/suplementos/no/12-3460-2008-06-19.html (accessed May 12, 2009).
Rolley, Katrina. 1993. Vested interests. Review of *Vested interests: Cross-dressing and cultural anxiety* by Marjorie Garber. *Feminist Review* 43:100–102.
Rosaldo, Renato. 1997. Cultural citizenship, inequality, and multiculturalism. In *Latino cultural citizenship: Claiming identity, space, and rights*, ed. W. Flores and R. Benmayor, 27–38. Boston, MA: Beacon Press.

Rubin, Henry. 2003. *Self made men: Identity, embodiment, and recognition among transsexual men.* Nashville, TN: Vanderbilt University Press.
Rudacille, Deborah. 2005. *The riddle of gender: Science, activism, and transgender rights.* New York: Pantheon Books.
Russo, Vito. 1981.*The celluloid closet.* New York: Harper & Row.
Salessi, Jorge. 2000. *Médicos maleantes y maricas. Higiene, criminología y homosexualidad en la construcción de la nación argentina (Buenos Aires, 1871–1914).* 2nd ed. Rosario, Argentina: B. Viterbo Editora.
Salón México. 1949. Dir. Emilio Fernández. Perf.Marga López, Miguel Inclán, Rodolfo Acosta, and Roberto Cañedo. Mexico City: Clasa Films Mundiales.
Sandoval-Sánchez, Alberto, ed. 2003. A queer dossier: Mayra Santos-Febres' Sirena Selena vestida de pena. Special issue, *Centro: Journal of the Center for Puerto Rican Studies* 15 (2): 4–125.
Santiago, Fabiola. 2003. Cuban film director breathes much easier after defection. *Cubanet*, September 14. http://www.cubanet.org/CNews/y03/sep03/15e3.htm (accessed March 18, 2006).
Santos-Febres, Mayra. 1991a. *Anamú y manigua.* San Juan: Editorial La iguana dorada
———. 1991b. *El orden escapado.* San Juan: Ed. Tríptico
———. 1994. *Pez de vidrio.* Miami: North South Center of the University of Miami.
———. 1996. *El cuerpo correcto.* San Juan: R&R Editoras.
———. 1999. *Tercer mundo.* Mexico City: Trilce de México.
———. 2000. *Sirena Selena vestida de pena.* Barcelona: Mondadori.
———. 2004. *Cualquier miércoles soy tuya.* Barcelona: Mondadori
———. 2005a. *Boat People.* San Juan: Ediciones Callejón.
———. 2005b. *Sobre piel y papel.* San Juan: Ediciones Callejón,
———. 2006. *Nuestra señora de la noche.* Mexico City: Espasa Calpe Mexicana, S.A.
Sardá, Alejandra. 1998. Lesbians and the gay movement in Argentina. *NACLA Report on the Americas.* 3 (4): 40–41.
Sarduy, Severo. 1969. *Escrito sobre un cuerpo.* Buenos Aires: Editorial Sudamericana.
———. 1972. *Cobra.* Buenos Aires: Editorial Sudamericana.
———. 1980. *De donde son los cantantes.* Barcelona: Seix Barral.
———. 1982. *La simulación.* Caracas: Monte Ávila Editores.
———. 1984. *Colibrí.* España: Editorial Argos Vergara, S.A.
Sarmiento, Domingo Faustino. 1874. *Facundo o civilización y barbarie en las pampas argentinas.* 4th ed. París: Librería Hachette y Cía.
———. 1946. *Conflicto y armonías de las razas en América.* Buenos Aires: Intermundo.
Schaefer, Claudia. 1996. *Danger zones: Homosexuality, national identity, and Mexican culture.* Tucson: University of Arizona Press.
———. 2003. *Bored to distraction: Cinema of excess in end-of-the-century Mexico and Spain.* Albany, NY: State University of New York Press.
Scheper, Jeanne. 2007. "Of la Baker, I am a disciple": The diva politics of reception. *Camera Obscura* 22 (65): 72–101.
Sedgwick, Eve Kosofsky. 1993. *Tendencies.* Durham, NC: Duke University Press.
———. 1994. *Epistemology of the closet.* London: Penguin.
Seidman, Steven. 1997. *Difference troubles: Queering social theory and sexual politics.* Cambridge: Cambridge University Press.
Sepúlveda Montoya, Salvador. 2004. Mercado Gay? *Se piensa*, December 24. http://www.sepiensa.cl/edicion/index.php?option=content&task=view&id=448&Itemid=40 (accessed August 22, 2006).
Serano, Julia. 2007. *Whipping girl: A transsexual woman on sexism and the scapegoating of femininity.* Emeryville, CA: Seal Press.
Sexualidad: un derecho a la vida. 2004. Dir. Lizette Vila. Havana: Proyecto Palomas.

Shaw, Lisa. 2007. Afro-Brazilian identity, *Malandragem* and homosexuality in *Madame Satã*. In *Contemporary Latin American cinema: Breaking into the global market*. ed. Deborah Shaw, 87–104. New York: Rowman & Littlefield.
Showalter, Elaine. 1990. *Sexual anarchy: Gender and culture at the fin de siecle*. New York: Viking.
Sifuentes-Jáuregui, Ben. 2001. *Transvestism, masculinity, and Latin American literature: Genders share flesh*. New York: Palgrave Macmillan.
Signorelli Heise, Tatiana. 2006. *Rainha Diaba* e *Madame Satã*. Representações da violência e marginalidade social no cinema brasileiro. Phd diss., Universidade de São Paulo.
Sin dejar huella. 2000. Dir. Maria Novaro. Perf. Aitana Sánchez-Gijón, Tiaré Scanda, Jesús Ochoa, and Martín Altomaro. Mexico City: Altavista Films.
Skidmore, Thomas E., and Peter H. Smith. 2005. *Modern Latin America*. New York: Oxford University Press.
Smith, Paul Julian. 1996. *Vision machines: Cinema, literature, and sexuality in Spain and Cuba, 1983–93*. London: Verso.
Smith, Paula A. 1997. The status of women in Mexico. In *Economic dimensions of gender inequality. A global perspective*, ed. Janet M. Rives and Mahmood Yousefi, 119–37. Westport, CT: Praeger.
Sommer, Doris. 1991. *Foundational fictions: The national romances of Latin America*. Berkeley: University of California Press.
Sontag, Susan. 1964. *Against interpretation, and other essays*. New York: Picador.
———. 1991. *Illness as metaphor; and AIDS and its metaphors*. London: Penguin.
Soto, Francisco. 1998. *Reinaldo Arenas*. New York: Twayne Publishers.
Stone, Sandy. 1991. The empire strikes back. In *Body guards: The cultural politics of gender ambiguity*, ed. Kristina Straub and Julia Epstein, 208–304. New York: Routledge.
Stryker, Susan. 2006a. (De)subjugated knowledges: An introduction to Transgender Studies. In *The transgender studies reader*, ed. Susan Stryker and Stephen Whittle, 1–17. New York: Routledge.
———. 2006b. My words to Victor Frankenstein above the village of Chamounix: Performing transgender rage. In *The transgender studies reader*, eds. Susan Stryker and Stephen Whittle, 244–56. New York: Routledge.
Subero, Gustavo. 2008. Fear of the trannies: On filmic phobia of transvestism in the new Latin American cinema. *Latin American Research Review* 43 (2): 159–79.
Surratt, H. L., J. Inciardi, P. Telles, V. McCoy, C. McCoy, and N. Weatherby. 1996. HIV risks among transvestites and other men having sex with men in Rio de Janeiro: A comparative analysis. Presentation, International Conference on AIDS July 7–12; 11: 335 (abstract no. Tu.C.2403).
Sutherland, Romy. 2002. María Novaro. *Senses of Cinema*. http://archive.sensesofcinema.com/contents/directors/02/novaro.html (accessed March 12, 2010).
Taufic, Camilo. 2004. La era del sexo frío. *El periodista*, January 30. http://www.elperiodista.cl/newtenberg/1579/article-57867.html (accessed November 25, 2005).
Terán, Oscar. 1986. *José Ingenieros: Pensar la nación*. Buenos Aires: Alianza.
Treichler, Paula A. 1989. Biomedical discourse: An epidemic of signification. In *AIDS: Cultural analysis, cultural activism*, ed. Douglas Crimp, 31–70. Cambridge, MA: MIT Press.
Ugarteche, Oscar, ed. 1997. *India bonita (o, del amor y otras artes. Ensayos de cultura gay en el Perú*. Lima: Movimiento Homosexual de Lima.
Una novia para David. 1985. Dir. Orlando Rojas. Perf. María Isabel Díaz, Francisco Gattorno, Thais Valdés, and César Évora. Havana: Instituto Cubano del Arte e Industrias Cinematográficos (ICAIC).

Ulrichs, Karl Heinrich. 1869. *Memnon. Die Geschlechtsnatur des mannliebenden Urnings. Eine naturwissen-schaftliche Darstellung. Körperlich-seelischer Hermaphroditismus. Anima muliebris virili corpore inclusa.* Schleiz: Hübscher.
Valentine, David. 2007. *Imagining transgender: An ethnography of a category.* Durham, NC: Duke University Press.
Valenzuela, Luisa. 1983. *Cola de lagartija.* Argentina: Editorial Bruguerra Argentina.
Valocchi, Steve. 1999. The class-inflected nature of gay identity. *Social Problems* 46:207–24.
Valverde, Mariana. 1991. As if subjects existed: Analyzing social discourses. *Canadian Review of Sociology and Anthropology* 28 (2): 173–87.
Van Haesendonck, Kristian. 2003. *Sirena Selena vestida de pena* de Mayra Santos-Febres. ¿Transgresiones de espacio o espacio de transgresiones? In A Queer dossier: Mayra Santos-Febres' Sirena Selena vestida de pena, ed. Alberto Sandoval-Sánchez. Special issue, *Centro: Journal of the Center for Puerto Rican Studies* 15 (2): 79–96.
Varella, D., L. Tuason, M.R. Proffitt, N. Escaleira, A. Alquezarm, and R.M. Bukowski.1996. HIV infection among Brazilian transvestites in a prison population. *AIDS Patient Care STDs* 10 (5): 299–302. Vargas Llosa, Mario. 1984. *Historia de Mayta.* Barcelona: Seix Barral.
Vattimo, Gianni. 1988. *The end of modernity. Nihilism and hermeneutics in a postmodern culture.* Cambridge: Polity Press.
Vega, Kimberly A. 2003. The colonized subject in self-exile: Cultural dislocation and existential angst in mid-20th century Puerto Rican literature. *Ciberletras* 10. http://www.lehman.cuny.edu/ciberletras/v10/vega.htm (accessed May 20, 2007).
20 centímetros. 2005. Dir. Ramón Salazar. Perf. Mónica Cervera, Pablo Puyol, and Miguel O'Dogherty. Madrid: Sogepac S. A.
Vértiz, Columba. 2000. Las noches de Constantinopla de Rojas, hacia el repunte del cine cubano. *Proceso,* May 7.
Vice, Sue. 1997. *Introducing Bakhtin.* Manchester, UK: Manchester University Press.
Vidal-Ortiz, Salvador. 2008. "The Puerto Rican way is more tolerant": Constructions and uses of homophobia among *Santería* practitioners across ethno-racial and national identification. *Sexualities* 11 (4): 476–95.
Visiting Scholars. 2003–4. *Homepage of Center for Iberian and Latin American Studies.* University of California, San Diego. http://cilas.ucsd.edu/expert_sheet/Zapata_R.php (accessed October 22, 2005).
Vujosevich, Jorge, Liliana Giménez, Stella Maris Moreira, Cecilia Rodríguez Godoy, and Emilia Rodríguez Justo.1998. Trabajadores sexuales masculinos. *Biblioteca Virtual del Consejo Latinoamericano de Ciencias Sociales.* http:/sala.clacso.org.ar/gsdl/cgi-bin/library?e=d-000-00---0iifcsar--00-0-0--0prompt-10---4------0-1l-1-es-Zz-1---20-about---00031-001-0-0utfZz-8-10&cl=CL2.1&d=HASH012bc8b562a1cb4cfc2a11ae&hl=0&gc=0&gt=0 (accessed March 12, 2010).
Warren, Jonathan W., and Frances Winddance Twine. 2002. Critical race studies in Latin America: Recent advances, recurrent weaknesses. In *A companion to racial and ethnic studies,* ed. D. T. Goldberg and J. Solomos, 538–60. Oxford: Blackwell.
Wigozki, Karina. n.d. El discurso travesti o el travestismo discursivo en *La esquina es mi corazón: Crónica urbana* de Pedro Lemebel. *La Casa* 2. http://www.class.uh.edu/mcl/faculty/zimmerman/lacasa/Estudios%20Culturales%20Articles/Karina%20Wigozki.pdf (accessed May 8, 2006).
Wilchins, Riki Anne. 1997. *Read my lips. Sexual subversion and the end of gender.* Connecticut: Firebrand Books.
Williams, Gareth. 2002. *The other side of the popular. Neoliberalism and subalternity in Latin America.* Durham, NC: Duke University Press.

Wolfe, Barry Michael. 2006. Transsexuals of Brazil. *glbtq: an encyclopedia of gay, lesbian, bisexual, transgender & queer culture*. http://www.glbtq.com/social-sciences/transsexuals_brazil.html (accessed May 12, 2009).
XXY. 2007. Dir. Lucía Puenzo. Perf. Ricardo Darín, Valeria Bertuccelli, Germán Palacios, and Carolina Pelleritti. Buenos Aires: The Distributing Company.
Y hembra es el alma mía. 1992. Dir. Lizette Vila. Havana: Proyecto Palomas.
Young, Allen. 1981. *Gays under the Cuban revolution*. San Francisco: Grey Fox Press.
Yuval-Davis, Nira. 1997. *Gender and nation*. London: Sage.
Zapata, Luis. 1983. *Melodrama*. 1983. Mexico City: El Enjambre.
———. 1985. *En jirones*. 1985. Mexico City: Posada.
———.1989. *La hermana secreta de Angélica María*. Mexico City: Cal y Arena.
———. 1992. *¿Por qué mejor no nos vamos?* Mexico City: Cal y Arena.
Zavala, Iris. 2000. *El bolero. Historia de un amor*. Madrid: Celeste.
Zona roja. 1975. Dir. Emilio Fernández. Perf. Fanny Cano, Armando Silvestre, Víctor Junco, and Venetia Vianello. Mexico City: Corporación Nacional Cinematográfica (CONACINE).

Index

A casa assassinada, 76
active-passive paradigm, 37, 49, 52, 167, 175, 176, 233n20, 235n6
Adiós mariquita linda, 183
Ahmad, Aijaz, 229n3
AIDS: Cultural Analysis, Cultural Activism, 137
Aïnouz, Karim, 74, 95, 98, 224
A lira do delirio, 76
Allatson, Paul, 134, 189
Amor bandido, 76
Anamú y manigua, 159
Anderson, Benedict, 26
Antes que anochezca, 46, 49, 67, 70
Anzaldúa, Gloria, 230n7
Anzieu, Didier, 116, 117
Aparicio, Frances, 123, 141, 237n6
A personagem homossexual no cinema brasileiro, 75
Arenas, Reinaldo, 10, 45–71, 107, 181, 186, 197, 210, 222, 223, 235n6, 235n7, 236n10, 245n4, 246n7
Arguedas, Alcides, 23
Ariel, 162, 242n15
Arroyo, Jossianna, 33, 176
Arturo, la estrella más brillante, 46, 54, 66, 67, 70
asalto, El, 45, 60, 61, 62, 63, 64, 70
Austin, J. L., 170

Baker, Josephine, 102
Barbin, Hérculine, 146
Barriadas, Efraín, 176
Batista, Fulgencio, 47
Baudrillard, Jean, 64
Beauvoir, Simone de, 114
Bell, David, 192
Bellas de noche, 75
Bellatin, Mario, 11, 22, 42, 107, 108, 125–42
Benítez Rojo, Antonio, 227n1
Berkins, Lohana, 207, 211, 221
beso de la mujer araña, El, 2, 145, 216
Bettcher, Talia Mae, 10
Beverley, John, 229n3
Bhabha, Homi, 232n15
Binnie, Jon, 192
Birkenmaier, Anke, 1, 2
Black, Max, 34, 35, 67
Black Skin, White Masks, 97
Blanco, Fernando, 182, 244n1
Boat People, 159
Bodies That Matter, 33, 172, 232n16
bodily ego, 116
bolero, 85, 86, 168, 174, 177, 216, 223, 244n22
Bolero. Historia de un amor, 244n22
Bom Crioulo, 20
Borges, Jorge Luis, 239n9
Bornstein, Kate, 6, 248n20
Bourdieu, Pierre, 114, 224, 245n3
brothel, 21, 73
 brothel-cabaret, 74

bugarrón, 51, 52
Bustos-Aguilar, Pedro, 233n20
Butler, Judith, 18, 19, 28, 31–32, 33, 36, 66, 116, 151, 168, 170, 172, 173, 192, 232n16, 233n17, 240n3, 243n20, 244n21, 245n6

cabaret, 73, 78, 86, 87, 96, 97, 102, 103
cabaretera, 75, 77, 86
Califia, Patrick, 241n10
Caminha, Adolfo, 20
camp, 56
Camus, Albert, 134
Candia Cáceres, Iván, 212, 214, 216
Candomblé, 101, 116, 119, 120
carnival, 49, 73, 74
carnivalesque, 9, 43, 48, 49, 74, 76, 89
Carrie, 240n5
Carrier, Joseph, 7, 233n20
Carrillo, Hector, 233n20
Carter, Angela, 146, 153
Castro, Fidel, 45, 46, 49, 52, 57, 59, 61, 73, 88, 90, 91
Cauldwell, David O., 228n6
Cava, Fiorella, 38, 39, 65
Celestino antes del alba, 45
Celluloid Closet, The, 76
cerco de la pasión, El, 88
Cerrado por reformas, 88
Chauncey, George, 203
Chávez-Silverman, Susana, 123, 141, 237n6
chingada, la, 176
Cinemachismo: Masculinities and Sexuality in Mexican Film, 75
citizenship, 186, 187, 188, 192, 209
Clark, Stephen J., 109, 123, 237n5
Clavel, Ana, 227n1
Cobra, 3, 231n11
Cola de lagartija, 10, 70

Colibrí, 3, 231n11
Colombian Gold, 10, 70
Colón, Willy, 1
colonialism, 27
color del verano, El, 45, 48, 50, 52, 55, 59, 60, 61, 70
Connell, Raewyn, 213
Conner, Randy P., 120
Creed, Barbara, 151
Crónica de un desayuno, 78
Cruz, Sor Juana Inés de la, 2
Cruz-Malavé, Arnaldo, 164, 177, 239n2
Cuadros, Gil, 239n12
Cualquier miércoles soy tuya, 159
Cuban Revolution, 46, 52
cuerpo correcto, El, 159
Cuerpo náufrago, 227

Dafoe, Daniel, 134
Damas chinas, 125
Danzón, 11, 74, 78–87, 94, 104, 108
Dávila, Juan, 32, 33
De donde son los cantantes, 3, 231n11
De la Mora, Sergio, 73, 75, 76, 77, 86
De Lauretis, Teresa, 78
De la V., Florencia, 1
Deleuze, Gilles, 183, 184, 206, 247n16
Delgado-Costa, José, 175
De Lima, Paolo, 125, 139
Del Pino, Ángeles, 184
Del Río, Joel, 94
De Man, Paul, 42
Deneuve, Catherine, 152, 240n6
De perlas y cicatrices, 183
Derrida, Jacques, 42
día del compadre, El, 75
Díaz, Paola, 212
DiFranco, Ani, 221
Dirlik, Arif, 229n3

disease as metaphor, 22, 126, 134
Disidentifications, 244n21
Donoso, Claudia, 246n10
Donoso, José, 2, 3, 77, 227n2
Dore, Elizabeth, 82, 83
Dos Santos, João Francisco, 95, 97, 101, 102, 103
doxa, 114
duality, 58, 60
Duany, Jorge, 161, 163, 242n17
Dyer, Richard, 34, 75, 233n21

Edelman, Lee, 237n1
Efecto invernadero, 125
effeminacy, 6, 47, 48, 64, 73
ELA. *See* Estado Libre Asociado
Ellis, Havelock, 228n4
embodiment, 39
En jirones, 145
Epps, Brad, 47, 48, 55, 66, 235n7
erasure, 37
escuela del dolor humano de Sechuán, La, 125
Espinoza Carramiñana, Claudia, 38
esquina es mi corazón, La, 11, 181, 187, 188, 189, 190, 193, 195, 201, 205, 209, 213, 217, 225
Estado Libre Asociado (ELA), 161, 163, 177
Esterrich, Carmelo, 235n9
Eugenides, Jeffrey, 241n12
Evans, David, 192

Fanon, Frantz, 97
Feinberg, Leslie, 218, 248n19
Felski, Rita, 64
Fernández, Josefina, 27, 38, 40, 65, 129, 130, 224, 230n9
Fichera, 75, 77, 236n1
Flores, 125
Flores Bueno, Daniel 125
Foster, David William, 20, 75
Foucault, Michel, 65, 146
Franco, Jean, 23, 182

Fresa y chocolate, 89
Freud, Sigmund, 116
Freyre, Gilberto, 96

Garabano, Sandra, 196, 218
Garber, Marjorie, 18, 28, 30, 31, 33–34, 177, 232n15, 233n18
Garfinkel, Harold, 240n3
Gelpí, Juan, 244n1
Goffman, Erving, 194
González, Solange, 211
González Pérez, César O., 40, 194, 195
Gortari, Carlos Salinas de, 14
Gouveia Engel, Magali, 95
"gran varón, El," 1
Green, James, 21
Grompone, Romeo, 131
Grosz, Elizabeth, 210
grotesque, 55, 65, 68, 69, 134
Guattari, Félix, 183, 184
Guerra Cunningham, Lucía, 184, 201
Guibert, Hervé, 239n12
Gutiérrez, Pedro Juan, 42, 107, 108–24, 125, 126, 129, 138, 139, 224, 237n2, 237n5
Gutiérrez Alea, Tomás, 89, 90
Gutmann, Matthew, 230n7, 241n11
Guy, Donna, 18

habitus, 114, 209
Hall, Stuart, 16
Haraway, Donna, 64, 65, 222
Hausman, Bernice, 158
hegemonic masculinity, 213, 214, 215, 216, 218
Heller, Ben, 161, 162
hermana secreta de Angélica María, La, 11, 143, 144, 145–58
Hernández Cruz, Diley, 40
Herrero-Olaizola, Alejandro, 145
higienistas, 21, 24, 95
Hirschfeld, Magnus, 228n4

Historia de Mayta, 134
HIV/AIDS, 56, 99, 133, 139, 141, 165, 188, 190, 191, 193, 194, 198, 199, 202, 208, 209, 217, 218, 223, 225, 239n14
  metaphorical use of, 22, 126, 135, 136, 137
homosexuality, 6, 37, 49
hooks, bell, 173, 243n21,

Illness as Metaphor; and AIDS and Its Metaphors, 135
indios, 22, 23, 24
Instituto Cubano del Arte e Industria Cinematográficos (ICAIC), 88
Insularismo, 161
intersexuality, 149, 150, 151, 152, 153, 155, 179
invert, 20, 26, 27
Irigaray, Luce, 214
Irwin, Robert McKee, 25, 26, 230n8

Jacobo el mutante, 125
Jagose, Annamarie, 237n1
Jameson, Fredric, 175, 229n3
jardín de la señora Murakami, El, 125
Jarman, Derek, 239n12
Jiménez Leal, Orlando, 234n3
Joslin, Tom, 239n12
Journey of the Plague Year, A, 134

Kaebnick, Suzanne, 56
Kafka, Franz, 184
Kaminsky, Amy, 25, 26, 58, 162
katharsis, La, 17
Kertbeny, Karl-Maria, 228n4
Kessler, Suzanne, 240n3
King, Rosamond S., 7, 229n1
Klein, Charles, 209
Koo, Pedro, 110, 113, 237n2
Krafft-Ebing, Richard von, 228n4
Kristeva, Julia, 151
Kulick, Don, 7, 74, 209

Lacan, Jacques, 71, 172, 240n9
La Fountain-Stokes, Lawrence, 8, 97
Lampião da Esquina, 99
Lancaster, Roger, 57, 233n20
Language and Symbolic Power, 114
Leiner, Marvin, 47
Lemebel, Pedro, 11, 42, 138, 181, 224, 225, 244n1, 246n7, 247n13, 247n16, 248n18
L'Étranger, 134
Lezama Lima, José, 50, 245n4
Livingston, Jennie, 169, 172
Llanos, Bernadita, 182, 215
Loco afán: Crónicas de sidario, 11–12, 181, 188, 189, 190, 191, 197, 198, 199, 201, 205, 207, 208, 209, 217, 218, 225, 245n5, 246n7
Logic of Practice, 114
López, Ana, 73, 86
lugar sin límites, El
  film, 77
  novel, 77, 104
Lumsden, Ian, 47, 233n20

machismo, 14, 39, 82
Madame Satã, 11, 14, 95–105
malandro, 96, 97, 98
Manalansan, Martin F., 239n2
Manrique, Jaime, 70
Manzana de Adán, La, iv, 1, 246n10
María, Angélica, 148, 149, 240n4
marianismo, 14, 82
Mariposas en el andamio, 88, 122
Marqués, René, 161, 162, 163, 172, 177
Marrero, M. T., 122
Martino, Wayne, 204
Máscaras, 10, 70
mask, 51, 62, 67, 77, 114, 171, 177
McCarthy-Brown, Karen, 169, 173, 233n17
McKenna, Wendy, 240n3
McRuer, Robert, 136

Melgar, Francisco, 238n7
Melhuus, Marit, 82
Melodrama, 145
Mesa Peña, Janet, 40
metaphor, 33–34, 35, 43, 51, 62, 67, 222
Michaels, Eric, 239n12
Mignolo, Walter, 227n3
Millot, Catherine, 155, 241nn9–10
Mi novia el travesti, 236n2
Molloy, Sylvia, 48, 68, 114, 196, 234n4, 246n8
Monette, Paul, 239n12
Monro, Surya, 187, 192
monstrous feminine, 62, 65, 151
Montaigne, Michel de, 55
Moreno, Antonio, 75, 76, 77
Morgado, Marcia, 159, 241n13
Mosse, George, 24, 25
mother figure, 57, 61, 62, 65
Moulian, Tomás, 188, 195, 231n10
Movimento dos Trabalhadores Rurais Sem Terra, 99
Mujer en traje de batalla, 227n1
Muñecas de media noche, 76
Muñoz, Carlos Basilio, 115
Muñoz, José Esteban, 102, 244n21
Muñoz, Mario, 76, 77, 94
Murray, Stephen O., 237n3

Nabal, Eduardo, 234n5
NAFTA. *See* North American Free Trade Agreement
Nagel, Joanne, 24
Namaste, Viviane, 33, 34–35, 36, 37, 43, 58, 67, 179, 218, 219, 222, 233n19, 243n20, 248n20
nation
    national discourse, 9, 36, 135, 143, 144, 160, 164, 177
    nationalism, 25
Navalha na carne, 76
neoliberalism, 12, 13, 83, 97, 98, 103, 138, 186, 188, 193, 195, 196, 197, 198, 201, 202, 204

Noches de cabaret, 75
noches de Constantinopla, Las, 11, 43, 87–94, 104, 108
North American Free Trade Agreement (NAFTA), 14, 83, 236n3
Novaro, María, 11, 74, 78–87, 222, 223, 236n4
novia para David, Una, 88
Nuestra señora de la noche, 159
Núñez Noriega, Guillermo, 15, 40, 221

O anjo nasceu, 76
Obra reunida, 125
O casamento, 76
Ópera do malandro, 76
Operation Bootstrap, 163
orden escapado, El, 159
Orozco, José Clemente, 17–18
Orwell, George, 61
Otra vez el mar, 45, 59, 63

Padura, Leonardo, 70
palacio de las blanquísimas mofetas, El, 45
Palaversich, Diana, 136, 151, 153, 157, 184, 198, 233n20
Papeles secundarios, 88
Paris Is Burning, 32, 33, 169, 172, 173, 233n17
Parker, Andrew, 24
Parker, Richard, 101
Partido Revolucionario Institucional (PRI), 144
Passion of the New Eve, 146
Paz, Octavio, 230n7
Pedreira, Antonio S., 23, 161, 162, 163, 176, 177, 241n14
pentagonía, 45, 46, 69
Perlman, Janice E., 244n3,
Perlongher, Néstor 191, 205, 206, 213, 245n4
Perrera, La, 78
Perros héroes, 125

Pez de vidrio, 159
Phillips, John, 16
Piñera, Sebastián, 50
plague, 22, 134
Plaza Atenas, Dino, 183
Plummer, Ken, 192
¿Por qué mejor no nos vamos?, 145
Portela, Ena Lucía, 111
posing, 48
Pratt, Mary Louise, 138
Pravaz, Natasha, 101
Prieur, Annick, 38, 197
Prosser, Jay, 33, 36, 117, 157, 172, 218, 241n10
prostitution, 39, 40, 210, 224
Puenzo, Lucía, 241n12
Puig, Manuel, 3, 145, 178, 211, 227n2

Queer Dossier, A, 167, 168, 174, 176
Queer Issues in Contemporary Latin American Cinema, 75
queer theory, 35, 145, 151, 155, 159, 175, 179, 233n17

race
  mestizaje, 21–22, 24, 176
  mixing, 21
racial democracy, 98
Rainha Diaba, 99, 100
Ramos, Lazaro, 96
Ramos Otero, Manuel, 174
Raymond, Janice, 158
Regla del Ocha, 119
representation, 8, 41–43
Repulsion, 152
Rey de La Habana, El, 11, 42, 107, 108, 109–24, 129, 139, 208
Reyes, Los, 1
Richard, Nelly, 31, 34, 35, 174
Ríos Ávila, Rubén, 64
Robles, Víctor, 244n2, 246n9
Rodó, José Enrique, 162, 242n15

Rodríguez-Madera, Sheilla, 40, 242n18,
Rojas, Orlando, 74, 88, 222, 223
Rojo, María, 79
Roldán, Los, 1
Rolley, Katrina, 233n18
Rubin, Henry, 218
Russo, Vito, 76

Sacks, Oliver, 116
Salessi, Jorge, 21
Salinas de Gortari, Carlos, 83
Salón de belleza, 11, 22, 107, 108, 125–42, 208, 225
Salón México, 75
samba, 96, 98
Sánchez, Los, 1
Sandoval-Sánchez, Alberto, 239n12, 244n24
santería, 119, 120, 121, 122, 139, 141, 237n6
Santiago, Fabiola, 88
Santos-Febres, Mayra, 143, 144, 158–78, 208, 222, 223, 244n21
Sarduy, Severo, 28, 29–30, 35, 70, 71, 178, 231nn11–13, 232n14, 245n4
Sarmiento, Domingo Faustino, 23, 230n6
scandal, 27, 209
Schaefer, Claudia, 80, 158
Scheper, Jeanne, 102
Sedgwick, Eve Kosofsky, 48, 136, 210
Sepúlveda Montoya, Salvador, 247nn11–12
Serano, Julia, 10
Sex Change, Social Change, 219
sex/gender variance, 4–5
sex reassignment surgery (SRS), 7, 153, 154, 167, 173
sexual diversity, 4–5
Sexualidad: un derecho a la vida, 88
Shaw, Lisa, 97

Showalter, Elaine, 230n5
Sifuentes-Jáuregui, Ben, 3, 19, 27, 30, 31, 34, 229n2
Signorelli Heise, Tatiana, 99, 100, 103
Silva, Luiz Inácio Lula da, 14, 96, 99
Sirena Selena vestida de pena, 11, 14, 143, 144–78
Smith, Paul Julian, 48, 89
Sobre piel y papel, 159
Some Like It Hot, 94
Sommer, Doris, 24, 25
Sontag, Susan, 135, 136, 137, 235n8
Soto, Fernando, 57, 59
Sparks, David Hatfield, 120
Sparks, Mariya, 120
Special Period, 88, 92, 94, 109, 111, 139, 236n5
SRS. *See* sex reassignment surgery
Stone, Sandy, 64, 107
Streetcar Named Desire, A, 240n8
Stryker, Susan, 66, 228n4
Subero, Gustavo, 103
subjectivity, 8, 12, 19, 20, 36, 39, 40, 116, 126, 139, 167, 179, 180, 182, 194, 207, 208, 210, 212, 217, 218, 222
Sutherland, Romy, 79

Tendencies, 136
Tengo miedo torero, 12, 181, 185, 191, 197, 205, 208, 211, 212, 213, 218, 225
Tercer mundo, 159
testimonio, 184
third space, 31
Tlatelolco massacre, 144
Toro-Alfonso, José, 242n18
traición de Rita Hayworth, La, 145
transgender, 6–7, 25, 28, 228n5
Transgender Warriors, 218
transvestite, 6, 228n4
traveschile, 41

travestismo and travestizaje, 24, 33, 43
Treichler, Paula A., 137
Trilogía sucia de La Habana, 109
tropicalizations, 123, 124

Ulrichs, Karl Heinrich, 227n4
Unidades Militares de Ayuda a la Producción (UMAP), 47, 54, 199, 234n3
Uranian, 227n4

Valentine, David, 228n5, 229n7
Valenzuela, Luisa, 70, 71
Valocchi, Steven, 203
Van Haesendonck, Kristian, 31, 176, 177
Vargas, Getúlio, 22, 96, 98
Vargas Llosa, Mario, 134, 135
Vattimo, Gianni, 64
vedette, 130
vedettismo, 129, 139, 225
Vértiz, Columba, 89
Vested Interests, 33
Vice, Sue, 55, 57
Vidal-Ortiz, Salvador, 121
Vila, Lizette, 88
Vujosevich, Jorge, 129

Wigozky, Karina, 186, 194, 195
Wilchins, Riki, 248n20
Williams, Gareth, 12, 13
Wojnarowicz, David, 239n12

XXY, 241n12

Yeguas del Apocalipsis, 183
Y hembra es el alma mía, 88
Yuval-Davis, Nira, 25, 26, 58

Zanjón de la Aguada, 183
Zapata, Luis, 143, 144, 178, 222, 223, 240n3
Zapata, Roger, 138
Zavala, Iris, 174, 244n22
Zona roja, 75

GPSR Compliance

The European Union's (EU) General Product Safety Regulation (GPSR) is a set of rules that requires consumer products to be safe and our obligations to ensure this.

If you have any concerns about our products, you can contact us on

ProductSafety@springernature.com

In case Publisher is established outside the EU, the EU authorized representative is:

Springer Nature Customer Service Center GmbH
Europaplatz 3
69115 Heidelberg, Germany